Human Activity Recognition (HAR) in Healthcare

Human Activity Recognition (HAR) in Healthcare

Editors

Luigi Bibbò
Marley M. B. R. Vellasco

MDPI

Basel • Beijing • Wuhan • Barcelona • Belgrade • Novi Sad • Cluj • Manchester

Editors
Luigi Bibbò
University of Florence
Florence
Italy

Marley M. B. R. Vellasco
Pontifical Catholic University
of Rio de Janeiro
Rio de Janeiro
Brazil

Editorial Office
MDPI
St. Alban-Anlage 66
4052 Basel, Switzerland

This is a reprint of articles from the Special Issue published online in the open access journal *Applied Sciences* (ISSN 2076-3417) (available at: https://www.mdpi.com/journal/applsci/special_issues/A1K098AX9D).

For citation purposes, cite each article independently as indicated on the article page online and as indicated below:

Lastname, A.A.; Lastname, B.B. Article Title. *Journal Name* **Year**, *Volume Number*, Page Range.

ISBN 978-3-0365-9778-2 (Hbk)
ISBN 978-3-0365-9779-9 (PDF)
doi.org/10.3390/books978-3-0365-9779-9

Contents

About the Editors

Luigi Bibbò

Luigi Bibbò received a B.D. and an M.D. in Biomedical Engineering at the University of Naples "Federico II", Italy, in 2006 and 2009, repsectively, and a Ph.D. in Electronic Engineering and Computer Science at the Second University of Naples, Italy, in 2014. From Sept. 2013 to May 2014, he was a Visiting Scientist at Tufts University of Boston (USA) in the Ultrafast nonlinear Optics and Photonics Laboratory. From April 2016 to Nov. 2018, he was a postdoc researcher at the College of Electronics and Information Engineering of Shenzhen University (CHINA) for research on plasmonic metamaterials. From Feb. 2019 to July 2019, he was an OAM multiplexing research fellow at Nanophotonic Research Center (NCR). From August 2019 to August 2022, he was a Researcher at DIIES at the University "Mediterranea" of Reggio Calabria (Italy) and lecturer of the course Electronic Bioengineering. Since March 2023, he has been a researcher at the Department of Industrial Engineering of the University of Florence on the design, development, and validation of Robotics, IoT, and Artificial Intelligence technologies for biomedical applications. His research interests include computational intelligence methods and applications, including neural networks, virtual reality, and augmented reality. He is a reviewer of numerous international newspapers and Guest Editor of Frontiers and MDPI papers.

Marley M. B. R. Vellasco

Marley M. B. R. Vellasco received bachelor's and master's degrees in electrical engineering from the Pontifical Catholic University of Rio de Janeiro (PUC-Rio), Brazil, and a Ph.D. degree in computer science from the University College London (UCL). She is currently the Head of the Computational Intelligence and Robotics Laboratory (LIRA), PUC-Rio. She is the author of four books and more than four hundred scientific papers in the area of soft computing and machine learning. She has supervised more than 35 Ph.D. Thesis and 85 M.Sc. dissertations. Her research interests include computational intelligence methods and applications, such as neural networks, fuzzy logic, hybrid intelligent systems (neuro-fuzzy, neuro-evolutionary, and fuzzy-evolutionary models), robotics and intelligent agents, applied to decision support systems, pattern classification, time-series forecasting, and control, optimization, and data mining.

applied sciences

MDPI

Editorial

Human Activity Recognition (HAR) in Healthcare

Luigi Bibbò [1,*] and Marley M. B. R. Vellasco [2]

1 BioRobotics Lab, Department of Industrial Engineering, University of Florence, 50134 Florence, Italy
2 Department of Electrical Engineering, Pontifical Catholic University of Rio de Janeiro, Rio de Janeiro 22451-000, Brazil; marley@ele.puc-rio.br
* Correspondence: luigi.bibbo@unifi.it

1. Introduction

Developments in the medical and technological fields have led to a longer life expectancy. However, this improvement has led to an increase in the number of older people with critical health conditions who need care. Older people who cannot care for themselves need special assistance during their daily care. Long-term care involves medical, welfare, rehabilitative, and social services that significantly impact the national social and health system and involve a growing number of caregivers who are difficult to find [1]. Advances in information and communications technology (ICT), nanotechnology, and artificial intelligence (AI) have made it possible to develop efficient home care systems [2], contributing to the containment of public expenditure and the improvement of the living conditions of older adults. The creation of intelligent objects, ordinarily present in the home, the advent of IoT, and the existence of AI algorithms have created the right conditions for the creation of smart environments (AmI) [3] and ambient assisted living (AAL) [4]. These systems make the home active, intelligent, and safe, making it possible to carry out daily activities in the best possible way and with full autonomy, as well as ensuring timely intervention in critical situations. The innovations in care for older people, introduced by technological evolution, are evident in the creation of smartwatches [5] and fitness bracelets for monitoring vital parameters such as blood pressure, heart rate, and physical activity; telemedicine to remotely monitor health status and establish treatment plans [6]; and robots to support social care [7].

The automatic detection of physical activities performed by human subjects is identified as human activity recognition (HAR). Its goal is correctly classifying data or images into gestures, actions, and human-to-human or human–object interactions. Identification is achieved using AI that analyzes activity data captured from different sources. Sources range from wearable sensors [8] and smartphone sensors [9] to photographic devices or CCTV cameras [10]. HAR is used in different fields of application ranging from video surveillance systems, the assessment of the state of health or the analysis of patient behavior in a natural environment by monitoring the actions carried out, or even for the detection of anomalies predicting falls, to human–computer interaction and robotics. Depending on the area of application, the sensors used will be different.

From a functional point of view, HAR consists of the following phases:

- Automatic acquisition of data on activities performed and vital signs through wearable sensors and sensors connected to medical equipment.
- Data pre-processing (elimination of any noise or unwanted signals).
- Features extraction.
- Model training and testing.
- Activity recognition.

Two technologies can be used for activity recognition: recognition based on vision or sensor-based recognition. Inertial sensors are preferred over video-based sensors that

Citation: Bibbò, L.; Vellasco, M.M.B.R. Human Activity Recognition (HAR) in Healthcare. *Appl. Sci.* **2023**, *13*, 13009. https://doi.org/10.3390/app132413009

Received: 2 December 2023
Accepted: 4 December 2023
Published: 6 December 2023

require the installation of cameras in all rooms in a house for motion recording. In addition, they are expensive, and the accuracy of reconnaissance is affected by brightness problems and inevitable visual disturbances, as well as violating privacy. Sensors based on MEMS technology are miniaturized, economical, and have low power consumption [11]. Monitoring activities in the environment where older people live is relevant to evaluating their behavioral changes. Technology can help to detect and alert healthcare professionals or family members about a patient's behavioral changes, preventing serious problems. Ultimately, with the help of these systems, we can monitor the patient's status depending on the specific pathology, the tracking data, and the exact location.

This Research Topic aims to create a collection of articles illustrating different methodological approaches to the subject of HAR in an exciting scenario. It contains eleven articles that will be briefly described below to stimulate the reader's interest and to expand their understanding.

2. An Overview of Published Articles

Ojiako and Farrahi (contribution 1) experimented with an innovative predictive model of human activities (HAR). They demonstrated that the sensor-based MLP mixer architecture enables competitive performance in vision-based tasks with lower computational costs than other deep learning techniques. The MLP mixer recently created by Google Brain [12] does not use convolutions or self-attention mechanisms, and instead consists entirely of MLPs. The authors compared the performance of the MLP mixer with the existing state-of-the-art literature:

*Ensemble LSTM.
*CNN-BiGRU.
*AttenSense.
*Multi-agent attention.
*DeepConvLSTM.
*Triple attention.
*Self-Caution*CNN.
*b-LSTM-S.

The performance was 10.1% better in the Daphnet Gait dataset, 1% better in the PAMAP2 dataset, and 0.5% better in the Opportunity dataset.

Velasco et al. (contribution 2) used the HAR approach to understand human behavior by analyzing data representative of domestic routines. Their study is oriented towards establishing a connection between the activities of daily living, the spaces in which they take place, and the times related to the performance of the activities in a given place. Research has shown that this information is helpful for healthcare professionals to assess the health status of patients, for family members to keep track of the habits of relatives, and for home designers to assess the architectural characteristics of home interiors for accessibility and movement of residents. The authors used the knowledge discovery database (KDD) approach with the data analyst variant as a key player in the knowledge discovery process [13]. The KDD approach is an interactive and iterative knowledge discovery process that identifies relationships between data that must be valid, new, potentially useful, and understandable. The analyst gains a greater understanding of the domestic routine with each process iteration. The parameters used for the evaluation are the sequence of places visited, times of day at which they are visited, and average duration of visits; the signals are acquired using PIR sensors connected to a Raspberry Pi4, placed inside each room of the house. Transitions between positions are detected by measuring the RSSI power of the Bluetooth signal emitted by a BLE device worn by the subject being monitored. The evaluation of the method was verified through workshops with seventeen multidisciplinary participants: architects, engineers, health professionals, and caregivers. The feedback obtained was positive, confirming the validity of the method adopted as a source of significant information on the status of the monitored subjects.

In the third manuscript, Huang et al. (contribution 3) proposed a new multiscale hierarchical adaptive network structure for HAR called HMA Conv-LSTM. In this model, there are:

- a multi-scale hierarchical convolution module (HMC) that performs finer-grained feature extraction on the spatial information of feature vectors;
- an adaptive channel feature fusion module that can blend functionality at different scales, improving model efficiency and removing redundant information;
- a dynamic channel-selection module-LSTM based on the attention mechanism to extract time context information.

This multi-scale convolution module uses convolutional cores of different scales for extracting and splicing multi-scale features in both sensory and temporal dimensions. This strengthens the network's ability to recognize features of different scales, improves its adaptability, and enhances its ability to characterize features.

The diversity and duration of the actions detected by sensors placed on different body positions dictate longer sliding window sizes for segmentation. This sizing can result in some fine-grained subtle action processes being overlooked, thus affecting action recognition. In contrast, the proposed hierarchical architecture can split the action window and extract features from the sensor sequence data with finer granularity to recognize the finer action processes effectively. To validate the efficacy of the proposed model, the authors carried out experiments on several public HAR datasets: Opportunity, PAMAP2, USC-HAD, and Skoda. Their model was built using Google's open-source TensorFlow 2.9.0 deep learning framework. The proposed model achieves competitive performance compared to several state-of-the-art approaches. The evaluation results also show that the proposed HMA Conv-LSTM can effectively obtain the temporal context and spatial information from sensor sequence data.

Again, Mekruksavanich et al. (contribution 4) used an innovative approach based on a DL network and the nature of the data. Exploiting the potential offered by WiFi-based detection techniques, they used channel status information (CSI) [14] rather than the received signal strength indicator (RSSI). The authors proposed a hybrid deep learning network called CNN-GRU-AttNet that leverages the strengths of CNN and GRU to extract informative spatio-temporal features from raw CSI data automatically and to efficiently classify tasks. They also integrated an attention mechanism into the network that prioritizes important features and time steps, thereby improving recognition performance. The network consists of five layers: the input layer, two CNN layers, a GRU layer, an attention layer, a fully connected layer, and an output layer. To assess the effectiveness of the proposed model, the authors used two publicly accessible datasets, CSI-HAR and Stan WIFI. They refer to seven activities: walking, running, sitting, lying down, standing up, bending, and falling. Because these datasets did not have predefined training and test sets, they adopted the cross-validation technique five times to evaluate the model's performance. They also performed a comparative evaluation of the performance of five core deep learning models: CNN, LSTM, BiLSTM, GRU, and BiGRU.

The results show exceptional efficacy in the classification of HAR activities, superior to the five basic DL models, producing an average accuracy of 99.62%, an accuracy of 99.61%, and an F1 score of 99.61% in all movements.

Kim and Lee (contribution 5), aware that some physical activities may include similar features that lead the automatic classification phase to incorrect evaluations, proposed a new approach to improve recognition accuracy. Their proposed method uses a smartphone's three-axis acceleration and gyroscopic data to define activity patterns visually. In particular, the method expands the sensor data into 2D and 3D images. This generates new characteristics of human activities that cannot be detected in one-dimensional data. These new features allow, on the one hand, the recognition of more diverse types of human physical activity and, on the other hand, the identification of unique characteristics among similar types of activities. The raw values from the accelerometer and gyroscope that correspond to the breadth of the continuous data of the activities performed are used to represent 2D image models. Each time-series value is transformed into a luminosity value, obtaining the Brightness Intensity Distribution Model (BIDP) for each physical activity data. Each point is expressed as a distinct brightness value based on the measured value. This type of representation includes areas of intense and low brightness depending on the location of the data waveform that can degrade the model's performance. To overcome this problem, the authors carried out a processing step to generate a standardized visual image.

The image data were used in the training phase along with the raw 1D data to increase the precision and accuracy of the HAR. The sensor data from the triaxial accelerometer and gyroscope used in this study came from the "WISDM Activity and Biometrics for Smartphones and Smartwatches" published by Weiss [14]. The neural network used was of the multidimensional convolutional type. The model achieved a 90% or higher performance for all 18 classes of physical activity examined.

This model's HAR performance was superior to previous studies' corresponding performance.

Caramaschi et al. (contribution 6) experimented with a model for the recognition of human activity independent of the orientation of the worn device that classified five predefined activities within a range of actions that could occur in a clinical setting. Their proposal stems from the study of how changes in sensor orientation affect the classification of deep learning (DL) human activity recognition (HAR) targeting activities such as slow and assisted walking and wheelchair use. The HAR model is orientation-agnostic, uses data augmentation, and is trained with acceleration measurements recorded from five sensor positions on the participant's trunk. The wearable sensor data augmentation approach, first used by Ohashi et al. [15], positively affects time-series computing and potentially improves data-driven tasks such as HAR. They used two datasets. The first is the Wearing Position Study (WPS) acquired at Philips Research Laboratories (2022). It contains three-axis acceleration measurements from nineteen healthy volunteers, comprising ten males and nine females. The second is the Simulated Hospital Study (SHS) acquired at Philips Research Laboratories (2019). It includes ten healthy male and ten female volunteers. Five GENEActive (GA) sensors were used for monitoring: two in contact with the skin, two dangling from the neck, and one in the pocket of the clinical gown. The implemented HAR model is a modified version of the DNN proposed by Fridriksdottir et al. [16]. The main difference is replacing the long short-time memory layer with a convolutional layer. This change in architecture was introduced to simplify the model and did not generate significantly different results from the previous DNN. The performance achieved by the two sets was evaluated to choose the number of augmented rotation intervals to be applied to the training data. The first set consisted of seven rotations between 0 and 90 degrees, while the second set consisted of seven rotations between 0 and 180 degrees. In light of this preliminary analysis, the final augmentation settings for the augmented model's training set consisted of ten rotations from 0 to 180, with a 20-degree pitch on the frontal, longitudinal, and sagittal axes separately. Cross-validation was used five times to train both the base and augmented model. The cross-validation performance was used to evaluate the augmentation approach (i.e., the range of rotations) and the effect of rotation on the baseline model. The control data results confirmed the augmented model's good performance obtained during cross-validation. Testing showed that as the data increased, the model could learn additional configurations not provided by the initial dataset.

Adherence to cardiac rehabilitation does not currently produce the expected results, negatively affecting the health status of patients and the use of available resources. To improve this trend, Filos et al. (contribution 7) set up a study based on machine learning techniques to predict the adherence of patients with cardiovascular disorders to a six-month home cardiac telerehabilitation program. Their approach is based on the use of clinical information available before the start of a program and behavioral and cardiovascular fitness characteristics acquired during the preliminary phase of familiarization with the program. As a first step, the methodology applied involves classifying patients into different clusters. Hierarchical clustering, an algorithm that groups objects with similar characteristics in a tree hierarchy, was used for classification. The baseline data led to the formation of three groups of patients: an active, low-risk patient group, sedentary, high-risk patients, and a group of patients at high cardiovascular risk but who are fit and motivated. Familiarity with exercise showed three adherence behaviors (high adherence, low adherence, and transient adherence), while exercise sessions after the familiarization phase resulted in adherent and non-adherent clusters. Two model types, namely repetitive decision trees (DT) and random forest (RF), were used to predict long-term adherence. The data to develop the DT model were patient clusters created based on baseline characteristics and clusters related to adherence to the exercise program. Since the DT model is unstable, a slight variation in the training dataset can lead to changes in the tree. A random forest (RF) technique, which is more stable, was thus applied. The first model showed both high accuracy and high recall, at 80.2 ± 19.5% and 94.4 ± 14.5%, respectively, which were better than the performance of the second model, which displayed a precision of 71.8 ± 25.8% and a recall of 87.7 ± 24%. Network analysis was applied to discover correlations of their characteristics that relate to adherence. This study highlighted how important the combination of basic clinical data with the characteristics acquired during a brief familiarization phase is for the high-accuracy prediction of adherence to the long-term RC program. The proposed methodology can be generalized to facilitate the identification of patients who are more adherent to telerehabilitation programs.

Obesity increases the risk of many chronic diseases, especially cardiovascular disease, and is a cause of death. Faced with the rapid increase in obesity in the population, Vidal et al. (contribution 8) developed a cross-sectional analytical study of residents of the United States of America (USA) who have an Instagram account to determine whether using any meal tracking platform to record food consumption correlated with an improvement in body mass index (BMI). The survey was conducted on a sample of actual or graduate students from Mary Hardin Baylor University, Oakland University, the University of Kentucky, and Queens University in Charlotte. Eight hundred and ninety-six subjects with an Instagram account signed up to participate in an anonymous online survey, of which 78.7% were women, 20.6% were men, and 0.7% were classified as others. As for generations, 11.5% belonged to Generation Z, 75.6% to the Millennials, 11.4% to Generation X, and 1.6% to the Baby Boomers. Overall, 93.5% of the sample did not smoke, 2.3% smoked, and 4.1% smoked occasionally. Concerning academic qualifications, 3.7% had high school graduates, 6.1% had some university credits, 0.6% had technical training, 3.2% had an associate degree, 43.2% had a bachelor's degree, 15.1% had a master's degree and 28.1% had a doctorate. The information acquired through the questionnaire included the number of hours per week dedicated to Instagram or physical activity and the intensity of physical activity performed. In order to test the influence of using any meal tracking platform to record food intake on BMI, they were asked if they had used any digital platform in the past month. The chi-square test was used to study the relationships between the use of any digital platform in the last month and gender, generation, smoking habits, highest academic degree earned, and time spent on Instagram. The Mann–Whitney U test was adopted to compare BMI, weekly hours spent on Instagram looking at nutrition- or physical activity-related content, vigorous physical activity, moderate physical activity, time spent walking, and time spent sitting among participants who did not eat meals. The survey showed that the platform was used by 34.2% of the sample. Participants who used any meal tracking platform also had a higher BMI, invested more hours per week on Instagram looking at nutrition- or physical activity-related content, and performed more minutes per week of vigorous physical activity. The survey showed that participants rely on new technologies for optimal weight without obtaining practical results. The authors believe that combining care with digital app-based tools and support from healthcare professionals can help individuals to effectively achieve a healthy weight.

In the ninth paper, Alemayol et al. (contribution 9) proposed a gait and pose analysis study based on estimating the angle of the lower limb joint from a single inertial sensor. Gait analysis is critical in healthcare; it is mainly adopted for precise patient monitoring, the identification of movement abnormalities, the evaluation of surgical findings, and the detection of osteoarthritis of the knee and hip to diagnose Parkinson's disease. Gaits are interpreted through three types of parameters: spatiotemporal (e.g., stride speed and length/stride), kinematic (e.g., hip extension/flexion), or kinetic parameters (e.g., ground reaction moments and forces). The authors used kinematic parameters, the joint angles of the lower limb, and preferred wearable sensors for data collection. These sensors are preferred to non-wearable ones, which generally consist of optical motion acquisition systems with high position accuracy, as they are expensive and require longer installation times and specific skills. Motion analysis in a real-world environment requires precise and reliable sensors. The investigations identified the Xsens inertial sensors as the most suitable for this purpose. The literature has various testimonies on the number of sensors, their positioning and estimation methods, and the analysis of movement. The authors employed various neural network algorithms to determine the number and placement of sensors for estimating the joint angle of both legs. To calculate the actual values of the lower limb joint angle, seven individual Awinda sensors were mounted on the lower half of the body of each of the sixteen subjects, in particular one on the pelvis at the height of the anterior-superior iliac spine, another on each of the lateral thighs, two more on the upper parts of the tibiae and finally two more on the upper anterior parts of the feet. The goal was the estimation of leg kinematics (joint angles) from any of the sensors attached to the body. The authors used four different neural network models for the estimation: long-term bidirectional memory (BLSTM), convolutional neural network, wavelet neural network, and unidirectional LSTM. Two groups of target angles of the leg joint were examined. The first set contained only four corners of the leg joint in the sagittal plane, while the second included six angles of the leg joint in the sagittal plane and two angles of the leg joint in the coronal plane. By evaluating different combinations of networks and datasets, it was found that the BLSTM network was the best performer with both datasets, with an absolute mean error (MAE) of between 3.02° and 4.33° for the four dominant angles of the leg joint in the sagittal plane. The results improved with an increased number of sensors and the introduction of biometric information. From the investigation of the placement of the single sensor, it was found that the shin or thigh is the optimal position for estimating the angle of the leg joint. Actual leg movement was compared to a computer-generated simulation of leg joints, which demonstrated the possibility of estimating leg joint angles during walking with a single inertial sensor.

Bibbò et al. (contribution 10) developed an innovative model to detect subjects' emotional health using a self-normalizing neural network (SNN) containing an ensemble layer. In the context of HAR, computer vision technology can be applied to recognize emotional states through facial expressions using facial positions such as the nose, eyes, and lips. The recognition of facial emotions is important because, from the analysis of the face, it is possible to detect the subject's health status, such as anxiety, depression, stress, malaise, and neurodegenerative disorders, making facial diagnosis possible. This is a beneficial technique in caring for older adults; through the information provided, medical staff can evaluate the type of intervention required to reduce the subjects' discomfort. Some facial manifestations can be associated with the first pathological symptoms, preventing diseases that can degenerate. The innovation produced by the authors is the development of an AI classifier based on a set of classifier neural networks whose outputs are directed to an ensemble layer. In particular, the networks are self-normalizing neural networks (SNNs). The model comprises six SNNs, each trained to identify six emotions (anger, disgust, fear, happiness, sadness, and surprise). The networks cascade, and each is dedicated to detecting the presence or absence in the input image of a single specific emotion (among the six present in this study) assigned to and associated with it. Each neural network is trained with its images for a specific emotion. Each network produces two outputs, among which the first, identified with EM through a numerical enhancement (from 0 to 1), confirms the correspondence of the emotion detected with that assigned to the network. The second, identified with AM, similarly through a numerical enhancement (from 0 to 1), signals the presence of a different emotion from that assigned to the specific network. These outputs are then transferred to the ensemble layer, which provides an accurate result by analyzing the outputs of the individual networks according to statistical logic. Kaggle was used as the dataset. The authors used an approach to validate the results through the control network in the experiments. The results showed a success rate for almost all emotions of around 80%, with a peak of 95% for the emotion "Fear".

The exciting topic of the metaverse is addressed in the eleventh article of this collection. One of the areas in which the metaverse is applied is digital games. Virtual reality and animation allow virtual characters to take on natural roles and generate new immersive ways to live their lives. Oliveira et al. (contribution 11) aimed their research at understanding the impact of the concept of the metaverse on ordinary people's lives. The definition of the concept of the metaverse was first postulated by Neal Stephenson in his book *Snow Crash* in 1992. It was defined as a virtual world capable of reaching, interacting, and influencing human existence [17]. There currently needs to be a single definition.

The metaverse can be understood as a network of interconnected 3D virtual worlds rendered in real time that can be experienced synchronously and persistently by an unlimited number of users. This study is part of the research on the metaverse, virtual reality, and gaming. It was produced in three focus groups with Portuguese adults who are regular video game players. The focus group originated in the work of the Bureau of Applied Social Research at Columbia University in 1940. It is used in research in several disciplines. It is a qualitative method of collecting data on a particular topic in an informal discussion between selected people. During the discussion, information is gained about what people think or feel and how they act. The developed investigation has the following aims:

- To verify how the metaverse is represented and characterized;
- To identify which technologies stimulate the immersion experience;
- To identify the main dimensions that influence the acceptance of the metaverse concept;
- To understand perceptions of metaverse and VR regarding socialization and well-being;
- To test perceptions of a player's daily life regarding the concepts of the metaverse, virtual reality, and gaming;
- To understand the impact of social representations on the concept of play;
- To understand animation's perceived role in relation to the Metaverse, Virtual Reality, and gaming concepts.

The data collected during the focus groups are the answers provided by the 13 participants to the twenty-eight questions distributed across the three themes: games, animation, and metaverse. The results obtained from player responses produced accurate information on how the metaverse is represented and characterized and relates to virtual reality and gaming. In conclusion, the metaverse is considered a game that allows immersive experiences through virtual reality technology and the style and esthetics of animation. It is also seen as a means of socialization and communication, and a promoter of well-being.

In the future, its expansion into the world of social networks as a means of communication is foreseeable.

3. Conclusions

AI-based automated HAR monitoring systems are exceptional tools that can be integrated into current practices to improve quality of life. The role of AI is essential in HAR systems because of its ability to extract hidden information and the level of accuracy shown in its classification activities. However, using these innovative technologies raises several issues related to divergent considerations among stakeholders concerning security, privacy, and health implications due to the use of these technologies. The approach in the design phase to the role of AI, from the point of view of its responsibilities, needs to be sufficiently clear. It should be highlighted whether the ML model is assistive or autonomous. Assistive models provide healthcare professionals with treatment, diagnosis, and management suggestions, leaving them responsible for making decisions. Autonomous models provide direct diagnoses without any interpretation or supervision from the doctor. Since the developer's choice regarding the level of autonomy has clear implications for accountability, it should be the subject of dialogue and discussion between stakeholders. Implementing machine learning systems requires considering both clinical and ethical aspects to produce benefits in health care, facilitate independent living, and reduce healthcare spending. One of the biggest challenges we will see in the future is the development of increasingly high-performance artificial intelligence models in new application domains that comply with moral and ethical requirements [18].

Author Contributions: L.B.: Writing—original draft, Writing—review and editing. M.M.B.R.V.: Review and editing. All authors have read and agreed to the published version of the manuscript.

Conflicts of Interest: The authors declare no conflict of interest.

List of Contributions

1. Ojiako, K.; Farrahi, K. MLPs Are All You Need for Human Activity Recognition. *Appl. Sci.* **2023**, *13*, 11154. https://doi.org/10.3390/app132011154.
2. Arribas Velasco, A.; McGrory, J.; Berry, D. An Evaluation Study on the Analysis of People's Domestic Routines Based on Spatial, Temporal and Sequential Aspects. *Appl. Sci.* **2023**, *13*, 10608. https://doi.org/10.3390/app131910608.
3. Huang, Q.; Xie, W.; Li, C.; Wang, Y.; Liu, Y. Human Action Recognition Based on Hierarchical Multi-Scale Adaptive Conv-Long Short-Term Memory Network. *Appl. Sci.* **2023**, *13*, 10560. https://doi.org/10.3390/app131910560.
4. Mekruksavanich, S.; Phaphan, W.; Hnoohom, N.; Jitpattanakul, A. Attention-Based Hybrid Deep Learning Network for Human Activity Recognition Using WiFi Channel State Information. *Appl. Sci.* **2023**, *13*, 8884. https://doi.org/10.3390/app13158884.
5. Kim, C.; Lee, W. Human Activity Recognition by the Image Type Encoding Method of 3-Axial Sensor Data. *Appl. Sci.* **2023**, *13*, 4961. https://doi.org/10.3390/app13084961.
6. Caramaschi, S.; Papini, G.; Caiani, E. Device Orientation Independent Human Activity Recognition Model for Patient Monitoring Based on Triaxial Acceleration. *Appl. Sci.* **2023**, *13*, 4175. https://doi.org/10.3390/app13074175.
7. Filos, D.; Claes, J.; Cornelissen, V.; Kouidi, E.; Chouvarda, I. Predicting Adherence to Home-Based Cardiac Rehabilitation with Data-Driven Methods. *Appl. Sci.* **2023**, *13*, 6120. https://doi.org/10.3390/app13106120.
8. Tricás-Vidal, H.; Vidal-Peracho, M.; Lucha-López, M.; Hidalgo-García, C.; Monti-Ballano, S.; Márquez-Gonzalvo, S.; Tricás-Moreno, J. Association between Body Mass Index and the Use of Digital Platforms to Record Food Intake: Cross-Sectional Analysis. *Appl. Sci.* **2022**, *12*, 12144. https://doi.org/10.3390/app122312144.
9. Alemayoh, T.; Lee, J.; Okamoto, S. Leg-Joint Angle Estimation from a Single Inertial Sensor Attached to Various Lower-Body Links during Walking Motion. *Appl. Sci.* **2023**, *13*, 4794. https://doi.org/10.3390/app13084794.
10. Bibbo', L.; Cotroneo, F.; Vellasco, M. Emotional Health Detection in HAR: New Approach Using Ensemble SNN. *Appl. Sci.* **2023**, *13*, 3259. https://doi.org/10.3390/app13053259.
11. Oliveira, A.; Cruz, M. Virtually Connected in a Multiverse of Madness?—Perceptions of Gaming, Animation, and Metaverse. *Appl. Sci.* **2023**, *13*, 8573. https://doi.org/10.3390/app13158573.

References

1. Un'indagine Sugli Anziani non Autosufficienti: Le Scelte delle Famiglie tra Assistenza Domiciliare e RSA. I Luoghi della Cura Rivista Online Network Non Autosufficienza (NNA). 2022. Available online: https://www.luoghicura.it/dati-e-tendenze/2022/11 (accessed on 8 July 2021).
2. Bibbo, L.; Carotenuto, R.; Corte, F.D.; Merenda, M.; Messina, G. Home care system for the elderly and pathological conditions. In Proceedings of the 7th International Conference on Smart and Sustainable Technologies (SpliTech), Split/Bol, Croatia, 19 August 2022; pp. 1–7. [CrossRef]
3. Gams, M.; Gu, I.Y.-H.; Härmä, A.; Muñoz, A.; Tam, V. Artificial intelligence and ambient intelligence. *J. Ambient. Intell. Smart Environ.* **2019**, *11*, 71–86. [CrossRef]
4. Cicirelli, G.; Marani, R.; Petitti, A.; Milella, A.; D'Orazio, T. Ambient Assisted Living: A Review of Technologies, Methodologies and Future Perspectives for Healthy Aging of Population. *Sensors* **2021**, *21*, 3549. [CrossRef] [PubMed]
5. San-Segundo, R.; Blunck, H.; Moreno-Pimentel, J.; Stisen, A.; Gil-Martín, M. Robust Human Activity Recognition using smartwatches and smartphones. *Eng. Appl. Artif. Intell.* **2018**, *7*, 190–202. [CrossRef]
6. Şahin, E.; Yavuz Veizi, B.G.; Naharci, M.I. Telemedicine interventions for older adults: A systematic review. *J. Telemed. Telecare* **2021**. [CrossRef] [PubMed]

7. Bradwell, H.L.; Aguiar Noury, G.E.; Edwards, K.J.; Winnington, R.; Thill, S.; Jones, R.B. Design recommendations for socially assistive robots for health and social care based on a large-scale analysis of stakeholder positions: Social robot design recommendations. *Health Policy Technol.* **2021**, *10*, 100544. [CrossRef]
8. Uddin, M.Z.; Soylu, A. Human activity recognition using wearable sensors, discriminant analysis, and long short-term memory-based neural structured learning. *Sci. Rep.* **2021**, *11*, 16455. [CrossRef]
9. Straczkiewicz, M.; James, P.; Onnela, J.P. A systematic review of smartphone-based human activity recognition methods for health research. *NPJ Digit. Med.* **2021**, *4*, 148. [CrossRef]
10. Sharma, V.; Gupta, M.; Kumar Pandey, A.; Mishra, D.; Kumar, A. A Review of Deep Learning-based Human Activity Recognition on Benchmark Video Datasets. *Appl. Artif. Intell.* **2022**, *36*, 1. [CrossRef]
11. Demrozi, F.; Pravadelli, G.; Bihorac, A.; Rashidi, P. Human Activity Recognition using Inertial, Physiological and Environmental Sensors: A Comprehensive Survey. *IEEE Access* **2020**, *8*, 210816–210836. [CrossRef] [PubMed]
12. Tolstichin, I.O.; Houlsby, N.; Kolesnikov, A.; Beyer, L.; Zhai, X.; Unterthiner, T.; Yung, J.; Steiner, A.; Keyser, D.; Uszkoreit, J.; et al. MLP-Mixer: An all-MLP architecture for vision. In *Advances in Neural Information Processing Systems, Proceedings of the 35th Conference on Neural Information Processing Systems (NeurIPS 2021), Online, 6–14 December 2021*; Ranzato, M., Beygelzimer, A., Dauphin, Y., Liang, P., Wortman Vaughan, J., Eds.; Neural Information Processing Systems Foundation, Inc. (NeurIPS): Vancouver, BC, Canada, 2021; Volume 34, pp. 24261–24272. Available online: https://proceedings.neurips.cc/paper_files/paper/2021/file/cba0a4ee5ccd02fda0fe3f9a3e7b89fe-Paper.pdf (accessed on 8 July 2021).
13. Brachman, R.J.; Arnad, T. The Process of Knowledge Discovery in Databases: A First Sketch. In Proceedings of the 1994 {AAAI} Workshop, Seattle, WA, USA, 31 July–4 August 1994. Technical Report {WS-94-03}.
14. Weiss, G.M. UCI Machine Learning Repository: WISDM Smartphone and Smartwatch Activity and Biometrics Dataset. 2019. Available online: https://archive.ics.uci.edu/ml/machine-learning-databases/00507/WISDM-dataset-description.pdf (accessed on 8 July 2021).
15. Ohashi, H.; Al-Nasser, M.; Ahmed, S.; Akiyama, T.; Sato, T.; Nguyen, P.; Nakamura, K.; Dengel, A. Augmenting wearable sensor data with physical constraint for DNN-based human-action recognition. In Proceedings of the ICML 2017 Times Series Workshop, Sydney, NSW, Australia, 6–11 August 2017; pp. 6–11.
16. Fridriksdottir, E.; Bonomi, A.G. Accelerometer-based human activity recognition for patient monitoring using a deep neural network. *Sensors* **2020**, *20*, 6424. [CrossRef] [PubMed]
17. Ball, M. *The Metaverse: And How it Will Revolutionize Everything*; W.W. Norton & CO: New York, NY, USA, 2022.
18. Siau, K.; Wang, W. Artificial Intelligence (AI) Ethics: Ethics of AI and Ethical AI. *J. Database Manag.* **2020**, *31*, 74–87. [CrossRef]

applied sciences

MDPI

Article

MLPs Are All You Need for Human Activity Recognition

Kamsiriochukwu Ojiako * and Katayoun Farrahi

School of Electronics and Computer Science, University of Southampton, Southampton SO17 1BJ, UK; k.farrahi@soton.ac.uk

* Correspondence: kco1e20@soton.ac.uk

Abstract: Convolution, recurrent, and attention-based deep learning techniques have produced the most recent state-of-the-art results in multiple sensor-based human activity recognition (HAR) datasets. However, these techniques have high computing costs, restricting their use in low-powered devices. Different methods have been employed to increase the efficiency of these techniques; however, this often results in worse performance. Recently, pure multi-layer perceptron (MLP) architectures have demonstrated competitive performance in vision-based tasks with lower computation costs than other deep-learning techniques. The MLP-Mixer is a pioneering pureMLP architecture that produces competitive results with state-of-the-art models in computer vision tasks. This paper shows the viability of the MLP-Mixer in sensor-based HAR. Furthermore, experiments are performed to gain insight into the Mixer modules essential for HAR, and a visual analysis of the Mixer's weights is provided, validating the Mixer's learning capabilities. As a result, the Mixer achieves F_1 scores of 97%, 84.2%, 91.2%, and 90% on the PAMAP2, Daphnet Gait, Opportunity Gestures, and Opportunity Locomotion datasets, respectively, outperforming state-of-the-art models in all datasets except Opportunity Gestures.

Keywords: human activity recognition; MLP-Mixer; efficiency

Citation: Ojiako, K.; Farrahi, K. MLPs Are All You Need for Human Activity Recognition. *Appl. Sci.* **2023**, *13*, 11154. https://doi.org/10.3390/app132011154

Academic Editors: Luigi Bibbò and Marley M.B.R. Vellasco

Received: 6 September 2023
Revised: 28 September 2023
Accepted: 29 September 2023
Published: 11 October 2023

1. Introduction

The last two decades have witnessed the rapid growth of wearable devices, which are increasingly being used for ubiquitous health monitoring. Human activity recognition (HAR) aims at detecting simple behaviours, such as walking or gestures; more complex behaviours, like cooking or opening a door, with various use-cases that continue to grow as the field expands; and assistive technology, such as identifying odd behaviours in the elderly, including falls [1], skill assessment [2], helping with rehabilitation [3], sports injury detection, and ambient assisted living [4–6]. Accurately predicting human activities from sensor data is difficult due to the complexity of human behaviour and the noise in the sensor data [7].

With larger datasets and more computational power, deep learning has evolved, removing the need for manually created features and inductive biases from models and increasing the reliance on automatically learning features from raw labelled data [8]. Complex deep learning techniques, such as convolutions and attention-based mechanisms, are used increasingly with growing computational capacity. These techniques perform well with larger models, resulting in processes that are generally more expensive computationally and memory-wise than previous techniques. Although wearable devices and smartphones have rapidly increased in computation efficiency over the past two decades, they are still limited in power and storage; this prevents them from using state-of-the-art deep learning techniques in HAR.

MLP-Mixers, recently created by Google Brain [8], are simplistic and less computationally expensive models, yet they produce near state-of-the-art results in computer vision tasks. Wearable devices could produce competitive results in HAR without the significant computational demands that current state-of-the-art models impose if MLP-Mixers performed similarly in HAR, which would help advance HAR toward low-powered devices.

The main contributions of this paper are as follows:

- We investigate the performance of the MLP-Mixer in multi-sensor HAR, achieving competitive, and in some cases, state-of-the-art performance in HAR without convolution, recurrent, or attention-based mechanisms in the model. The accompanied code can be found here https://github.com/KMC07/MLPMixerHAR (accessed on 6 October 2023).
- We analyse the impact of each layer in the Mixer for HAR.
- We analyse the effect of the sliding windows on the Mixer's performance in HAR.
- We perform a visual analysis of the Mixer's weights to validate that the Mixer is successfully recognising different human activities.

2. Related Work

Four main categories of deep-learning architecutres have been used in HAR, convolution-based architectures, recurrent networks, hybrid models, and attention-based models [9]. Evaluation is performed on benchmark HAR datasets, including Opportunity [10], Daphnet Gait [11], PAMAP2 [12], Skoda Checkpoint [13], WISDM [14], MHEALTH [15], and UCI-HAR [16].

With the recent success of CNNs in feature detection, Zeng et al. [17] first proposed using CNNs in HAR, but they only used a basic CNN on a single accelerometer. Next, Hammerla et al. [18] thoroughly investigated CNN use in HAR and established its viability. However, good performance requires large CNN models; this increases the computational cost, constraining their use on low-power devices. To solve this, Tang et al. [19] looked into the performance and viability of an efficient CNN that uses a tiny Lego filter inspired by Yang et al. [20]. The paper investigated a resource-constrained CNN model for HAR on mobile and wearable devices, achieving an F_1 score of 91.40% and 86.10% in the PAMAP2 and Opportunity datasets, respectively. However, this work had the drawback of having slightly worse performance when compared to conventional CNNs when using small Lego filters instead of traditional filters.

Recurrent networks are good at capturing long-term dependencies, and because of their architecture, they can pick up temporal features in sequenced data. Hammerla et al. [18] took advantage of these benefits and proposed three LSTM models: two uni-directional LSTM and a bi-directional LSTM model, which trains on both historical and upcoming data. The models were trained and evaluated on the PAMAP2, Opportunity, and Dapnet Gait datasets. This work described how to train similar recurrent networks in HAR and introduced a brand-new regularisation method. The bi-LSTM model outperformed state-of-the-art models in the Opportunity Gestures dataset, achieving an F_1 score of 92.7%. Murad et al. [21] showcased the performance of uni-directional, bi-directional, and cascaded LSTM models. The bi-direction LSTM performed best on the Opportunity dataset, with an accuracy of 92.5%. The cascaded LSTM performed the best on Daphnet, with an accuracy of 94.1%. However, the work did not evaluate the models on extensive and complex human activities; additionally, resource efficiency was not considered when designing the model.

CNNs effectively extract spatial features from a local area; however, these models do not have "memory", making it hard to learn long-term dependencies between different samples. RNNs, on the other hand, due to their specific structure, have memory allowing them to learn long-term dependencies; however, they are challenging to train. Researchers have created hybrid deep learning models to address the shortcomings of both CNN and RNN neural networks.

Recently, attention mechanisms have been applied in models to improve performance in HAR. Attention mechanisms allow the model to learn what to focus on in the dataset and understand the relationship between each input element. Ma et al. [22] combined attention mechanisms with a CNN-GRU. This architecture provides the benefits of CNNs, GRUs, and attention, enabling spatial and temporal understanding of the dataset. The model had good performance on all the datasets explored. However, the model is unsuitable for low-powered devices due to the computational complexity of combining all these models. Gao et al. [23] combined temporal and sensor attention in residual networks using a novel dual attention technique to enhance the capacity for feature learning in HAR datasets. The temporal attention focuses on the target activity sequence and chooses where in the sequence to concentrate, whereas the sensor attention is vital in selecting which sensor to focus on, obtaining accuracy scores of 82.75% and 93.16% on Opportunity and PAMAP2, respectively. Although this model performed well, it was constrained by the shortage of labelled multimodal training samples. Additionally, this work did not consider this model's computation and memory requirements, which decreases its potential for use in low-powered devices.

MLP Architectures

In a different area of study, with the arrival of the MLP-Mixer, pure deep MLP architectures have started appearing in computer vision tasks. The MLP variants have similar structures to the MLP-Mixer, usually with only the internal layers being modified to improve the model. These MLPs work by using a "token-mixing" or/and "channel-mixing" layer to capture relevant information from the input, followed by stacking these layers N times. The MLP-Mixer achieved competitive results in computer vision tasks; however, CNNs and Transformer-based models such as Vision Transformers (ViT) [24] outperform the Mixer. To overcome this, Liu et al. [25] proposed a new MLP model called gMLP that introduces a spatial gating unit into MLP layers to enable cross-token interactions. The gMLP performs spatial and channel projections similar to the MLP-Mixer; however, there is no channel-mixing layer. The gMLP has 66% fewer parameters than the MLP-Mixer yet has a 3% performance improvement.

Another method involves using only channel projections. Removing the token-mixing layer prevents MLPs from gaining context from the input and stops the tokens from interacting with one another. Instead, to regain context, the feature maps are spatially interacted with using channel projections after being shifted to align them between the various channels [24]. Yu et al. [26] proposed the S^2-MLP. This model uses spatial shift operations to communicate between patches. This method is computationally efficient with low complexity. This model achieves high performance even with its simplicity, outperforming the MLP-Mixer and remaining competitive with ViT. Finally, Wei et al. [27] proposed ActiveMLP. This is a token-mixing mechanism that enables the model to learn how to combine the current token with useful contextual information from other tokens within the global context of the input. This mechanism allows the model to learn diverse patterns successfully in vision-based tasks, achieving an accuracy of 82% in ImageNet-1K.

The token-Mixer uses static operations. This prevents the token-Mixer from adapting to the varying content contained in the different tokens. Methods have been proposed to add adaptability, allowing the varying information in the tokens to be mixed [24]. Tang et al. [28] try to overcome the static token-mixing layer by viewing each token as an amplitude and phase-varying wave. The phase is a complex number that controls the influence of how tokens and fixed weights are related in the MLP, whereas the amplitude is a real number that represents each token's content. The combined output of these tokens is affected by the phase difference between them, and tokens with similar phases tend to complement one another. WaveMLP limits the fully connected layers to only tokens connected within a local window to address the issue of input resolution sensitivity; however, this prevents the MLP from taking global context across the entire input. WaveMLP is among the best MLP architectures, achieving 82.6% top 1-accuracy in ImageNet-1K. It achieves competitive results with CNNs and Transformers but is still outperformed by them. To improve on this, Wang et al. [29] proposed the DynaMixer; by considering the contents of each set of tokens to be mixed, DynaMixer can dynamically generate mixing matrices. The DynaMixer mixes the tokens row-wise and column-wise to improve the computation speed. In each iteration of the DynaMixer, feature dimensionality occurs to produce the Mixer matrices; additionally, substantially reducing the number of dimensions has little impact on the performance. These feature spaces are separated into various segments for token-mixing. The DynaMixer currently produces state-of-the-art performance among MLP vision architectures, achieving 82.7% top-1 in Imagenet-1k.

3. Methodology

3.1. MLP-Mixer

The MLP-Mixer (Mixer) does not use convolutions or self-attention mechanisms and is instead made up entirely of MLPs. Even with a simpler architecture than CNNs and transformers, the Mixer produces competitive results in computer vision tasks against state-of-the-art models. The Mixer only uses basic matrix multiplication, changes to data layout, and scalar non-linearities, resulting in a simpler and faster model. The Mixer has a similar architecture to the ViT; however, the Mixer's structure has benefits in terms of speed by allowing linear computation scaling when increasing the number of input patches instead of quadratic scaling in the case of the ViT.

Figure 1 illustrates the MLP-Mixer architecture. The input is divided into unique patches that do not overlap. The patches are linearly projected into an embedding space. In contrast to the transformer and ViT, the input does not need positional embeddings as the Mixer is sensitive to the position of the inputs in the token-mixing MLPs [8]. The Mixer consists of two types of MLP layers: the token-mixing layer and the channel-mixing layer. The inspiration behind this is that modern vision neural architectures, according to [8], (1) mix their features at a given spatial location across channels and (2) mix their features between different spatial locations. CNNs implement (1) with a convolution layer through the 1×1 convolution operation; and (2) using large kernels and by adding multiple convolution layers with pooling, which decreases the input spatially. In attention-based models, both (1) and (2) are performed within each self-attention layer. The Mixer's purpose is to separate per-location operations (1) and cross-location operations (2). These features are achieved through two layers, called "token-mixing" and "channel-mixing", representing the per-location and the cross-location operations, respectively.

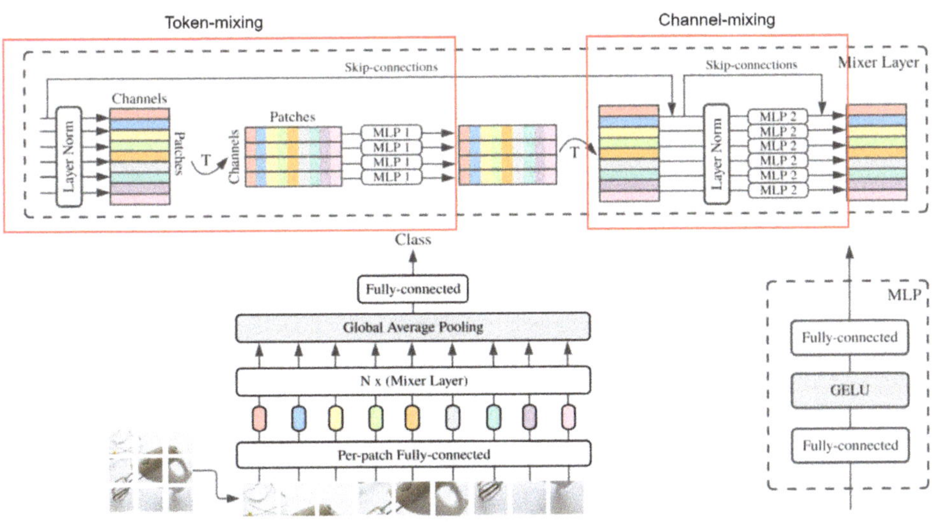

Figure 1. Annotated MLP-Mixer architecture with token-mixing annotated on the left and channel-mixing annotated on the right. Image from [8].

Each unique patch has identical dimensions. The number of patches is calculated by dividing the input dimensions (H, W) by the patch resolution (P, P), $S = HW/P^2$. The sequence of non-overlapping patches is projected into an embedding space with dimension C, resulting in a matrix of dimensions $S \times C$. The layers in the Mixer are all the same size and are made up of two MLP blocks each.

- The first block is the token-mixing MLP; the input matrix is normalised and transposed to allow the data to mix across each patch. The MLP(MLP1) will act on each column of the input matrix, sharing its weights across the columns. The matrix is transposed back into its original form. The overall context of the input is obtained by feeding each patch's data into the MLP. This token-mixing block essentially allows different patches in the same channel to communicate.
- The second block is the channel-mixing MLP; this receives residual connections from its pre-normalised original input to prevent information from being lost during the training process. The result is normalised, and a different MLP(MLP2) performs the channel-mixing with a separate set of weights. The MLP acts on each input matrix row, and its weights are shared across the rows. A single patch's MLP receives data from every channel, enabling communication between the information from various channels.

Each MLP block contains two feed-forward layers with a GELU [30] activation function applied to each row of the input data. The Mixer layers are calculated in Equation (1) (the layer index is not included), and the GELU function is demonstrated in Equation (2).

$$\begin{aligned} U_{*,i} &= X_{*,i} + W_2\sigma(W_1 LayerNorm(X)_{*,i}), \quad for\ i = 1 \ldots C, \\ Y_{j,*} &= U_{j,*} + W_4\sigma(W_3 LayerNorm(U)_{j,*}), \quad for\ j = 1 \ldots S. \end{aligned} \tag{1}$$

$$GELU(x) = xP(X \leq x) = x\Phi(x) \tag{2}$$

It is intuitive to share the weights in each layer of the channel-mixing MLPs as this offers positional invariance, a key characteristic of convolution layers in CNNs. However, it is less intuitive to share the weights across channels in the token-mixing MLPs. For instance, some CNNs use separable convolutions [31], which apply convolutions to each channel independently of the others. However, these convolutions apply different filters to each channel, in contrast to the token-mixing MLPs, which use the same filter for all channels. Additionally, sharing weights in the token-mixing and channel-mixing layers prevents the Mixer from growing in size quickly when the number of patches, S, or the dimensions of the embedding space, C, increases, leading to substantial memory savings. Furthermore, the empirical performance of this model is unaffected by this characteristic.

4. Datasets

To evaluate the performance of the MLP-Mixer in classifying a variety of activities, three datasets are used for benchmarking.

4.1. Opportunity

The opportunity dataset [10] contains complex labelled data collected from multiple body sensors. It consists of data from four subjects recorded in a daily living scenario designed to create multiple activities in a realistic manner. Each subject had six sets of data.

The opportunity dataset consists of all three types of human activities: recurrent, static, and spontaneous. The subjects wore a body jacket that contained five inertial measurement units (IMU), made up of a 3D accelerometer, a gyroscope, and a magnetic sensor; two inertial sensors for both feet; and 12 wireless accelerometers sensors, which suffered from data loss due to their Bluetooth connection. In this dataset, only sensor data without packet loss was used. This included data from the inertial sensors on both feet and the accelerometer sensors on the back and upper limbs, resulting in each sample containing 77 dimensions of sensor data when combining all the sensor data together. The sensors recorded the data at a sampling rate of 30 Hz. The Mixer is trained, validated, and tested on are similar to that in the previous literature [18,32–34] for consistency and fair comparison.

The Mixer was tested on ADL4 and AD5 from subjects 2 and 3, ADL2 from subject 1 was used as the validation set, and the rest of the ADLs and all the drill sessions were used for training the Mixer. The Opportunity dataset has multiple benchmark HAR tasks, including:

- **Opportunity Gestures:** This involves successfully classifying different gestures being performed by the subjects from both arm sensors. There are 18 different gesture classes.
- **Opportunity Locomotion:** This involves accurately classifying the locomotion of the subjects using full body sensors. There are five different locomotion classes.

4.2. PAMAP2

The PAMAP2 dataset [12] contains complex labelled data collected from chest, hand, and ankle sensors. This consisted of data recorded from nine subjects. Each subject followed a routine of 12 different actions and optionally performed an addition of 6 activities, resulting in 18 recorded activities each, 19 if you include the null class.

The PAMAP2, similar to the Opportunity dataset, contains all three types of human activities. The nine subjects wore IMUs on their hands, ankles, and chest. The IMU recorded multimodal data, which consisted of an accelerometer, gyroscope, heart rate, temperature, and magnetic data. In total, the data contains 40 sensor recordings and 12 IMU orientation data points, resulting in each sample containing 52 dimensions of sensor data when combined. Each sensor sampled the data at a sampling rate of 100 Hz, and the dataset was downsampled to approximately 33.3 Hz to have a similar sampling rate to the opportunity dataset. There were missing data present in the dataset from the packet loss of the wireless sensors. To account for this, only the heart rate sensor was interpolated; afterwards, samples with missing values were excluded from the dataset. The parts of the dataset that are trained, tested, and validated are identical to the previous literature [34,35]. The Mixer was tested on subject 6 and validated on subject 5, and the rest were used for training; however, subject 9 was dropped due to significantly less sensor data compared to the rest of the subjects. Additionally, the orientation data points were not used as they were unimportant for this problem, leaving the dataset with a dimension of 40 features. To make the experiments performed on PAMAP2 comparable with the previous literature, the optional activities and the null activities are excluded while training the Mixer, resulting in a total of 12 classes to be classified.

4.3. Daphnet Gait

The daphnet gait dataset [11] contains labelled data collected from accelerometer sensors. It consists of data collected from 10 subjects who are affected with Parkinson's disease (PD). The subjects are instructed to carry out three types of tasks, walking in a straight line; walking while turning; and realistic ADL scenarios, which involve tasks such as getting coffee. These tasks were designed to frequently induce gait freezing in the subjects. Freezing is a common symptom of PD, which causes difficulty starting movements, such as taking steps, for a short period of time [18]. The goal of the dataset is to detect whether the subjects are freezing or doing the specified actions (walk, turn). This is a binary classification problem since the specified action are combined into one class, "No Freeze", and the "Null" class is excluded from the experiment.

Accelerometers were used to capture information about the subjects. They were placed on the chest, above the ankle, and above the knee, resulting in each sample containing nine dimensions of sensor data when combined. Each sensor sampled the data at a sampling rate of 64 Hz, and the dataset was downsampled to 32 Hz for temporal comparison with the other datasets. A fair comparison was maintained by splitting the dataset into training, validation, and testing sets identical to the early literature [18]. The Mixer was tested on data from subject 2, validated on subject 9, and trained using the rest of the information.

4.4. Sliding Windows

For the datasets to be trained and tested by the Mixer, a sliding window approach is used on the dataset. This splits the dataset into multiple sequences with the dimensions ($D_f \times S_L$), where D_f is the number of features in the dataset and S_L is the sliding window length. These 2D sequences, in the case of the Mixer, are treated as images. The length of the sliding window maintains a fixed length throughout each separate training process but varies across the different datasets and experiments. As mentioned in Section 3.1, the Mixer takes an input image with dimensions (H, W) that is split into patches with identical dimensions (P, P). This requires the patch resolution, P, to be fully divisible by both dimensions of the input. This limits the length of the sliding window to either be divisible by the number of features in the dataset or divisible by the patch resolution.

The Mixer outputs a prediction of the activity for every sliding window interval after observing it; however, there would be multiple predictions in the sliding window instead of a single ground truth prediction. There are multiple methods around this [35], which involve using the prediction at the end of the sliding window, max-pooling all of the sequence predictions over time, or returning the most frequent predictions. The Mixer benefits from mixing its features at a given spatial location across channels and between different spatial locations. In addition, the token-mixing MLP provides a global context of the input to the model. Therefore, using the most frequent predictions as the ground truth prediction is preferred to other methods since the Mixer learns context from the whole input. The details of the sliding window for each dataset are briefly described below, and the summary of their parameters is tabulated in Table 1.

- **Opportunity:** The dataset was fit into a sliding window with an interval of 2.57 s. This duration represents 77 samples, which makes the input dimensions identical, allowing the patch resolution to be a factor of 77. The dataset was normalised to account for the wide range of sensors used in the dataset. After preprocessing the data, there were no labels of "close drawer 2" activity in the test set (ADL4 and AD5 from subjects 2 and 3).
- **PAMAP2:** Before downsampling, the dataset was fitted into a sliding window interval of 0.84 s, which corresponds to 84 samples. The "rope-jumping" activity in subject 6 had a very small number of samples. After preprocessing, there were no labels of this activity present in the test set (subject 6).
- **Daphnet Gait:** Before downsampling, a sliding window interval of 2.1 s was used to fit the dataset; this interval corresponds to 126 samples. Daphnet Gait contains a lot of longer activities, so a wider sliding window interval was chosen to provide the Mixer with more information.

Table 1. The parameters used for each dataset. Note, the parameters are chosen in order to make them comparable to prior literature for a fair comparison.

	Opportunity	**PAMAP2**	**Daphnet Gait**
Parameters			
Number of Activities	18	19	2
Number of Features	77	40	9
Sliding Window Length	77	84	126
Sampling Rate	30 Hz	100 Hz	64 Hz
Downsampling	1	3	2
Step Size	3	3	3
Normalisation	True	False	False
Interpolation	False	True	False
Includes Null activities	True	False	False

Large sliding windows were used to give the Mixer access to more information and enable the sequence to be divided into patches correctly and in an error-free manner. Smaller step sizes were used because the Mixer tends to overfit, giving it more training points and ensuring that there were enough data points for adequate testing on the various activities in each dataset.

4.5. Data Sampler and Generation

A class balance sampler was applied to the training dataset to give similar probability to the classes during training, allowing the Mixer to learn from each class equally in the imbalanced datasets. The different samples are stored based on their labelled class. During each batch, the sampler accesses the training samples based on their weights. The samples are weighted based on the proportion of their class in the training dataset.

4.6. Patches

The MLP-Mixer requires a sequence of input patches. This layer converts the input sensor data into separate patches. The patch resolution has to be fully divisible by both the input height and width dimensions. The patch resolution differed between datasets, and the resolution for each dataset is tabulated in Table 2. This was implemented using a strided Conv2D layer in Pytorch. A strided Conv2D layer produces the same results as the per-patch fully-connected layer used in [8]. This layer reshapes the input from number of samples, number of channels, input height, and input width to number of samples, number of patches, and patch-embedding dimensionality.

Table 2. Specification of the Mixer architecture for each dataset.

	Opportunity	PAMAP2	Daphnet Gait
Specifications			
Number of Layers	10	10	10
Patch Resolution	11	4	9
Input Sequence Length	49	210	14
Patch-Embedding Size	512	512	512
Token Dimension	256	256	256
Channel Dimension	2048	2048	512
Learnable Parameters (M)	21	21	5

5. Experimental Setup

The Mixer was trained using the Adam optimiser with the cross-entropy loss as the criterion and hyperparameters $\beta_1 = 0.9$, $\beta_2 = 0.999$. The Mixer has a tendency to overfit, so a weight decay of 1×10^{-3} was used. The gradient clipping at the global norm was set to 1, and the batch size for the training and testing dataset was 64. A learning rate scheduler was used, and the learning rate was set to 0.01. For the first 500 steps, the learning rate scheduler used a linear warm-up rate. Then, until the training was finished, it used a cosine decay.

The specifications of the Mixer architecture used to produce the main results in Section 6 is tabulated in Table 2. The experiments were run five times with the best specifications, and the mean of the results was taken.

5.1. Ablation Study

The Mixer is ablated to compare the importance of different design choices of the MLP-Mixer in HAR. The different design choices involve the architecture of the Mixer (token-mixing MLP, channel-mixing MLP) and the RGB embedding layer. The macro F_1 score is used in the ablation study to assess the model. This prevents high evaluation scores by simply choosing the majority class in imbalanced datasets and provides accurate insight into the model's learning capabilities across class activities.

The MLP-Mixer without RGB Embedding: The Mixer saw a slight decrease in performance, which meant that this layer made some contribution to the Mixer's learning capabilities. This allows the sensor data to simulate the RGB channels in images. This produces three sets of features for the Mixer to project into its embedding space instead of a single set of features from the single sensor channel. The results are tabulated in Table 3.

Table 3. Mixer ablation study.

	Opportunity	PAMAP2	Daphnet
Metric	F_m	F_m	F_m
Base Mixer	0.68	0.971	0.85
Mixer with no RGB Embedding	0.63	0.940	0.79
Mixer with no Token-Mixing	0.05	0.165	0.12
Mixer with no Channel-Mixing	0.569	0.82	0.795

The MLP-Mixer without the Token-Mixing MLPs: The model had a significant decrease in performance in all the datasets without the token-mixing MLPs. The Mixer uses token-mixing to learn global context from the input and communicate information between patches; without this layer, the Mixer cannot effectively capture the spatial and temporal information of the activities in the datasets. The results tabulated in Table 3 indicate the Mixer loses its capabilities to learn relevant features of the dataset; hence, it can be concluded that the token-mixing MLP is necessary for the Mixer to perform well in HAR benchmark datasets.

The MLP-Mixer without the Channel-Mixing MLPs: The channel-mixing MLPs allow the model to communicate between channels, essentially acting as a 1×1 convolution. This enables the Mixer to detect features between channels, and without it, only spatial information between the various patches will be learned. The results tabulated in Table 3 showcase substantial performance loss, which indicates that the channel-mixing MLP is important for HAR. However, the performance loss is lower than the performance loss in the absence of the token-mixing MLPs. This indicates that the channel-mixing MLP is a supplement to the token-mixing MLP, communicating the information learned from the token-mixing layer across channels rather than capturing core features needed for accurate prediction in HAR.

5.2. Measuring Performance

When evaluating classification problems, accuracy can be used as a metric that determines the percentage of correct predictions the model made; this works very well in most problems, but in classification problems with imbalanced datasets, this metric is no longer as valuable. For example, in a binary classification task, the dataset could be imbalanced with a ratio of 1:100 for the minority and majority classes, respectively. Accurately predicting the majority class but failing to classify all of the minority classes would still lead to an accuracy of approximately 99%, which does not evaluate the model's ability to predict different classes. Fortunately, there are other metrics that can be used on imbalanced datasets to evaluate the model's performance. The following possibilities arise when a model predicts classes:

- **True Positive (TP):** the model accurately predicts that the class is an activity.
- **True Negative (TN):** the model accurately predicts that the class is not an activity.
- **False Positive (FP):** the model inaccurately predicts that the class is an activity.
- **False Negative (FN):** the model inaccurately predicts that the class is not an activity.

5.2.1. Precision

Precision is the ratio of positive classification for class i over all positive predictions. It answers the following question: How many samples recognised and predicted as class i, were correctly classified? The precision is calculated below:

$$Precision = \frac{TP}{TP + FP} \tag{3}$$

5.2.2. Recall

Recall or the true positive rate is the ratio of positive classification prediction for class i over all predictions of class i. It answers the following question: How many times was class i correctly classified? The recall is calculated below.

$$Recall = \frac{TP}{TP + FN} \tag{4}$$

5.2.3. F_1-Score

The F_1 score combines recall and precision to create a new accuracy-like measurement. It is the harmonic mean of precision and recall, accounting for the false positives (precision) and the false negatives (recall) in the different classes. The F_1 score is calculated below:

$$F_1 = 2 \cdot \frac{Precision \cdot Recall}{Precision + Recall} \tag{5}$$

In a multi-classification problem, having an F_1 score for each class is not preferable to a single score that gives insight into the overall performance of the model. This single score is obtained using average techniques over all the F_1 scores [36].

5.2.4. Macro F_1-Score

The macro F_1 score computes the unweighted mean of all the F_1 scores. It treats all classes equally, which is very useful in imbalanced datasets since the imbalance is not taken into account when averaging the F_1 scores.

5.2.5. Weighted F_1-Score

The weighted F_1 score computes the weighted mean of all the F_1 scores. It weighs each class based on the number of true occurrences (true positives and false negatives) it has, which is very useful in imbalanced datasets where you want to give classes with more instances in the dataset a higher weightage in the F_1 score.

6. Results

The Mixer is compared with the following state-of-the-art architectures:

- **Ensemble LSTMs [32]:** combines multiple LSTMs using ensemble techniques to produce a single LSTM.
- **CNN-BiGRU [37]:** CNN connected with a biGRU.
- **AttenSense [22]:** a CNN and GRU are combined using an attention mechanism to learn spatial and temporal patterns.
- **Multi-Agent Attention [38]:** combines multi-agent collaboration with attention-based selection.
- **DeepConvLSTM [35]:** combines an LSTM to learn temporal information with a CNN to learn spatial features.
- **BLSTM-RNN [33]:** a bi-LSTM, with its weights and activation functions binarized.
- **Triple Attention [39]:** a ResNet, using a triple-attention mechanism.
- **Self-Attention [40]:** a self-attention-based model without any recurrent architectures.
- **CNN [18]:** a CNN with three layers and max pooling.
- **b-LSTM-S [18]:** bidirectional LSTM that uses future training data.

Table 4 shows the performance comparison between the Mixer and existing state-of-the-art literature. Table 4 shows that the MLP-Mixer performs better than previous techniques in the Opportunity Locomotion, PAMAP2, and Daphnet Gait datasets. Despite the model's shortcomings in the Opportunity Gestures dataset, it is still competitive with most of the previously developed methods. Sliding window techniques were used in all the previous techniques, with only the sliding window lengths and overlaps differing. Although the Mixer beats the previous techniques in Opportunity Locomotion, most previous work that used the Opportunity dataset for performance evaluation only focused on the gesture classification task while disregarding the locomotion task.

The sliding window lengths used were similar to or larger than previous techniques, allowing the model to capture more information from each interval. Therefore, it can be concluded that the MLP-Mixer model can learn the spatial and temporal dynamics of the sensor data more effectively than the previous models. The Mixer performs better than existing attention and convolution-based models in PAMAP2. The macro-score of the Mixer is slightly higher (0.97) than the triple-attention model [39] (0.96) and significantly higher than the best convolution-based model [18] (0.937), and it performed better than the state-of-the-art by 1%. In the daphnet-gait dataset, the model also performed better than convolution and recurrent models, producing a macro-score of 0.842 compared to 0.741. It performed better than the state-of-the-art by 10.1%. However, the existing literature using the Daphnet Gait focuses more on future prediction [41–43] instead of recognition and uses different evaluation metrics; therefore, it cannot be directly compared to the Mixer. In the Opportunity Gestures, the Mixer remains competitive but does not perform better than the b-LSTM-S. The opportunity dataset was particularly challenging for the MLP-Mixer, due to shorter activities combined with a larger sliding window necessary for the image to be split into patches. As a result, there were several activities in the training sliding window, making it more difficult for the Mixer to learn and harder for it to predict activities in the test sliding window. The b-LSTM-S performed 1.7% better than the Mixer in this dataset.

Table 4. State-of-the-art comparison for MLP-Mixer scores with bold font showing the best performing cases. Mixer results in the format mean ± std. F_w is the weighted F_1 score, and F_m is the F_1 macro score.

	Opportunity Locomotion	Opportunity Gestures	PAMAP2	Daphnet Gait
Metric	F_w	F_m	F_m	
Ensemble LSTMs [32]	-	0.726	0.854	-
CNN-BiGRU [37]	-	-	0.855	-
AttenSense [22]	-	-	0.893	-
Multi-Agent Attention [38]	-	-	0.899	-
DeepConvLSTM [35]	0.895	0.917	-	-
BLSTM-RNN [33]	-	-	0.93	-
Triple Attention [39]	-	-	0.932	-
Self-Attention [40]	-	-	0.96	-
CNN [18]	-	0.894	0.937	0.684
b-LSTM-S [18]	-	**0.927**	0.868	0.741
MLP-Mixer	**0.90 ± 0.005**	0.912 ± 0.002	**0.97 ± 0.002**	**0.842 ± 0.007**

7. Discussion

Convolutions capture the spatial information in a local area of the data. However, they are not effective at learning long-term dependencies (temporal data) [24], unlike recurrent networks, which specialise in long-term dependencies. The self-attention mechanism learns the entire context of input patches. Additionally, it learns what to pay attention to based on its weights [40], allowing it to learn the relationship between the sensors and the different activities. The token-mixing MLPs can be considered a convolution layer that captures information about the entire input, combining spatial information from a single channel and distributing channel weights to increase efficiency, which allows the Mixer to perform better than previous techniques when an adequate amount of data is provided and the invariant features of the input are coherent.

The normalised confusion matrices of the PAMAP2, Opportunity, and Daphnet datasets are illustrated in Figures 2–4, respectively. The model's ability to distinguish between activities in the PAMAP2 confusion matrix showed that it had learned the various spatial and temporal characteristics of each activity. The model did have some trouble distinguishing between the "ironing" and "standing" activities; this is probably because the sensor data for these actions are similar in the chest and ankle regions but only slightly different in the hand regions. With further inspection, standing consisted of talking while gesticulating, further validating the possibility of similarities in the hand sensors. Furthermore, the model had little trouble differentiating between "walking", "vacuum cleaning", and "descending stairs" activities; this is understandable since it mistook these activities for similar ones.

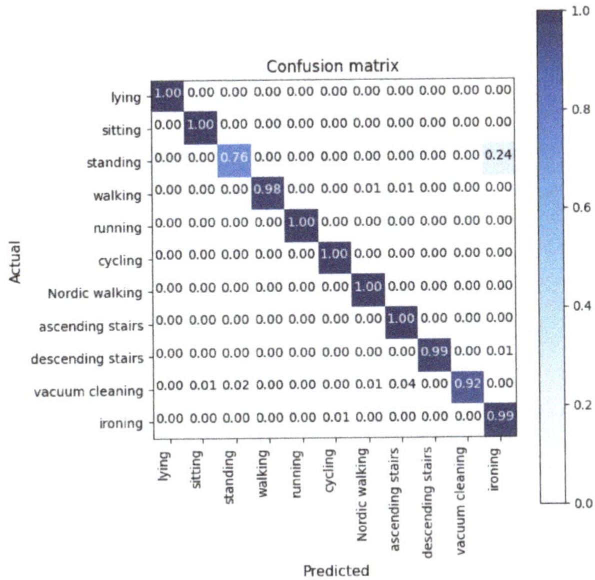

Figure 2. Normalised confusion matrix of the PAMAP2 dataset.

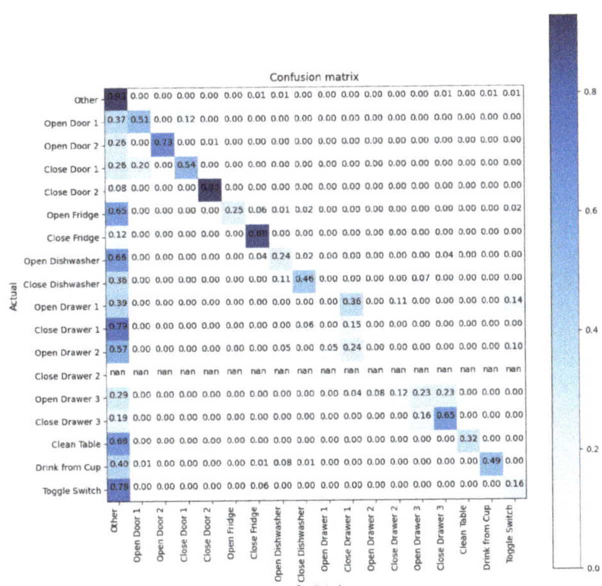

Figure 3. Normalised confusion matrix of the opportunity dataset.

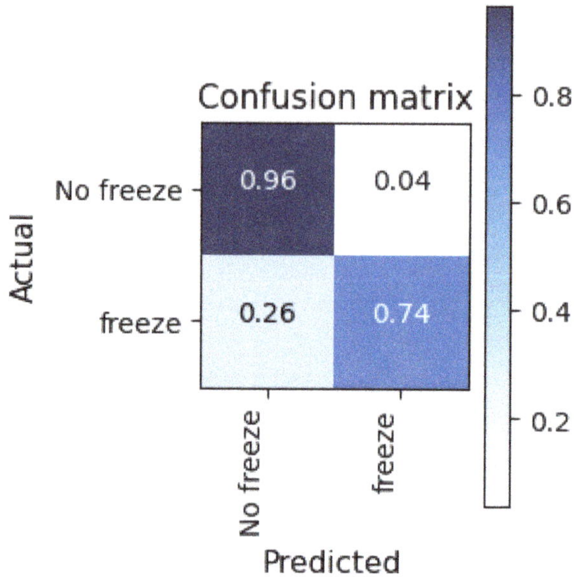

Figure 4. Normalised confusion matrix of the Daphnet Gait dataset.

It was more difficult for the model to distinguish between different activities in the Opportunity dataset. Because there were significantly more samples of Null activities than any other activity, the Opportunity confusion matrix, Figure 3, shows that the model frequently mistook activities for being unrelated. Furthermore, because the activities were short, the model had a more challenging time figuring out where a given activity began and ended in the sliding window. The confusion matrix demonstrates that the model was could pick up on some of the "open door 2" and "close fridge" activity characteristics. However, the model did not successfully capture features of "open drawer 1" and mistook this activity for "close drawer 1". Further investigation revealed that the activity, which consisted of opening and closing the drawer, took place in a single sequence, suggesting that the model could not determine when the activity began and, therefore, could not correctly distinguish between the two.

There was a significant imbalance between the two activities in the Daphnet Gait dataset, much like in the opportunity dataset. As shown in Figure 4, the Mixer was trained on an adequate sample size for the majority class", No Freeze", allowing it to learn when the participants were not freezing correctly. However, in the minority case, there was insufficient data from the Mixer to properly learn relevant features, resulting in the Mixer incorrectly classifying the participants as not freezing 26% of the time.

7.1. Performance of Sliding Window Parameters

Each dataset contains a different range of activity lengths and repetition rates. The sliding window length has a significant impact depending on how long the activities are in the dataset. The sliding window's parameters were altered to study its effect on the Mixer performance. The model's parameters were fixed, and the step size was constant instead of using an overlap percentage of the window length to prevent the number of samples from affecting the results. Small window intervals contain insufficient data for the Mixer to learn from and make decisions. On the other hand, if the sliding window interval is large relative to the activities in the window, it allows information from multiple activities to be present in a single sliding window, making it harder for the Mixer to determine which activity the sliding window represents among the multiple activities.

Performance generally improves with increasing overlap, but as there are more samples to train and test, the computational complexity of training the Mixer also rises. In contrast, little to no overlap significantly reduces the sample size, particularly for larger sliding window sizes, which causes the Mixer to over-fit on the dataset.

Figures 5–7 illustrate the changes in the Mixer's performance when the sliding window length is changed. In datasets with more extended activities, such as PAMAP2 and Daphnet, larger sliding windows increase the model's capability to learn by providing more information. On the other hand, in the Opportunity dataset, which contains shorter activities, the model's performance decreases with larger window lengths. The sliding window figures indicate that the sliding window has a slight effect on the Mixer's performance, but overall the model is not sensitive to the sliding window length.

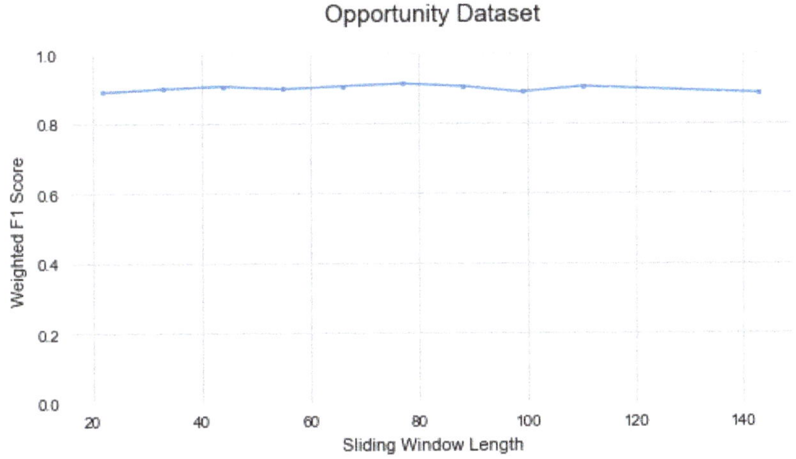

Figure 5. Evaluation of sliding window length on the Opportunity dataset

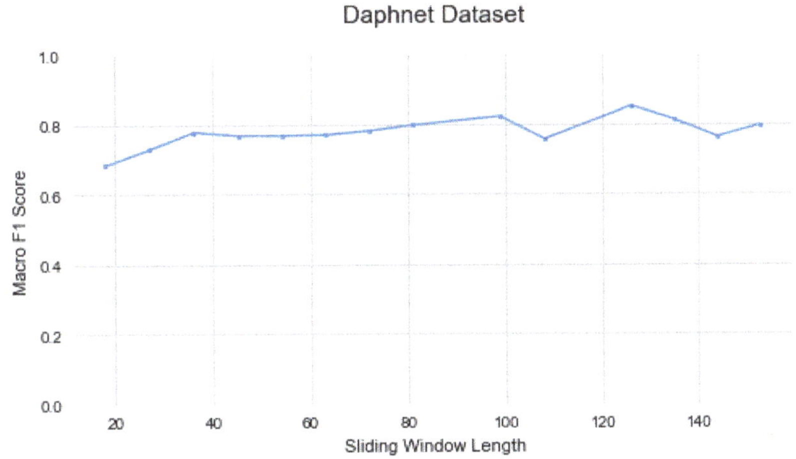

Figure 6. Evaluation of sliding window length on the Daphnet Gait dataset

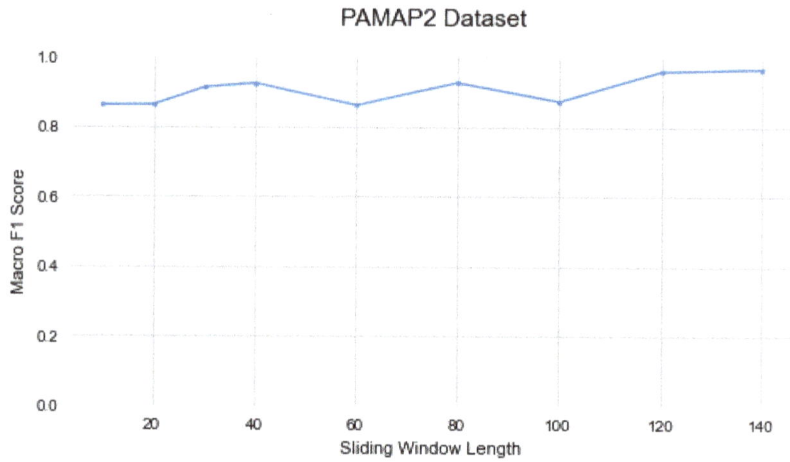

Figure 7. Performance evaluation of sliding window length on the PAMAP2 dataset

7.2. Weight Visualisation

The models' weights are visualised to provide insight into which sensors the model considers necessary for different activities. This experiment aims to confirm that the Mixer is capturing relevant features and to offer some interpretation of how the Mixer categorises the activities. The analysis is performed on the PAMAP2 dataset to showcase various simple and complex activities. Six different activities and their associated weights are illustrated in Figure 8.

Figure 8 shows how the Mixer associates various sensors with various activities. The Mixer not only learns which sensors are crucial but also when they are crucial as the emphasis of the sensors changes throughout the sliding window. For example, in ascending stairs, the hand (X, Y), chest (X), and ankle sensors have essential features that the Mixer emphasises, typical when climbing a staircase with handrails. Cycling focuses on the hand (Y) sensor, most likely for steering, and the chest and ankle sensors, likely for pedalling. The Mixer prioritises the hand's (X, Z) sensors when ironing, as expected. While lying down, the Mixer considers all sensors important, except for the ankle (Z) and hand (Y), which is to be expected given that the participants had complete freedom to change their lying positions. Finally, the Mixer values the hand (X, Z) and chest (X) sensors for vacuum cleaning and the ankles (X, Y) and chest (X) sensors for running activities, which is consistent with common sense. This analysis concludes that the Mixer is successfully learning the spatial and temporal characteristics of the various activities because the weight assignments for these activities are understandable and in tune with common sense.

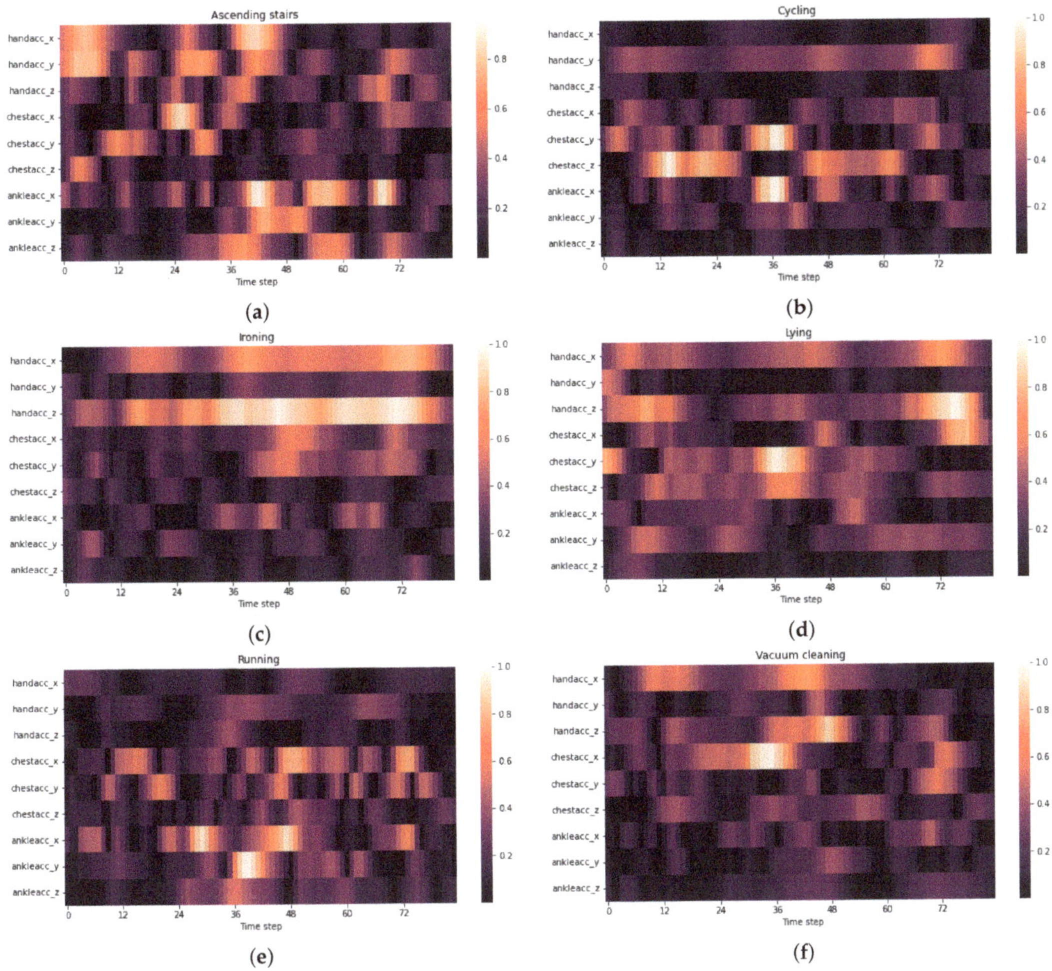

Figure 8. The Mixer's weight visualisation for each accelerometer sensors in the sliding window. Each figure represents a different activity: (**a**) Ascending stairs, (**b**) cycling, (**c**) ironing, (**d**) lying, (**e**) running, and (**f**) vacuum cleaning.

8. Conclusions

In this paper, the MLP-Mixer performance is investigated for HAR. The Mixer does not use convolutions or self-attention mechanisms and instead relies solely on MLPs. It uses token-mixing and channel mixing layers to communicate between patches and channels, learning the global context of the input and enabling excellent spatial and temporal pattern recognition in HAR. Experiments were performed on three popular HAR datasets: Opportunity, PAMAP2 and Daphnet Gait. The Mixer was assessed using sliding windows on the dataset. This paper demonstrates that pure-MLP architectures can compete with convolutional and attention-based architectures in terms of HAR viability and performance. We demonstrate that the MLP-Mixer outperforms current state-of-the-art models in the test benchmarks for all datasets except for Opportunity Gestures. It performs 10.1% better in the Daphnet Gait dataset, 1% better in the PAMAP2 dataset, and 0.5% in the Opportunity Locomotion dataset. The Mixer was outperformed in the Opportunity Gestures; however, it remained competitive with the state-of-the-art results. To the best of my knowledge, vision-based MLP architectures have not been applied to HAR tasks. It is interesting to see the performance of a pure-MLP architecture outperform and remain competitive with state-of-the-art models in HAR.

Author Contributions: Conceptualization, K.O. and K.F.; methodology, K.O. and K.F.; software, K.O.; validation, K.O.; investigation, K.O.; writing—original draft preparation, K.O.; writing—review and editing, K.O. and K.F.; supervision, K.F. All authors have read and agreed to the published version of the manuscript.

Funding: This research received no external funding.

Informed Consent Statement: Informed consent was obtained from all subjects involved in the study.

Data Availability Statement: The links to the publicly available datasets used in this paper are provided in Section 4 of the paper (Datasets).

Conflicts of Interest: The authors declare no conflict of interest.

References

1. Parker, S.J.; Strath, S.J.; Swartz, A.M. Physical Activity Measurement in Older Adults: Relationships With Mental Health. *J. Aging Phys. Act.* **2008**, *16*, 369–380. [CrossRef] [PubMed]
2. Kranz, M.; Möller, A.; Hammerla, N.; Diewald, S.; Plötz, T.; Olivier, P.; Roalter, L. The mobile fitness coach: Towards individualized skill assessment using personalized mobile devices. *Pervasive Mob. Comput.* **2013**, *9*, 203–215. [CrossRef]
3. Patel, S.; Park, H.S.; Bonato, P.; Chan, L.; Rodgers, M. A Review of Wearable Sensors and Systems with Application in Rehabilitation. *J. Neuroeng. Rehabil.* **2012**, *9*, 21. [CrossRef]
4. Cedillo, P.; Sanchez-Zhunio, C.; Bermeo, A.; Campos, K. A Systematic Literature Review on Devices and Systems for Ambient Assisted Living: Solutions and Trends from Different User Perspectives. In *2018 International Conference on eDemocracy & eGovernment (ICEDEG)*; IEEE: New York, NY, USA, 2018. [CrossRef]
5. De Leonardis, G.; Rosati, S.; Balestra, G.; Agostini, V.; Panero, E.; Gastaldi, L.; Knaflitz, M. Human Activity Recognition by Wearable Sensors: Comparison of different classifiers for real-time applications. In Proceedings of the 2018 IEEE International Symposium on Medical Measurements and Applications (MeMeA), Rome, Italy, 11–13 June 2018; pp. 1–6. [CrossRef]
6. Park, S.; Jayaraman, S. Enhancing the quality of life through wearable technology. *IEEE Eng. Med. Biol. Mag.* **2003**, *22*, 41–48. [CrossRef] [PubMed]
7. Lara, O.D.; Labrador, M.A. A Survey on Human Activity Recognition using Wearable Sensors. *IEEE Commun. Surv. Tutorials* **2013**, *15*, 1192–1209. [CrossRef]
8. Tolstikhin, I.O.; Houlsby, N.; Kolesnikov, A.; Beyer, L.; Zhai, X.; Unterthiner, T.; Yung, J.; Steiner, A.; Keysers, D.; Uszkoreit, J.; et al. MLP-Mixer: An all-mlp architecture for vision. *Adv. Neural Inf. Process. Syst.* **2021**, *34*, 24261–24272.
9. Le, V.T.; Tran-Trung, K.; Hoang, V.T. A comprehensive review of recent deep learning techniques for human activity recognition. *Comput. Intell. Neurosci.* **2022**, *2022*, 8323962. [CrossRef]
10. Roggen, D.; Calatroni, A.; Rossi, M.; Holleczek, T.; Förster, K.; Tröster, G.; Lukowicz, P.; Bannach, D.; Pirkl, G.; Ferscha, A.; et al. Collecting complex activity datasets in highly rich networked sensor environments. In Proceedings of the 2010 Seventh International Conference on Networked Sensing Systems (INSS), Kassel, Germany, 15–18 June 2010; pp. 233–240. [CrossRef]
11. Bächlin, M.; Plotnik, M.; Roggen, D.; Maidan, I.; Hausdorff, J.; Giladi, N.; Troster, G. Wearable Assistant for Parkinson's Disease Patients with the Freezing of Gait Symptom. *Inf. Technol. Biomed. IEEE Trans.* **2010**, *14*, 436–446. [CrossRef]
12. Reiss, A.; Stricker, D. Introducing a New Benchmarked Dataset for Activity Monitoring. In Proceedings of the 2012 16th International Symposium on Wearable Computers, Newcastle, UK, 18–22 June 2012; pp. 108–109. [CrossRef]
13. Zappi, P.; Lombriser, C.; Stiefmeier, T.; Farella, E.; Roggen, D.; Benini, L.; Tröster, G. Activity Recognition from On-Body Sensors: Accuracy-Power Trade-Off by Dynamic Sensor Selection. In *Proceedings of the Wireless Sensor Networks*; Verdone, R., Ed.; Springer: Berlin/Heidelberg, Germany, 2008; pp. 17–33.
14. Weiss, G.M.; Yoneda, K.; Hayajneh, T. Smartphone and Smartwatch-Based Biometrics Using Activities of Daily Living. *IEEE Access* **2019**, *7*, 133190–133202. [CrossRef]
15. Banos, O.; García, R.; Holgado-Terriza, J.; Damas, M.; Pomares, H.; Rojas, I.; Saez, A.; Villalonga, C. *mHealthDroid: A Novel Framework for Agile Development of Mobile Health Applications*; Proceedings 6; Springer International Publishing: Berlin/Heidelberg, Germany, 2014; Volume 8868, pp. 91–98. [CrossRef]
16. Anguita, D.; Ghio, A.; Oneto, L.; Parra, X.; Reyes-Ortiz, J.L. A Public Domain Dataset for Human Activity Recognition using Smartphones. In Proceedings of the European Symposium on Artificial Neural Networks (ESANN), Computational Intelligence and Machine Learning, Bruges, Belgium, 24–26 April 2013.
17. Zeng, M.; Nguyen, L.T.; Yu, B.; Mengshoel, O.J.; Zhu, J.; Wu, P.; Zhang, J. Convolutional Neural Networks for human activity recognition using mobile sensors. In Proceedings of the 6th International Conference on Mobile Computing, Applications and Services, Austin, TX, USA, 6–7 November 2014; pp. 197–205. [CrossRef]

18. Hammerla, N.Y.; Halloran, S.; Ploetz, T. Deep, Convolutional, and Recurrent Models for Human Activity Recognition using Wearables. *arXiv* **2016**, arXiv:1604.08880.
19. Tang, Y.; Teng, Q.; Zhang, L.; Min, F.; He, J. Layer-Wise Training Convolutional Neural Networks with Smaller Filters for Human Activity Recognition Using Wearable Sensors. *IEEE Sens. J.* **2021**, *21*, 581–592. [CrossRef]
20. Yang, Z.; Wang, Y.; Liu, C.; Chen, H.; Xu, C.; Shi, B.; Xu, C.; Xu, C. Legonet: Efficient convolutional neural networks with lego filters. In Proceedings of the International Conference on Machine Learning. PMLR, Long Beach, CA, USA, 9–15 June 2019; pp. 7005–7014.
21. Murad, A.; Pyun, J.Y. Deep Recurrent Neural Networks for Human Activity Recognition. *Sensors* **2017**, *17*, 2556. [CrossRef]
22. Ma, H.; Li, W.; Zhang, X.; Gao, S.; Lu, S. AttnSense: Multi-level Attention Mechanism For Multimodal Human Activity Recognition. In Proceedings of the Twenty-Eighth International Joint Conference on Artificial Intelligence (IJCAI), Macao, China, 10–16 August 2019; pp. 3109–3115. [CrossRef]
23. Gao, W.; Zhang, L.; Teng, Q.; He, J.; Wu, H. DanHAR: Dual Attention Network for multimodal human activity recognition using wearable sensors. *Appl. Soft Comput.* **2021**, *111*, 107728. [CrossRef]
24. Liu, R.; Li, Y.; Tao, L.; Liang, D.; Zheng, H.T. Are we ready for a new paradigm shift? A survey on visual deep MLP. *Patterns* **2022**, *3*, 100520. [CrossRef] [PubMed]
25. Liu, H.; Dai, Z.; So, D.R.; Le, Q.V. Pay Attention to MLPs. *Adv. Neural Inf. Process. Syst.* **2021**, *34*, 9204–9215.
26. Yu, T.; Li, X.; Cai, Y.; Sun, M.; Li, P. S2-MLP: Spatial-Shift MLP Architecture for Vision. In Proceedings of the 2022 IEEE/CVF Winter Conference on Applications of Computer Vision (WACV), Waikoloa, HI, USA, 3–8 January 2022; pp. 3615–3624. [CrossRef]
27. Wei, G.; Zhang, Z.; Lan, C.; Lu, Y.; Chen, Z. ActiveMLP: An MLP-like Architecture with Active Token Mixer. *arXiv* **2022**, arXiv:2203.06108.
28. Tang, Y.; Han, K.; Guo, J.; Xu, C.; Li, Y.; Xu, C.; Wang, Y. An Image Patch is a Wave: Phase-Aware Vision MLP. In Proceedings of the IEEE/CVF Conference on Computer Vision and Pattern Recognition, New Orleans, LA, USA, 18–24 June 2022; pp. 10935–10944.
29. Wang, Z.; Jiang, W.; Zhu, Y.; Yuan, L.; Song, Y.; Liu, W. DynaMixer: A Vision MLP Architecture with Dynamic Mixing. In Proceedings of the 39th International Conference on Machine Learning, PMLR, Baltimore, MD, USA, 17–23 July 2022; Volume 162, pp. 22691–22701.
30. Hendrycks, D.; Gimpel, K. A baseline for detecting misclassified and out-of-distribution examples in neural networks. *arXiv* **2016**, arXiv:1610.02136.
31. Chollet, F. Xception: Deep Learning with Depthwise Separable Convolutions. In Proceedings of the IEEE Conference on Computer Vision and Pattern Recognition (CVPR), Honolulu, HI, USA, 21–26 July 2017.
32. Guan, Y.; Ploetz, T. Ensembles of Deep LSTM Learners for Activity Recognition using Wearables. In *Proceedings of the ACM on Interactive, Mobile, Wearable and Ubiquitous Technologies*; Association for Computing Machinery: New York, NY, USA, 2017; pp. 1–28.
33. Edel, M.; Köppe, E. Binarized-BLSTM-RNN based Human Activity Recognition. In Proceedings of the 2016 International Conference on Indoor Positioning and Indoor Navigation (IPIN), Alcala de Henares, Spain, 18–21 September 2016; pp. 1–7. [CrossRef]
34. Moya Rueda, F.; Grzeszick, R.; Fink, G.A.; Feldhorst, S.; Ten Hompel, M. Convolutional Neural Networks for Human Activity Recognition Using Body-Worn Sensors. *Informatics* **2018**, *5*, 26. [CrossRef]
35. Ordóñez, F.J.; Roggen, D. Deep Convolutional and LSTM Recurrent Neural Networks for Multimodal Wearable Activity Recognition. *Sensors* **2016**, *16*, 115. [CrossRef]
36. Pedregosa, F.; Varoquaux, G.; Gramfort, A.; Michel, V.; Thirion, B.; Grisel, O.; Blondel, M.; Prettenhofer, P.; Weiss, R.; Dubourg, V.; et al. Scikit-learn: Machine Learning in Python. *J. Mach. Learn. Res.* **2011**, *12*, 2825–2830.
37. Mekruksavanich, S.; Jitpattanakul, A. Deep Convolutional Neural Network with RNNs for Complex Activity Recognition Using Wrist-Worn Wearable Sensor Data. *Electronics* **2021**, *10*, 1685. [CrossRef]
38. Chen, K.; Yao, L.; Zhang, D.; Guo, B.; Yu, Z. Multi-agent Attentional Activity Recognition. *arXiv* **2019**, arXiv:1905.08948.
39. Tang, Y.; Zhang, L.; Teng, Q.; Min, F.; Song, A. Triple Cross-Domain Attention on Human Activity Recognition Using Wearable Sensors. *IEEE Trans. Emerg. Top. Comput. Intell.* **2022**, *6*, 1–10. [CrossRef]
40. Mahmud, S.; Tonmoy, M.T.H.; Bhaumik, K.K.; Rahman, A.K.M.M.; Amin, M.A.; Shoyaib, M.; Khan, M.A.H.; Ali, A.A. Human Activity Recognition from Wearable Sensor Data Using Self-Attention. *arXiv* **2020**, arXiv:2003.09018.
41. Li, B.; Yao, Z.; Wang, J.; Wang, S.; Yang, X.; Sun, Y. Improved Deep Learning Technique to Detect Freezing of Gait in Parkinson's Disease Based on Wearable Sensors. *Electronics* **2020**, *9*, 1919. [CrossRef]
42. Thu, N.T.H.; Han, D.S. Freezing of Gait Detection Using Discrete Wavelet Transform and Hybrid Deep Learning Architecture. In Proceedings of the 2021 Twelfth International Conference on Ubiquitous and Future Networks (ICUFN), Jeju Island, Republic of Korea, 17–20 August 2021; pp. 448–451. [CrossRef]
43. El-ziaat, H.; El-Bendary, N.; Moawad, R. A Hybrid Deep Learning Approach for Freezing of Gait Prediction in Patients with Parkinson's Disease. *Int. J. Adv. Comput. Sci. Appl.* **2022**, *13*, 766–776. [CrossRef]

applied sciences

MDPI

Article

An Evaluation Study on the Analysis of People's Domestic Routines Based on Spatial, Temporal and Sequential Aspects

Aitor Arribas Velasco *, John McGrory and Damon Berry

School of Electrical and Electronic Engineering, Technological University Dublin, Grangegorman Lower, D07 H6K8 Dublin, Ireland; john.mcgrory@tudublin.ie (J.M.); damon.berry@tudublin.ie (D.B.)
* Correspondence: aitor.arribasvelasco@tudublin.ie

Abstract: The concept of collecting data on people's domestic routines is not novel. However, the methods and processes used to decipher these raw data and transform them into useful and appropriate information (i.e., sequence, duration, and timing derived from monitoring domestic routines) have presented challenges and are the focus of numerous research groups. But how are the results of the decoded transposition received, interpreted and used by the various professionals (e.g., occupational therapists and architects) who consume the information? This paper describes the inclusive evaluation process undertaken, which involved a selected group of stakeholders including health carers, engineers and end-users (not the occupants themselves, but more so the care team managing the occupant). Finally, our study suggests that making accessible key spatial and temporal aspects derived from people's domestic routines can be of great value to different professionals. Shedding light on how a systematic approach for collecting, processing and mapping low-level sensor data into higher forms and representations can be a valuable source of knowledge for improving the domestic living experience.

Keywords: behaviour analysis; domestic environments; activities of daily living; knowledge discovery in databases

Citation: Arribas Velasco, A.; McGrory, J.; Berry, D. An Evaluation Study on the Analysis of People's Domestic Routines Based on Spatial, Temporal and Sequential Aspects. *Appl. Sci.* **2023**, *13*, 10608. https://doi.org/10.3390/app131910608

Academic Editors: Marley M.B.R. Vellasco and Luigi Bibbò

Received: 28 August 2023
Revised: 16 September 2023
Accepted: 22 September 2023
Published: 23 September 2023

1. Introduction

People spend most of their time indoors. The Irish people spend an average of 90% of their time in indoors [1–3]. Human Activity Recognition (HAR) approaches are increasingly being employed to understand human behaviour through the analysis of data representative of resident's domestic routines. Current research indicates that healthcare professionals, as well as family members of vulnerable older people, and professionals from the built environment, could potentially benefit from information regarding how householders transit between the different domestic spaces. The term domestic space has been used to refer to the private space of the house [4]. Based on the interaction between people and houses, this research focuses on two perspectives.

On the one hand, if we look at the design of a house, although there are generic spaces, such as an entrance/exit area to the house, a kitchen, bedrooms, bathrooms, etc., their physical characteristics differ from one another, such as the number of rooms and floors, their dimensions and orientation, and thus the way they are connected and distributed. Space syntax, a set of techniques and theories for the study of spatial configurations, is used to predict possible effects of architectural spaces on users, particularly, how people make and use spatial configurations [5]. For example, space syntax has been used to assess the impact of different proposals for extending the existing layout of the Tate Britain Museum [6]. In addition, research has shown that various applications can benefit from occupant information, such as improvements in energy efficiency and indoor air quality, space utilisation and optimisation, occupants' comfort enhancement, and healthcare systems [7]. Iweka et al. showed how information about people's behaviour in relation to the use of domestic spaces is needed to ensure an effective transition towards optimal energy use in private dwellings [8]. Ayalp pointed out the importance and the need to use information representative of domestic human's behaviour when designing new homes [9]. In addition, Mahmoud noted how the interior architectural characteristics of a space impact the accessibility and circulation of people [10].

On the other hand, domestic routines help family members to organise themselves, what they have to do when, as well as in what order and how often. Basic household activities may include bedtime routine, cooking, using the toilet, etc. The skills required to perform these routine tasks have been measured by clinicians to assess the health status of patients in order to independently care for oneself [11]. The term used in this domain is activities of daily living (ADLs) [12]. Basic ADLs include: ambulating, feeding, dressing, personal hygiene, continence and toileting [11]. ADLs are traditionally assessed by healthcare professionals through face-to-face interviews with patients [13]. Although the aim of this research is not to provide a method to replace existing ADL assessment techniques, the focus is on the connection between these activities and the spaces of the house in which they take place, which is of relevant interest in order to provide supporting evidence. For example, ambulating refers to the ability of the patient to move from one position to another and walk independently. Others, such as personal hygiene and toileting, can be inferred based on the use of the bathroom space. Also, feeding is intrinsically related to the amount of time the person spends in the kitchen. Bouchachia and Mohsen, who designed a smart home approach to support caregivers working with people with dementia, remarked that family members can use smart home information to keep track on a daily basis of their loved one's day to day routines, while occupational health professionals could use this information to improve their knowledge of patients [14].

Both previously described views are characterised by temporal information derived from people's domestic routines, in addition to the characteristics of the spaces of the house wherein they take place—spatial information. Spatial and temporal properties have been used to get insights about people's interaction with domestic spaces. Thiago and Gershon defined a human-sensing taxonomy that includes five components that can be measured through spatial and temporal sensing information to analyse the occupancy of buildings and how people interact with them: presence (is there at least one person present?), count (how many people are present?), location (where is each person?), track (where was this person before?) and identity (who is each person?) [15]. Based on these components, Wael al. defined three lenses through which to analyse building occupancy: occupancy resolution (refers to different occupancy levels, for example, resident presence or absence), temporal resolution (refers to the frequencies over time with which events take place) and spatial resolution (refers to the building structure, rooms, floors, and the building as a whole) [7]. These lenses align with major components of this research:

- The movements of people as a result of household routines in domestic buildings;
- Locations as parts of the whole design of the house through which people move, and timeliness as the times of the day, duration and the frequency of events in different spaces of the house;
- Occupancy of buildings. This is used to refer to the presence and movements of people indoors. The term *indoor positioning* can include crude binary PIR detection (i.e., occupancy of a space), or a finer resolution of a location of a person within the space (i.e. positioning location), especially in areas where GPS signal is not present [16].

This paper presents a systematic approach, based on the knowledge discovery in databases (KDD) process, which uses sensor data that reflect the transitioning between locations in a home (e.g., moving from the bedroom to the bathroom) and provides time-based information about the use of different rooms by a monitored resident (e.g., at 2 a.m. moved from the bedroom to the kitchen and stayed for 5 min). The data are then transposed to a set of data visualisations to provide supporting evidence on the following aspects of the monitored household's domestic routines:

- What is the frequency of the visits to the locations?
- What are the most common transitions between locations of the house?

- Which hours of the day are most representative of an activity taking place in a particular location?
- How long on average does the monitored subject spend in a location?

This information is not fully representative of activities such as brushing teeth or preparing food, but is intended to be useful to carers or observers who need to understand the spatial and temporal aspects of other person's routines in their home. It can also inform designers on space usage and areas that have the highest numbers of transition, for example, kitchen to dining room, so increased care can be taken during the design of these spaces, or perhaps more wear-resistant materials can be used.

We present an overview of the proposed overall methodological KDD process in Section 2. In Section 3, the evaluation study conducted to gather feedback and first impressions from the main consumers of the information made available is described. The responses collected through the evaluation study are analysed in Section 4. Finally, Section 5 presents the conclusions based on the results of the thematic analysis carried out.

2. Proposed Method

The mapping of low-level sensor data into other forms, which may be more compact, more abstract, or more useful, involves various steps that go beyond the computational reasoning of the datasets. There are several questions that need to be addressed as a part of this process, including what types of data are needed, how the data will be stored, how the data will be processed, and how the results will be presented. In 1996, Fayyad et al. described the knowledge discovery in databases process as the "non-trivial process of identifying novel, potentially useful, and ultimately understandable patterns or relationships within a dataset in order to make important decisions" [17]. So, KDD is a systematic and iterative way of uncovering structures of information, understandable patterns, from data that can be interpreted as valid. In addition, these entities should be valid for new data with some degree of certainty, resulting in some benefit to the end user or task [18].

As a result of this successful methodology proposed by Fayyad et al., a number of different KDD approaches were developed, derived mainly for business uses [18]. The five steps (Sample, Explore, Modify, Model and Assess—SEMMA) constitute the data mining process developed by the SAS Institute for enterprises to solve different business problems [19]. Two Crows Consulting also proposed a data mining process model very similar to the original KDD process [20]. Anand and Buchner proposed an internet-enabled knowledge discovery process model adapted to the web mining project [21]. Similarly, in 1997, Cabena et al. suggested a business-oriented KDD process that included most of the steps involved in the original KDD process [22]. Brachman and Anand introduced an alternative perspective, a human-centred process, focusing on the data analyst as the key actor in the overall KDD process [23]. One of the main reasons for this argument was that the extraction of valuable knowledge requires prior background knowledge (i.e., an expertise) beyond the data and their analysis, and this background knowledge of the study area, according to the authors, resides only in the analyst.

Depending on the KDD approach studied, the number of steps can vary; nonetheless, the generic steps involved in KDD are: (1) developing an understanding of the end goal, (2) collecting data, (3) selecting a target dataset, (4) cleaning and preprocessing data, (5) creating sub-sets of interest, (6) data mining, and ultimately, (7) producing outputs for evaluation (Figure 1).

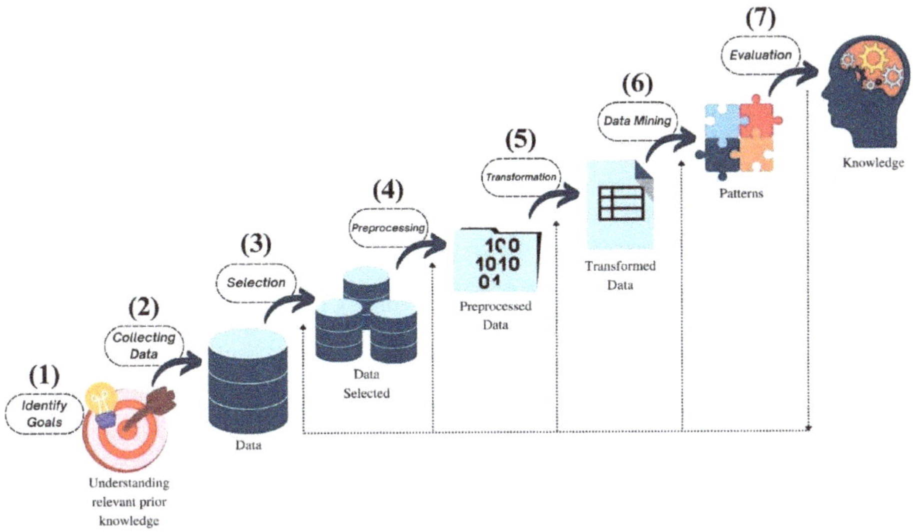

Figure 1. Knowledge discovery in databases steps.

Traditionally, the KDD process has used data mining algorithms to automate the extraction of patterns. Generally, data mining techniques developed in the field of HAR in domestic environments have been classified into two main groups: data-driven and knowledge-driven approaches, as well as hybrid methods [7]. Regardless of the approach undertaken, the activity recognition process focusses on the creation of models that accurately map human activities. Reusability and scalability are the main challenges of these approaches, as the nature of human activities involves the sequencing of events, and a particular start time and duration for each step. Additionally, domestic environments vary in shape, form, and materials, and these factors influence, among other things, the way in which they are used by their inhabitants. Nonetheless, regardless of the computational method used, the results of the data mining step need to be presented in a meaningful way and in a form that can be dynamically adapted by an analyst through iterations so that conclusions can be drawn.

Our KDD approach follows the idea put forward by Brachman and Anand; we propose a human-centred approach that brings the analyst's background knowledge into the knowledge discovery process. The aim, therefore, is to make the background knowledge in the knowledge discovery process a key element in the elaboration of assumptions derived from the study of the sensor data. Our KDD process mimics the scientific method, as it offers the possibility to explore observations and answer questions. Hence, the process starts with a question formulated by the analyst; for example, what is the resident's night-time routine? This leads to the formulation of a hypothesis, via deduction, perhaps that the night-time routine of the resident includes the use of the bathroom and the bedroom, that a minimum duration is expected for these events, and that the frequency of visits to the bathroom should not exceed 2 min on average. To test the hypothesis derived from the analyst's background knowledge, four modes of data visualisation, described in the following section, were adapted. These visualisations are flexible based on different parameter modifications undertaken by the analyst to show different key spatial and temporal aspects of the sensor data. By iteratively examining these data visualisations, a conclusion can be drawn. Table 1 shows the comparison between the main steps of our KDD process and the generic KDD steps previously listed.

Table 1. Comparison between our KDD steps and generic KDD steps.

Our KDD Steps	Generic KDD Steps
1. Identify goals	1. Identify goals
2. Collecting data	2. Collecting data
3. Selection	3. Selection
4. Preprocessing	4. Preprocessing
5. Transformation	5. Transformation
6. The question addressed (Developing a hypothesis)	6. Data mining
7. Testing the hypothesis using data visualisations	
8. Evaluation (examining results and drawing conclusions)	7. Evaluation (examining results and drawing conclusions)

Through each iteration of the KDD process, the analyst is expected to gain a deeper understanding of the routine analysed. The key spatial and temporal parameters used to analyse the daily routines include:

- Order in which locations are transited (e.g., between 1 a.m. and 7 a.m.: (1)—bedroom, (2)—corridor, (3)—bathroom, (4)—corridor, (5)—bedroom etc.);
- Times of the day when locations are visited (e.g., between 1 a.m. and 7 a.m.: bathroom at 1:45 a.m. and at 5:50 a.m.);
- Average duration of the visits (e.g., between 1 a.m. and 7 a.m.: average duration of visits to the bathroom is 3 min).

This information can then be used, for example, by healthcare professionals and family members to better understand the behavioural aspects of a monitored loved one. But also, it can be of great value to architects seeking to understand how people use spaces, and thus how the design of the interior affects the way people conduct their daily routines.

The purpose of the survey discussed in this paper was to collect feedback and first insights from a selected group of professional stakeholders that could benefit from the information reported at the end of the process, and thus how the approach described in this paper can contribute to the field of HAR by providing a systematic tool with which the data containing the architectural characteristics of the house, the collected sensor data showing the transitions of a monitored householder between the different locations of the house, and the placement of the sensing technology, can be decoupled in a reusable and structured way. This enables the migration of these low-level data inputs into a set of data visualisations adapted to display key spatial and temporal aspects, including the sequencing between the most frequently occupied areas of the house and the duration and timing of events, related to the use of the space by a monitored householder.

The remaining steps, including data collection, data cleaning and pre-processing techniques, and data transformation, were not examined in this evaluation study so as to avoid confusing the volunteer participants due to the technical nature of these steps.

3. Evaluation

The workshops developed aimed to engage the study participants with a prototype of the step-by-step data analysis process in order to address the extent to which low-level sensor-based data could be a meaningful source of information. The evaluation study was conducted using Google Forms and involved architects, engineers, healthcare professionals and end-users (not the occupant, but the care team managing the occupant). The evaluation consisted of the following sections.

3.1. Section A: Understanding the Data and Metadata

In the first part, the participant was given a brief introduction to the research and what was expected of them in this study. They were presented with a sample of the anonymised CSV file containing the data analysed (Figure 2). Each entry contains the date and time of an event, the location ID corresponding to a particular space of the house, and the sensor status, with "1" representing that the sensor was activated.

Date	Timestamp	LocationID	SensorStatus
09/05/2021	00:03:43	2	1
09/05/2021	00:07:38	2	1
09/05/2021	00:38:43	7	1
09/05/2021	00:42:54	7	1
09/05/2021	00:52:29	7	1

Figure 2. Sample extracted from the CSV dataset.

The custom-built tracker was a (Passive Infrared) PIR sensor attached to a Raspberry Pi 4. This tracker device was placed in each room of the house to continuously, anonymously and unobtrusively monitor the transitions between locations by measuring the RSSI strength of the Bluetooth signal emitted by a BLE device worn by the monitored subject. The novel linking of the PIR and RSSI was imposed to avoid false positives due to the proximity of the rooms and fluctuations in RSSI signal measurements. The indoor tracking system and the collection of data for testing and evaluation were approved by the Research Ethics and Integrity Committee of the TU Dublin.

Then, they were shown a representation of the layout of the house where the monitored subject lived. This Tube-map visualisation of the house is a digitised pseudo map designed to make it easier to understand the possible transitions between rooms, e.g., adjacent rooms. To this end, the rooms are represented by circles of different colours, i.e., every bathroom is coloured pink and every bedroom green, and the possibility to move between two locations (which we define as a transition) is represented by a straight line (which we define as an edge), as shown in Figure 3. In addition, the average distance in metres between two rooms is also shown, calculated as the distance from the centre point of one room to the transitioning area, i.e., door, open wall, lift, or staircase, and from this point to the centre of the adjacent room. Finally, the average time it would take to cover this distance for a 70- to 80-year-old person is also indicated. It was explained to the participants that this information is obtained from the expanded Building Information Model (BIM) based on the original BIMXML model, which is a key enabler for the reusability of the process, regardless of the architectural characteristics of the house.

Based on this information, the participant was asked to rate, on a scale from 0—Very difficult to 4—Very easy, their ability to understand the possible movements that can be made by a resident based on the floor plan of the house.

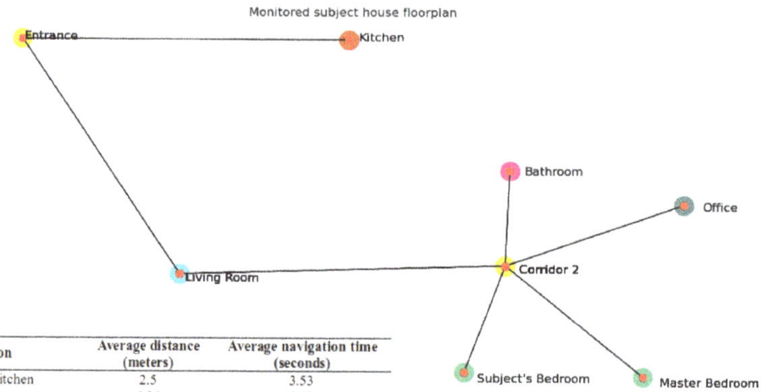

Transition	Average distance (meters)	Average navigation time (seconds)
Entrance - Kitchen	2.5	3.53
Entrance – Living room	6.06	8.63
Living room – Corridor 2	9	12.82
Corridor 2 – Subject's bedroom	2.12	3.02
Corridor 2 – Bathroom	2.25	3.2
Corridor 2 - Office	2.98	4.25
Corridor 2 - Master bedroom	3.3	4.71

Figure 3. Tube-map visualisation.

3.2. Section B: Adding Context to the Dataset and Establishing a Daily Routine Hypothesis

This section provided a brief explanation of the context in which the dataset analysed was created, i.e., the age of the monitored resident, whether s/he lived independently or with other family members, and the time over which the data were collected. Then, the volunteer participant was asked the following question: based on your own background knowledge, could you describe how you imagine the sleeping night routine of the resident being monitored? For example, what locations of the house do you think are occupied/visited? Further, if there is any timing associated, such as time of arrival to a specific location, or minimum time spent in it. The answers provided by the analyst (volunteer participant in this study) would be used as the hypothesis to be verified or refined during the visual data exploration. Ultimately, this will help the analyst to gain a deeper understanding of the resident's behaviour as derived from domestic routines.

3.3. Section C: Understanding the Data Visualisations

This section introduced the participant of the study to the data visualisations selected and adapted to enable the analysis of the data. The data visualisations used in this work have been chosen for displaying key spatial and temporal aspects previously discussed.

(a) Visualisation 1: This diagram shows a summary of the average percentage of sensor events (monitored resident visits) per time interval of 1 h in a selected location from the dataset. Overall, this visualisation aims to provide an insight into the times of day when the monitored subject is most likely to visit the location selected for the analysis, for example the bedroom in Figure 4. This visualisation uses a dynamic variable, the target location (e.g., the bathroom), which can be manually modified to adapt the information presented.

(b) Visualisation 2: This graph shows a summary of the average duration of the sensor events (monitored resident visits) at a selected location in 5 min time intervals for a selected time window (Figure 5). This diagram uses three dynamic variables that allow the information presented to be manually adjusted. These variables are the target location, and the start time and the end time of the time window requested for analysis (e.g., bathroom, from 00:00 to 00:25).

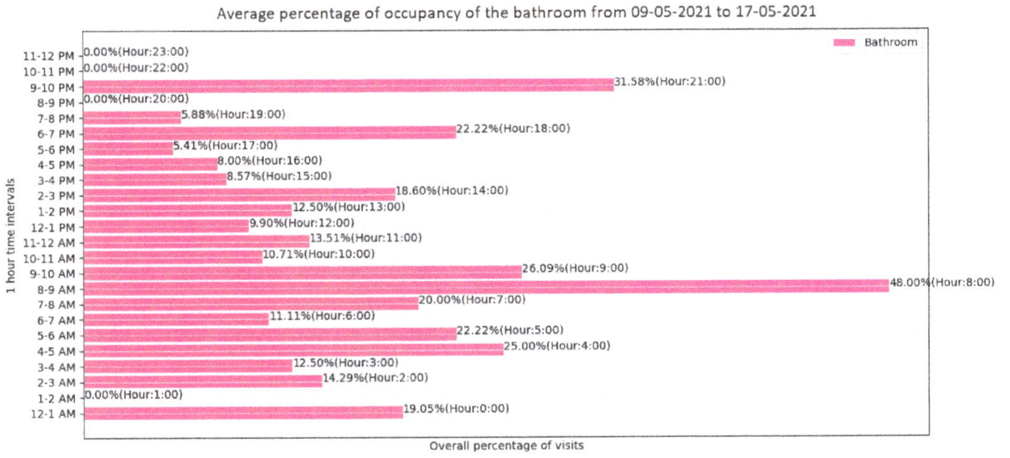

Figure 4. Side–by–side graph proposed for analysing the average number of sensor events representing the occupancy of a selected location per hour within the 24 h of a day.

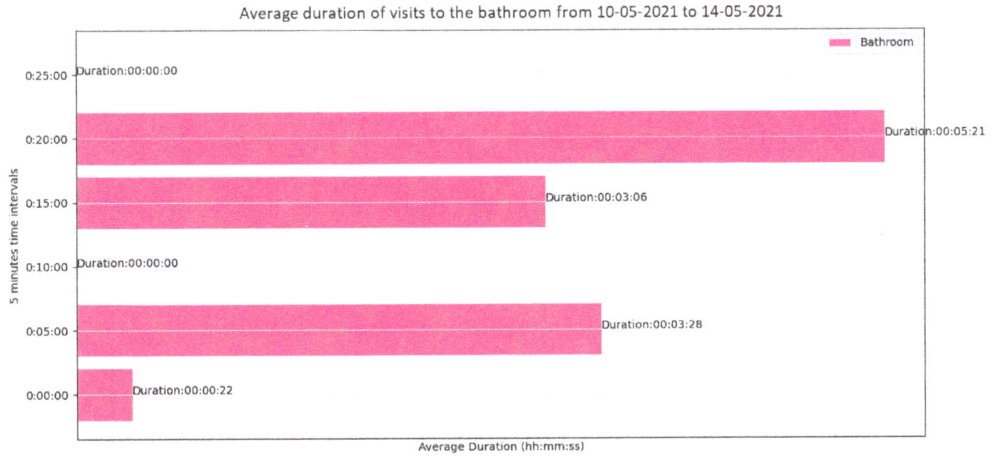

Figure 5. Side–by–side graph proposed for analysing the average duration of the sensor events (monitored resident visits) in a selected location per 5 min within a selected time window.

The aim was to use this information in combination with the previous information shown in visualisation 1. Thus, it is possible to determine how often on average the monitored resident visits the selected location and how long he/she spends there on average.

(c) Visualisation 3: This graph shows the sequence or order of locations that the monitored resident passed through between different days. In order to simplify the content of this graph, no time information about the duration of the events is shown. The time window over which the sequences are drawn can be manually selected by specifying the start and end times, e.g., from 05:00:00 to 06:00:00, Figure 6.

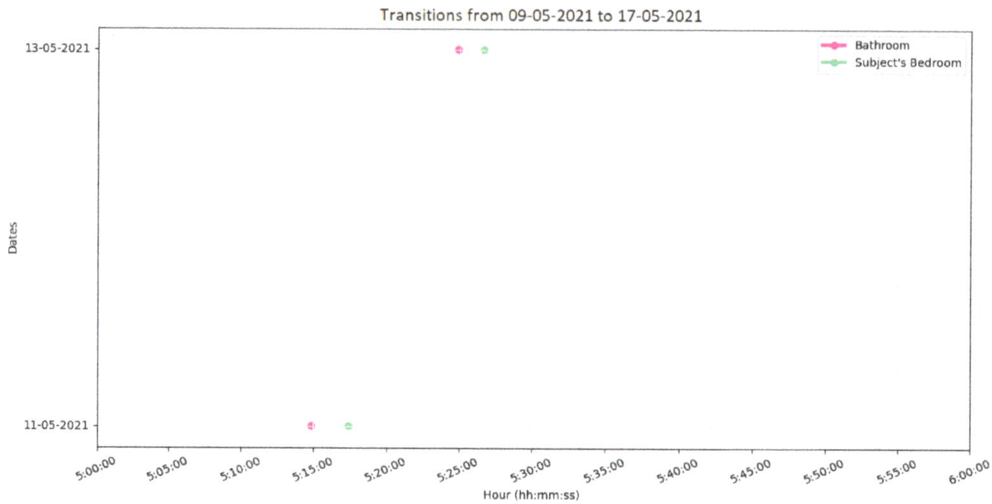

Figure 6. Node graph proposed to display the sequence of visits to different locations of a monitored resident.

(d) Visualisation 4: The aim of this diagram is to show additional temporal information to the previously shown sequences for a selected day. Therefore, a layer of temporal context is added, which can be used to estimate the start time, duration and end time of each event on a selected day (Figure 7). The date can be manually selected, e.g., 12 May 2021.

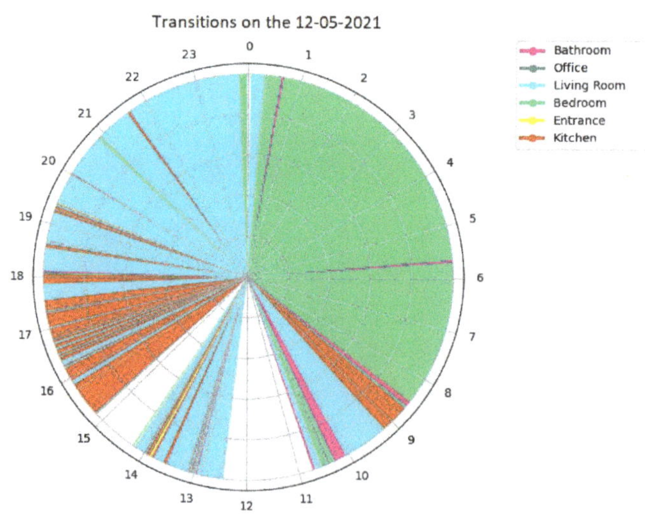

Figure 7. 24 h clock visualisation proposed for the study of temporal information associated with the daily routine of a monitored resident.

After completing the description of these visualisations, participants were asked the following questions to assess the process and the data visualisations evaluated:

- Would you have been able to identify the identity of the monitored resident or other people from the dataset used?
- Were the data visualisations useful in accepting or refining your preliminary hypothesis?

- Could you please explain why the information provided through this process is important and could be useful to you, based on your personal or professional experience?
- To conclude, volunteers were given the option to submit further comments or suggestions.

Their answers and feedback are discussed in the following section.

4. Results and Discussion

The evaluation study was conducted by 17 multidisciplinary participants including architects, engineers, and end-users. They were selected based on their professional backgrounds. The qualitative data collected were analysed based on the thematic analysis approach developed by Braun and Clarke [24]. In this line, the process involved the following steps:

- Familiarisation with the data;
- Creating initial codes;
- Collating codes with supporting data;
- Grouping codes into themes;
- Reviewing themes;
- Writing the narrative as follows.

Through these steps, we intended to characterise and identify repeated patterns or themes from the data collected. As a result, we found six dominant themes in the data that support the decisions made during the design of the process. These themes are:

- Human behaviour concerns;
- Temporal awareness related to resident's domestic routines;
- Spatial awareness related to resident's domestic routines;
- Architectural applications;
- Healthcare applications;
- Improvement suggestions.

As described in the first section of the paper, the value and importance of understanding people's behaviour in the home is supported by a wide range of authors. The first theme, human behaviour concerns, could be said to focus on the how things are done at home. For example, different responses said:

> *"With the information derived from the graphs and diagrams we can get a real idea of the routine of any person."*
>
> *"These routines help us to identify different behaviours and study each case individually."*
>
> *"In the case of visualisation 4, at a glance you understand the daily routine of the subject. Simple and very informative. I find this one very useful."*

It also sheds light on health disorders that may appear during a person's life:

> *"This process could be useful to better understand the night routines of a friend who had sleepwalking episodes."*

More obvious is the fact that older adults living independently need special attention. Knowing how a loved one's week has been offers peace of mind when they live independently. We could see this, for example, in the answers of the volunteers:

> *"I find this research incredibly useful especially for those who live alone and still need some kind of assistance."*
>
> *"I immediately thought about elder people and how their life and safety may be improved via this monitoring process."*
>
> *"Simple and very informative. I find this approach very useful. Mainly for monitoring elderly and dependent people. For example, an increase in visits to the bathroom may indicate that the subject has a health problem."*

Once the importance of how we do things at home is highlighted, we need to find parameters that accurately reflect people's behaviour. So *how* requires knowing *where* and *when*. In order words, spatial and temporal information. Human behaviour resulting from activities of daily living can take many different forms. However, there are common things that we all expect to see. For example, different people may have different sleeping routines, but we can all agree that a person is expected to sleep in her or his bedroom for at least 7 to 8 h a night. This was confirmed by the responses:

> *"Visualisation 4 is quicker to understand, and provides more information, where, when and for how long."*

> *"Repeated visits to the kitchen, short or not, may indicate an eating disorder (ED)."*

> *"It is important to understand where most of our time is spent in our home to see maybe where we are most productive, where we "waste" a lot of our time, how we can improve/maximize our spatial use and temporal dimensions within the home."*

From the literature, we are aware of the value of this information to two main groups of stakeholders, building professionals and health professionals. For the former, the use of the space could be an advantage in terms of optimising future designs and the impact they could have on householders. The latter might be able to benefit from this information, for example, to support what has been said by a patient in a traditional assessment. In order to verify these assumptions, we invited different members of each group among the participants. Their feedback supports the previous statements. For example, a researcher on energy-efficient buildings said:

> *"One of the biggest uncertainties that any control strategy get effected by is the occupancy behaviour and movement. For example, the adaptive thermally insulated blind was found to be ineffective if the human behaviour not talking into account in the control strategy. This research is beneficial when it comes to controlling building systems and in other building systems such as the lighting system and heating system."*

Also, another architectural researcher pointed out the following:

> *"As an architect I think it is very important to understand the users requirements. This information will be really useful in tailored space design, especially for people with special needs."*

Healthcare professionals also noted the value of this information in their daily work. A worker experienced with people with disabilities said:

> *"As a professional in the health care area with experience with people with disabilities, it brings new possibilities for me when it comes to studying behaviours of people with some intellectual and/or physical disability, since most of the time we cannot simply ask the subjects directly."*

A healthcare professional working with older adults pointed out:

> *"I think it would be useful given that many older adults have falls at night and lay on the floor for long periods until someone visits in the morning. If this data was available it could help trigger an alarm/alert a next of kin if a family member left a bedroom at night (for example to use the toilet) and did not return within 5 min, they may have fallen and this could help them be found faster and possibly prevent further damage and trauma and allow them to seek help quicker."*

A background psychologist commented on the importance of the use of this information as evidence in the assessment of patients.

> *"It could also help to understand moods by analysing where and when patients feel happy/sad/anxious and see if changing the spatial/temporal dimensions in the house could affect their mood. This could then be applied for other settings such as offices or even coffee shops to maximize employee well-being and productivity based on spaces, time spent in those spaces and time to move between those spaces."*

An occupational therapist noted that:

"It seems to me a necessity tool, since relying on human attention to detect unusual patterns of behaviour would, in my opinion, lead to errors."

Despite the positive feedback, it is also important to highlight the limitations that some volunteers found when carrying out the evaluation. The diagrams were designed to tell a story in a language that people could understand. However, some responses suggested that certain aspects could be improved to make them more accessible and effective. For example, visualisation 3, described in the previous section, shows the order in which places are visited, and it was designed to minimise the complexity of the information by removing the duration of the events. However, this visualisation encountered more difficulties in getting the message across:

"The graph illustrating the transitions might be improved by using a continuous line between dots to show previous locations not present in the current form. For example, if you view from midnight to 3am, and the person was in the bedroom prior to midnight, this would not be obvious from the transition dot showing the new location."

"Visualisation 3 I think provides less data to an end user without previous knowledge, because seeing only points in a graph is not understandable for everyone, especially when there is more data and the graph is complicated with many more points."

"I found some of the graphs difficult to interpret and had to look at them a number of times."

In addition, the evaluation of the simplified Tube-map of the house layout described in Figure 3 shows a high level of acceptance among the study participants. From the 16 responses, 11 gave a score of "4—Very easy" regarding their ability to understand the possible movements that can be made by the monitored resident through the premises. The other five participants rated the visualisation with a score of "3—Easy". These results suggest that a simplified representation of the layout of a house can improve the interpretation and understanding of the physical space in which the monitored resident lives. It is important to emphasise that this graph was developed to this end and to avoid unnecessary complexity in traditional house floor plans for non-technical people.

5. Conclusions

In this paper, we evaluated the KDD process to promote awareness about spatial, temporal and transitional aspects resulting from monitoring domestic routines. The feedback collected from stakeholders in the construction industry suggests that this information can be of great interest, for example, in the development of energy-efficient building solutions, and to architects to consider the post-occupancy of the building during the design phase. In addition, potential end-users such as family members of vulnerable population living independently, including the elderly and people with physical and mental disabilities, commented on the value of increased awareness of temporal and locational transit information in better understanding how their loved one is doing on a daily basis. The feedback obtained also shows the positive usability of the Tube-map, which was created to help people understand the topology of the building.

Finally, future work will focus on further evaluations to gain a deeper understanding of the value of understanding how people conduct their daily routines at home.

Author Contributions: Conceptualisation, A.A.V., J.M. and D.B.; methodology, A.A.V.; validation, A.A.V.; formal analysis, A.A.V., J.M. and D.B.; investigation, A.A.V.; resources, A.A.V.; data curation, A.A.V.; writing—original draft preparation, A.A.V.; writing—review and editing, A.A.V., J.M. and D.B.; visualisation, A.A.V.; supervision, J.M. and D.B.; project administration, A.A.V., J.M. and D.B.; funding acquisition, J.M. and D.B. All authors have read and agreed to the published version of the manuscript.

Funding: This research received no external funding.

Institutional Review Board Statement: Not applicable.

Informed Consent Statement: Informed consent was obtained from all subjects involved in the study.

Data Availability Statement: Data available on request.

Conflicts of Interest: The authors declare no conflict of interest.

References

1. Irish Green Building Council. Indoor Air Quality in Irish Homes Raised as Key Concern at Irish Green Building Council's Conference. November 2018.. Available online: http://tiny.cc/k8r8vz (accessed on 7 July 2023).
2. Kiernan, R.; Quintyne, D.K.I.; Kelly, I.; McDermott, R.; Kelly, C. Indoor air quality. 2022. Available online: file:///C:/Users/MDPI/Downloads/position-paper-on-indoor-air-quality-1.pdf (accessed on 7 July 2023).
3. Spengler, J.D.; Sexton, K. Indoor Air Pollution: A Public Health Perspective. *Science* **1983**, *221*, 9–17. [CrossRef] [PubMed]
4. Cieraad, I. Domestic Spaces. In *International Encyclopedia of Geography: People, the Earth, Environment and Technology*; Wiley Online Library: Hoboken, NJ, USA, 2017. [CrossRef]
5. Hillier, B.; Tzortzi, K. Space Syntax. In *A Companion to Museum Studies*; John Wiley & Sons, Ltd.: Hoboken, NJ, USA, 2006; pp. 282–301. [CrossRef]
6. Dursun, P. Space syntax in architectural design. In Proceedings of the 6th International Space Syntax Symposium, Istanbul, Turkey, 12–15 June 2007.
7. Alsafery, W.; Rana, O.; Perera, C. Sensing within Smart Buildings: A Survey. *ACM Comput. Surv.* **2023**, *55*, 1–35. [CrossRef]
8. Iweka, O.; Liu, S.; Shukla, A.; Yan, D. Energy and behaviour at home: A review of intervention methods and practices. *Energy Res. Soc. Sci.* **2019**, *57*, 101238. [CrossRef]
9. Ayalp, N.U.R. Cultural identity and place identity in house environment: Traditional Turkish house interiors. *TOBB ETU Univ.* **2012**, *64*, 69.
10. Mahmoud, H.-T.H. Interior Architectural Elements that Affect Human Psychology and Behavior. *Acad. Res. Community Publ.* **2017**, *1*, 10. [CrossRef]
11. Edemekong, P.F.; Bomgaars, D.L.; Sukumaran, S.; Schoo, C. *Activities of Daily Living*; StatPearls: Treasure Island, FL, USA, 2020; Available online: http://www.ncbi.nlm.nih.gov/books/NBK470404/ (accessed on 9 June 2021).
12. Katz, S. Assessing self-maintenance: Activities of daily living, mobility, and instrumental activities of daily living. *J. Am. Geriatr. Soc.* **1983**, *31*, 721–727. [CrossRef] [PubMed]
13. Mlinac, M.E.; Feng, M.C. Assessment of Activities of Daily Living, Self-Care, and Independence. *Arch. Clin. Neuropsychol.* **2016**, *31*, 506–516. [CrossRef] [PubMed]
14. Amiribesheli, M.; Bouchachia, H. A tailored smart home for dementia care. *J. Ambient Intell. Humaniz. Comput.* **2018**, *9*, 1755–1782. [CrossRef]
15. Teixeira, T.; Dublon, G. A Survey of Human-Sensing: Methods for Detecting Presence, Count, Location, Track, and Identity. *ACM Comput. Surv.* **2010**, *5*, 59.
16. Clough, M. Indoor Positioning Glossary. 2023. Available online: https://www.pointr.tech/blog/indoor-positioning-glossary (accessed on 1 January 2023).
17. Fayyad, P.S.U.; Piatesky-Shapiro, G. From Data Mining to Knowledge Discovery in Databases. *AI Mag.* **1996**, *17*, 37.
18. Mariscal, G.; Marbán, Ó.; Fernández, C. A survey of data mining and knowledge discovery process models and methodologies. *Knowl. Eng. Rev.* **2010**, *25*, 137–166. [CrossRef]
19. SAS Institute. Introduction to SEMMA. August 2017. Available online: https://documentation.sas.com/doc/en/emref/14.3/n061bzurmej4j3n1jnj8bbjjm1a2.htm (accessed on 24 February 2023).
20. Two Crows Corporation. *Introduction to Data Mining and Knowledge Discovery*, 3rd ed.; Two Crows Corp.: Potomac, MD, USA, 1999.
21. Buchner, A.G.; Mulvenna, M.; Anand, S.S.; Hughes, J. An internet-enabled knowledge discovery process. In Proceedings of the 9th International Database Conference on Heterogeneous and Internet Databases, Hong Kong, China, 6 May 1999.
22. Cabena, P.; Hadjinian, P.; Stadler, R.; Verhees, J.; Zanasi, A. *Discovering Data Mining: From Concept to Implementation*; Prentice-Hall, Inc.: Upper Saddle River, NJ, USA, 1997.
23. Brachman, R.J. The Process of Knowledge Discovery in Databases: A First Sketch. In Proceedings of the 3rd International Conference on Knowledge Discovery and Data Mining, Seattle, WA, USA; 1996; pp. 1–11.
24. Braun, V.; Clarke, V. Using thematic analysis in psychology. *Qual. Res. Psychol.* **2006**, *3*, 77–101. [CrossRef]

applied sciences

MDPI

Article

Human Action Recognition Based on Hierarchical Multi-Scale Adaptive Conv-Long Short-Term Memory Network

Qian Huang [1,2,*], Weiliang Xie [1], Chang Li [1], Yanfang Wang [1] and Yanwei Liu [2]

1 School of Computer and Information, Hohai University, Nanjing 211106, China; xieweiliang@hhu.edu.cn (W.X.); lichang@hhu.edu.cn (C.L.); yanfang_wang08@hhu.edu.cn (Y.W.)
2 Nanjing Huiying Electronic Technology Co., Ltd., Nanjing 211100, China; liuyanwei@iie.ac.cn
* Correspondence: huangqian@hhu.edu.cn

Abstract: Recently, human action recognition has gained widespread use in fields such as human–robot interaction, healthcare, and sports. With the popularity of wearable devices, we can easily access sensor data of human actions for human action recognition. However, extracting spatio-temporal motion patterns from sensor data and capturing fine-grained action processes remain a challenge. To address this problem, we proposed a novel hierarchical multi-scale adaptive Conv-LSTM network structure called HMA Conv-LSTM. The spatial information of sensor signals is extracted by hierarchical multi-scale convolution with finer-grained features, and the multi-channel features are fused by adaptive channel feature fusion to retain important information and improve the efficiency of the model. The dynamic channel-selection-LSTM based on the attention mechanism captures the temporal context information and long-term dependence of the sensor signals. Experimental results show that the proposed model achieves Macro F1-scores of 0.68, 0.91, 0.53, and 0.96 on four public datasets: Opportunity, PAMAP2, USC-HAD, and Skoda, respectively. Our model demonstrates competitive performance when compared to several state-of-the-art approaches.

Keywords: multi-scale analysis; attention mechanism; feature fusion; human action recognition

Citation: Huang, Q.; Xie, W.; Li, C.; Wang, Y.; Liu, Y. Human Action Recognition Based on Hierarchical Multi-Scale Adaptive Conv-Long Short-Term Memory Network. *Appl. Sci.* **2023**, *13*, 10560. https://doi.org/10.3390/app131910560

Academic Editors: Antonio Fernández-Caballero, Marley M.B.R. Vellasco and Luigi Bibbò

Received: 30 August 2023
Revised: 13 September 2023
Accepted: 16 September 2023
Published: 22 September 2023

1. Introduction

Human Action Recognition (HAR) is gradually attracting attention, and it is widely used in the fields of human–robot interaction, elderly care, healthcare, and sports [1–3]. In addition, it plays an important role in areas such as biometrics, entertainment, and intelligent-assisted living. Examples include fall behavior detection for the homebound elderly population, rehabilitative exercise training for patients, and exercise action assessment for athletes [4,5]. HAR can be performed from both visual and non-visual modalities [6–8], where the visual modalities are mainly data modalities such as RGB video, depth, bone, and point cloud; and the non-visual modalities are mainly data modalities such as sensor signals, radar, magnetic field, and Wi-Fi signals based on wearable devices [9]. These data modalities encode different sources of information, and different modalities have their own advantages and characteristics in different application scenarios.

Visual-modality-based approaches perform feature extraction from video streams captured by cameras; although this approach can visualize the characteristics of human actions, its performance is affected by the viewing angle, camera occlusion, and the quality of the background illumination, and there may be privacy issues. On the contrary, the non-visual modality-based approach, which acquires sensor data of human actions through wearable devices, does not suffer from privacy issues, has a relatively small amount of data, does not have occlusion issues, and is adaptable to the environment. Better results are expected by processing and analyzing sensor data for HAR. This paper focuses on sensor-based HAR.

Sensor-based HAR is a fundamental component in human–robot interaction and pervasive computing [10]. It achieves HAR by acquiring sequence data from embedded sensor devices (accelerometers, magnetometers, gyroscopes, etc.) of multiple sensor modalities worn at different body locations for data processing and analysis. Generally, the data collected by the sensors in a HAR system form a time series of information. After noise reduction and normalization of the data sequence, it is segmented into individual windows by a sliding window method with a fixed window size and overlap rate. Then, each window is categorized as an action by the HAR method. Figure 1 illustrates an example of window action on the PAMAP2 dataset. In daily life, human physical actions include not only some simple actions, but also some complex actions consisting of multiple microscopic processes. For example, the action of running includes many microscopic processes, such as starting, accelerating, maintaining, sprinting, decelerating, and so on.

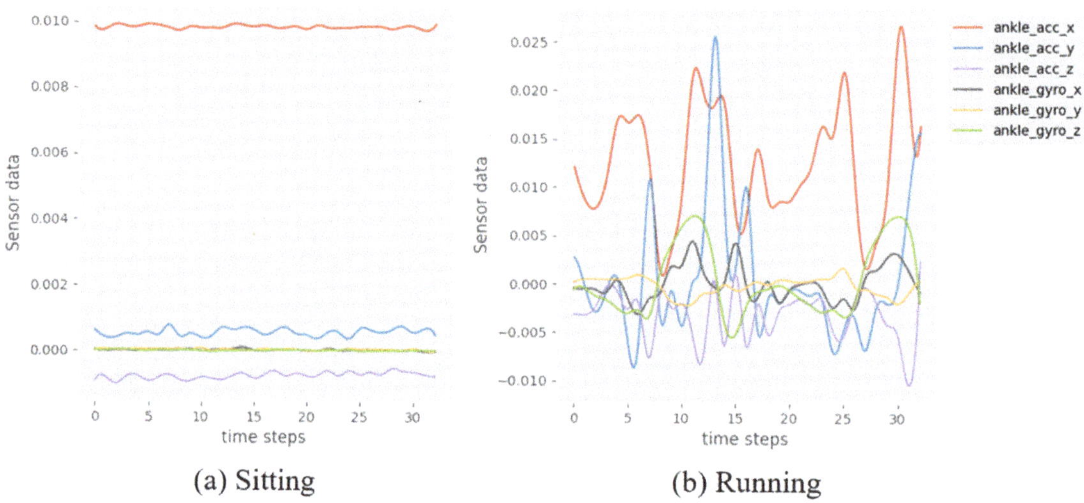

Figure 1. Example of a window of "Sitting" (**a**) and "Running" (**b**) actions on the PAMAP2 dataset, timestep = 1 s.

Traditional machine learning methods [11,12] rely heavily on hand-crafted features and expert knowledge [13] and only capture shallow features, making it difficult to perform HAR accurately. Recently, deep learning methods have provided promising results in the field of HAR [14]. It can learn feature representations for classification tasks without involving domain-specific knowledge, which achieves more accurate HAR. Therefore, many researchers have applied CNNs and RNNs to HAR to effectively perform feature extraction, automatic learning of feature representations, and removal of hand-crafted features [15–17]. However, since action recognition is a time-series classification problem, CNNs may have difficulty in capturing time-dimensional information. The Long Short-Term Memory (LSTM) network can effectively capture the temporal context information and long-term dependency of sequence data, so some works successfully apply LSTM to HAR [18–20].

In addition, since CNNs can extract local spatial feature information and LSTMs can capture temporal context information, hybrid models can effectively capture spatio-temporal motion patterns from sensor signals. Some recent work combining hybrid models of CNNs and RNNs has shown promising results [21–24]. However, since LSTMs compress all the input information into the network, this will lead to the incorporation of noise from the sensor data acquisition when extracting features, which will affect the effectiveness of action recognition. Based on this, there are some works to solve this problem by introducing the attention mechanism [25–29]. The attention mechanism enables the model to focus more on the parts that are relevant to the current recognition to improve accuracy. Also, some works optimize the action recognition and window segmentation problems by multi-task learning for HAR [30]. Although these models have achieved significant results on HAR, they do not adequately consider fine-grained features, which may lead to some confusion in action classification.

To address these issues, we proposed a novel hierarchical multi-scale adaptive Conv-LSTM network structure called HMA Conv-LSTM, where we attentively weight sensor signals by sensor feature selection, extract finer-grained spatial features using hierarchical multi-scale convolution, and extract temporal contextual information by a dynamic channel-selection-LSTM network. Meanwhile, we employ adaptive channel feature fusion to process multi-channel feature maps. The main contributions of this paper are as follows:

1. We propose a novel HMA Conv-LSTM network, which realizes HAR that can well distinguish confusing actions of subtle processes. Extensive experiments on four public datasets of Opportunity, PAMAP2, USC-HAD, and Skoda show the effectiveness of our proposed model.
2. We propose the hierarchical multi-scale convolution module, which performs finer-grained feature extraction by hierarchical architecture and multi-scale convolution on spatial information of feature vectors.
3. In addition, we propose the adaptive channel feature fusion module is capable of fusing features at different scales, which improve the efficiency of the model and remove redundant information.
4. For the multi-channel feature maps extracted by adaptive channel feature fusion, we propose the dynamic channel-selection-LSTM module based on the attention mechanism to extract the temporal context information.

The rest of the paper is organized as follows: Section 2 reviews previous work related to us. Section 3 details the methodology proposed in this paper. Section 4 describes the experimental setup and the four HAR benchmark datasets and compares the proposed model with state-of-the-art methods. Section 5 explores the selection of model parameters and ablation experiments, discusses the results, and analyzes the confusion matrix as well as visualizes the attention weights. Finally, Section 6 concludes the paper.

2. Related Work

Research work on sensor-based HAR can be categorized into two types: machine learning methods and deep learning methods. Earlier research works on HAR were mainly based on traditional machine learning methods such as the Random Forest (RF), Support Vector Machine (SVM), and Hidden Markov Model (HMM). Gomes et al. [31] compared the performances of three classifiers: SVM, RF, and KNN. Kasteren et al. [32] proposed a sensor that can automatically recognize actions and data labeling system; they demonstrated the performance of a HMM in recognizing actions. Tran et al. [33] constructed a HAR system via an SVM that was able to recognize six human actions by extracting 248 features. However, traditional machine learning methods rely heavily on hand-crafted features such as mean, maximum, variance, and fast Fourier transform coefficients [34]. Since extracting hand-crafted features relies on human experience and expert knowledge and only captures shallow features, the accuracy is limited.

Unlike traditional machine learning methods, deep learning can learn the feature representation of a classification task without involving domain-specific knowledge, and HAR can be achieved without extracting hand-crafted features. Yang et al. [15] proposed that CNNs can effectively capture salient features in the spatial dimension and outperform traditional machine learning methods. Jiang et al. [35] proposed a CNN model that arranges raw sensor signals into signal images as model inputs and learns low-level to high-level features from action images to achieve effective HAR.

Meanwhile, since action recognition is a time-series classification problem, it may be difficult for CNNs to capture time dimension information. In contrast, Hammerla et al. [18] and Dua et al. [19] used the LSTM network for HAR, which can effectively capture contextual information and long-term dependencies of the temporal dimension of the sensor sequence data. Ullah et al. [36] proposed a stacked LSTM network for recognizing six types of human actions using smartphone data, with 93.13% recognition accuracy. Mohsen et al. [37] used GRU to classify human actions, achieving 97% accuracy on the WISDM dataset. Gaur et al. [38] achieved a high accuracy in classifying repetitive and non-repetitive actions over time based on LSTM–RNN networks. Although the above methods can recognize some simple human actions (e.g., cycling, walking) well, the recognition of some complex actions (e.g., stair up/down, open/close door) is still challenging, which is due to the difficulty in capturing the spatio-temporal correlation of sensor signals using a single CNN or RNN network.

Recently, much of the work in HAR has focused on hybrid models of CNN and RNN. Ordóñez et al. [21] combined an CNN and an LSTM to achieve significant results in capturing spatio-temporal features from sensor signals. Yao et al. [22] constructed separate CNNs for the different types of data in the sensor inputs, and then merged them to form global feature information; they then extracted temporal relationships through an RNN to achieve HAR. Nafea et al. [39] used CNN with varying kernel dimensions and BiLSTM to capture features with different resolutions. They effectively extracted spatio-temporal features from sensor data with high accuracy.

In addition, some works address the problem that LSTMs may compress the noise of sensor data into the network. They introduce the attention mechanism to prevent the incorporation of noisy and irrelevant parts when extracting features, thus improving the effectiveness of HAR. Murahari et al. [27] added an attention layer to the DeepConvLSTM architecture proposed in Ordóñez et al. [21] to learn the correlation weight of the hidden state outputs of the LSTM layer to create context vectors, instead of directly using the last hidden state. Ma et al. [25] also proposed an architecture based on attention-enhanced CNNs and GRUs, which uses attention to augment the weight of the sensor modalities and encapsulate the temporal correlation and temporal context information of specific sensor signal features. In contrast, Mahmud et al. [26] completely discarded the recurrent structure and adapted the transformer architecture [40] proposed in the field of machine translation to use a self-attention-based neural network model to generate feature representations for classification to better recognize human actions. Zhang et al. [41] proposed a hybrid model ConvTransformer for HAR, which can fully extract local and global information of sensor signals and use attention to enhance the model feature characterization capability. Xiao et al. [42] proposed a two-stream transformer network to extract sensor features from temporal and spatial channels that effectively model the spatio-temporal dependence of sensor signals.

The attention mechanism enables the model to pay more attention to the parts that are relevant to the current recognition when processing sequence data, helping the model to capture long-term dependencies. Although these models perform well on HAR, they do not sufficiently consider fine-grained features, which may lead to the actions of some fine-grained processes being confused during classification. Therefore, we propose the HMA Conv-LSTM network for human action recognition.

3. Proposed Method

In this section, we introduce the data preprocess and explain the proposed HMA Conv-LSTM network, whose framework is shown in Figure 2.

3.1. Data Preprocess

Public datasets are usually collected by sensors under real-life conditions and may contain inconsistent, incomplete, and noisy data. To enable deep learning networks to process multidimensional sensor timing information for HAR, we perform preprocessing operations such as data complementation, normalization, and segmentation.

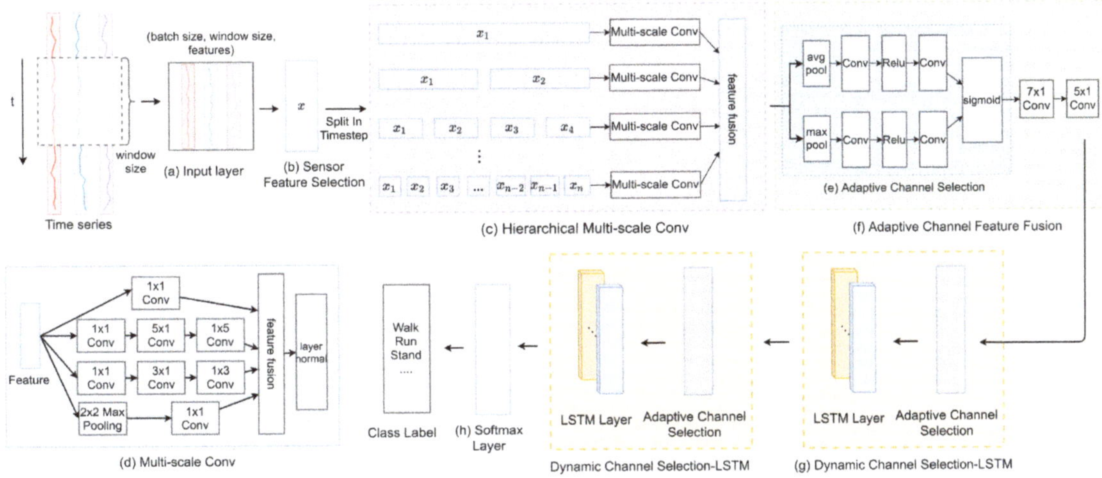

Figure 2. Overview of HMA Conv-LSTM. Input layer (**a**) reads the windowed data from the segmented sensor sequence; Sensor Feature Selection (SFS) (**b**) performs feature selection on input data based on attention mechanism; Hierarchical Multi-scale Convolution (HMC) (**c**) performs finer-grained feature extraction on the spatial information of the features; Multi-scale Conv (**d**) uses different scale convolution kernels to extract features from different hierarchical levels of data; Adaptive channel selection (ACS) (**e**) improves the discrimination and sensitivity of the model to the features of each channel; Adaptive Channel Feature Fusion (ACFF) (**f**) can retain important information and improve model efficiency; dynamic channel-selection-LSTM (DCS-LSTM) (**g**) can establish the linkage between feature vectors at different timesteps; Softmax Layer (**h**) obtains the probability distribution of the predicted values of each category, and finally takes the category with the largest predicted value as the classification result.

3.1.1. Data Completion

HAR datasets are typically acquired using inertial sensors at different body parts. The data at each sampling point are spliced according to the timestep. During the acquisition process, data may be missing at certain sampling timesteps. Although missing data at a single timestep has limited impact on the overall data, it can affect the integrity of the timing data. Therefore, linear interpolation is used to fill in missing values. Let (x, y) represent missing data, where (x_0, y_0) represents the previous non-missing data and (x_1, y_1) represents the next non-missing data. Since the timestep x is known, the missing value y can be obtained by using linear interpolation:

$$y = y_0 + (x - x_0)\frac{y_1 - y_0}{x_1 - x_0} \tag{1}$$

3.1.2. Data Normalization

Since different sensing unit data often use different units of measure, the range of values can vary. If raw data are used directly as input to the model, it may result in data items with large values that sway the model's classification effect. Additionally, fluctuating unprocessed data may affect the model's performance [43]. Therefore, we need to normalize raw data by scaling it to fall within an interval of -1 to 1. It eliminates differences in the range between different sensor channel types. Data normalization also speeds up model convergence and improves its training rate and accuracy.

For the collected dataset $D = \{d_1, d_2, d_3, \ldots, d_n\}$, each data sample contains multi-featured sensor data $d_i = \{x_1, x_2, \ldots, x_K\}$, where K represents the number of features. To determine the maximum and minimum values for all features in the dataset, we form the vectors x_{max} and x_{min}. And then, we perform the normalization operation:

$$x_i = 2 \times \frac{|x_i - x_{min}|}{|x_{max} - x_{min}|} - 1 \tag{2}$$

3.1.3. Data Segmentation and Downsampling

In real-life scenarios, different sampling devices and sensors have varying sampling rates. To accommodate most sensor devices, we need to downsample the data that are sampled at a higher rate. For datasets, matching the sampling rates across all data allows for a more accurate comparison of model performance on different datasets. In this case, we downsample the PAMAP2, Skoda, and USC-HAD datasets to approximately 33 Hz to match the sampling rate of the Opportunity dataset.

In this paper, our proposed model is to perform feature extraction for each action window after segmenting the sensor data sequence. The two dimensions of an action window are the timestep and the number of sensor features, respectively. Suppose the sensor data sequence is segmented using a sliding window of width W and a certain overlap rate. Each window obtained can be denoted as $V = [v_1, \ldots, v_t, \ldots, v_W]$, where $v_t = [v_1^t, \ldots, v_K^t]$ represents K features of the sensor at timestep t. In addition, the action ground truth label for each window is defined as the label with the most occurrences of each sensor data within the window. Window-wise and Sample-wise are two methods used to segment action data [26]. In our study, we uniformly use the Window-wise method on the training, validation, and test sets to ensure consistent results.

Window size and sliding window overlap rate are important factors in action recognition because different actions can vary in duration and complexity. To better evaluate and explore the impact of these factors on our model's overall effectiveness, we deploy window size and window overlap rate as hyperparameters in our project. We specifically evaluate and explore optimal hyperparameters in Section 5.

3.2. Sensor Feature Selection

Different types of sensor features play varying roles in recognizing different actions. Using unimportant sensor features may significantly impact recognition due to noise [44]. To capture the contribution weights and potential importance of different types of sensor features, we perform the SFS operation based on the attention mechanism on the sensor input data. Not all sensor features contribute equally when performing action classification. For example, the sensor at the subject's ankle may not contribute much when performing the "Open Drawer" action. In addition, this weight not only assigns importance to sensor input features, but also demonstrates the effectiveness of feature selection by visualizing how much attention is paid to specific features for a particular action.

The SFS operation uses a two-dimensional convolution across sensor feature values and timesteps to extract dependencies between them. First, it takes as input the sensor's feature vectors $[v_1^t, v_2^t, \ldots v_i^t, \ldots, v_K^t]$ and reshapes them into a single-channel vector, which is then processed using k convolutional filters to output a k-channel image. This is then converted back to a single channel using a 1×1 convolutional kernel and the attention weights of the individual sensor feature values are obtained by the softmax operation defined in (4). The whole process can be formalized as

$$q_i^t = \tanh(W_1 v_i^t + b_1) \tag{3}$$

$$s_i^t = \frac{\exp((q_i^t)^T w_1)}{\sum_K \exp((q_i^t)^T w_1)} \tag{4}$$

$$c^t = \sum_K s_i^t v_i^t \tag{5}$$

where i denotes the i-th sensor feature value, and K denotes the number of features of a single timestep sensor. We first obtain the hidden representation of v_k^t as q_i^t from the convolutional layer, then compute the similarity between q_i^t and the context vector w_1, and obtain the normalized attention weight s_i^t by a softmax operation. $\{W_1, w_1, b_1\}$ is the trainable parameter of the attention network, and c^t is the unified feature representation of all K sensor features obtained after the weighted vector.

3.3. Hierarchical Multi-Scale Convolution

We proposed the HMC module to perform finer-grained feature extraction on the spatial information of the feature vectors. In the following, we will introduce the multi-scale convolution module and the entire hierarchical architecture separately.

3.3.1. Multi-Scale Convolution

In deep convolutional structures, single-size convolutional kernels often fail to provide diverse features and lack the ability to decompose on multi-scales. Since the overall process of some confusable behaviors (e.g., open/close door) is relatively similar, it is often difficult to focus on both global and local features if the network is constructed using only a single-scale convolutional kernel. Inspired by the work of Szegedy et al. [45], we use the multi-scale convolutional neural network. It utilizes convolutional kernels of different scales for multi-scale feature extraction and splicing in both sensor and temporal dimensions. This strengthens the network's ability to recognize features of different scales, enhances its adaptability, and improves its feature characterization ability. In addition, we separate the common $N \times N$ two-dimensional convolution kernel, first convolve the temporal information by the $N \times 1$ convolution kernel, and then use the $1 \times N$ convolution kernel to convolve the information of different sensor dimensions at the same timestep. The specific structure is shown in Figure 2d.

In our network structure, 1×1 convolution kernels are used to organize information across channels and perform dimensionality reduction on input channels. It improves the network's expressive power and adds a layer of features and nonlinear variations. By using convolution kernels of different sizes, we can analyze raw sensor data at multi-scales. To address the issue of vanishing and exploding gradients during network training, we perform batch normalization after weighted multi-scale feature fusion. This accelerates the network's convergence process while keeping the distribution of test and training data the same and improving the generalization ability of the network.

3.3.2. Hierarchical Architecture

HAR relies on sequential data captured by sensors placed at various body locations, which contain spatial and temporal information about physical actions. Due to the varying durations and complexities of different actions, some actions may require longer sliding window sizes for segmentation to achieve good recognition results. However, sliding window sizes that are too large may cause the general network model to overlook some fine-grained subtle action processes, thereby affecting action recognition. In contrast, our proposed hierarchical architecture can split the action window and extract features from the sensor sequence data at a finer granularity to effectively recognize the finer action processes. The specific structure of the whole HMC module is shown in Figure 2c.

To construct the HMC network architecture, we divide the sensor feature sequence weighted by the SFS module in the time dimension, as shown in Figure 3. The HMC can capture some subtle changes of actions in human motion. By capturing the sub-actions in the sensor feature sequences, the model can obtain more detailed information, thus realizing a finer-grained HAR. In this work, we have tested experimentally and finally selected the hierarchical architecture with 2 layers of division, and the experiments show good results, as detailed in Section 5.

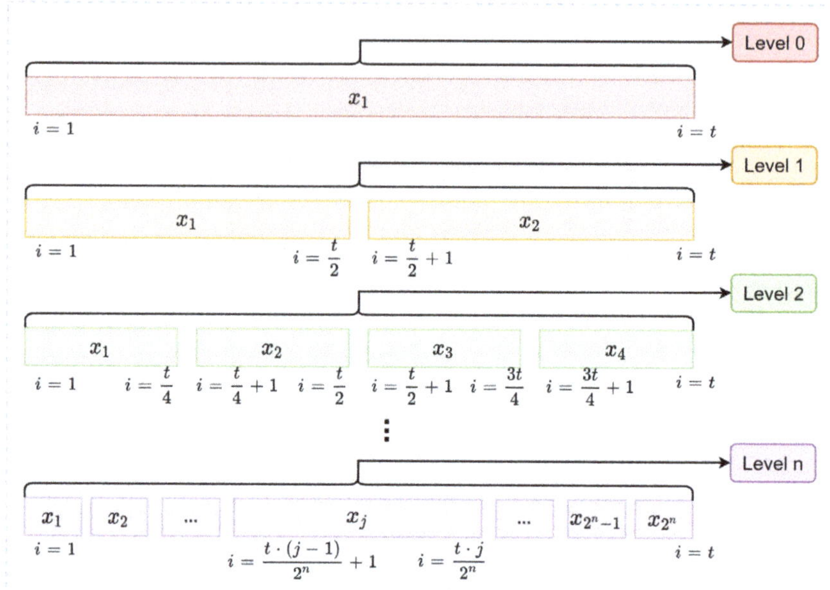

Figure 3. Delineation of the Hierarchical Architecture.

For the sensor feature sequence $x = [c^1, c^2, \ldots c^i, \ldots, c^t]$ weighted by the SFS module, each feature vector c_i consists of $[c_1^i, c_2^i, \ldots c_j^i, \ldots, c_K^i]$, where t denotes the number of timesteps, and K denotes the number of features of a single timestep sensor. When the hierarchical number of partitions $level = 0$, the sequence is not hierarchical and the feature sequence is unchanged and defaults to 1 partition, $x_1^0 = x$; when the number of partitions $level = 1$, the sequence is divided into 2 partitions, i.e.,

$$x_1^1 = \left[c^1, c^2, \ldots, c^{\frac{t}{2}}\right],\ x_2^1 = \left[c^{\frac{t}{2}+1}, \ldots, c^{t-1}, c^t\right] \tag{6}$$

When the number of strata $level = 2$, the sequence is divided into 4 partitions, i.e.,

$$x_1^2 = \left[c^1, c^2, \ldots, c^{\frac{t}{4}}\right], x_2^2 = \left[c^{\frac{t}{4}+1}, \ldots, c^{\frac{t}{2}}\right], x_3^2 = \left[c^{\frac{t}{2}+1}, \ldots, c^{\frac{3}{4}t}\right], x_4^2 = \left[c^{\frac{3}{4}t+1}, \ldots, c^t\right] \tag{7}$$

When the number of strata $level = n$, the sequence is divided into 2^n partitions, i.e.,

$$x_i^n = \left[c^{\frac{t*(i-1)}{2^n}+1}, c^{\frac{t*(i-1)}{2^n}+2}, \ldots, c^{\frac{t*i}{2^n}}\right], i \in \{1, \ldots, 2^n - 1, 2^n\} \tag{8}$$

In fact, we divide the features into two each time, so the i-th sub-partition of the l-th layer comes from the $\lfloor \frac{i+1}{2} \rfloor$ parent partition of the l-1-th layer; the formulaic expression is

$$x_j^{l-1} = \left[x_{i*2-1}^l, x_{i*2}^l\right] \tag{9}$$

After the hierarchical division, all sub-partitions are presented as a pyramidal tree structure. We perform multi-scale convolutional operations on each partition of the division. We use multi-scale convolutional neural networks to extract and splice features in the sensor dimension and time dimension to strengthen the network's ability to recognize features at different scales by multi-scale mining of the data to improve the characterization ability of the final acquired features.

Then, we first splice the multi-scale features extracted from each partitioned layer in the time dimension, and then perform feature superposition; the final features are fused to a multi-channel feature y' of the same dimension as that obtained from the original feature x through the multi-scale convolutional network, which serves as the output of the whole HMC network. For layer l, the features can be represented as

$$y^l = concat\left(x_1^l, x_2^l, \ldots, x_{2^l}^l\right) \tag{10}$$

And the final fusion feature obtained is

$$y' = y^1 + y^2 + \cdots + y^n \tag{11}$$

where y' is fused from n layers of hierarchical multi-scale features. By using the Hierarchical architecture, we can capture some of the subtle changes in action during human movement. The model obtains more detailed information by acquiring sub-actions in the sequence of sensor features, thus enabling finer-grained HAR.

3.4. *Adaptive Channel Feature Fusion*

After acquiring the multi-scale features by HMC module, we perform ACFF operations on them. The ACS module and the multi-scale channel feature fusion operation will be described separately in the following section.

3.4.1. Adaptive Channel Selection

We proposed the ACS module to process the multi-channel feature maps, adaptively learn the weight coefficients of each channel, improve the overall model's discriminative ability and sensitivity to each channel feature, and strengthen the channel features that are beneficial to model classification while suppressing the useless channel feature information. Its structure is shown in Figure 2e.

The ACS module mainly contains extraction operations and squeeze operations. Assume that the output vector x of the multi-scale convolutional layer is of size $C \times W \times H$, where C is the number of channels, and $W \times H$ denotes the size of the feature map of each channel. The extraction operation inputs x into a global average pooling layer and a global maximum pooling layer to compress the features, resulting in channel-level statistical information Z_{avg} and Z_{max}. This information encodes the spatial features on each channel as a real number with a global receptive field representing the global features of the feature maps. The output dimensions match the number of feature channels input. The formulas for finding Z_c^{avg} and Z_c^{max} for each channel are as follows:

$$Z_c^{avg} = \frac{1}{W \times H} \sum_{i=1}^{W} \sum_{j=1}^{H} x_c(i,j) \tag{12}$$

$$Z_c^{max} = \max_{1 \le i \le W} \max_{1 \le j \le H} x_c(i,j) \tag{13}$$

where $x_c(i,j)$ represents the value of row i and column j in the c-channel feature map. After the extraction operation, the global description features are obtained for each channel. And the activation operation aims to obtain the relationship between the channels, which is achieved by using two fully connected layers. The first fully connected layer plays the role of dimensionality reduction, downgrading the channel dimensions of Z_c^{avg} and Z_c^{max} to 1/16 of their original dimensions to change the capacity and computational cost of the ACS module in the network. It is then activated by the ReLU function and upscaled to the original channel dimensions using a second fully connected layer. Finally, the normalized weights are obtained using the Sigmoid activation function after superimposing the channel dimensions computed by the two branches of global average pooling and global maximum pooling. The formula for the activation operation is expressed as

$$s = Sigmoid(W_1 \cdot ReLU(W_0 \cdot Z_{avg}) + W_1 \cdot ReLU(W_0 \cdot Z_{max})) \tag{14}$$

where $W_0 \in R^{\frac{C}{16} \times C}$ and $W_1 \in R^{C \times \frac{C}{16}}$; finally, the learned weights s_c for each channel are multiplied by the original individual channel features x_c:

$$y_c = s_c \times x_c \tag{15}$$

The output dimensions of the extraction and squeeze operations of the ACS module are unchanged, and the whole process can be viewed as learning the weight coefficients of each channel adaptively to improve the overall model's discriminative ability and sensitivity to the features of each channel.

3.4.2. Multi-Scale Channel Feature Fusion

We propose the ACFF module to process the acquired multi-scale feature maps. The module consists of an ACS module and two convolutional layers. Its structure is shown in Figure 2f. Using different sizes of convolutional kernels can extract features at different scales. Here, we use a convolutional layer containing 64 convolutional kernels of sizes 7×1 and 5×1 to extract local time-domain features and ultimately achieve ACFF at different scales. For the multi-channel feature map x_1, assuming the size of $C \times W \times H$, the whole process is formulaically expressed as

$$f_1(x_1) = \sum_{c=1}^{C} \sum_{r=1}^{7} x_1(c,\ i, j+r-1) W_1(c,k,r) \tag{16}$$

$$f_2(x_2) = \sum_{c=1}^{64} \sum_{r=1}^{5} x_2(c,\ i, j+r-1) W_2(c,k,r) \tag{17}$$

$$y = f_2(f_1(x_1)) \tag{18}$$

where W_1 and W_2 denote the convolution kernels of the two convolutional layers, respectively, and $x_1(c,i,j)$ denotes the value of input x_1 in the c-th channel of row i and column j. r denotes the convolution width. k denotes the number of convolution kernels, which is the number of output channels of the convolutional layer. Finally, after two convolution layers, the output feature is y.

In conclusion, the ACFF module performs multi-scale feature extraction and fusion of multi-channel feature maps. It can reduce the amount of computation while retaining important spatial information. Moreover, it can improve the efficiency and interpretability of the model, remove redundant information, and realize the fusion of features at different scales.

3.5. *Dynamic Channel-Selection-LSTM*

For the channel feature maps obtained after ACFF, to establish the connection between different timestep feature vectors, we use two proposed DCS-LSTM modules to extract the temporal context information of the sensor signals, the structure of which is shown in Figure 2g. In addition, Karpathy et al. [46] pointed out that models containing at least two recurrent layers work better in processing sequence data. Here, we similarly use the ACS operation to obtain the contributions of different channels, adaptively learn the weight coefficients of each channel, and strengthen the ability to characterize features for the classification of confusable behaviors. The structure of the basic LSTM network cell is shown in Figure 4.

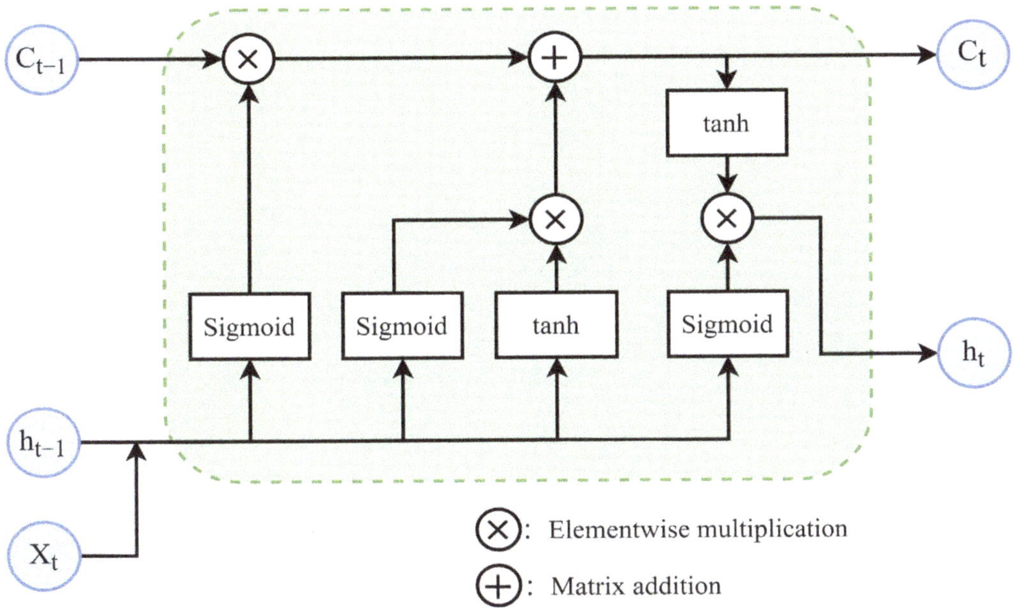

Figure 4. Structure of the LSTM cell unit. It updates the state of the unit through input gates, output gates, and forgetting gates. The upper horizontal line ensures that vectors pass through the neurons with only a few linear operations, enabling long memory retention.

The forgetting gate decides what information to let continue through that neuron. The input gate decides how much information to update to the state matrix. The output gate combines the neuron's state vectors, the input vectors, and the output vectors of the previous neuron to arrive at the output value for the current moment. Its vector update operation is represented as

$$i_t = \sigma(W_{ai}a_t + W_{hi}h_{t-1} + W_{ci}c_{t-1} + b_i) \tag{19}$$

$$f_t = \sigma(W_{af}a_t + W_{hf}h_{t-1} + W_{cf}c_{t-1} + b_f) \tag{20}$$

$$o_t = \sigma(W_{ao}a_t + W_{ho}h_{t-1} + W_{co}c_t + b_o) \tag{21}$$

$$c_t = f_t c_{t-1} + i_t\sigma(W_{ac}a_t + W_{hc}h_{t-1} + b_c) \tag{22}$$

$$h_t = o_t\sigma(c_t) \tag{23}$$

where i_t, f_t, and o_t are the output vectors of the input, forgetting, and output gates of the LSTM cell at time t, respectively; c_t is the state vector of the LSTM cell at time t; σ is a sigmoid nonlinear excitation function that introduces a nonlinear factor; a_t is the input vector of the LSTM cell at time t; W stands for the weight matrix for the connection between different gates; and b is the bias vector.

LSTM can record the feature representation of longer sequence data. Therefore, we proposed the DCS-LSTM network to implement the time-series modeling work on the data to facilitate the extraction of temporal contextual information of the sensor signals and weight the channel features by an ACS module to improve the model's ability to discriminate individual channel features and classify confusable behaviors. The hidden cells of the LSTM are set to 128.

4. Experiments

In this section, we conduct comprehensive experiments on several public HAR datasets to validate the effectiveness of our proposed framework. First, we describe the experimental setup, training measures, and evaluation metrics. Then, we present the benchmark datasets used. Finally, we compare our proposed model with state-of-the-art methods from recent years and report on the performance of HMA Conv-LSTM.

4.1. Experimental Setup

We build the model using Google's open-source deep learning framework TensorFlow 2.9.0, implement it using Python 3.8, and train it on an Intel Xeon Platinum 8255C CPU and an RTX 3080 GPU with 10 GB of memory. In addition, we used the Adam optimizer [47] to minimize the cross-entropy loss function for model training. The learning rate adopts Adam's default parameter of 0.001 as the initial training parameter of the model. We also use a cosine learning rate scheduling strategy to dynamically adjust the learning rate according to the cosine function in each epoch. The batch size of the four datasets is set to 128, and the number of training epochs is 80. Details of the hyperparameters used for model training are shown in Table 1.

Table 1. Hyperparameters of the model trained.

Hyperparameters	Value
Optimizer	Adam
Loss function	Cross entropy
Batch size	128
Learning rate	0.001
Learning rate scheduler	Cosine
Training epoch	80
Dropout rate	0.3

4.2. Dataset Description

We conducted experiments on the proposed HMA Conv-LSTM model on four benchmark datasets [48] with the same experimental setup as in the previous work. Table 2 shows the basic information statistics of the four datasets. Figure 5 shows the distribution of sample categories for the four benchmark datasets.

Table 2. Summary of the datasets. Here A = Accelerometer, G = Gyroscope, M = Magnetometer.

Dataset	Action Number	Validation Subject ID	Test Subject ID	Sampling Rate	Downsampling	Sensors Used
Opportunity	18	1(Run 2)	2, 3(Run 4, 5)	30 Hz	100%	A, G, M
PAMAP2	12	105	106	100 Hz	33%	A, G
USC-HAD	12	11, 12	13, 14	100 Hz	33%	A, G
Skoda	11	1(10%)	1(10%)	98 Hz	33%	A

Opportunity dataset [49] mainly contains daily household and kitchen actions. Subjects recorded data using inertial measurement units (IMUs) such as accelerometers, gyroscopes, and magnetometers at 12 locations on the body. The dataset is annotated for 18 mid-level actions (e.g., opening/closing the refrigerator), with one null category exceeding 76% of the data. It makes the dataset highly unbalanced in terms of the distribution of action categories.

PAMAP2 dataset [50] mainly contains multiple household actions. A total of nine subjects were instructed to perform 12 actions of daily living. Subjects recorded complete IMU data, temperature, and heart rate data using three wearable sensors located on the hand, chest, and ankle.

USC-HAD dataset [51] includes six readings from three-axis accelerometers and gyroscopes worn on the subjects' bodies. It contains 12 different action categories from 14 subjects, including walking, running, elevator up/down, etc. In addition, the sensor locations and division of action categories in this dataset make classification using feature representation learning challenging. For example, it is difficult to discriminate between actions such as walking to the left or right using only accelerometers and gyroscopes.

Skoda dataset [52] mainly consists of 10 actions performed by workers in an automotive production environment, such as opening/closing doors and check steering wheel. It also includes labeled empty categories. It consisted of one subject wearing an accelerometer in several different positions on their arm to perform manual maintenance and quality checks on automotive parts.

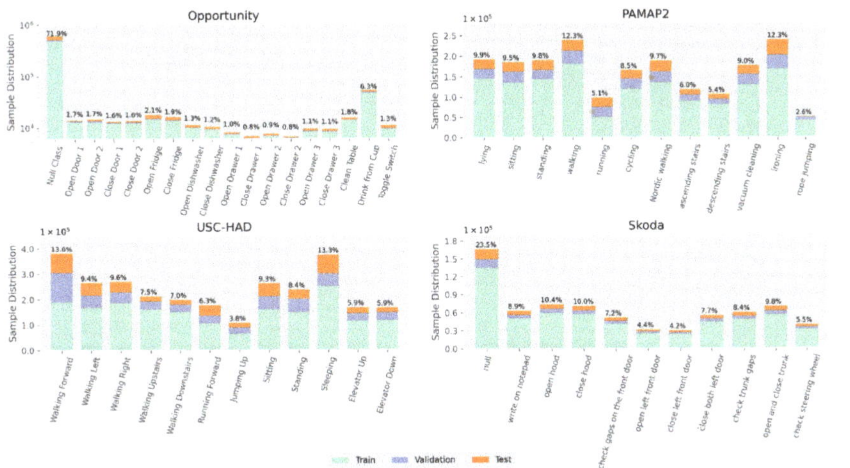

Figure 5. Distribution of sample categories across training, validation, and test sets in the four benchmark datasets, as well as the proportion of the overall number of samples accounted for by each category. The ratio of training, validation, and test sets is approximately 80:10:10%.

4.3. Performance Metric

In our experiments, we use the Macro average F1-score as the evaluation metric to compare the performance of our proposed method with other methods. In particular, for the Opportunity dataset, accuracy is not a suitable measure due to its highly uneven categorization. Since the traditional F1-score measures the performance of binary classification, we use the mean F1-score, which is F_m, weighted to categories according to their sample proportions.

$$F_m = \frac{1}{C}\sum_{i=1}^{C} \frac{2 \times Precision_i \times Recall_i}{Precision_i + Recall_i} \tag{24}$$

where C is the number of action categories. For category i, $Precision_i = \frac{TP_i}{TP_i + FP_i}$, $Recall_i = \frac{TP_i}{TP_i + FN_i}$. TP_i and FP_i are the number of true positives and false positives, respectively, while FN_i refers to the number of false negatives.

4.4. Comparison with State-of-the-Art Methods

In this section, we compare our proposed model with related work from recent years. The selected baseline approach is based on the four public datasets in Table 2. Firstly, our model outperforms SVM because earlier machine learning methods relied heavily on hand-crafted features, which limited their accuracy. Additionally, our model outperforms CNN and LSTM, which only consider either temporal contextual relevance or spatial relevance. Secondly, our model is more accurate than the DeepConvLSTM and

DeepConvLSTM + Attention models because our HMC structure effectively captures finer-grained information about tiny action processes. Furthermore, our model is more accurate than recently proposed methods such as ConvAE, AttnSense, and Self-Attention that incorporate attention mechanism. It reflects that our model outperforms most existing models and illustrates the effectiveness of our hierarchical architecture for feature extraction. In addition, Table 3 is categorized by network type, which are traditional models, LSTM-based, and attention mechanism-based models, and, finally, our proposed model.

Table 3. Macro F1-score of different methods on the benchmark set.

Methods	Opportunity	PAMAP2	USC-HAD	Skoda
SVM [53]	-	0.71	-	0.82
RF [54]	-	0.74	-	0.83
CNN [55]	0.59	0.82	0.41	0.85
LSTM [56]	0.63	0.75	0.38	0.89
b-LSTM [18]	0.68	0.84	0.39	0.91
DeepConvLSTM [21]	0.67	0.75	0.38	0.91
DeepConvLSTM + Attention [27]	0.71	0.88	-	0.91
LSTM + Continuous Attention [57]	-	0.90	-	0.94
ConvAE [48]	**0.72**	0.80	0.46	0.79
SADeepSense [58]	0.66	0.66	0.49	0.90
AttnSense [25]	0.66	0.89	0.49	0.93
Self-Attention * [26]	0.63	0.84	0.51	0.87
HMA Conv-LSTM	**0.68**	**0.91**	**0.53**	**0.96**

Models with * indicate that the performance is obtained by our replication. The bold parts represent our proposed model and the best performance on each dataset.

As shown in Table 3, the recognition performance of HMA Conv-LSTM significantly outperforms the other baselines. Despite USC-HAD being a challenging dataset, our model performs better than other models such as DeepConvLSTM (0.38) and AttnSense (0.49). Additionally, our proposed model outperforms other models which are based on attention mechanisms. On the PAMAP2 dataset, our model achieves better results (0.91) than DeepCovnLSTM + Attention (0.88), LSTM + Continuous Attention (0.90), and AttnSense (0.89). For the Skoda dataset, our model achieves high performance and outperforms other well-performing models such as AttnSense (0.93) and LSTM + Continuous Attention (0.94). In addition, compared to other methods, our model performs well on the Opportunity dataset (0.68), which contains complex actions. Due to the short duration of some of these mid-level gestures, the hierarchical architecture does not improve the current results much. However, when considering more complex and confusing gestures, the effect of our model is evident.

In conclusion, our proposed model outperforms other baseline methods on all datasets except the Opportunity dataset. It demonstrates the effectiveness and contribution of our model. The evaluation results further show that our proposed HMA Conv-LSTM can effectively obtain both temporal context information and spatial information from sensor sequence data. It can also recognize some subtle action processes with fine-grained detail, ultimately achieving good results.

5. Ablation Study and Discussion

We evaluate the effectiveness of our proposed HMA Conv-LSTM model. First, we explored the effect of the choice of model hyperparameters on performance. Second, we evaluated the effectiveness and contribution of each module of the model through ablation experiments. Then, we analyzed the confusion matrix obtained by testing the model on some of these datasets. Finally, we visualized the feature weights in SFS when recognizing some actions to improve the interpretability of the model.

5.1. Parameter Selection

To evaluate the impact of hyperparameters on the model's overall performance, we explored the sliding window size, sliding window overlap rate, and the number of hierarchical layers. We adjusted them sequentially and finally chose the optimal parameters. First, we analyzed the effect of sliding window size on the model's recognition performance. The four datasets were previously downsampled uniformly to a sampling rate of about 33 Hz per second. Since the repetition period of different actions varies, we experimented by changing the window size in seconds.

In Figure 6, our proposed model is more stable to changes in window size compared to other models. It also indicates that some complex actions require longer sliding window sizes for segmentation to achieve good recognition results. When the initial window size is small, the performance is average because the HMC structure has difficulty capturing information on multi-scales. As the window size increases, the model's performance improves, demonstrating the effectiveness of the hierarchical architecture and multi-scale convolution for feature extraction at different scales. The DCS-LSTM can also better capture temporal context information. Considering the performance, we chose a sliding window size of 1 s for the PAMAP2 and USC-HAD datasets, while the Opportunity and SKODA datasets chose a sliding window size of 1.5 s for action recognition.

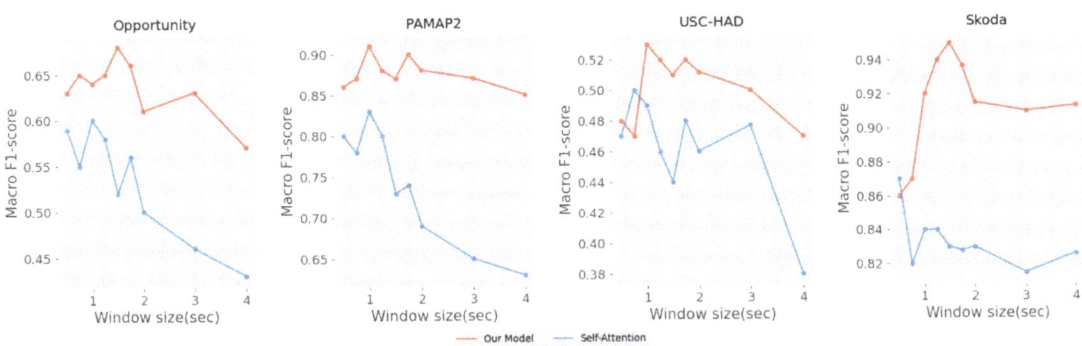

Figure 6. Performance of different window sizes, which shows the performance comparison of our proposed model with the self-attention model.

Then, based on the optimal sliding window size, we also discussed the impact of sliding window overlap rate on model performance. Due to the varying durations and complexities of different actions, the sliding window overlap rate is also critical in affecting action recognition. In Figure 7a, the model's performance on most datasets increases as the window overlap rate starts to increase, and the model reaches its best result when the overlap rate reaches 0.5. As the overlap rate continues to increase, the model's performance starts to decrease. This suggests that an appropriate overlap ratio can help the model better capture local patterns and relationships in time series data, maximizing the information in the data while ensuring computational efficiency. Therefore, we chose 50% as the window overlap rate for model training. Finally, based on the optimal configuration, we explored the number of layers in the hierarchical architecture of our proposed model.

In Figure 7b, as the number of layers increases from zero to two, the model's performance improves on each dataset. This indicates that our proposed HMA Conv-LSTM network can effectively capture multi-scale features and some fine-grained subtle action processes. However, when the number of layers reaches three, the performance starts to deteriorate. The window size may be the cause of this situation. When the number of layers is three, the minimum division of the partition length is small, and the multi-scale convolution operation can no longer capture finer features. The model's best results are obtained when the number of layers is two. Therefore, we choose two as the number of hierarchical layers for model construction.

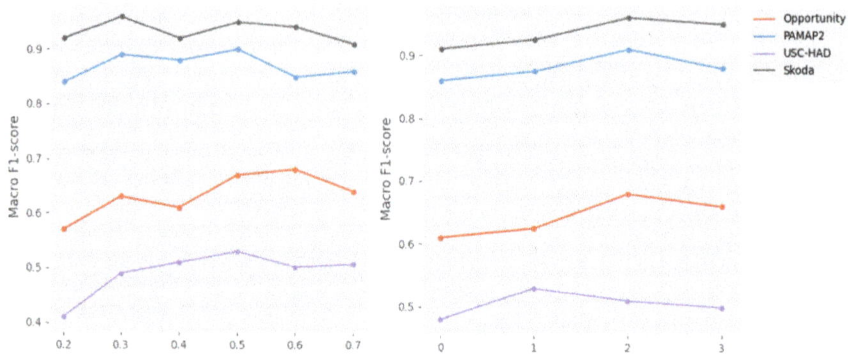

Figure 7. Performance of different window overlap rates (**a**) and different hierarchical numbers (**b**).

5.2. Effectiveness of the Proposed Modules

We conducted an ablation study on the proposed model, based on the optimal parameter configurations of the previous model, to evaluate the contributions of the proposed modules. The results of the ablation experiments are shown in Table 4. In each experiment, we removed specific modules from the proposed model. Additionally, we replaced the ablated modules with alternative modules in some experiments for further testing. For example, we replaced the entire HMC with multi-scale convolution and replaced DCS-LSTM with LSTM. We also deleted ACS in ACFF and used the remaining two convolutional layers instead.

Table 4. Ablation study results compared with the full HMA Conv-LSTM model (Macro F1-score).

Model	Opportunity		PAMAP2		USC-HAD		Skoda	
	F1-Score	Δ	F1-Score	Δ	F1-Score	Δ	F1-Score	Δ
HMA Conv-LSTM	**0.68**	-	**0.91**	-	**0.53**	-	**0.96**	-
-SFS	0.65	−0.03	0.87	−0.04	0.51	−0.02	0.93	−0.03
-ACFF (+Two Convolution Layer)	0.65	−0.03	0.89	−0.02	0.50	−0.03	0.94	−0.02
-DCS-LSTM (+LSTM)	0.66	−0.02	0.89	−0.02	0.51	−0.02	0.93	−0.03
-HMC	0.61	−0.07	0.86	−0.05	0.48	−0.05	0.91	−0.05
-HMC (+Multi-scale Convolution)	0.64	−0.04	0.87	−0.04	0.50	−0.03	0.93	−0.03

The bold parts represent the performance of our proposed model before ablation on each dataset.

From Table 4, it is evident that HMC significantly contributes to improving recognition. Its ablation leads to about 0.05 performance degradation across datasets. While the ablation of SFS leads to about 0.03 performance degradation. When we replaced the HMC component with a single multi-scale convolution component, the model performance also decreased by about 0.03, illustrating the importance and effectiveness of the hierarchical architecture and suggesting that multi-scale feature maps captured by the multi-scale convolution are effective.

Regarding DCS-LSTM, replacing it with a standard LSTM network resulted in a performance decrease of about 0.02, indicating that the ACS operation effectively captures contributions from different channels and learns each channel's weights adaptively. When ACS was ablated from the ACFF component, performance decreased by about 0.02, further demonstrating ACS operation's effectiveness. In conclusion, all components in our proposed model significantly contribute to its performance, as evidenced by the results of our ablation experiments. In addition, our study also has some limitations. Our model depends on the quality of the sensor signal. If there are a lot of noise or data missing, it may affect the model's performance.

5.3. Comparison of Specific Actions

Figures 8 and 9 shows the confusion matrix of our proposed model on the PAMAP2, USC-HAD, Skoda, and Opportunity datasets. The confusion matrix is used to measure the effectiveness of a classifier in recognizing different categories. The row and column labels of a confusion matrix represent the true and predicted categories, respectively. The diagonal elements of the confusion matrix indicate the correct recognition rate for each action, while the off-diagonal elements represent the proportion of actions that are incorrectly recognized as other categories.

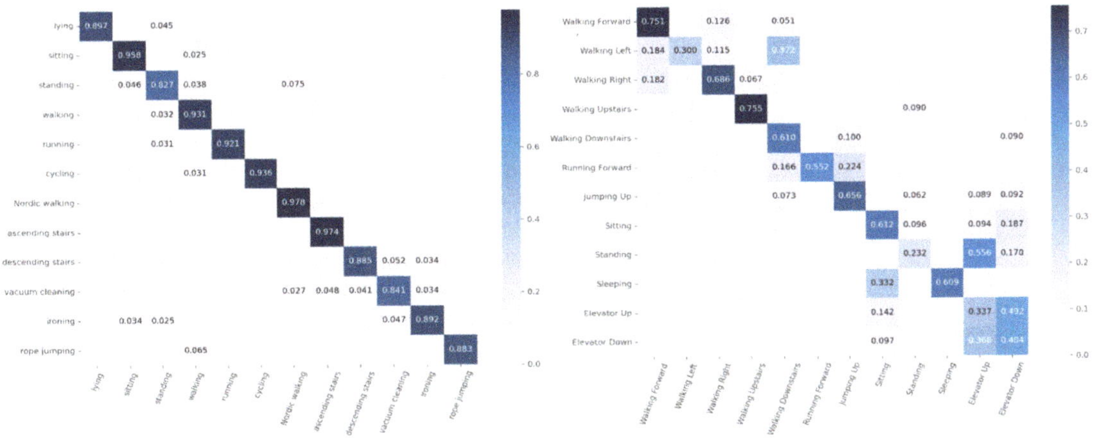

(a) PAMAP2 (b) USC-HAD

Figure 8. Confusion matrix of the proposed model on the PAMAP2 (**a**) and USC-HAD (**b**) datasets.

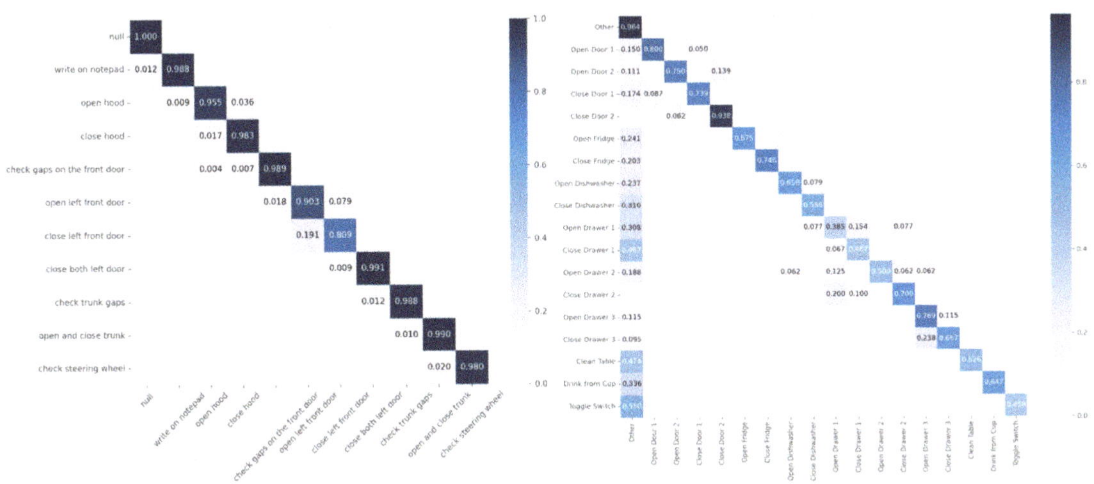

(a) Skoda (b) Opportunity

Figure 9. Confusion matrix of the proposed model on the Skoda (**a**) and Opportunity (**b**) datasets.

In Figure 8a, there is some confusion between "standing" and "sitting", which is reasonable because the two actions are relatively similar. Other categories such as "walking", "running", and "descending stairs" are well recognized. In Figure 8b, there is some confusion about the type of action due to the division of the sensor's position and action category at the time of data acquisition. However, for some categories such as "Walking Forward", "Walking Right", "Walking Upstairs", etc., our model is still able to distinguish the confusing actions well.

In Figure 9a, there is some confusion between the actions "open left front door" and "close left front door" due to the similarity of the two actions, resulting in similar data collected by the accelerometer. However, other action categories, such as "open hood", "close hood", and "close both left doors" were well recognized. This is because these actions are process-oriented and can be distinguished without serious confusion, and the model is more sensitive to the data collected by the sensors. In Figure 9b, human action recognition on the Opportunity dataset is challenging due to the highly unbalanced sample distribution. Nevertheless, our model can still distinguish some easily confused actions, such as "Open Door 1" and "Open Door 2", "Close Door 1" and "Close Door 2", "Open Drawer 3" and "Close Drawer 3", etc. This shows that our proposed model can effectively and accurately recognize some complex actions with subtle processes and can also distinguish some confusing actions well.

In addition, the evaluation metrics scores for each category on the Skoda and Opportunity datasets are presented in Tables 5 and 6, respectively. The main focus here is to analyze the performance of the Macro F1-score. In Table 5, the "close left front door" action has the lowest Macro F1-score of 0.85; while the actions such as "write on notepad" and "check steering wheel" have a higher Macro F1-score of 0.99. In Table 6, the Macro F1-score performance of confusing actions such as "Open Door 1", "Open Door 2", "Close Door 1", and "Close Door 2" all reached above 0.79, while the Macro F1-score performance of "Open Drawer 2", "Close Drawer 2", "Open Drawer 3", and "Close Drawer 3" also reached above 0.6, which is generally a good performance. These results indicate that our proposed model has good action recognition performance.

Table 5. Evaluation metrics for each action of the proposed model on the Skoda dataset.

Action of Skoda Dataset	Precision	Recall	Macro F1-Score
null	0.996	0.999	0.998
write on notepad	0.989	0.988	0.989
open hood	0.980	0.955	0.968
close hood	0.959	0.983	0.970
check gaps on the front door	0.989	0.989	0.989
open left front door	0.834	0.903	0.867
close left front door	0.890	0.809	0.848
close both left door	0.987	0.991	0.989
check trunk gaps	0.989	0.988	0.988
open and close trunk	0.988	0.991	0.989
check steering wheel	0.999	0.980	0.990

Table 6. Evaluation metrics for each action of the proposed model on the Opportunity dataset.

Action of Opportunity Dataset	Precision	Recall	Macro F1-Score
Other	0.949	0.964	0.956
Open Door 1	0.842	0.800	0.821
Open Door 2	0.844	0.750	0.794
Close Door 1	0.944	0.739	0.829
Close Door 2	0.750	0.938	0.833
Open Fridge	0.800	0.675	0.732
Close Fridge	0.733	0.746	0.740

Table 6. *Cont.*

Action of Opportunity Dataset	Precision	Recall	Macro F1-Score
Open Dishwasher	0.595	0.658	0.625
Close Dishwasher	0.486	0.586	0.531
Open Drawer 1	0.294	0.385	0.333
Close Drawer 1	0.539	0.467	0.500
Open Drawer 2	0.889	0.500	0.640
Close Drawer 2	0.636	0.700	0.667
Open Drawer 3	0.606	0.769	0.678
Close Drawer 3	0.560	0.667	0.609
Clean Table	0.909	0.526	0.667
Drink from Cup	0.762	0.647	0.700
Toggle Switch	0.857	0.450	0.590

5.4. Visualizing Sensor Feature Selection Weights

We visualized the attentional weights in the SFS module to evaluate the effects of different sensor features on different parts of the human body and different actions. Figure 10a shows the IMU inertial sensing units in different parts of the human body in the PAMAP2 dataset; Figure 10b,c shows the attentional weights of the different sensor features for the actions of "running" and "ironing", respectively.

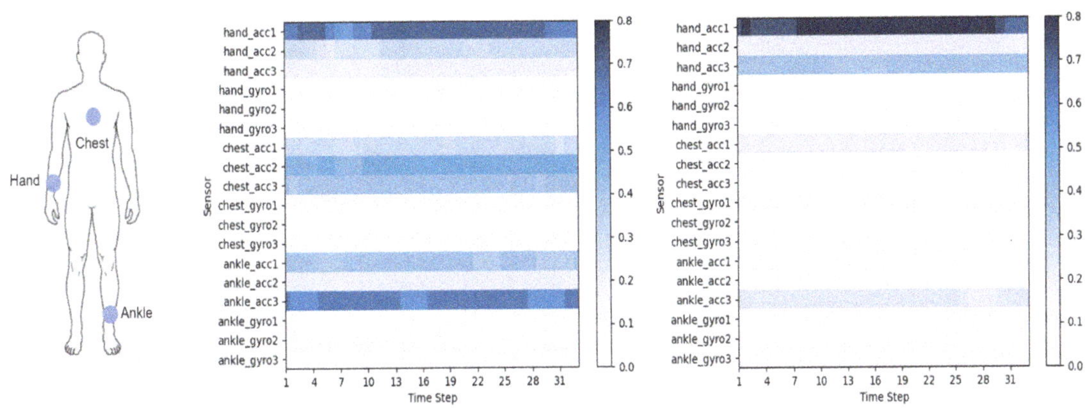

(a) Position of sensors (b) running (c) ironing

Figure 10. Visualization of attention weights for "running" (**b**) and "ironing" (**c**) actions of the PAMAP2 dataset, and the position of sensors (**a**).

In Figure 10b, the "hand_acc", "chest_acc", and "ankle_acc" three-axis sensors in the IMU have a significant impact on the running action. This is reasonable and intuitively understandable because all parts of the human body are coordinated to complete actions during running, and different types of sensor features play different roles in recognizing different actions. In Figure 10c, the "hand_acc" sensor in the IMU is given more weight, which is also reasonable because ironing is mainly performed with the hand.

Not all sensor features have the same contribution when performing action classification. Our SFS module can automatically learn the weights of different sensor features in the HAR task, capturing their contributions and potential importance. In short, our module effectively identifies sensor features that contribute to the HAR task, providing a more accurate basis for action classification.

6. Conclusions

In this paper, we proposed the HMA Conv-LSTM, a novel hierarchical multi-scale adaptive Conv-LSTM network for HAR. This network attentively weights sensor signals by SFS, extracts finer-grained spatial features using HMC, and employs ACFF to process multi-channel feature maps. It extracts temporal context information through a DCS-LSTM network. The model fuses spatial features at different scales with time series information at different levels to effectively capture the spatio-temporal motion patterns of the sensor signals and accurately recognize some actions with fine-grained processes. Extensive experiments on four public datasets demonstrate that HMA Conv-LSTM achieves competitive performance when compared to several state-of-the-art approaches.

In future work, we will continue to improve our model by experimenting with new network structures and techniques to improve the performance of the model. We will also consider using some data noise reduction and data augmentation operations to improve the data quality, reduce the impact of noise on the model performance, and improve the model's generalization ability.

Author Contributions: Conceptualization, W.X.; Methodology, W.X. and C.L.; Software, W.X.; Validation, W.X.; Formal analysis, C.L. and Q.H.; Resources, Q.H. and Y.W.; Writing—original draft, W.X.; Writing—review & editing, C.L. and Q.H.; Supervision, C.L., Q.H. and Y.L.; Project administration, Q.H., Y.W. and Y.L. All authors have read and agreed to the published version of the manuscript.

Funding: This work is supported by the Key Research and Development Program of China (No. 2022YFC3005401), the Key Research and Development Program of China, Yunnan Province (No. 202203AA080009), the Fundamental Research Funds for the Central Universities (No. B230205027), Postgraduate Research & Practice Innovation Program of Jiangsu Province (No. 422003261), the 14th Five-Year Plan for Educational Science of Jiangsu Province (No. D/2021/01/39), the Jiangsu Higher Education Reform Research Project (No. 2021JSJG143).

Institutional Review Board Statement: Not applicable.

Informed Consent Statement: Not applicable.

Data Availability Statement: Not applicable.

Acknowledgments: The authors express gratitude to the funding institutions.

Conflicts of Interest: The authors declare no conflict of interest.

References

1. Anagnostis, A.; Benos, L.; Tsaopoulos, D.; Tagarakis, A.; Tsolakis, N.; Bochtis, D. Human activity recognition through recurrent neural networks for human–robot interaction in agriculture. *Appl. Sci.* **2021**, *11*, 2188. [CrossRef]
2. Asghari, P.; Soleimani, E.; Nazerfard, E. Online human activity recognition employing hierarchical hidden Markov models. *J. Ambient Intell. Humaniz. Comput.* **2020**, *11*, 1141–1152. [CrossRef]
3. Ramos, R.G.; Domingo, J.D.; Zalama, E.; Gómez-García-Bermejo, J.; López, J. SDHAR-HOME: A sensor dataset for human activity recognition at home. *Sensors* **2022**, *22*, 8109. [CrossRef] [PubMed]
4. Khan, W.Z.; Xiang, Y.; Aalsalem, M.Y.; Arshad, Q. Mobile phone sensing systems: A survey. *IEEE Commun. Surv. Tutor.* **2012**, *15*, 402–427. [CrossRef]
5. Taylor, K.; Abdulla, U.A.; Helmer, R.J.; Lee, J.; Blanchonette, I. Activity classification with smart phones for sports activities. *Procedia Eng.* **2011**, *13*, 428–433. [CrossRef]
6. Zhang, S.; Wei, Z.; Nie, J.; Huang, L.; Wang, S.; Li, Z. A review on human activity recognition using vision-based method. *J. Healthc. Eng.* **2017**, *2017*, 3090343. [CrossRef]
7. Dang, L.M.; Min, K.; Wang, H.; Piran, M.J.; Lee, C.H.; Moon, H. Sensor-based and vision-based human activity recognition: A comprehensive survey. *Pattern Recognit.* **2020**, *108*, 107561. [CrossRef]
8. Abdel-Salam, R.; Mostafa, R.; Hadhood, M. Human activity recognition using wearable sensors: Review, challenges, evaluation benchmark. In Proceedings of the International Workshop on Deep Learning for Human Activity Recognition, Montreal, QC, Canada, 21–26 August 2021; pp. 1–15.
9. Sun, Z.; Ke, Q.; Rahmani, H.; Bennamoun, M.; Wang, G.; Liu, J. Human action recognition from various data modalities: A review. *IEEE Trans. Pattern Anal. Mach. Intell.* **2022**, *45*, 3200–3225. [CrossRef]
10. Bulling, A.; Blanke, U.; Schiele, B. A tutorial on human activity recognition using body-worn inertial sensors. *ACM Comput. Surv. (CSUR)* **2014**, *46*, 1–33. [CrossRef]

11. Bao, L.; Intille, S.S. Activity recognition from user-annotated acceleration data. In Proceedings of the International Conference on Pervasive Computing, Nottingham, UK, 7–10 September 2004; pp. 1–17.
12. Plötz, T.; Hammerla, N.Y.; Olivier, P.L. Feature learning for activity recognition in ubiquitous computing. In Proceedings of the Twenty-Second International Joint Conference on Artificial Intelligence, Barcelona, Spain, 16–22 July 2011.
13. Bengio, Y. Deep learning of representations: Looking forward. In Proceedings of the Statistical Language and Speech Processing, Tarragona, Spain, 29–31 July 2013; pp. 1–37.
14. Islam, M.M.; Nooruddin, S.; Karray, F.; Muhammad, G. Human activity recognition using tools of convolutional neural networks: A state of the art review, data sets, challenges, and future prospects. *Comput. Biol. Med.* **2022**, *149*, 106060. [CrossRef]
15. Yang, J.; Nguyen, M.N.; San, P.P.; Li, X.; Krishnaswamy, S. Deep convolutional neural networks on multichannel time series for human activity recognition. In Proceedings of the Twenty-Fourth International Joint Conference on Artificial Intelligence, Buenos Aires, Argentina, 25–31 July 2015; pp. 3995–4001.
16. Ha, S.; Yun, J.-M.; Choi, S. Multi-modal convolutional neural networks for activity recognition. In Proceedings of the 2015 IEEE International Conference on Systems, Man, and Cybernetics, Hong Kong, China, 9–12 October 2015; pp. 3017–3022.
17. Guan, Y.; Plötz, T. Ensembles of deep lstm learners for activity recognition using wearables. *Proc. ACM Interact. Mob. Wearable Ubiquitous Technol.* **2017**, *1*, 1–28. [CrossRef]
18. Hammerla, N.Y.; Halloran, S.; Plötz, T. Deep, convolutional, and recurrent models for human activity recognition using wearables. *arXiv* **2016**, arXiv:1604.08880.
19. Dua, N.; Singh, S.N.; Semwal, V.B. Multi-input CNN-GRU based human activity recognition using wearable sensors. *Computing* **2021**, *103*, 1461–1478. [CrossRef]
20. Zhao, Y.; Yang, R.; Chevalier, G.; Xu, X.; Zhang, Z. Deep residual bidir-LSTM for human activity recognition using wearable sensors. *Math. Probl. Eng.* **2018**, *2018*, 7316954. [CrossRef]
21. Ordóñez, F.J.; Roggen, D. Deep convolutional and lstm recurrent neural networks for multimodal wearable activity recognition. *Sensors* **2016**, *16*, 115. [CrossRef]
22. Yao, S.; Hu, S.; Zhao, Y.; Zhang, A.; Abdelzaher, T. Deepsense: A unified deep learning framework for time-series mobile sensing data processing. In Proceedings of the 26th International Conference on World Wide Web, Perth, Australia, 3–7 April 2017; pp. 351–360.
23. Nan, Y.; Lovell, N.H.; Redmond, S.J.; Wang, K.; Delbaere, K.; van Schooten, K.S. Deep learning for activity recognition in older people using a pocket-worn smartphone. *Sensors* **2020**, *20*, 7195. [CrossRef]
24. Radu, V.; Tong, C.; Bhattacharya, S.; Lane, N.D.; Mascolo, C.; Marina, M.K.; Kawsar, F. Multimodal deep learning for activity and context recognition. *Proc. ACM Interact. Mob. Wearable Ubiquitous Technol.* **2018**, *1*, 1–27. [CrossRef]
25. Ma, H.; Li, W.; Zhang, X.; Gao, S.; Lu, S. AttnSense: Multi-level attention mechanism for multimodal human activity recognition. In Proceedings of the International Joint Conference on Artificial Intelligence, Macao, China, 10–16 August 2019; pp. 3109–3115.
26. Mahmud, S.; Tonmoy, M.; Bhaumik, K.K.; Rahman, A.M.; Amin, M.A.; Shoyaib, M.; Khan, M.A.H.; Ali, A.A. Human activity recognition from wearable sensor data using self-attention. *arXiv* **2020**, arXiv:2003.09018.
27. Murahari, V.S.; Plötz, T. On attention models for human activity recognition. In Proceedings of the 2018 ACM International Symposium on Wearable Computers, Singapore, 8–12 October 2018; pp. 100–103.
28. Haque, M.N.; Tonmoy, M.T.H.; Mahmud, S.; Ali, A.A.; Khan, M.A.H.; Shoyaib, M. Gru-based attention mechanism for human activity recognition. In Proceedings of the 2019 1st International Conference on Advances in Science, Engineering and Robotics Technology (ICASERT), Dhaka, Bangladesh, 3–5 May 2019; pp. 1–6.
29. Al-qaness, M.A.; Dahou, A.; Abd Elaziz, M.; Helmi, A. Multi-ResAtt: Multilevel residual network with attention for human activity recognition using wearable sensors. *IEEE Trans. Ind. Inform.* **2022**, *19*, 144–152. [CrossRef]
30. Duan, F.; Zhu, T.; Wang, J.; Chen, L.; Ning, H.; Wan, Y. A Multi-Task Deep Learning Approach for Sensor-based Human Activity Recognition and Segmentation. *IEEE Trans. Instrum. Meas.* **2023**, *72*, 2514012. [CrossRef]
31. Gomes, E.; Bertini, L.; Campos, W.R.; Sobral, A.P.; Mocaiber, I.; Copetti, A. Machine learning algorithms for activity-intensity recognition using accelerometer data. *Sensors* **2021**, *21*, 1214. [CrossRef] [PubMed]
32. Van Kasteren, T.; Noulas, A.; Englebienne, G.; Kröse, B. Accurate activity recognition in a home setting. In Proceedings of the 10th International Conference on Ubiquitous Computing, Seoul, Republic of Korea, 21–24 September 2008; pp. 1–9.
33. Tran, D.N.; Phan, D.D. Human activities recognition in android smartphone using support vector machine. In Proceedings of the 2016 7th International Conference on Intelligent Systems, Modelling and Simulation (Isms), Bangkok, Thailand, 25–27 January 2016; pp. 64–68.
34. Figo, D.; Diniz, P.C.; Ferreira, D.R.; Cardoso, J.M. Preprocessing techniques for context recognition from accelerometer data. *Pers. Ubiquitous Comput.* **2010**, *14*, 645–662. [CrossRef]
35. Jiang, W.; Yin, Z. Human activity recognition using wearable sensors by deep convolutional neural networks. In Proceedings of the 23rd ACM International Conference on Multimedia, Brisbane, Australia, 26–30 October 2015; pp. 1307–1310.
36. Ullah, M.; Ullah, H.; Khan, S.D.; Cheikh, F.A. Stacked lstm network for human activity recognition using smartphone data. In Proceedings of the 8th European Workshop on Visual Information Processing (EUVIP), Roma, Italy, 28–31 October 2019; pp. 175–180.
37. Mohsen, S. Recognition of human activity using GRU deep learning algorithm. *Multimed. Tools Appl.* **2023**, 1–17. [CrossRef]

38. Gaur, D.; Kumar Dubey, S. Development of Activity Recognition Model using LSTM-RNN Deep Learning Algorithm. *J. Inf. Organ. Sci.* **2022**, *46*, 277–291.
39. Nafea, O.; Abdul, W.; Muhammad, G.; Alsulaiman, M. Sensor-based human activity recognition with spatio-temporal deep learning. *Sensors* **2021**, *21*, 2141. [CrossRef]
40. Vaswani, A.; Shazeer, N.; Parmar, N.; Uszkoreit, J.; Jones, L.; Gomez, A.N.; Kaiser, Ł.; Polosukhin, I. Attention is all you need. *arXiv* **2017**, arXiv:1706.03762.
41. Zhang, Z.; Wang, W.; An, A.; Qin, Y.; Yang, F. A human activity recognition method using wearable sensors based on convtransformer model. *Evol. Syst.* **2023**, 1–17. [CrossRef]
42. Xiao, S.; Wang, S.; Huang, Z.; Wang, Y.; Jiang, H. Two-stream transformer network for sensor-based human activity recognition. *Neurocomputing* **2022**, *512*, 253–268. [CrossRef]
43. Zhao, C.; Huang, X.; Li, Y.; Yousaf Iqbal, M. A double-channel hybrid deep neural network based on CNN and BiLSTM for remaining useful life prediction. *Sensors* **2020**, *20*, 7109. [CrossRef]
44. Zeng, M.; Wang, X.; Nguyen, L.T.; Wu, P.; Mengshoel, O.J.; Zhang, J. Adaptive activity recognition with dynamic heterogeneous sensor fusion. In Proceedings of the 6th International Conference on Mobile Computing, Applications and Services, Austin, TX, USA, 6–7 November 2014; pp. 189–196.
45. Szegedy, C.; Liu, W.; Jia, Y.; Sermanet, P.; Reed, S.; Anguelov, D.; Erhan, D.; Vanhoucke, V.; Rabinovich, A. Going deeper with convolutions. In Proceedings of the IEEE Conference on Computer Vision and Pattern Recognition, Boston, MA, USA, 7–12 June 2015; pp. 1–9.
46. Karpathy, A.; Johnson, J.; Fei-Fei, L. Visualizing and understanding recurrent networks. *arXiv* **2015**, arXiv:1506.02078.
47. Kingma, D.P.; Ba, J. Adam: A method for stochastic optimization. *arXiv* **2014**, arXiv:1412.6980.
48. Haresamudram, H.; Anderson, D.V.; Plötz, T. On the role of features in human activity recognition. In Proceedings of the 2019 ACM International Symposium on Wearable Computers, New York, NY, USA, 9–13 September 2019; pp. 78–88.
49. Roggen, D.; Calatroni, A.; Rossi, M.; Holleczek, T.; Förster, K.; Tröster, G.; Lukowicz, P.; Bannach, D.; Pirkl, G.; Ferscha, A. Collecting complex activity datasets in highly rich networked sensor environments. In Proceedings of the 2010 Seventh International Conference on Networked Sensing Systems (INSS), Kassel, Germany, 15–18 June 2010; pp. 233–240.
50. Reiss, A.; Stricker, D. Introducing a new benchmarked dataset for activity monitoring. In Proceedings of the 2012 16th International Symposium on Wearable Computers, Newcastle, UK, 18–22 June 2012; pp. 108–109.
51. Zhang, M.; Sawchuk, A.A. USC-HAD: A daily activity dataset for ubiquitous activity recognition using wearable sensors. In Proceedings of the 2012 ACM Conference on Ubiquitous Computing, Pittsburgh, PA, USA, 5–8 September 2012; pp. 1036–1043.
52. Stiefmeier, T.; Roggen, D.; Ogris, G.; Lukowicz, P.; Tröster, G. Wearable activity tracking in car manufacturing. *IEEE Pervasive Comput.* **2008**, *7*, 42–50. [CrossRef]
53. Hearst, M.A.; Dumais, S.T.; Osuna, E.; Platt, J.; Scholkopf, B. Support vector machines. *IEEE Intell. Syst. Their Appl.* **1998**, *13*, 18–28. [CrossRef]
54. Liaw, A.; Wiener, M. Classification and regression by randomForest. *R News* **2002**, *2*, 18–22.
55. LeCun, Y.; Bengio, Y.; Hinton, G. Deep learning. *Nature* **2015**, *521*, 436–444. [CrossRef]
56. Hochreiter, S.; Schmidhuber, J. Long short-term memory. *Neural Comput.* **1997**, *9*, 1735–1780. [CrossRef]
57. Zeng, M.; Gao, H.; Yu, T.; Mengshoel, O.J.; Langseth, H.; Lane, I.; Liu, X. Understanding and improving recurrent networks for human activity recognition by continuous attention. In Proceedings of the 2018 ACM international symposium on wearable computers, New York, NY, USA, 8–12 October 2018; pp. 56–63.
58. Yao, S.; Zhao, Y.; Shao, H.; Liu, D.; Liu, S.; Hao, Y.; Piao, A.; Hu, S.; Lu, S.; Abdelzaher, T.F. Sadeepsense: Self-attention deep learning framework for heterogeneous on-device sensors in internet of things applications. In Proceedings of the IEEE INFOCOM 2019-IEEE Conference on Computer Communications, Paris, France, 29 April–2 May 2019; pp. 1243–1251.

applied sciences

MDPI

Article

Attention-Based Hybrid Deep Learning Network for Human Activity Recognition Using WiFi Channel State Information

Sakorn Mekruksavanich [1], Wikanda Phaphan [2], Narit Hnoohom [3,*] and Anuchit Jitpattanakul [4,5,*]

1 Department of Computer Engineering, School of Information and Communication Technology, University of Phayao, Phayao 56000, Thailand; sakorn.me@up.ac.th
2 Department of Applied Statistics, Faculty of Applied Science, King Mongkut's University of Technology North Bangkok, Bangkok 10800, Thailand; wikanda.p@sci.kmutnb.ac.th
3 Department of Computer Engineering, Faculty of Engineering, Mahidol University, Nakhon Pathom 73170, Thailand
4 Department of Mathematics, Faculty of Applied Science, King Mongkut's University of Technology North Bangkok, Bangkok 10800, Thailand
5 Intelligent and Nonlinear Dynamic Innovations Research Center, Science and Technology Research Institute, King Mongkut's University of Technology North Bangkok, Bangkok 10800, Thailand
* Correspondence: narit.hno@mahidol.ac.th (N.H.); anuchit.j@sci.kmutnb.ac.th (A.J.)

Abstract: The recognition of human movements is a crucial aspect of AI-related research fields. Although methods using vision and sensors provide more valuable data, they come at the expense of inconvenience to users and social limitations including privacy issues. WiFi-based sensing methods are increasingly being used to collect data on human activity due to their ubiquity, versatility, and high performance. Channel state information (CSI), a characteristic of WiFi signals, can be employed to identify various human activities. Traditional machine learning approaches depend on manually designed features, so recent studies propose leveraging deep learning capabilities to automatically extract features from raw CSI data. This research introduces a versatile framework for recognizing human activities by utilizing CSI data and evaluates its effectiveness on different deep learning networks. A hybrid deep learning network called CNN-GRU-AttNet is proposed to automatically extract informative spatial-temporal features from raw CSI data and efficiently classify activities. The effectiveness of a hybrid model is assessed by comparing it with five conventional deep learning models (CNN, LSTM, BiLSTM, GRU, and BiGRU) on two widely recognized benchmark datasets (CSI-HAR and StanWiFi). The experimental results demonstrate that the CNN-GRU-AttNet model surpasses previous state-of-the-art techniques, leading to an average accuracy improvement of up to 4.62%. Therefore, the proposed hybrid model is suitable for identifying human actions using CSI data.

Keywords: human activity recognition; WiFi sensing; deep learning; attention mechanism; channel state information

Citation: Mekruksavanich, S.; Phaphan, W.; Hnoohom, N.; Jitpattanakul, A. Attention-Based Hybrid Deep Learning Network for Human Activity Recognition Using WiFi Channel State Information. *Appl. Sci.* **2023**, *13*, 8884. https://doi.org/10.3390/app13158884

Academic Editors: Luigi Bibbò and Marley M.B.R. Vellasco

Received: 29 May 2023
Revised: 27 July 2023
Accepted: 29 July 2023
Published: 1 August 2023

1. Introduction

Over the last decade, human activity recognition (HAR) research has advanced significantly. It has proven successful in several areas, such as healthcare, smart homes, sports performance tracking, and human–computer interaction [1]. The primary goal of HAR is to detect and understand user actions, enabling computing systems to provide proactive assistance [2,3]. There are two main categories of HAR: vision-based and sensor-based. Firstly, vision-based HAR (V-HAR) holds great promise, benefiting from the rapid advancements in computer vision techniques and the high resolution offered by optical sensors [4–6]. Despite its success, V-HAR still faces challenges such as illumination, occlusion, and privacy concerns. However, sensor-based HAR (S-HAR) has become increasingly popular due to the rapid advancement in sensor technology [7–9]. S-HAR collects data from low-level sensors, such as accelerometers, gyroscopes, magnetometers, and acoustic sensors, to extract high-level information about human behavior. However, S-HAR has limitations in terms of environmental requirements, and people may object to using sensors due to their bothersome or cumbersome nature. V-HAR and S-HAR have challenges to overcome, but they can potentially provide valuable insights into human behavior.

Despite the numerous methods developed in recent years, WiFi-based sensing techniques have gained significant attention due to their widespread availability, versatility, and high performance [10]. WiFi-based sensing has the potential to integrate sensing and communication functions, as channel information can be utilized for both purposes [11]. Compared to V-HAR and S-HAR techniques, WiFi-based HAR systems provide several advantages. WiFi-based HAR systems differ from V-HAR systems in that they are not influenced by lighting conditions or variations in human body shapes, and they also respect user privacy. Additionally, these systems provide a more convenient option for smart home and healthcare applications since they do not rely on users wearing sensors. Consequently, researchers have actively engaged in investigating and developing WiFi-based HAR methods in recent times.

Wi-Fi-based human HAR systems offer a cost-effective and seamless integration solution within existing Wi-Fi infrastructures in both residential and commercial environments, with minimal additional expenses. These systems can be arranged into two main types [12] based on their utilization of the received signal strength indicator (RSSI) [13], while the other type relies on channel state information (CSI) [10,14] for activity recognition tasks. The CSI provides a comprehensive characterization of the radio frequency (RF) signal propagation, encompassing aspects such as amplitude attenuation, time lag, and phase shift across various carrier frequencies. Prior research has consistently demonstrated the superior performance of CSI-based HAR systems compared to RSSI-based alternatives [14], primarily due to the increased richness and informational content provided by CSI data.

Learning-based approaches have emerged as potent tools for classification and prediction, occupying a crucial role in HAR and the implementation of recognition models. Researchers have extensively employed conventional machine learning (ML) techniques, including Hidden Markov Model [15], Random Forest [16], Support Vector Machine [17], and K-Nearest Neighbor [18], to achieve HAR objectives. In conventional activity recognition methods, ML algorithms manually extract features from sensor data, often relying on statistical or structural attributes such as means, medians, and standard deviations. Extracting the most relevant manual features often demands domain expertise. While these handcrafted features demonstrate satisfactory performance in scenarios with limited training data, their extraction becomes increasingly intricate as the number of sensors escalates.

Deep learning (DL), a cutting-edge approach within the realm of ML, has gained significant traction due to its remarkable capability to extract features and perform classification simultaneously. In contrast to traditional ML methods, DL leverages artificial neural networks with multiple layers to process data and address intricate problems. Promising outcomes have been observed across various domains through DL models including Convolutional Neural Networks (CNN), Long Short-Term Memory (LSTM), and Recurrent Neural Networks (RNN). CNN effectively overcomes high dimensionality by employing filters capable of convolving and sharing weights. On the other hand, RNN, a type of neural network, leverages previous outputs as inputs in the present step and incorporates hidden states, making it particularly suitable for solving sequential concerns and operating time series data. DL presents distinct advantages over traditional ML approaches as it surpasses the limitations of manual feature extraction and exhibits enhanced efficiency in handling large datasets. Additionally, Graphics Processing Units (GPUs) can be employed to accelerate the computational speed of DL models.

Over the past few years, the improvement of DL techniques has become increasingly prominent in CSI-based HAR [19]. Among these techniques, the LSTM method has emerged as a notable strategy that relies solely on the current state of CSI for learning. LSTM excels at autonomously learning representative features and capturing temporal data during the feature learning process. To attain superior performance in HAR utilizing CSI measurements, researchers have developed an attention-based bidirectional LSTM method. This method combines a Bidirectional LSTM (BLSTM) [20] with an attention model that assigns increased weights to specific time steps, effectively enhancing recognition efficiency.

The conventional LSTM is limited to processing sequential CSI measurements in a single direction, such as forward, and it solely relies on historical CSI information for the current hidden state. However, we emphasize the significance of incorporating future CSI data to enable accurate HAR. Additionally, the sequentially learned features of a conventional LSTM can have varying effects on the HAR task. In the conventional LSTM method, each learned characteristic contributes equally to the final identification of human activities. Real-time applications can benefit from employing advanced DL approaches and models to enhance the accuracy of these methods.

Therefore, this article presents CNN-GRU-AttNet, an innovative DL network specifically designed for extracting spatial-temporal features from raw WiFi CSI data. The network architecture comprises convolution layers and a gated recurrent unit (GRU) layer. Moreover, we incorporate an attention mechanism that dynamically assigns weights to important features and time steps, thereby enhancing the model's generalization performance for HAR. To evaluate the effectiveness of our proposed model, we conduct a comprehensive set of experiments and compare its performance against existing benchmark approaches. The main contributions of this research can be succinctly summarized as:

- Development of a novel DL framework that enables HAR using WiFi CSI measurements, eliminating the need for manual feature extraction.
- Introduction of a hybrid DL network, CNN-GRU-AttNet, that leverages the strengths of CNN and GRU to automatically extract spatial and temporal features, leading to highly accurate HAR results.
- Integration of an attention mechanism into the CNN-GRU-AttNet network, allowing for the prioritization of important features and time steps, thereby enhancing recognition performance.
- Thorough evaluation of the proposed approach through a series of rigorous experiments, demonstrating its superior performance in HAR using WiFi CSI data.

The paper follows the subsequent structure: Section 2 presents an extensive review of existing research on HAR utilizing WiFi CSI data. In Section 3, we introduce the framework for automatic learning and selection of features in the HAR process, along with the detailed description of the proposed CNN-GRU-AttNet model. The experimental setup and the results obtained under various scenarios are outlined in Section 4. Section 5 provides an in-depth discussion of the experimental findings, analyzing their implications and significance. Lastly, Section 6 concludes the study by summarizing the key findings and suggesting possible avenues for planned research endeavors.

2. Related Works

2.1. CSI-Based HAR

Within the existing literature, numerous WiFi-based HAR systems have been researched and analyzed, capitalizing on the widespread availability of WiFi signals. Notably, Abdelnasser et al. [21] presented a system called WiGest, which consists of three integral components: initial feature extraction, gesture recognition, and motion mapping. This system employs RSS measurements for accurate gesture identification. Additionally, Gu et al. [22] proposed an alternative approach that leverages WiFi RSS to recognize human activities. Through manual extraction of significant features from raw RSS measurements, they introduced a fusion algorithm capable of identifying essential movements such as standing and walking.

The efficacy of activity recognition mechanisms based on RSS measurements is limited by the presence of instability and disorder caused by multi-path and fading effects, even when considering basic activities. While RSS provides a broad understanding of communication links, CSI offers more intricate details about the condition of the communication channel [23]. Notably, the enhanced reliability and informativeness of WiFi CSI have attracted considerable attention. Zhang et al. [24] devised a Fresnel zone model for HAR that employs WiFi CSI signals, enabling the assessment of WiFi signals' sensing capabilities. Through their proposed model, they achieved remarkable accuracy in detecting human behaviors at centimeter and decimeter scales, such as respiration rate and the orientation of walking. Furthermore, Wang et al. [25] introduced a location-based movement identification system that utilizes WiFi CSI readings.

Previous studies relied on hand-crafted features, which obligate expert knowledge and may not capture the implicit features necessary for accurate HAR using WiFi CSI. To address this issue, some researchers have proposed using DL techniques to automatically learn essential features for this task.

2.2. DL for HAR

DL techniques have gained significant traction in utilizing WiFi CSI for the purposes of localizing and classifying human actions, leveraging the wealth of wireless link information it offers. Wang et al. [26] presented an indoor localization of the HAR system based on a multitasking 1D-CNN architecture enhanced with residual connections. Their model achieved a notable accuracy of 95.68% when tested on a dataset comprising six distinct categories of human behavior. Moshiri et al. [27] gathered CSI data from various human activities and converted them into RGB images, which were then passed through a 2D-CNN layer for classification. Their best-performing model obtained an accuracy of 95%. Chahoushi et al. [28] presented a MIMO-AE for physical activity classification, which achieved a high accuracy of 94.49% using only 50% of the training data.

In HAR, RNNs and their subsets, such as LSTM, have been commonly used for CSI data analysis. However, when analyzing long sequences, these networks face problems, leading to vanishing gradients. Even with the inclusion of long memory and switch gates in LSTM, the problem persists [20]. The memory bandwidth requirements of LSTMs are substantial by reason of the complexity of their sequential direction and MLP layers. Furthermore, these models encounter difficulties when confronted with sequences comprising a large number of terms, as their performance becomes compromised beyond 100 terms [29]. Additionally, LSTMs are restricted to analyzing sequential data in a single direction, limiting their ability to capture bidirectional dependencies. Therefore, they cannot differentiate between activities such as lying and sitting down.

To overcome these limitations, researchers have developed new methods for HAR. Yousefi et al. [19] created the StanWiFi dataset, extracted statistical features, and used hidden Markov models, LSTM, and RF models to classify activities with reported accuracies of 64.6%, 73.3%, and 90.5%, respectively. The BiLSTM architecture was meticulously designed to leverage both historical and prospective CSI data [30], facilitating effective feature learning in the realm of classification. Additionally, the ABLSTM algorithm [20] underwent rigorous evaluation and comparative analysis against alternative algorithms. Zhang et al. [31] introduced the Dense-LSTM method, which demonstrated a remarkable accuracy of approximately 90% while employing a reasonable amount of CSI data. Shang et al. [32] proposed a DL model that combined LSTM-CNN with WiFi CSI signals, yielding an average performance of 94.14% on a publicly available dataset. Moreover, Santosh et al. [33] presented CSITime, an adjusted InceptionTime structure customized for HAR tasks using WiFi CSI signals, achieving an impressive accuracy of 98% on the StanWiFi dataset.

As discussed earlier, several researchers have explored different techniques for HAR, including feature extraction, CNN, and RNN-based models, as shown in Table 1. The presence of spatial and temporal characteristics within WiFi CSI-based HAR data necessitates the utilization of a model capable of effectively capturing both aspects of human behavior. To address this, our study introduces a hybrid DL model that is proficient in learning spatial-temporal features, all while maintaining a streamlined parameter count. This model offers enhanced precision and accuracy for HAR tasks.

Table 1. Previous works analysis using DL approaches for HAR based on CSI data.

Year	Classifier Model	Dataset	Physical Activities	Accuracy
2019	1D-CNN [26]	Private	six casual activities	88.13%
2017	LSTM [19]	StanWiFi	lie down; fall; walk; run; sit down; stand up	90.50%
2019	ABLSTM [20]	StanWiFi	lie down; fall; walk; run; sit down; stand up	97.30%
		Private	empty; jump; pick up; run; sit down; wave hand; walk	
2020	Dense-LSTM [31]	Private	make phone call; check wristwatch; walk normal and fast; run; jump; lie down; play guitar and piano; play basketball	90.00%
2021	LSTM-CNN [32]	Private	stand; sit, falling; standing up; stepping	94.14%
2021	2D-CNN [27]	CSI-HAR	lie down; fall; bend; run; sit down; stand up; walk	95.00%
2022	CSITime [33]	StanWiFi	lie down; fall; walk; run; sit down; stand up	98.00%
2023	MIMI-AE [28]	CSI-HAR	lie down; fall; bend; run; sit down; stand up; walk	94.49%

3. Proposed Methodology

This research introduces an HAR system that utilizes a hybrid DL network called CNN-GRU-AttNet based on WiFi CSI data. The first step involves collecting raw CSI data for DL networks. The raw CSI data are pre-processed in the second step using denoising and segmentation techniques. Following that, the pre-processed CSI data are partitioned into separate training and evaluating sets utilizing a five-fold cross-validation methodology. Subsequently, the data samples undergo a process of high-dimensional embedding to generate features by employing convolutional layers and a GRU layer within the CNN-GRU-AttNet model. Finally, the system's performance is evaluated using standard assessment techniques, such as accuracy, precision, recall, and F1-score. Figure 1 illustrates the overall organization of the framework.

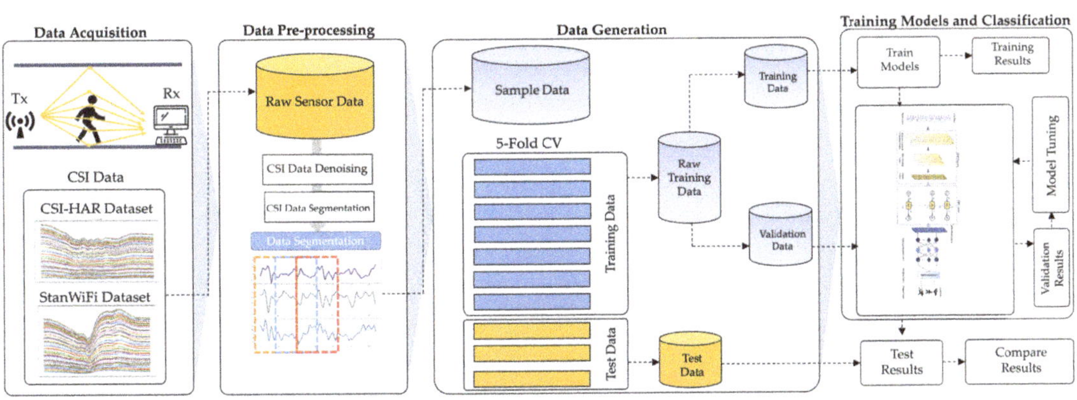

Figure 1. A CSI-based HAR framework using a hybrid DL network.

3.1. Data Acquisition

This study conducted experiments using two publicly available datasets: CSI-HAR and StanWiFi. The details of both datasets are presented in Table 2.

Table 2. Summary of the CSI datasets used in this study.

Dataset	No. of Participants (Age Range)	Collection Tools	Bandwidth and Number of Subcarries	Activities	No. of Samples
CSI-HAR	3 (25 to 70 yrs)	Raspberry Pi-4B Nexmon CSI Tool	40 MHz and 52 Subcarriers	Lie down	405
				Fall	437
				Bend	415
				Run	449
				Sit down	413
				Stand up	348
				Walk	398
StanWiFi	6 (unidentified)	Intel 5300 NIC	20 MHz and 30 Subcarriers	Lie down	657
				Fall	443
				Run	1209
				Sit down	400
				Stand up	304
				Walk	1465

3.1.1. CSI-HAR Dataset

The proposed model's performance and comparable baseline models for WiFi-based HAR were evaluated using the publicly available CSI-HAR dataset [27]. The dataset was collected by building in the Nexmon tool on a Raspberry Pi-4GB, which allowed for collecting and storing CSI data based on transmitted and received information. The dataset contains 4000 CSI samples collected over 20 s, with each line representing 5 ms. The activity-related parts of the data were separated and stored in CSV files as matrices with 52 columns and 600 to 1100 rows, depending on the activity time. Along with the CSI samples, label files were provided to distinguish the lines for each action. The dataset consists of seven discrete activities, namely walk, run, sit down, lie down, stand up, bend, and fall. These actions were operated a total of twenty repetitions by three participants across different age groups within a controlled homeroom environment.

3.1.2. StanWiFi Dataset

Within the StanWiFi dataset [19], there are seven distinct activities: lie down, fall, walk, run, sit down, stand up, and pick up. These activities were performed by 6 participants, and each activity was repeated 20 times. The data gathering involved a Wi-Fi router with a single antenna transmitting signals, while a laptop equipped with NIC-5300 Intel's network interface card and three antennas received the signals. The transmitter and receiver were positioned 3 m away from each other in a line-of-sight scenario, and the duration of each activity was set at 20 s. With a sampling frequency of 1000 Hz, the dataset incorporated an input feature vector that encompassed both raw CSI amplitude data and a 90-dimensional vector. This vector consisted of 3 antennas and 30 subcarriers. The original dataset had seven categories, but only six were used in this study to facilitate comparison with previous works. The majority of methods proposed in the literature (e.g., [19,20,33]) have been evaluated on six activity classes from the dataset, with the "pick up" activity class being excluded. In our case, to ensure fair comparison, we evaluate our proposed CNN-GRU-AttNet on the same six daily activity classes of the StanWiFi dataset. A single training datapoint is the number of samples × the number of features (500) × the number of timestamps (90).

3.2. Data Pre-Processing

3.2.1. Data Denoising

To effectively address the impact of noise on the CSI and overcome the potential lack of discernible characteristics for different activities, it is crucial to employ ML techniques for noise filtering and feature extraction. Various noise reduction techniques can be utilized, such as the implementation of Butterworth low-pass filters [34]. Nonetheless, the presence of high-bandwidth burst and impulse noises in the CSI, using low-pass filters alone, is not feasible for achieving a seamless CSI stream.

Based on empirical evidence, there are more effective approaches to achieve this objective, including employing principal component analysis (PCA) for noise denoising [34]. PCA is a method that reduces the complexity of a system by identifying key features where a significant portion of relevant information is concentrated. In the context of PCA-based denoising, this study adheres to the recommendation proposed in [34]. It involves excluding the initial principal component and instead selecting the subsequent five principal components for feature extraction. The reason behind this choice is that the noises arising from internal state transitions are present in all CSI streams. These noises, which show a strong correlation, get mixed into the initial principal component, along with the signal generated by human motion. However, it is important to note that all the human motion signal data present in the initial principal component are also captured within the remaining principal components. In the context of PCA, the components derived from PCA show no correlation with each other. As a result, the initial principal component solely represents one of these orthogonal components, while the rest are preserved within the subsequent PCA components. Therefore, removing the initial principal component does not compromise any relevant data. The decision to choose five principal components for feature extraction is supported by empirical evidence. The aim is to find a balance between classification effectiveness and computational overhead.

To mitigate noise, the initial principal component is excluded, and the subsequent five components are utilized for feature extraction. This approach preserves data related to the dynamic reflection of the mobile target, as it is also captured in other primary components. Following the application of PCA denoising to the CSI data, specific characteristics are extracted to enhance its usability for classification purposes. To demonstrate the denoising performance, we compared the PCA denoising method using the Signal-to-Noise Ratio (SNR), which represents the ratio of signal power (meaningful information) to noise power. The denoising results are presented in Figures 2 and 3.

Figure 2 illustrates the amplitude received from all subcarriers of CSI data obtained from the CSI-HAR dataset after noise reduction using the PCA denoising method. Notably, the denoised CSI signals exhibit higher SNR values compared to the raw CSI samples. These findings indicate the successful reduction of noise from the raw CSI data.

Figure 3 presents the raw and smoothed CSI signals for six human activities from the StanWiFi dataset. The visualizations reveal similar SNR results across all subcarriers of the CSI data after noise reduction using the PCA denoising method. Similar to the previous investigation, the SNR value of the denoised CSI data is higher than the SNR value of the raw data.

3.2.2. Segmentation

Segmentation is a crucial process that involves dividing a signal into smaller sections or windows. In our research, we utilize segmentation for two primary purposes. The first challenge we encounter is the variability in the captured CSI signals, which can differ in length and belong to different subjects. This variability hinders the identification procedure. The second challenge relates to the temporal aspect of processing an extensive volume of CSI data, which requires significant time and computational resources.

To address these challenges effectively, our study adopts a predetermined window size. This window size allows us to partition the denoised CSI signal into multiple smaller signals. By doing so, we can treat each small signal as an independent instance during the training phase of the CNN-GRU-AttNet model. This approach not only enhances efficiency but also improves the accuracy of our results.

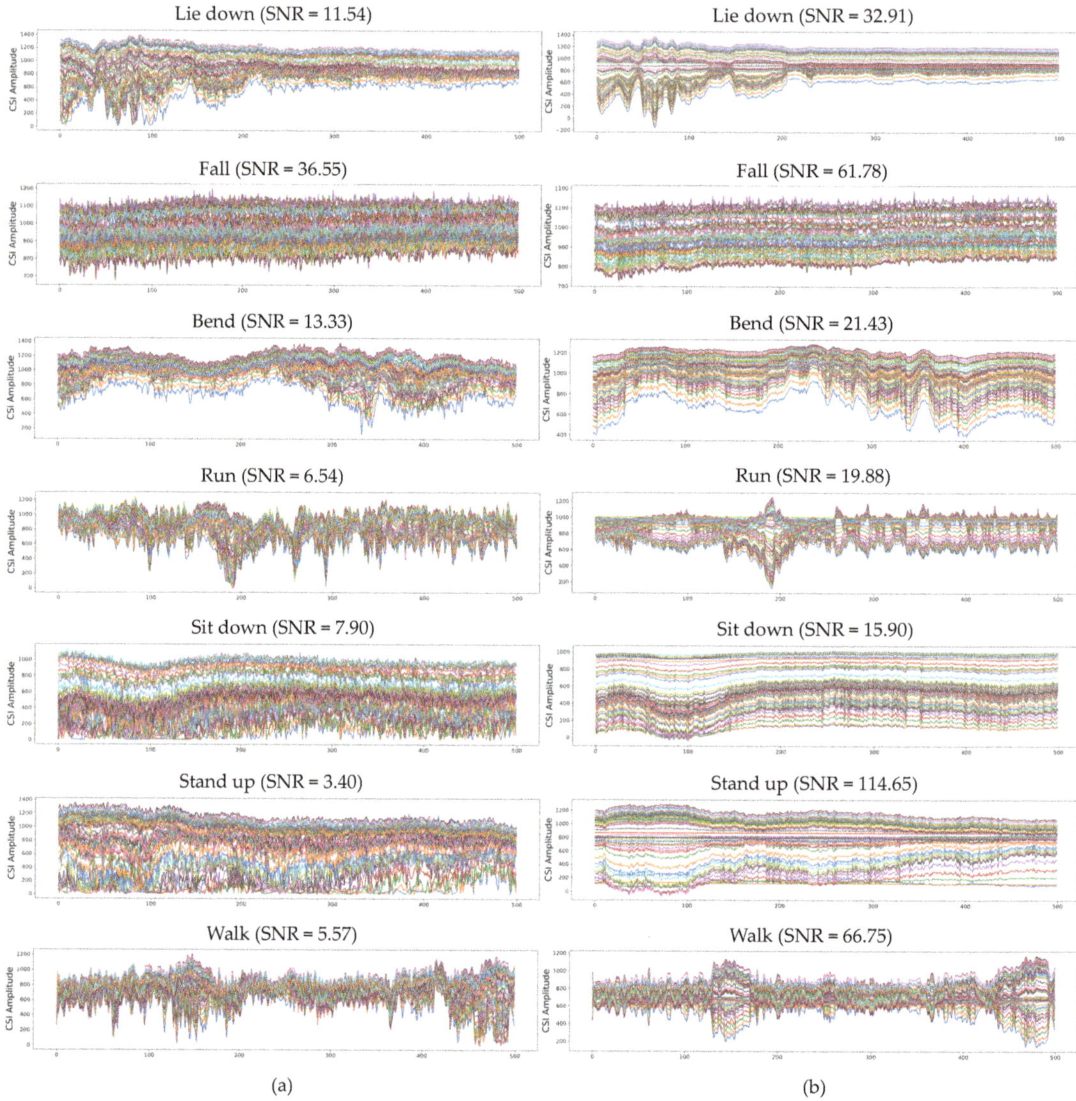

Figure 2. Some CSI signal representations from CSI-HAR dataset after pre-processing: (**a**) before denoising; (**b**) after denoising.

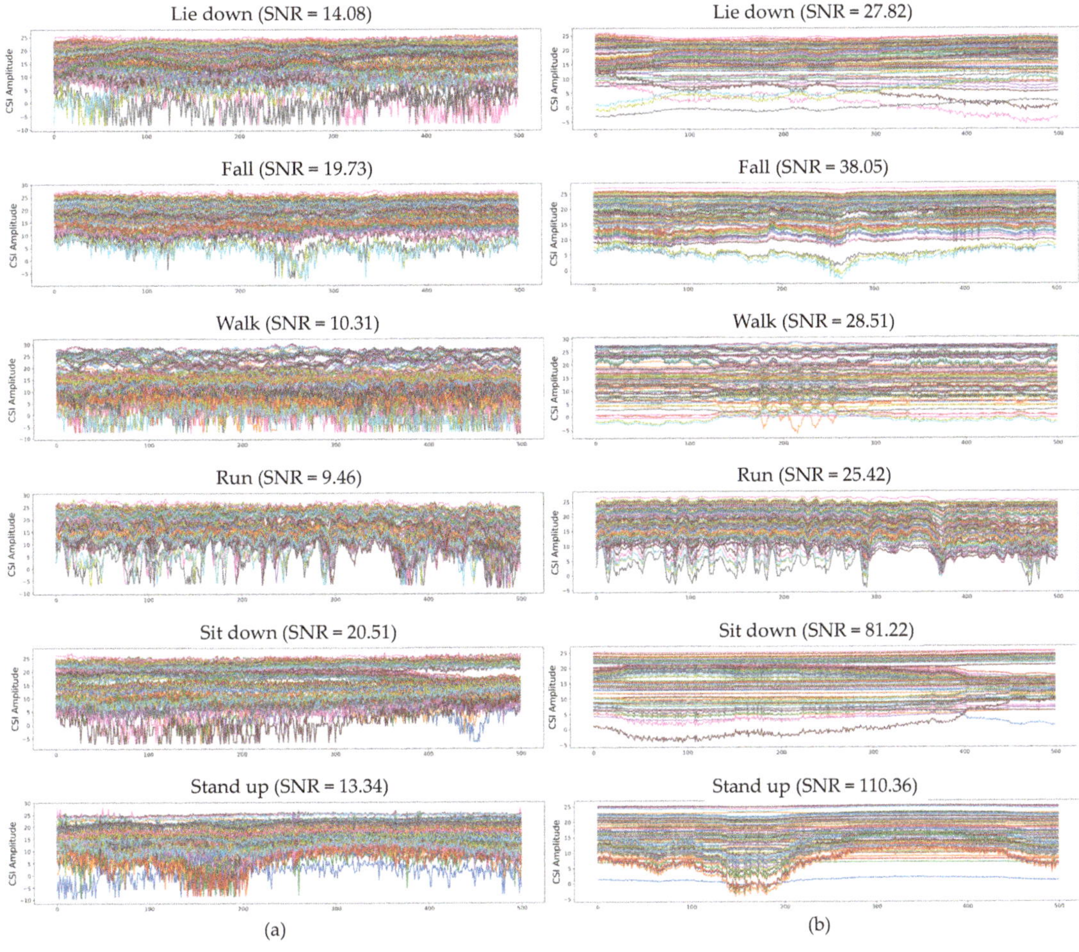

Figure 3. Some CSI signal representations from StanWiFi dataset after pre-processing: (**a**) before denoising; (**b**) after denoising.

3.3. Recognition Model

This section presents CNN-GRU-AttNet, an attention-based neural network designed for recognizing human activities using WiFi CSI data, as illustrated in Figure 4. The proposed CNN-GRU-AttNet comprises five layers: the input layer, two CNN layers, a GRU layer, an attention layer, a fully connected layer, and an output layer. Each of these layers will be described in detail below.

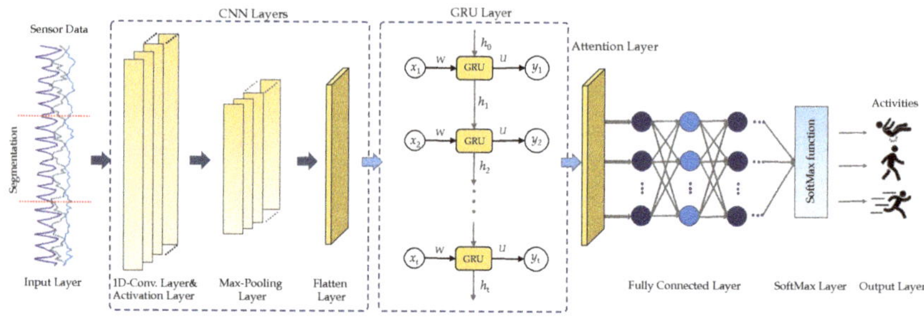

Figure 4. The proposed CNN-GRU-AttNet architecture for CSI-based HAR in this work.

CNNs extensively employ DL models with robust feature extraction capabilities. They can effectively and automatically extract features from input data, especially two-dimensional image data, and process them quickly. The convolutional layers in CNN are different from traditional neural network models since they are not fully connected. Instead, the inputs are linked to the following layers, and subregions in the input sets have the exact weights, resulting in spatially related outputs. In contrast, traditional neural network models have different weights for each input, increasing the input dimensionality and making the network more intricate. CNN addresses this issue by reducing the number of connections and weights through weight sharing and downsampling operations.

This study utilized a CNN with two layers. The first layer contained 64 filters and a kernel size of 3, while the second layer had 64 filters and a kernel size of 5. The max-pooling layers had a uniform pool size of 2. To connect the CNN and GRU layers, a flattened layer was inserted. Table 3 displays the detailed parameters of the CNN used in this research.

Table 3. Parameters of each layer of the CNN network.

Layer Name	Kernel Size	Kernel Number	Padding	Stride
Conv1D-1	5	64	2	4
Maxpooling-1	2	None	0	1
Conv1D-2	7	64	2	1
Maxpooling-2	2	None	0	1

While CNNs have proven to be highly effective in feature extraction, their performance in tasks involving time-dependent inputs, such as the analysis of biometric signal data in this study, may be relatively limited. In scenarios where sequential data are processed, the network's prediction of future states is influenced by the previous state of the input. Therefore, the network needs to consider both the current and preceding inputs. To address this challenge, the RNN model is capable of analyzing each element of the temporal sequence and incorporating both the current and preceding inputs for the current input of the RNN. The output of an RNN at a specific time step t depends on the output of the RNN at the previous time step, $t-1$.

Theoretically, RNNs are capable of acquiring knowledge from time series data with arbitrary lengths. However, when dealing with extensive time series in real-world applications, RNNs encounter the problem of gradient disappearance, which impedes the learning of long-term dependencies. To tackle this issue, we integrated a GRU as the memory component within the RNN architecture. The organization of the GRU cell's internal structure is visualized in Figure 5.

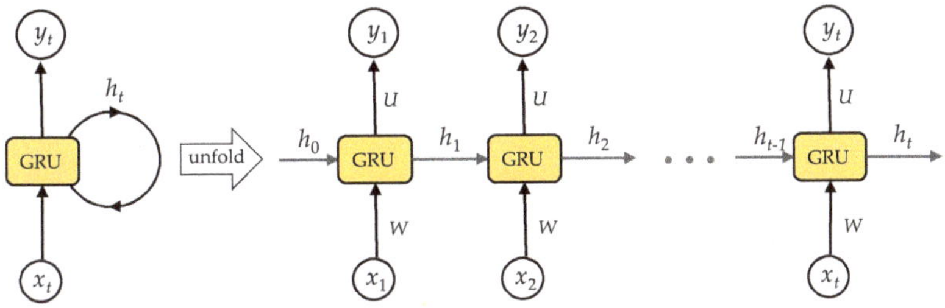

Figure 5. The structure of a GRU network.

GRU networks can be considered as a simplified form of LSTM networks within the class of RNNs, as illustrated in Figure 6. They offer enhanced computational efficiency while preserving the effectiveness of LSTM networks.

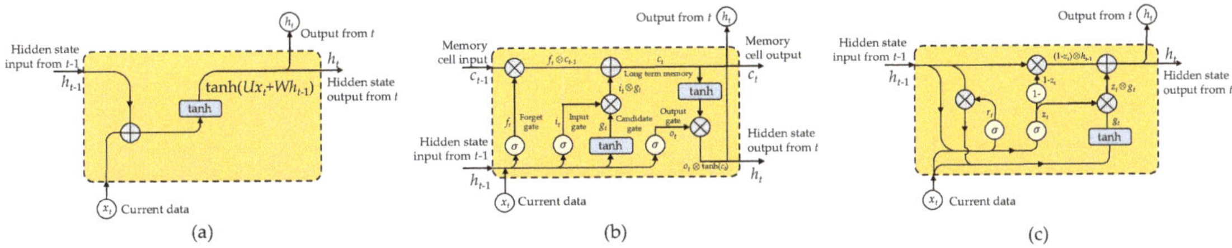

Figure 6. Comparison of RNN-based models: (**a**) simple RNN, (**b**) LSTM, and (**c**) GRU.

The architectural representation of a GRU unit, as shown in Figure 6c, consists of an update gate and a reset gate that control the extent of modification for each hidden state. These gates serve as mechanisms to regulate the flow of relevant and irrelevant information between consecutive states in a computational model. Computation of the hidden state h_t at a specific time t incorporates the update gate output z_t, the reset gate output r_t, and the current input x_t. Additionally, the preceding hidden state h_{t-1} is taken into account, as demonstrated below:

$$z_t = \sigma(W_z x_t \oplus U_z H_{t-1}) \tag{1}$$

$$r_t = \sigma(W_r x_t \oplus U_r H_{t-1}) \tag{2}$$

$$g_t = \tanh(W_g x_t \oplus U_g(r_t \otimes h_{t-1})) \tag{3}$$

$$h_t = ((1 - z_t) \otimes h_{t-1}) \oplus (z_t \otimes g_t) \tag{4}$$

The symbol σ denotes the sigmoid function, $\oplus$ denotes the elementwise addition operation, and $\otimes$ denotes the elementwise multiplication operation.

Once the GRU network has captured the contextual features, this study proposes using a self-attention mechanism to capture crucial information further. This mechanism assigns more weight to important information, leading to a more precise understanding of sequence semantics. The calculation process for the self-attention mechanism is depicted in Figure 7.

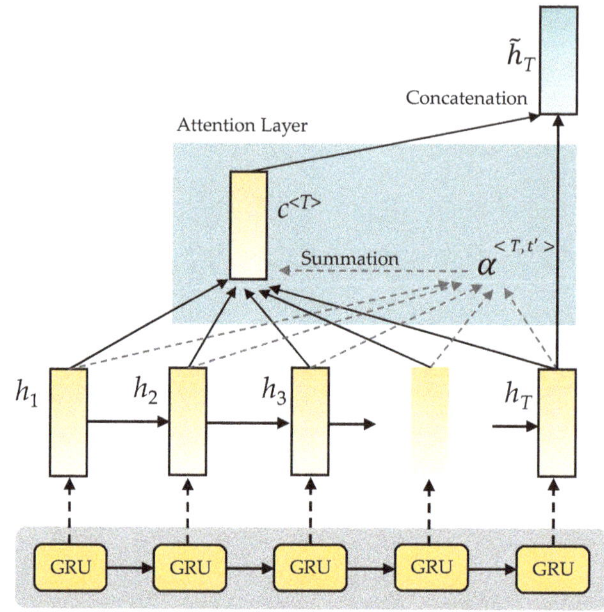

Figure 7. Attention-based GRU for the classification process.

Once the GRU layer has computed the pre-processed data $X = (x_1, x_2, ..., x_T)$, we can derive the vector $H = [h_1, h_2, h_3, ..., h_t, ..., h_T]$, where T denotes the length of the vector data X, and h_t denotes the hidden state of the GRU at time step t. We can build the self-attention mechanism for the GRU using the following steps:

$$\gamma_t = \tanh(w_2 h_t + b_2) \tag{5}$$

$$\beta_t = \frac{\exp((\gamma_t)^T w_2)}{\sum_t \exp((\gamma_t)^T w_2)} \tag{6}$$

$$\delta = \sum_t \beta_t h_t, \tag{7}$$

where w_2 is a contextual vector at the time level, β_t is a weight normalized through a softmax function, and δ represents the uniform representation of the entire sequence, which is calculated by summing all the hidden states weighted by their corresponding attention weights.

Following the attention layer, the neural network incorporates three dense layers with dropout regularization. The initial layer consists of 128 neurons and utilizes a dropout rate of 0.25. This is followed by a layer of 64 neurons with a dropout rate of 0.25 as well. Finally, the output layer of the model consists of two neurons. The rectified linear unit (ReLU) activation function is employed in all layers of the model. To achieve the best results during the training process, a configuration of 200 epochs and a batch size of 32 were utilized. The categorical cross-entropy loss function was used, and optimization was performed using the Adam optimizer [35].

3.4. Hyperparameter and Training

A three-step process is involved in building any statistical classification model. Firstly, the model development phase involves choosing hyperparameters such as batch size, activation function, learning rate, number of iterations, etc. that influence how well the model is built and trained. Adequate variation and a sufficient quantity of data are necessary for this phase. Secondly, model training and validation are carried out, with the training set being used to select hyperparameters, and the validation set to evaluate performance. In this particular instance, the training hyperparameters were carefully chosen. They consisted of a learning rate of 1×10^{-3}, 100 epochs, and a batch size of 128. To ensure efficient learning, a callback monitor was utilized to adjust the learning rate, reducing it by 75% if no progress was made for ten successive epochs. The training process incorporated data shuffling by randomizing the order of the data before the beginning of each epoch, introducing diversity. The hyperparameters were determined through an iterative process of experimentation and refinement, aiming to achieve the highest level of accuracy.

In order to assess the efficacy of the proposed model, we utilized two publicly accessible datasets, CSI-HAR and StanWiFi. Since these datasets did not have predefined training and testing sets, we adopted the five-fold cross-validation technique [36] to assess the model's performance. This technique involved randomly dividing the complete dataset into ten equally sized subsets that were mutually exclusive. The model fitting process followed an iterative procedure, where nine subsets were used for training, while the remaining subset was used for evaluating the performance. This testing and training process was repeated ten times to ensure that each subset underwent a precise testing phase. The overall performance of the model was evaluated by computing the mean value of the outcomes obtained from all iterations.

The Adam optimizer [35] played a crucial role in our methodology by updating the weights of our model. Moreover, we employed the cross-entropy loss function to quantify the error or loss during the training phase.

3.5. Network Training and Evaluation Metrics

A valuable tool for assessing the recognition performance of DL models is the confusion matrix, which provides a clear and visual representation of their performance. The multi-class confusion matrix can be mathematically represented: the rows represent the instances in the predicted class, while the columns represent the instances in the actual class.

$$C = \begin{bmatrix} c_{11} & c_{12} & c_{13} & \cdots & c_{1n} \\ c_{21} & c_{22} & c_{23} & \cdots & c_{2n} \\ c_{31} & c_{32} & c_{33} & \cdots & c_{3n} \\ \vdots & \vdots & \vdots & \ddots & \vdots \\ c_{n1} & c_{n2} & c_{n3} & \cdots & c_{nn} \end{bmatrix}$$

The confusion elements for each class are given by:

- True positive: $TP(C_i) = C_{ii}$;
- False positive: $FP(C_i) = \sum_{l=1}^{n} c_{li} - TP(C_i)$;
- False negative: $FN(C_i) = \sum_{l=1}^{n} c_{il} - TP(C_i)$;
- True negative: $TN(C_i) = \sum_{l=1}^{n} \sum_{k=1}^{n} c_{lk} - TP(C_i) - FP(C_i) - FN(C_i)$.

The evaluation of the DL models utilized in this study involved analyzing a confusion matrix and calculating four commonly used metrics: accuracy, precision, recall, and F1-score.

Accuracy is a measure of systematic error and is calculated by dividing the sum of true positive and true negative by the total number of records. Precision is determined by computing the ratio of examples that are correctly classified as belonging to a specific smartwatch user's class to all examples that are classified as belonging to that class. Recall is evaluated as the ratio of examples that are classified as belonging to a specific smartwatch user's class to all examples that actually belong to that class. Lastly, the F1-score is a metric that blends precision and recall using the harmonic mean.

The mathematical expressions for these evaluation metrics were written as:

$$Accuracy = \frac{1}{|Class|} \times \sum_{i=1}^{|Class|} \frac{TP_i + TN_i}{TP_i + FP_i + TN_i + FN_i} \quad (8)$$

$$Precision = \frac{1}{|Class|} \times \sum_{i=1}^{|Class|} \frac{TP_i}{TP_i + FP_i} \quad (9)$$

$$Recall = \frac{1}{|Class|} \times \sum_{i=1}^{|Class|} \frac{TP_i}{TP_i + FN_i} \quad (10)$$

$$F1\text{-}score = 2 \times \frac{Precision \times Recall}{Precision + Recall} \quad (11)$$

4. Experiments and Findings

In this section, we provide a detailed analysis of the experiments conducted and the results obtained using the CNN-GRU-AttNet model on two distinct datasets: CSI-HAR and StanWiFi. Our aim is to demonstrate the effectiveness of the proposed model. Furthermore, we perform a comparative evaluation by assessing the performance of five baseline deep learning models (CNN, LSTM, BiLSTM, GRU, and BiGRU), along with other contemporary models, on the same datasets. This comparative analysis allows us to gain insights into the relative strengths and weaknesses of different models in the context of the given datasets.

4.1. Experimental Setting

The deep learning networks employed in this study were exclusively developed and trained on the Google Colab Pro+ platform. To expedite the model training procedure, we utilized the Tesla V100-SXM2-16GB graphics processor component. The proposed model and the standard deep learning models were implemented using the Python programming language, with Tensorflow and CUDA backend frameworks serving as the backbone. Throughout the investigation, we focused on the following Python libraries:

- To facilitate the comprehension, manipulation, and analysis of sensor data, we employed Numpy and Pandas for efficient data manipulation.
- For effective presentation and visualization of data exploration and model evaluation results, we utilized Matplotlib and Seaborn.
- In our experimental procedures, we leveraged the Scikit-learn library as a tool for data sampling and generation.
- The instantiation and training of the DL models were carried out utilized the TensorFlow, Keras, and TensorBoard frameworks.

4.2. Experimental Findings on CSI-HAR Dataset

The results of the CSI-based HAR dataset demonstrate the superior classification capabilities of the CNN-GRU-AttNet model, as presented in Table 4. The findings highlight the CNN-GRU-AttNet model's outstanding performance, with an average accuracy of 99.62%, precision of 99.61%, recall of 99.61%, and F1-score of 99.61% across all human movements. Furthermore, a comparative analysis indicates that the CNN-GRU-AttNet model exhibits exceptional efficacy in classifying HAR tasks, surpassing the achievement of the five baseline DL models.

Table 4. Performance results of both the proposed CNN-GRU-AttNet model and the five baseline models on the CSI-HAR dataset.

Model	Recognition Performance (Mean ± Std)			
	Accuracy	Precision	Recall	F1-Score
CNN	95.67% (±1.57%)	95.97% (±1.46%)	95.76% (±1.51%)	95.66% (±1.60%)
LSTM	84.12% (±1.22%)	84.56% (±1.14%)	84.17% (±1.24%)	84.10% (±1.18%)
BiLSTM	90.44% (±0.86%)	90.49% (±0.86%)	90.38% (±0.84%)	90.34% (±0.88%)
GRU	89.21% (±2.86%)	89.14% (±2.92%)	89.12% (±2.87%)	89.06% (±2.89%)
BiGRU	95.39% (±0.92%)	95.38% (±0.94%)	95.37% (±0.96%)	95.31% (±0.95%)
CNN-GRU-AttNet	99.62% (±0.26%)	99.61% (±0.26%)	99.61% (±0.27%)	99.61% (±0.26%)

Figure 8 illustrates the confusion matrix of the CSI-HAR dataset based on the proposed CNN-GRU-AttNet model. The matrix's diagonal elements correspond to the model's accuracy in identifying individual human actions. The findings indicate that the CNN-GRU-AttNet model is effective in capturing both the spatial and temporal features of the WiFi CSI signal. Specifically, the model achieves 100% accuracy in recognizing run, sit down, standup, and walk activities. However, there needs to be more clarification between lie down and sit down activities. The misclassification could be explained by the overlapping patterns between sit down activities, characterized by sudden sitting and prolonged immobility, and lie down activities.

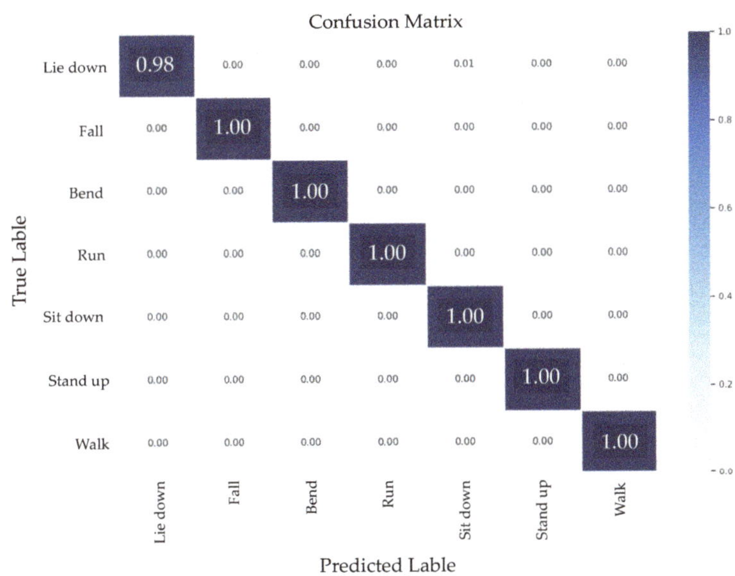

Figure 8. Confusion matrix of the proposed model on CSI-HAR dataset.

The accuracy and loss metrics of the CNN-GRU-AttNet model are illustrated in Figure 9. The graph in Figure 9a depicts the accuracy values for both the training and validation data. Notably, the model achieves convergence within a relatively short timeframe, specifically within 100 epochs. Additionally, Figure 9b demonstrates that the training loss exhibits higher values compared to the validation loss, which is a reasonable observation. This elevated training loss can be attributed to the multi-phase learning process aimed at understanding the distinct characteristics of CSI signals associated with various human actions.

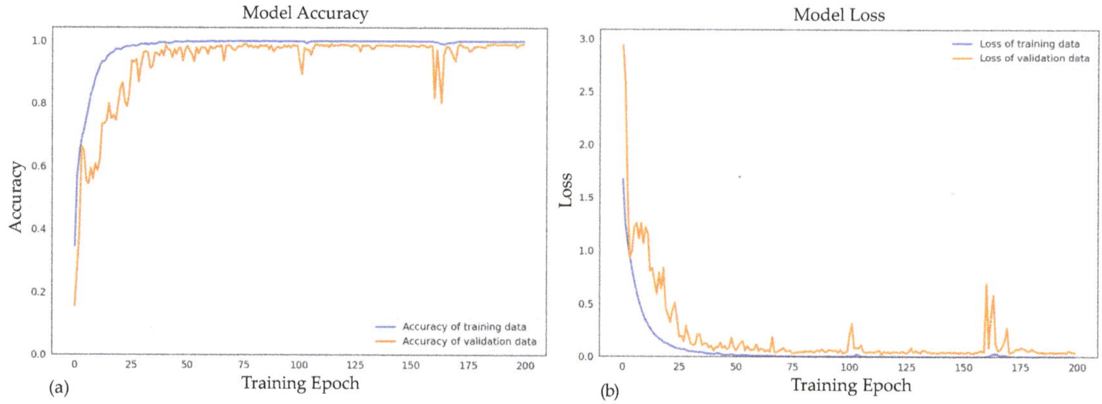

Figure 9. The accuracy and loss metrics of the CNN-GRU-AttNet model on the CSI-HAR dataset: (**a**) train and validation accuracy curves; (**b**) train and validation loss curves.

4.3. Experimental Findings on StanWiFi Dataset

Table 5 presents the experimental results of the CNN-GRU-AttNet model applied to HAR on the StanWiFi dataset. The table clearly demonstrates that the proposed model achieves impressive performance with an average accuracy of 98.66%, precision of 98.43%, recall of 97.88%, and F1-score of 98.14%. These results show that the CNN-GRU-AttNet model performs well in recognizing human activities. Furthermore, compared to five other baseline DL models, the CNN-GRU-AttNet model achieves the highest recognition accuracy.

Table 5. Performance results of both the proposed CNN-GRU-AttNet model and the five baseline models on the StanWiFi dataset.

Model	Recognition Performance (Mean ± Std)			
	Accuracy	**Precision**	**Recall**	**F1-Score**
CNN	89.08% (±4.61%)	87.52% (±5.47%)	89.49% (±3.48%)	87.55% (±4.74%)
LSTM	93.95% (±2.15%)	91.32% (±2.66%)	94.80% (±1.64%)	92.75% (±2.25%)
BiLSTM	94.73% (±1.73%)	92.25% (±2.15%)	94.74% (±1.18%)	93.18% (±1.77%)
GRU	94.84% (±2.52%)	92.68% (±3.44%)	94.84% (±2.32%)	93.35% (±3.12%)
BiGRU	95.73% (±2.64%)	94.70% (±2.39%)	95.02% (±3.78%)	94.62% (±3.38%)
CNN-GRU-AttNet	98.66% (±0.26%)	98.43% (±0.29%)	97.88% (±0.59%)	98.14% (±0.42%)

The confusion matrix of the CNN-GRU-AttNet model on the StanWiFi dataset is illustrated in Figure 10. The results demonstrate that the model has high recognition accuracy for lie down, walk, and stand up activities, achieving over 96% accuracy. In contrast, fall and run activities show slightly lower performance, around 94%. Additionally, sit down activities have a recognition accuracy of 92% or higher. However, there needs to be more clarification between lie down and sit down activities, and this may be due to the similarity in signal patterns between the two activities. Figure 11 illustrates the accuracy and loss metrics of the CNN-GRU-AttNet model applied to the StanWiFi dataset.

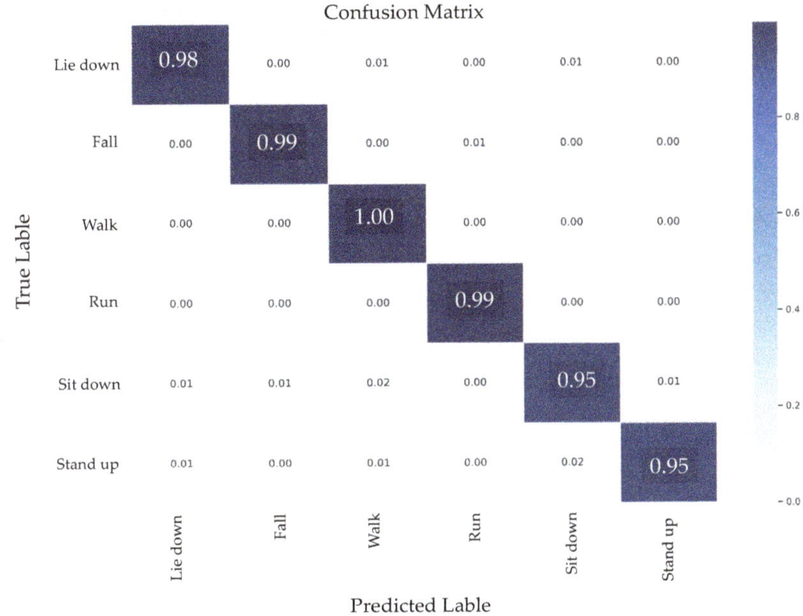

Figure 10. Confusion matrix of the proposed model on the StanWiFi dataset.

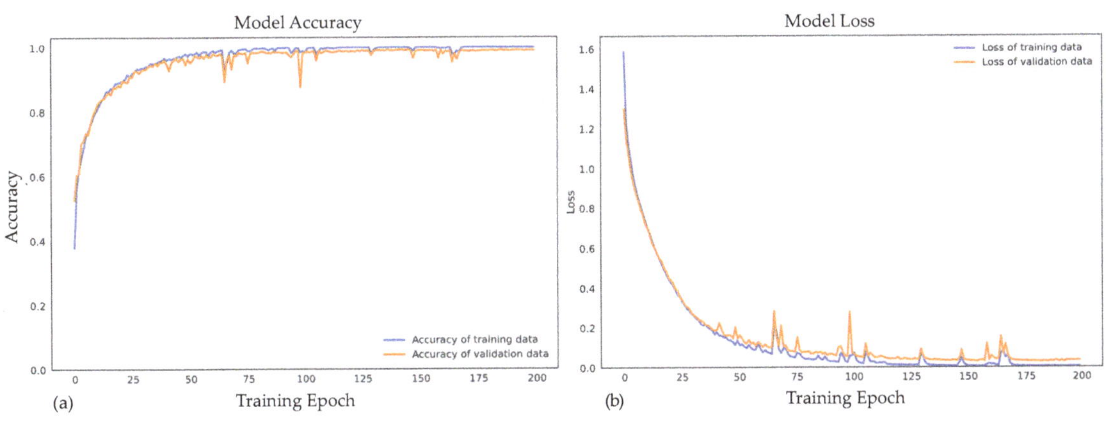

Figure 11. The accuracy and loss metrics of the CNN-GRU-AttNet model on the StanWiFi dataset: (**a**) train and validation accuracy curves; (**b**) train and validation loss curves.

5. Discussion

This section discusses the experimental outcomes achieved by utilizing the proposed CNN-GRU-AttNet model on two distinct datasets.

5.1. *Performance Comparison*

Assessing the overall effectiveness of a model presents a significant challenge, as it requires comparing different models using the same dataset. Therefore, we evaluate the efficacy of the proposed model through a comparative analysis with other models using the CSI-HAR and StanWiFi datasets. The comparative results are provided in Table 6. Our study demonstrates that the proposed CNN-GRU-AttNet model outperforms other models on the CSI-HAR dataset in terms of recognition capability. The CNN-GRU-AttNet model achieved an average accuracy of 99.62%, precision of 99.61%, recall of 99.61%, and F1-score of 99.61%. Furthermore, our proposed CNN-GRU-AttNet model exhibits a remarkable accuracy improvement of 4.62% compared to the leading-edge model currently available on the CSI-HAR dataset.

The proposed CNN-GRU-AttNet model has demonstrated a superior level of accuracy, achieving a score of 98.66% on the StanWiFi dataset, which represents a 0.66% improvement over the best state-of-the-art performance [33]. Upon analyzing the performance of various existing models presented in Table 6, it is evident that our proposed CNN-GRU-AttNet outperforms all others in terms of recognition outcomes on both datasets. This observed enhancement can be attributed to the recently suggested framework, which adeptly captures and utilizes spatial and temporal characteristics extracted from unprocessed CSI data for the purpose of HAR.

Table 6. Comparison between the proposed model and other existing works.

Dataset	Classifier	Accuracy	Precision	Recall	F1-Score
CSI-HAR	2D-CNN [27]	95.00%	-	-	-
	MIMI-AE [28]	94.49%	-	-	-
	CNN-GRU-AttNet	99.62%	99.61%	99.61%	99.61%
StanWiFi	LSTM [19]	90.50%	-	-	-
	ABLSTM [20]	97.30%	-	-	-
	CSITime [33]	98.00%	-	-	-
	CNN-GRU-AttNet	98.66%	98.43%	97.88%	98.14%

5.2. Impact of the Attention Mechanism

The ability to obtain an interpretable representation is crucial for many ML applications. While DL techniques excel at extracting features from raw data, understanding the relative importance of the input data can be challenging. This issue has been addressed in prior research through the introduction of attention mechanisms. In our study, we enhanced the classification algorithm by incorporating an attention mechanism originally designed for neural network machine translation tasks, as presented by Luong et al. [37]. This approach allowed us to develop an interpretable representation that highlighted the significance of individual input data segments within the model. The findings of our study demonstrate that the inclusion of the attention mechanism led to improved recognition effectiveness across all scenarios, as evidenced by the data presented in Figure 12. The CNN-GRU-AttNet model exhibited notable performance improvements on both benchmark datasets.

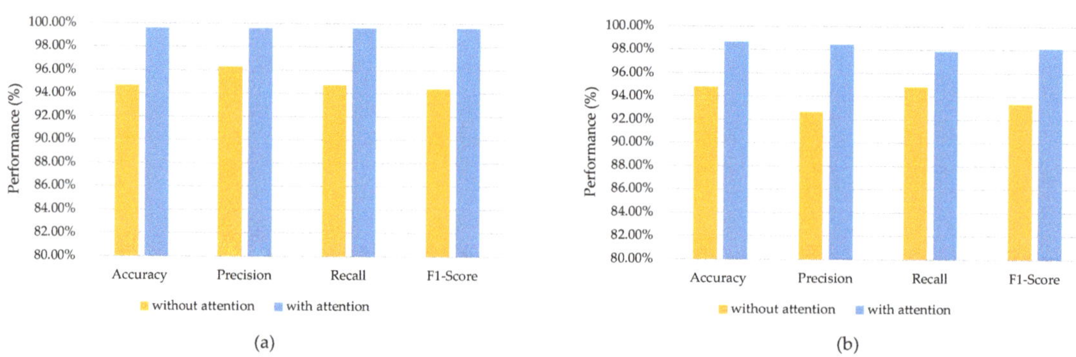

Figure 12. Improved performance of the proposed network with/without the attention mechanism: (**a**) CSI-HAR dataset; (**b**) StanWiFi dataset.

5.3. Impact of the PCA Denoising Method

In the proposed methodology, we employed the PCA denoising method to effectively eliminate noisy signals from the CSI data. Through experimentation, we observed that PCA leverages the correlated variations present in the CSI time series of different subcarriers, thereby effectively removing noise from the signals. This process specifically targets the elimination of uncorrelated noisy components that cannot be adequately filtered out through traditional low-pass filtering.

General-purpose denoising methods, such as low-pass filters or median filters, unfortunately, do not perform well in handling impulse and bursty noises for two reasons. Firstly, these methods typically require much higher sampling rates than the frequency of the WiFi signal, making them less suitable for this scenario. Secondly, the noise density in CSI values is too high for traditional filters to efficiently handle [34].

To thoroughly investigate the impact of the PCA denoising method, we conducted additional experiments. The comparative results presented in Table 7 clearly demonstrate that denoising the CSI data using PCA leads to notable improvements in the recognition performances of our proposed CNN-GRU-AttNet. Specifically, we achieved an accuracy increase of up to 1.43% for the CSI-HAR dataset and 1.00% for the StanWiFi dataset. As a result, it becomes evident that the PCA-based noise reduction plays a significant role in achieving the high recognition accuracies observed in our proposed methodology.

Table 7. Comparison between the proposed model using CSI data before and after denoising by the PCA denoising method.

Dataset	Classifier	Accuracy	Precision	Recall	F1-Score
CSI-HAR	CNN-GRU-AttNet using CSI data without the PCA denosing method	98.19%	98.27%	98.17%	98.17%
	CNN-GRU-AttNet using denoised CSI data with the PCA denosing method	99.62%	99.61%	99.61%	99.61%
StanWiFi	CNN-GRU-AttNet using CSI data without the PCA denosing method	97.66%	97.13%	97.00%	97.04%
	CNN-GRU-AttNet using denoised CSI data with the PCA denosing method	98.66%	98.43%	97.88%	98.14%

5.4. Performance Analysis for Different Subjects

To analyze performances across different subjects, we conducted an additional experiment using the CSI data from the CSI-HAR dataset, which includes detailed information about the subjects involved in data collection. Specifically, the CSI-HAR dataset contains records of each activity performed 20 times by 3 voluntary subjects of varying ages, ranging from 25 to 70 years old. The subjects represent a diverse group, consisting of an adult, a middle-aged person, and an elderly person.

Table 8 presents an analysis of the performance of the proposed CNN-GRU-AttNet model on individual subjects. Notably, the F1-scores of subject 2 (a middle-aged person) show consistently high values, exceeding 95% for all activities. On the other hand, when using the CSI data of subject 1 (an adult), the F1-scores for some activities (lie down, bend, sit down, stand up, and walk) are found to be lower than 95%. These findings strongly suggest that there are notable differences in the CSI data captured from different subjects.

5.5. Limitations of the Proposed Method

Due to the absence of a conventional dataset that incorporates the CSI data obtained from settings with substantial interference, we could not evaluate the suggested model's efficacy in such an environment. However, we aim to investigate this aspect in our future research.

Table 8. Recognition performances of the proposed CNN-GRU-AttNet based on CSI data from different subjects.

Subject	Activity	Recognition Performance		
		Accuracy	Recall	F1-Score
Subject 1 (an adult)	Lie down	82.4%	100.0%	90.3%
	Fall	100.0%	96.6%	98.2%
	Bend	86.2%	100.0%	92.6%
	Run	92.1%	100.0%	95.9%
	Sit down	100.0%	76.9%	87.0%
	Stand up	100.0%	87.0%	93.0%
	Walk	100.0%	89.3%	94.3%
Subject 2 (a middle-aged person)	Lie down	100.0%	96.3%	98.1%
	Fall	100.0%	100.0%	100.0%
	Bend	100.0%	100.0%	100.0%
	Run	100.0%	100.0%	100.0%
	Sit down	96.6%	96.6%	96.6%
	Stand up	100.0%	100.0%	100.0%
	Walk	96.7%	100.0%	98.3%
Subject 3 (an elderly person)	Lie down	100.0%	100.0%	100.0%
	Fall	100.0%	93.3%	96.6%
	Bend	88.9%	100.0%	94.1%
	Run	100.0%	95.5%	97.7%
	Sit down	100.0%	92.9%	96.3%
	Stand up	92.6%	100.0%	96.2%
	Walk	100.0%	100.0%	100.0%

6. Conclusions for Future Research

This study introduces a DL model called CNN-GRU-AttNet, designed to automatically recognize human behavior from WiFi CSI signals. Human activity can be represented as time-series data with temporal and spatial characteristics. The CNN-GRU-AttNet model addresses this challenge by extracting spatial and significant features simultaneously using convolutional blocks and attention modules, respectively. Additionally, the GRU block is employed to capture latent temporal patterns within the CSI signals. By combining these three components, the model effectively represents the CSI signal's characteristics and focuses its attention on activity-related information. Consequently, the CNN-GRU-AttNet model improves the accuracy of activity recognition. Evaluations were conducted on two distinct datasets, CSI-HAR and StanWiFi, resulting in recognition accuracies of 99.62% and 98.66%, respectively. A comparative analysis with existing approaches demonstrated the superiority of the proposed model, achieving improvements of 4.62% and 0.66% in accuracy, respectively.

There are potential plans to collect and analyze empirical datasets obtained from environments with significant interference. The task of identifying multi-user activity in real-world situations poses a more realistic and complex challenge compared to identifying single-user activity. As a result, this study's research will be expanded to include HAR for multiple users. Publicly available datasets often contain common activities that do not accurately represent real-world situations, as individuals engage in a variety of activities on a daily basis. Therefore, the acquisition of a WiFi dataset that includes a broader range of indoor human activities will be deferred for future research.

Author Contributions: Conceptualization, S.M. and A.J.; methodology, S.M.; software, A.J.; validation, W.P. and A.J.; formal analysis, S.M.; investigation, S.M. and A.J.; resources, N.H.; data curation, S.M.; writing—original draft preparation, S.M. and N.H.; writing—review and editing, N.H. and A.J.; visualization, W.P.; supervision, A.J.; project administration, N.H.; funding acquisition, S.M. and A.J. All authors have read and agreed to the published version of the manuscript.

Funding: This project was funded by the Thailand Science Research and Innovation Fund; University of Phayao (Grant No. FF66-UoE001); National Science, Research and Innovation Fund (NSRF); and King Mongkut's University of Technology North Bangkok with Contract no. KMUTNB-FF-66-07.

Institutional Review Board Statement: Not applicable.

Informed Consent Statement: Not applicable.

Data Availability Statement: All data were presented in the main text.

Conflicts of Interest: The authors declare no conflict of interest.

References

1. Hnoohom, N.; Mekruksavanich, S.; Jitpattanakul, A. An Efficient ResNetSE Architecture for Smoking Activity Recognition from Smartwatch. *Intell. Autom. Soft Comput.* **2023**, *35*, 1245–1259. [CrossRef]
2. Thanarajan, T.; Alotaibi, Y.; Rajendran, S.; Nagappan, K. Improved wolf swarm optimization with deep-learning-based movement analysis and self-regulated human activity recognition. *AIMS Math.* **2023**, *8*, 12520–12539. [CrossRef]
3. Mekruksavanich, S.; Jitpattanakul, A. RNN-based deep learning for physical activity recognition using smartwatch sensors: A case study of simple and complex activity recognition. *Math. Biosci. Eng.* **2022**, *19*, 5671–5698. [CrossRef]
4. Jalal, A.; Kim, Y.H.; Kim, Y.J.; Kamal, S.; Kim, D. Robust human activity recognition from depth video using spatiotemporal multi-fused features. *Pattern Recognit.* **2017**, *61*, 295–308. .: 10.1016/j.patcog.2016.08.003. [CrossRef]
5. Sharma, V.; Gupta, M.; Pandey, A.K.; Mishra, D.; Kumar, A. A Review of Deep Learning-based Human Activity Recognition on Benchmark Video Datasets. *Appl. Artif. Intell.* **2022**, *36*, 2093705. [CrossRef]
6. Vrskova, R.; Kamencay, P.; Hudec, R.; Sykora, P. A New Deep-Learning Method for Human Activity Recognition. *Sensors* **2023**, *23*, 2816. [CrossRef]
7. Shoaib, M.; Bosch, S.; Incel, O.D.; Scholten, H.; Havinga, P.J.M. Complex Human Activity Recognition Using Smartphone and Wrist-Worn Motion Sensors. *Sensors* **2016**, *16*, 426. [CrossRef]
8. Reyes-Ortiz, J.L.; Oneto, L.; Samà, A.; Parra, X.; Anguita, D. Transition-Aware Human Activity Recognition Using Smartphones. *Neurocomputing* **2016**, *171*, 754–767. .: 10.1016/j.neucom.2015.07.085. [CrossRef]
9. Mekruksavanich, S.; Hnoohom, N.; Jitpattanakul, A. A Hybrid Deep Residual Network for Efficient Transitional Activity Recognition Based on Wearable Sensors. *Appl. Sci.* **2022**, *12*, 4988. [CrossRef]
10. Yan, H.; Zhang, Y.; Wang, Y.; Xu, K. WiAct: A Passive WiFi-Based Human Activity Recognition System. *IEEE Sensors J.* **2020**, *20*, 296–305. [CrossRef]
11. Liu, F.; Cui, Y.; Masouros, C.; Xu, J.; Han, T.X.; Eldar, Y.C.; Buzzi, S. Integrated Sensing and Communications: Toward Dual-Functional Wireless Networks for 6G and Beyond. *IEEE J. Sel. Areas Commun.* **2022**, *40*, 1728–1767. [CrossRef]
12. Wang, W.; Liu, A.X.; Shahzad, M.; Ling, K.; Lu, S. Device-Free Human Activity Recognition Using Commercial WiFi Devices. *IEEE J. Sel. Areas Commun.* **2017**, *35*, 1118–1131. [CrossRef]
13. Sigg, S.; Scholz, M.; Shi, S.; Ji, Y.; Beigl, M. RF-Sensing of Activities from Non-Cooperative Subjects in Device-Free Recognition Systems Using Ambient and Local Signals. *IEEE Trans. Mob. Comput.* **2014**, *13*, 907–920. [CrossRef]
14. Muaaz, M.; Chelli, A.; Pätzold, M. WiHAR: From Wi-Fi Channel State Information to Unobtrusive Human Activity Recognition. In Proceedings of the 2020 IEEE 91st Vehicular Technology Conference (VTC2020-Spring), Antwerp, Belgium, 25–28 May 2020; pp. 1–7. [CrossRef]
15. Cheng, X.; Huang, B. CSI-Based Human Continuous Activity Recognition Using GMM–HMM. *IEEE Sensors J.* **2022**, *22*, 18709–18717. [CrossRef]
16. Dang, X.; Cao, Y.; Hao, Z.; Liu, Y. WiGId: Indoor Group Identification with CSI-Based Random Forest. *Sensors* **2020**, *20*, 4607. [CrossRef] [PubMed]
17. Alsaify, B.A.; Almazari, M.M.; Alazrai, R.; Alouneh, S.; Daoud, M.I. A CSI-Based Multi-Environment Human Activity Recognition Framework. *Appl. Sci.* **2022**, *12*, 930. [CrossRef]
18. Moghaddam, M.G.; Shirehjini, A.A.N.; Shirmohammadi, S. A WiFi-based System for Recognizing Fine-grained Multiple-Subject Human Activities. In Proceedings of the 2022 IEEE International Instrumentation and Measurement Technology Conference (I2MTC), Ottawa, ON, Canada, 16–19 May 2022; pp. 1–6. [CrossRef]
19. Yousefi, S.; Narui, H.; Dayal, S.; Ermon, S.; Valaee, S. A Survey on Behavior Recognition Using WiFi Channel State Information. *IEEE Commun. Mag.* **2017**, *55*, 98–104. [CrossRef]
20. Chen, Z.; Zhang, L.; Jiang, C.; Cao, Z.; Cui, W. WiFi CSI Based Passive Human Activity Recognition Using Attention Based BLSTM. *IEEE Trans. Mob. Comput.* **2019**, *18*, 2714–2724. [CrossRef]
21. Abdelnasser, H.; Youssef, M.; Harras, K.A. WiGest: A ubiquitous WiFi-based gesture recognition system. In Proceedings of the 2015 IEEE Conference on Computer Communications (INFOCOM), Kowloon, Hong Kong, 26 April–1 May 2015; pp. 1472–1480. [CrossRef]
22. Gu, Y.; Quan, L.; Ren, F. WiFi-assisted human activity recognition. In Proceedings of the 2014 IEEE Asia Pacific Conference on Wireless and Mobile, Bali, Indonesia, 28–30 August 2014; pp. 60–65. [CrossRef]

23. Yang, Z.; Zhou, Z.; Liu, Y. From RSSI to CSI: Indoor Localization via Channel Response. *ACM Comput. Surv.* **2013**, *46*, 1–32. [CrossRef]
24. Zhang, D.; Wang, H.; Wu, D. Toward Centimeter-Scale Human Activity Sensing with Wi-Fi Signals. *Computer* **2017**, *50*, 48–57. [CrossRef]
25. Wang, Y.; Liu, J.; Chen, Y.; Gruteser, M.; Yang, J.; Liu, H. E-Eyes: Device-Free Location-Oriented Activity Identification Using Fine-Grained WiFi Signatures. In Proceedings of the 20th Annual International Conference on Mobile Computing and Networking (MobiCom '14), New York, NY, USA, 2014; pp. 617–628. [CrossRef]
26. Wang, F.; Panev, S.; Dai, Z.; Han, J.; Huang, D. Can WiFi Estimate Person Pose? *arXiv* **2019**, arXiv:1904.00277.
27. Moshiri, F.; Parisa.; Shahbazian.; Reza.; Nabati.; Mohammad.; Ghorashi, S.A. A CSI-Based Human Activity Recognition Using Deep Learning. *Sensors* **2021**, *21*, 7225. [CrossRef]
28. Chahoushi, M.; Nabati, M.; Asvadi, R.; Ghorashi, S.A. CSI-Based Human Activity Recognition Using Multi-Input Multi-Output Autoencoder and Fine-Tuning. *Sensors* **2023**, *23*, 3591. [CrossRef] [PubMed]
29. Elbayad, M.; Besacier, L.; Verbeek, J. Pervasive Attention: 2D Convolutional Neural Networks for Sequence-to-Sequence Prediction. *arXiv* **2018**, arXiv:1808.03867.
30. Schuster, M.; Paliwal, K. Bidirectional recurrent neural networks. *IEEE Trans. Signal Process.* **1997**, *45*, 2673–2681. [CrossRef]
31. Zhang, J.; Wu, F.; Wei, B.; Zhang, Q.; Huang, H.; Shah, S.W.; Cheng, J. Data Augmentation and Dense-LSTM for Human Activity Recognition Using WiFi Signal. *IEEE Internet Things J.* **2021**, *8*, 4628–4641. [CrossRef]
32. Shang, S.; Luo, Q.; Zhao, J.; Xue, R.; Sun, W.; Bao, N. LSTM-CNN network for human activity recognition using WiFi CSI data. *J. Phys. Conf. Ser.* **2021**, *1883*, 012139. [CrossRef]
33. Yadav, S.K.; Sai, S.; Gundewar, A.; Rathore, H.; Tiwari, K.; Pandey, H.M.; Mathur, M. CSITime: Privacy-preserving human activity recognition using WiFi channel state information. *Neural Networks* **2022**, *146*, 11–21. [CrossRef] [PubMed]
34. Wang, W.; Liu, A.X.; Shahzad, M.; Ling, K.; Lu, S. Understanding and Modeling of WiFi Signal Based Human Activity Recognition. In Proceedings of the 21st Annual International Conference on Mobile Computing and Networking (MobiCom '15), New York, NY, USA, 2015; pp. 65–76. [CrossRef]
35. andJimmy Ba, D.P.K. Adam: A Method for Stochastic Optimization. In Proceedings of the 3rd International Conference on Learning Representations, ICLR 2015, San Diego, CA, USA, 7–8 May 2015.
36. Stone, M. Cross-Validatory Choice and Assessment of Statistical Predictions. *J. R. Stat. Soc. Ser. B (Methodol.)* **1974**, *36*, 111–147. [CrossRef]
37. Luong, T.; Pham, H.; Manning, C.D. Effective Approaches to Attention-based Neural Machine Translation. In Proceedings of the 2015 Conference on Empirical Methods in Natural Language Processing, Lisbon, Portugal, 17–21 September 2015; pp. 1412–1421. [CrossRef]

applied sciences

MDPI

Article

Virtually Connected in a Multiverse of Madness?—Perceptions of Gaming, Animation, and Metaverse

Abílio Oliveira * and Mónica Cruz *

Instituto Universitário de Lisboa (ISCTE-IUL), ISTAR-IUL, 1649-026 Lisboa, Portugal
* Correspondence: abilio.oliveira@iscte-iul.pt (A.O.); monica_susana_cruz@iscte-iul.pt (M.C.)

Abstract: Few studies analyze what are the common representations of the metaverse. Regarding what has been said about this concept, our research aims to verify how adults perceive and represent the metaverse. We carried out a study with focus groups, having as participants Portuguese adults all considered habitual gamers (or users of digital games). The objectives for this study were seven: verify how the metaverse is being represented and characterized; identify which technologies stimulate the immersion experience; identify the main dimensions that influence the acceptance of the metaverse concept; understand the perceptions of the metaverse and virtual reality regarding socialization and wellbeing; verify the perceptions of a gamer's daily life regarding the metaverse, virtual reality, and gaming concepts; understand the impact of social representations on the gaming concept; and to understand the perceived role of animation regarding the metaverse, virtual reality, and gaming concepts. Our results reveal a common understanding of the metaverse, despite some confusion about this concept. We also verified the high importance of wellbeing and social dimensions in metaverse immersive experiences provided by technology or gaming characteristics. This exploratory study gave us essential findings about the perceptions of the metaverse and a deep understanding of the relations between the metaverse, virtual reality, animation, and gaming.

Keywords: metaverse; virtual reality; animation; digital games; gaming; qualitative research

Citation: Oliveira, A.; Cruz, M. Virtually Connected in a Multiverse of Madness?—Perceptions of Gaming, Animation, and Metaverse. *Appl. Sci.* **2023**, *13*, 8573. https://doi.org/10.3390/app13158573

Academic Editors: Juan-Carlos Cano and Christos Bouras

Received: 28 May 2023
Revised: 11 July 2023
Accepted: 21 July 2023
Published: 25 July 2023

1. Introduction

Over the years, the gaming industry has become a fulcrum for technological development with the premise of reaching higher player engagement. With this evolution, our reality has been transformed by virtual reality through animation, where virtual characters assume almost real roles and new realities are generated, as well as languages and new types of communication [1]. Whether a single individual or global, the perception must be understood ethically and even politically [2].

This virtual reality brought by animation through the gaming world is considered a dream [3] by the author Heilig of its power to transform reality. And so we become aware of how digital transformation has come into our lives because of the metaverse [4]. The gaming industry has founded this concept because we are enveloped with alternate worlds [5], considered the first areas where metaverse solutions were applied [5]. In this way, the Metaverse concept has brought us a whole new perspective of reality, uniting the technology to create new immersive ways to live our lives [6].

Nevertheless, only a few studies focus on trying to understand real perceptions, of ordinary people, of the concept of the metaverse. Do regular people understand the impact of the metaverse on their lives and how important this can be in the future? Until the present date, even the authors have yet to come up with a precise definition for this concept, so if a consensus between them is still waiting to happen, should we expect that other people will understand this concept better? As investigators, we aim to understand the balance between scientific knowledge of this concept and common understanding.

So, we ask what are the thoughts of the gamers? What are their common thoughts regarding this concept? Is scientific knowledge aligned with common thoughts? Or are two apart visions being created?

This research aims to contribute to a better understanding of how this metaverse concept is being perceived, giving the scientific knowledge of how common assumptions could or should be explored regarding the definition of this concept. And to provide the technology and gaming industry with crucial ideas on which concepts they should be guided to evolve in the future. This study may also be useful for common users or gamers to reflect on their motivation to seek the metaverse and on how they use games and virtual reality, considering their socialization in the real world versus immersion in virtual environments—understanding people's perceptions may contribute to better communication linking the real and virtual worlds to proportionate a better involvement and socialization (beyond any distance or physical barrier).

This explorative study is part of extensive research on the metaverse, virtual reality, and gaming concepts. So, we ask: how is the metaverse being perceived and represented by gamers?

Since this is an explorative study and a part of a Ph.D. in development, the objectives proposed for this study were elaborated using previous investigations already made, and objectives were predefined according to our Ph.D. thesis.

With this context, we aim to: (1) verify how the metaverse is being represented and characterized; (2) identify which technologies stimulate the immersion experience; (3) identify the main dimensions that influence the acceptance of the metaverse concept; (4) understand perceptions of the metaverse and virtual reality regarding socialization and wellbeing; (5) verify the perceptions of a gamer's daily life regarding the metaverse, virtual reality, and gaming concepts; (6) understand the impact of social representations on the gaming concept; (7) to understand the perceived role of animation regarding the metaverse, virtual reality, and gaming concepts.

This study consisted of three focus groups with Portuguese adults who are all considered regular gamers (or users of digital games). The qualitative data gathered were analyzed using frequencies. We aimed to identify the main emerging themes and concepts, helping us explore what can be done in the future and discover more about these concepts.

The present study is framed in a general introduction and a brief literature review. After these, we present a detailed exploration of the methodology applied to the frequent themes and main concepts that result from the focus groups we analyzed. After this, we present the findings of this study, followed by a discussion considering the present results and a conclusion, including suggestions for future work.

2. Background

2.1. Gaming

The gaming notion begins with technological evolution and engagement with video or digital games. The gaming area has been with us for a long time [7], and with its evolution, it has responded to all our wishes, offering new environments, experiences, and opportunities [8]. Gaming has been considered the founder of the metaverse as an entertainment tool since it was one of the first solutions where this concept was applied [5].

To understand the gaming concept, we must embrace ourselves through the notion of playing. Playing is a free activity where joy and fun exist [9]. However, it does not need to have a goal. All the rules created rely only on the imaginations of the person or persons playing [9]. So, another view of playing is being in this world to comprehend what is around us, who we are, and a way to interact with others [10].

In this way, we can understand that the gaming area is something that has been present for a long time [7] and has responded to our wishes and experience needs [8] to become more social and share experiences [11]. The gaming world allows us to explore different experiences where we free ourselves from the limits of our bodies and our previous experiences and extend ourselves to infinite possibilities [12].

It is also essential to understand the social importance of the gaming area because most people play video games with others [13]. Players prefer to play with other players [14] and communication is more fun, involved, and bonding when people are connected [15]. There is a unique opportunity for sociability and social games, making them the only media that allow this activity together [16].

With this understanding, we can see the gaming industry's efforts continuously growing through the years, allowing new concepts to be born because of technological development. As humans, we are continually staged by our social contexts, and we cannot centre or surpass them. However, the gaming world offers alternative worlds that distance the social rules and quotidian.

2.2. Virtual Reality

Virtual reality has been one of the concepts and development technology that was launched through the gaming area. The term engineers use is virtual, which means substitute computers and peripherical devices instead of human senses [17]. So, virtual reality can be seen as a technology that can replace a user's primary senses for computer data [18]. It is also considered an electronic simulation of experienced environments [19], allowing users to get different sensory experiences of real things through simulation, but it does not mean a new experience can occur [17]. It can be seen as an artificial reality from the actual world [17].

Virtual reality relies on computer graphic systems combined with different displays and interface devices that allow immersion through a 3D computer-generated environment [20]. It is considered a new medium which is only possible through the technological advances creating practical applications and new ways of communication [21]. Virtual reality profoundly impacts daily human lives because humans will constantly challenge the limits of existing technology and optimize the combination of resources to push the progress of science and technology forward [22]. Virtual tools provide various means of accessing, viewing, and analyzing data within a focal point to offer spatiality, immersion, and interaction [23].

To understand virtual reality best, we must understand its key important elements. One key element is the participants because all the virtual reality magic happens in their minds. This experience is not the same for each participant because of their experiences, culture, and history [21]. Then we have the creators, as the second key element, who are the person or team that designs and implements the created work to be experienced [21]. The third key element is the virtual world. It is considered the content of a given medium and can exist without being displayed in a virtual reality system. When we observe that world through the possibility of bringing objects and interactions in a physically immersive, interactive way, we experience it via virtual reality [21]. The fourth key element is immersion, the sensation of being in an environment that can be a mental state or accomplished physically. Physical immersion is considered a characteristic that defines virtual reality [21]. The fifth, and last key element, is interactivity because it allows alternate realities through computers, games, and other systems or devices [21].

Virtual reality is seen as an advanced human–computer interaction interface that allows the simulation of realistic environments [24]. This interactivity can also be defined as communication media because users can modify a form or content mediated by the environment in real time [19]. This concept can have different forms, such as cab simulation, projected reality, augmented reality, telepresence (the feeling of being physically somewhere other than where the user is [25]), and desktop virtual reality (keyboard, mouse, monitor, headphones) [24].

2.3. Animation

We now understand virtual reality existing in the gaming world; however, we must take some time to understand the core of the gaming existence, which is the animation.

The connection between the gaming area and the animation started because of the economy around them. The first to explore this relationship was Walt Disney [26], and by seventy years, commercial license became a possibility [27]. By this means, digital technology with special effects such as animation broke an essential psychological barrier because it allowed virtual worlds [26] to exist.

Animation has brought to the gaming world and virtual reality all its meaning "to give life". It is an extraordinary audiovisual expression that transforms nonreal events and takes the audience there [28]. Animation has excellent potential and importance because of its ability to establish transversal communication with any age, gender, culture, religion, or nationality [29]. Because of this ability, animation is considered a creative strategy [30] and a new model of communication for the future [28].

2.4. Metaverse

After our dive through the gaming area and the technological development (virtual reality and animation concepts), we arrive at the main concept of this investigation, the metaverse.

The metaverse concept definition appeared for the first time by the author Neal Stephenson in his book Snow Crash in 1992. It was defined as a virtual world that could reach, interact, and affect human existence [31]. However, until today, there has yet to be a consensus about the definition of the metaverse, but there will be definitions near agreement in the future. The metaverse can be defined as a massive dimension network of interconnected 3D virtual worlds rendered in real time that can be experienced synchronously and persistently by an unlimited number of users with a unique sense of presence and data continuity, who have identity, history, rights, objects communication and payments [31]. It is also a 3D experience where we can interact with virtual and augmented reality through headsets, sensory gloves, cameras, and sensors registering our bodily movements [8].

The metaverse has its inner world that continues to exist even if we are not connected [8]. It can be described as the layer between us and the reality [32], where a 3D virtual world is shared, and the experiences can be experienced through virtual and augmented reality [33]. It is based on the real world but without physical limitations [34]. The users can involve themselves socially, economically, and culturally through their avatars [35] because the metaverse unites platforms of socially immersive virtual realities compatible with video games with massive online multiplayers, open gaming worlds, and collaborative spaces of augmented reality [36]. It is also seen as a digital universe that mixes online gaming elements with social networks and virtual reality, allowing users to engage digitally [37].

The metaverse social application will transform social networks [18], and we can see that the gaming world is the founder of this concept because gamers could tie it to the screen and envelop it with alternative worlds [6]. The gaming experience has increasingly become a lived experience, and the limits between the metaverse and what is gaming and what is not have disappeared [8]. The metaverse can be achieved via the internet through augmented reality devices, game consoles, computers, tablets, or mobile phones [4]. In this way, the metaverse concept is present consciously or unconsciously in our lives.

2.5. Related Work—A Comprehensive Review of Main Concepts

To understand the relationships between the main concepts, in this section, we connect these concepts with the objectives of the present study. Tables 1–4 were structured to help us to observe the relations of the concepts (gaming, virtual reality, animation, and metaverse) and their definitions studied by scientific authors according to our objectives, which are to: (1) verify how the metaverse is being represented and characterized; (2) identify which technologies stimulate the immersion experience; (3) identify the main dimensions that influence the acceptance of the metaverse concept; (4) understand the perceptions of the metaverse and virtual reality regarding socialization and wellbeing; (5) verify the perceptions of a gamer's daily life regarding the metaverse, virtual reality, and gaming concepts; (6) understand the impact of social representations on the gaming concept; and (7) to understand the perceived role of animation regarding the metaverse, virtual reality, and gaming concepts.

Table 1. Related Work—Concept Gaming.

Author	Description	Concept Relation	Objective Alignment
[8]	has responded to all our wishes, offering new environments, experiences, and opportunities	Gaming	(3) (4)
[5]	Gaming has been considered the founder of the metaverse as an entertainment tool since it was one of the first solutions where this concept was applied	Gaming vs. Metaverse	(3) (4) (5)
[9]	Playing is a free activity where joy and fun exist	Gaming	(4)
[11]	becoming more social and sharing experiences	Gaming	(4) (5) (6)
[13]	It is also essential to understand the social importance of the gaming area because most people play video games with others	Gaming	(4) (5)
[15]	communication is more fun, involvement, and bond when people are connected	Gaming	(2) (4) (5) (6)

Table 2. Related Work—Concept Virtual Reality.

Author	Description	Concept Relation	Objective Alignment
[17]	The term engineers use is virtual, which means substitute computers and peripherical devices instead of human senses	Virtual Reality	(2) (4)
[18]	virtual reality can be seen as a technology that can replace a user's primary senses for computer data	Virtual Reality	(2)
[19]	considered an electronic simulation of experienced environments	Virtual Reality	(2)
[20]	Virtual reality relies on computer graphic systems combined with different displays and interface devices that allow immersion through a 3D computer-generated environment	Virtual Reality	(2) (5)
[21]	It is considered a new medium only possible by the technological advances creating practical applications and new ways of communication	Virtual Reality	(2) (4) (5)
[21]	Physical immersion is considered a characteristic that defines virtual reality	Virtual Reality	(2) (4) (5)
[19]	This interactivity can also be defined as communication media because users can modify a form or content mediated by the environment in real time	Virtual Reality	(2) (4) (5)
[25]	This concept can have different forms, such as cab simulation, projected reality, augmented reality, telepresence (the feeling of being physically somewhere other than where the user is)	Virtual Reality	(2)
[24]	desktop virtual reality (keyboard, mouse, monitor, headphones)		(2)

Table 3. Related Work—Concept Animation.

Author	Description	Concept Relation	Objective Alignment
[26]	The connection between the gaming area and the animation started because of the economy around them. The first to explore this relationship was Walt Disney	Animation	(6)
[26]	By this means, digital technology with special effects such as animation broke an essential psychological barrier because it allowed virtual worlds	Animation	(3) (7)
[28]	It is an extraordinary audiovisual expression that transforms nonreal events and takes the audience there	Animation	(7)

Table 3. *Cont.*

Author	Description	Concept Relation	Objective Alignment
[29]	has excellent potential and importance because of its ability to establish transversal communication with any age, gender, culture, religion, or nationality	Animation	(6) (7)
[30]	of this ability, the animation is considered a creative strategy	Animation	(7)
[28]	new model of communication for the future	Animation	(7)

Table 4. Related Work—Concept Metaverse.

Author	Description	Concept Relation	Objective Alignment
[31]	virtual world that could reach, interact, and affect human existence	Metaverse vs. Virtual Reality	(1) (2) (4) (7)
[31]	The metaverse can be defined as a massive dimension network and interconnected 3D virtual worlds rendered in real time that can be experienced synchronously and persistently by an unlimited number of users with a unique sense of presence and data continuity, has identity, history, rights, objects communication and payments	Virtual Reality	(1) (4) (5)
[8]	It is also a 3D experience where we can interact with virtual and augmented reality through headsets, sensory gloves, cameras, and sensors registering our bodily movements	Metaverse vs. Virtual Reality	(1) (2) (7)
[8]	its inner world that continues to exist even if we are not connected		(1)
[32]	It can be described as the layer between us and the reality		(1) (4) (5)
[33]	where a 3D virtual world is shared, and the experiences can be experienced through virtual and augmented reality		(1) (2) (7)
[34]	based on the real world but without physical limitations		(1) (4) (5)
[35]	The users can involve themselves socially, economically, and culturally through their avatars		(1) (3) (4) (5)
[36]	Metaverse unites platforms of socially immersive virtual realities compatible with video games with massive online multi-players, open gaming worlds, and collaborative spaces of augmented reality		(1) (2) (4) (5) (7)
[37]	It is also seen as a digital universe that mixes online gaming elements with social networks and virtual reality, allowing users to engage digitally		(1) (2) (3) (4) (7)
[8]	The gaming experience has increasingly become a lived experience, and the limits between the metaverse and what is gaming and what is not have disappeared		(1) (3) (4) (5) (7)
[4]	The metaverse can be achieved via the internet through augmented reality devices, game consoles, computers, tablets, or mobile phones		(1) (2) (5)

2.6. Qualitative Research—Focus Group

The focus group originated in the work of the Bureau of Applied Social Research at Columbia University in 1940 [38]. It has become common in research since 1990. It can be applied to various disciplines such as education, communication and media, health, youth, ecology and conservation, feminism, sociology, and social psychology [39]. The focus group is a qualitative data collection method that engages a small number of people in an informal discussion around a particular topic [39]. It is considered a nonstandard technique to gather information based on what appears to be an informal discussion among a group of selected people [40]. This discussion occurs in the presence of a moderator that leads and focuses the discussion on the research issues [40]. There must be prior planning, leaving it up to the researcher to determine which questions to approach and discuss, with attention to the group. These questions are scheduled, and the moderator is responsible for facilitating participation amongst the discussion group members [39]. The focus group stimulates the creation of discourses between the participants that may never occur in real life, quickly achieving a large amount of data. This method is considered very efficient for gathering data [41]. Discussion groups are defined by a small number of individuals gathered for a discussion, making them more valuable overall than a sample representative [42]. In a group, collective discussion brings together each individual's sphere of life, and these are confronted with disagreements, making this method more critical than any other. Human behavior remains normative, what changed are the sources of normative influence that are more diverse, complex, and interactive [43].

Focus group discussion effectively provides information about what people think or feel and how they do it [44]. A group, per se, is not considered good or bad but reflects human capabilities. Any discussion group can be viewed as a focus group if the investigator actively encourages and listens to group interaction [45]. The interactions within the discussion group enable the exploration of stabilized forms of socially shared knowledge, tensions, and different meanings within the same shared understanding and the reinterpretations of the symbolic forms of the social knowledge [40]. The great potential of focus groups is the explicit use of group interaction to produce data and thoughts that would be less accessible without the interaction found in a group [41]. It can be used as a single-method investigation or in combination with other methods. This helps guide a study to generate hypotheses based on the informants' opinions, thoughts, and feelings, assessing different populations, or developing questionnaires—as in our case—based on the participants' views, suggestions, and interpretations.

The focus group can be used as a simulation of speech and conversations of everyday life or as an almost natural method to study the generation of social representations or social knowledge in general [46]. This discussion type is considered closer to everyday communication [40]. This method generates discussion and therefore reveals the meanings that people read in the topic of debate and how they negotiate these meanings. It creates diversity and difference within or between the group, revealing the dilemmas of everyday arguments [46]. The number of focus groups to be carried out should be evaluated according to the interests and objectives being researched [47]. We need to remember that within a group chosen to represent a social category, the individual participants identify as part of a specific social group [40]. And the group is also considered a unit of analysis because it represents the social group the researcher wants to investigate [40]. Depending on the type of investigation, focus groups can be used as a method on their own or in combination with other methods (e.g., surveys, observations, and single interviews) [48].

The development of communication and information research practice technologies has been significantly impacted [48], and the focus group has been naturally transferred to internet research [40]. The online focus group can be distinguished into synchronous (real-time) or asynchronous (nonreal-time) groups. Synchronous groups require all participants to be online simultaneously using a chatroom or conferencing software [48]. In this case, a possible issue could be the reduced flow of the discussion and the availability of visual information [49]. However, some software can enable the transmission of relatively nuanced expressions and emotions in video mode [50] and are able to replicate real-time, face-to-face interaction [51]. The asynchronous groups must be provided with the software on their computer, and the participants do not have to be all online. This has some disadvantages causing technical issues or hesitation to install this software [48]. The number of participants in the real-time focus group should be limited, causing the discussion to be too fast and superficial [48]. Differences between online and face-to-face focus group research concerning group interaction and the ability to obtain information are eroded as technology provides more significant opportunities to create a social presence online [49].

Online focus groups have advantages, such as logistical issues, because the difficulty of having all participants at the same place and time is reduced by technology [52,53]. Recording and transcriptions were also facilitated by built-in online interfaces, which can be downloaded almost immediately [49,50], and automatic recording allows the possibility of preclassifying the collected information [40]. Sensitive issues and the anonymity of virtual groups can create a high sense of psychological safety for sensitive or embarrassing topics [51]. Regarding the limitation of interaction biases, online interaction can control some tendencies and prevent participant conflicts or competitiveness [40]. Regarding adaptability for specific targets, online focus groups can be appropriate for particular types of participants, such as teens, low-incidence groups, professionals, policymakers, and disabled individuals [49].

As for the disadvantages, we can point to the digital gap, choosing participants with some familiarity concerning technology implied in an online focus group. The artificiality of the interaction situation is that participants may feel concerns about sharing personal information with strangers in an electronic context [50]. And the lack of nonverbal communication may reduce the nonverbal communication that plays a crucial role in eliciting responses [49].

Nevertheless, the online focus group may lead to more disclosure than real-world groups. Data are easier to document, and the loss of contributions due to audibility problems during the transcript can be reduced [48]. Online focus groups make data analysis relatively easy through coding and categorization [48].

Regarding the sample size of the focus group, we already know that this method is considered a qualitative technique that collects data very efficiently [54]. But when do we know it is enough?

We can make out a little in qualitative research because we do not try to generalize a population but instead identify social processes [55]. It is also essential to consider the saturation point concept, considering the point at which gathering new data does not provide any new theoretical insights into the studied phenomenon [56,57]. So, it does not matter how little data we have collected, we have to consider the generalizations that can be made from just one single case. We should focus on our interactive units (such as social relationships, encounters, and organizations) because these units allow a direct and deeper analysis of the characteristic observed [58]. The saturation concept is important in previous studies regarding focus group samples. In a study whose objective was to assess the saturation and guidance on focus group research, it was found that one focus group generated 64% of the theme/concepts and that three focus groups generated 84%, concluding that three focus groups are enough to identify the most prevalent concepts [59]. In another study relating to influence saturation, the authors concluded through their research that only a few groups are required to capture the breadth of the main issues [60].

For this reason, we decided that three focus groups were enough to collect the main concepts for our explorative study.

3. Methods

3.1. Data Gathering—Focus Group

This study consists of three synchronous online focus groups, with a total of 13 participants of Portuguese nationality. For choosing the participants, we used as inclusion criteria: (1) being a gamer (plays digital or video games regularly); (2) being young adults or adults; (3) having some knowledge regarding video-conference tools. As for the exclusion criteria: (1) did not match all the inclusion criteria mentioned; (2) needed access to a computer with internet to participate in the online focus group. There were seven males and six females, with an average age of twenty-nine. Google Meet was the software chosen to make the video conference.

The questions were revised for each focus group depending on difficulties observed and on the understanding of what was asked in the previous focus group made. However, we never interfered with the line of ideas or suggested a response. For example, one question clarified the meaning of metaverse because participants asked directly if the metaverse was the concept itself mentioned or if it was the Facebook company changing their name to Meta. In a general way, all the participants understood what was questioned immediately.

The focus groups comprised twenty-eight questions, divided into three main themes: gaming, animation, and metaverse.

For the gaming theme, we had these questions prepared:

1. What is it for you to play?
2. What is the gaming world for you?
3. What is a gamer for you?
4. What do you think about there being different types of gamers?
5. How do you feel/think that the gaming world is present in our daily lives?
6. What do you think/feel about the statement "a game is a virtual reality"?
7. What do you think/feel about the possibility of social reality being an important factor in choosing a game in favor of others?
8. When you play, do you feel immersed ("inside") in the game?
9. How do you relate playing with your everyday reality?
10. How do you relate playing with animation and the metaverse?
11. To what extent do you feel immersed in a virtual world while playing the game? As? Why?
12. What are the most fascinating features for you to play?
13. What are the most important features in a game to feel more immersed?
14. Do you know or use any objects/technologies that provide immersion in a game?

For the animation theme, the questions were:

1. What do you think/feel about the statement "animation is present in all games"?
2. Do you consider animation an important factor in a game?
3. What features do you like/look for in a gaming animation?
4. What do you think about the statement "an animation is a kind of virtual reality"?

For the main theme of metaverse the questions were:

1. What is the metaverse for you? Refer to at least three words about what it means.
2. What do you think about the metaverse? What do you think the metaverse is for?
3. Have you ever been immersed in the Metaverse? What made you feel/think?
4. For which population do you think the metaverse is more directed? (adults, teens, children, or seniors/elderly?)
5. How is the metaverse present in your daily life?
6. Do you think the metaverse is a virtual reality? Why?
7. How do you think/feel about the metaverse's relation to our social reality?
8. What do you think about the possibility of social reality being an important factor in interacting with the metaverse?
9. Is a game a metaverse?

3.2. Data Gathering and Analysis

In each online focus group, the participants were informed before the discussion that their participation was voluntary, confidential, and anonymous, and they could decide to leave anytime. We also obtained a verbal agreement from the participants to allow the recording of the online focus group session for posterior data analysis.

During the focus group, there were many participants who answered the questions with only one or two words or small sentences, which allow us to categorize in a frequency of results.

All the qualitative data was gathered in a transcript in a Word file, which summarized and categorized (e.g., fun and enjoy fun—joint categorization fun) the concepts mentioned and analyzed the frequencies of responses from the participants, considering categories and main themes. After this categorization, we calculated the frequencies and percentages of the answers given.

3.3. Data Results

For the gaming questions:

1. What is it for you to play?

As we can observe (see Table 5), according to the meaning of playing, all the participants considered it fun (N = 13, 100%). Some participants felt something that allowed an escape from reality and a relaxing activity (N = 6, 46.2%). This gives us essential concepts such as good mood and new game experiences, reinforcing gaming as something that promotes the wellbeing of the players.

Table 5. Gaming—What is it for you to play?

Categories	Total	%
Fun	13	100
Escape reality	6	46.2
Relax	6	46.2
Socialization	5	38.5
Hobby	3	23.1
Therapy	1	7.7

2. What is the gaming world for you?

Table 6 shows that the gaming world is considered something that gathers people, such as a community (53.8%) and those who enjoy games (46.2%). These results show us that the players consider the gaming world as a social and wellbeing world.

Table 6. Gaming—What is the gaming world for you?

Categories	Total	%
Community	7	53.8
The specific group enjoys games	6	46.2
Digital Games	4	30.8
Games categories	3	23.1
Specific group	2	15.4
Join of concepts	2	15.4
Games Industry	2	15.4
Society stereotype	1	7.7
Culture	1	7.7

3. What is a gamer for you?

Most participants responded that a gamer plays games (61.5%, Table 7) and that gamer is a word used to classify a group of people (46.2%, Table 7). So, we can observe that for these participants, a gamer can be anyone playing games, giving a generic or simple consideration regarding a common synonym of a gamer without preconcepts.

Table 7. Gaming—What is a gamer for you?

Categories	Total	%
A person that plays games	8	61.5
The name given to a group of people	6	46.2
A person that likes any games	5	38.5
A person that regularly plays games	2	15.4
A person that plays games has hobbies	1	7.7
The person who likes computers	1	7.7
A person who likes technology	1	7.7
Synonym of nerd expression	1	7.7

4. What do you think about there being different types of gamers?

On this question, we can see that the participants were unanimous, considering that there are different types of gamers (100%, Table 8), meaning that they play frequently or occasionally (84.6%, Table 9). They also considered this question the premise of the professional gamer (46.2%, Table 9). These show us that from common perception, a gamer is characterized by their playing frequency.

Table 8. Gaming—What do you think about there being different types of gamers?

Categories	Total	%
Yes	13	100
No	0	0

Table 9. Gaming—What do you think about there being different types of gamers?

Categories	Total	%
Frequent or daily gamer	11	84.6
Occasional gamer	11	84.6
Professional gamer	6	46.2
Semiprofessional	1	7.7

5. How do you feel/think that the gaming world is present in our daily lives?

For the participants, the gaming world is present in their daily lives (N = 13, 100%, Table 10) because it is mainly a source that provides fun (N = 7, 53.8%, Table 11). These results are expected since all these participants are considered gamers, but most of these results show us the need for fun, relaxation, and socialization in a gamer's life.

Table 10. Gaming—How do you feel/think that the gaming world is present in our daily lives?

Categories	Total	%
Yes	13	100
No	0	0

Table 11. Gaming—How do you feel/think that the gaming world is present in our daily lives?

Categories	Total	%
Provides fun	7	53.8
Relaxation	4	30.8
Socialization	4	30.8
Provides positive emotions (happiness, cheerfulness)	3	23.1
Part of the personality of a person	2	15.4
Escape reality	1	7.7
Necessity to play	1	7.7

6. What do you think/feel about the statement "a game is a virtual reality"?

For this question, we can see that most participants consider a game as a promotor of virtual reality (N = 10, 76.9%, Table 12) because it can create an alternative reality (N = 3, 23.1%, Table 13). Through these results, we can understand that most gamers understand the meaning of the virtual reality concept and observe some confusion or no awareness regarding this.

Table 12. Gaming—What do you think/feel about the statement "a game is a virtual reality"?

Categories	Total	%
Yes	10	76.9
No	3	23.1

Table 13. Gaming—What do you think/feel about the statement "a game is a virtual reality"?

Categories	Total	%
Creates an alternative reality	3	23.1
Virtual reality does not apply to games	1	7.7
This applies to augmented reality	1	7.7
Reality provided by computers	1	7.7
Provides experiences	1	7.7

7. What do you think/feel about the possibility of social reality being an important factor in choosing a game in favor of others?

In this question, the social reality of a game was considered almost unanimous as something important when these participants consider a game (N = 12, 92.3%, Table 14), mainly because friends and close people play the same game (N = 12, 92.3%, Table 15) and because the game itself has a social component (ex: chat, community, blog, multiplayer) (N = 10, 76.9%, Table 15). Social connection is essential when choosing the game type to reinforce, be around friends, or make new connections.

Table 14. Gaming—What do you think/feel about the possibility of social reality being an important factor in choosing a game in favor of others?

Categories	Total	%
Yes	12	92.3
No	1	7.7

Table 15. Gaming—What do you think/feel about the possibility of social reality being an important factor in choosing a game in favor of others?

Categories	Total	%
Friends and close people playing the same game	12	92.3
Social component	10	76.9
Unites people	5	38.5
Friends reference	4	30.8
Gameplay of the game	2	15.4
Games classification (magazines or tv shows)	2	15.4
Price	1	7.7

8. When you play, do you feel immersed ("inside") in the game?

According to this question, we can understand that almost all the participants feel immersed in a game (N = 12, 92.3%, Table 16). However, they also answered that it could be only sometimes (N = 6, 46.2%, Table 16), mainly because they considered that it depends on the type of the game (N = 6, 46.2%, Table 17). So, we can consider that although all the games provide an immersed feeling, this immersion feeling can be stronger or weaker depending on the type of game. Nevertheless, all the games offer immersion feelings.

Table 16. Gaming—When you play, do you feel immersed ("inside") in the game?

Categories	Total	%
Yes	12	92.3
Sometimes	6	46.2
No	1	7.7

Table 17. Gaming—When you play, do you feel immersed ("inside") in the game?

Categories	Total	%
It depends on the game type	6	46.2
Identification with the game characters	5	38.5
Game history	4	30.8
It depends on the game context	1	7.7

9. How do you relate playing with your everyday reality?

As we already saw in the questions above, the playing action is considered by most participants playing games as something that provides fun (N = 7, 53.8%, Table 18). Fun is considered as an essential theme in the life of a gamer.

Table 18. Gaming—How do you relate playing with your everyday reality?

Categories	Total	%
Provides fun	7	53.8
Relaxation	4	30.8
Socialization	4	30.8
Provides positive emotions (happiness, cheerfulness)	3	23.1
Part of the personality of a person	2	15.4
Escape reality	1	7.7
Necessity to play	1	7.7

10. How do you relate playing with animation and the metaverse?

With this question, in Table 19, we can see that concepts such as metaverse and animation are considered connected (N = 13, 100%) and important (N = 9, 69.2%) in the gaming world. We can see a conscient understanding of gaming, animation, and metaverse concepts and their relation.

Table 19. Gaming—How do you relate playing with animation and the metaverse?

Categories	Total	%
Concepts are connected	13	100
Important concept	9	69.2

11. To what extent do you feel immersed in a virtual world while playing the game? As? Why?

The participants on this question, Table 20, showed us that the history (N = 7, 53.8%), the possibility to create/build things (N = 6, 46.2%), and the gameplay (N= 6, 46.2%) has the main characteristic of them to feel more immersed in the virtual world given by the game. We can observe that the attributes mentioned for immersion are engaging and fun promoters.

Table 20. Gaming—While playing the game, to what extent do you feel immersed in a virtual world? As? Why?

Categories	Total	%
History	7	53.8
Build/create things	6	46.2
Gameplay	6	46.2
Fun	5	38.5
Price	5	38.5
Person's state of mind	4	30.8
Visual graphics	4	30.8
Socialization	3	23.1
Emotions (ability to create)	2	15.4
Characters	2	15.4
Music/Audios	2	15.4
Community	2	15.4
Curiosity	1	7.7
Immersive	1	7.7

12. What are the most fascinating features for you to play?

In Table 21, the same characteristic is explored in the above question so that we can see when the participants relate to the most liked features of a game, history (N = 7, 53.8%), the possibility to create/build things (N = 6, 46.2%), and the gameplay (N = 6, 46.2%). We can also understand that a gamer seeks a game's engagement and fun promotion.

Table 21. Gaming—What are the most fascinating features for you to play?

Categories	Total	%
History	7	53.8
Build/create things	6	46.2
Gameplay	6	46.2
Fun	5	38.5
Price	5	38.5
Person's state of mind	4	30.8
Visual graphics	4	30.8
Socialization	3	23.1
Emotions (ability to create)	2	15.4
Characters	2	15.4
Music/Audios	2	15.4
Community	2	15.4
Curiosity	1	7.7
Immersive	1	7.7

13. What are the most important features in a game to feel more immersed?

As for the important feature of feeling more immersed in a game, we can see the history and gameplay (N = 6, 46.2%, Table 22), characters, ability to build/create things, and visual graphics (N = 5, 38.5%, Table 22). Once again, engagement and fun-promoting features are the most important for immersion.

Table 22. Gaming—What are the most important features in a game to feel more immersed?

Categories	Total	%
History	6	46.2
Gameplay	6	46.2
Characters	5	38.5
Build/create things	5	38.5
Visual graphics	5	38.5

Table 22. *Cont.*

Categories	Total	%
Socialization	4	30.8
Music/Audios	4	30.8
Price	4	30.8
Emotions	2	15.4
Fun	2	15.4
Curiosity	1	7.7
Person's state of mind	1	7.7

14. Do you know or use any objects/technologies that provide immersion in a game?

Most participants considered the headphones the leading provider as a technology object of immersion in a game (N = 9, 69.2%, Table 23). These results show us that headphones are a significant technology that emphasizes the sense of immersion. Compared with other technologies, these results make us wonder if the simple or cheaper technologies already have tremendous power to provide this immersion feeling. Expensive technology is not available for everybody, but it does not mean they are less immersive than cheaper ones.

Table 23. Gaming—Do you know or use any objects/technologies that provide immersion in a game?

Categories	Total	%
Headphones	9	69.2
Keyboard	5	38.5
VR goggles	4	30.8
Monitors	4	30.8
Chair	3	23.1
Interactive game commands	1	7.7
Computer Software that controls the environment	1	7.7
Mousepads	1	7.7

For the animation questions:

1. What do you think/feel about the statement "animation is present in all games"?

In this question, we can see that for most participants, the animation is present in all games (N = 11, 84.6%, Table 24) and is mandatory to be present (N = 7, 63.6%, Table 25). The results show us that the definition of what is animation and its importance are current in the gamer's mind.

Table 24. Animation—What do you think/feel about the statement "animation is present in all games"?

Categories	Total	%
Yes	11	84.6
No	2	15.4

Table 25. Animation—What do you think/feel about the statement "animation is present in all games"?

Categories	Total	%
Has to be mandatorily present	7	63.6
Makes characters more real	2	18.2

2. Do you consider animation an important factor in a game?

According to this question, all participants considered animation an important game factor (N = 13, 100%, Table 26). Some of the participants revealed their thoughts about animation being adapted to the gameplay of each game (N = 5, 38.5%, Table 27). It is clear that the animation is part of a game; without it, there would be no games.

Table 26. Animation—Do you consider animation an important factor in a game?

Categories	Total	%
Yes	13	100
No	0	0

Table 27. Animation—Do you consider animation an important factor in a game?

Categories	Total	%
It has to be adapted to the gameplay of a game	5	38.5
Graphics can influence the desire to play	3	23.1
It has to be adapted to the game	3	23.1
Can determine a game's success	1	7.7

3. What features do you like/look for in a gaming animation?

The main feature that the participants look for in a gaming animation is style/aesthetics (N = 6, 46.2%, Table 28). Animation is something that has to be well thought about in its style and aesthetics.

Table 28. Animation—What features do you like/look for in a gaming animation?

Categories	Total	%
Style/aesthetics	6	46.2
It has to be adapted to the game	5	38.5
Gameplay	5	38.5
Socialization	1	7.7

4. What do you think about the statement "an animation is a kind of virtual reality"?

On this question, is animation a kind of virtual reality, we can see a clear division (Table 29) between yes (N = 6, 46.2%) and no (N = 7, 53.8%). However, if we see the answers given by the participants that responded yes, animation is seen as something that creates/part (N = 3, 50%, Table 30) of the virtual reality. These results show an inevitable confusion or no awareness of the definition or relation between animation and virtual reality concepts.

Table 29. Animation—What do you think about the statement "an animation is a kind of virtual reality"?

Categories	Total	%
Yes	6	46.2
No	7	53.8

Table 30. Animation—What do you think about the statement "an animation is a kind of virtual reality"?

Categories	Total	%
It is part of but not one	3	50
Creates virtual reality	3	50

For the metaverse questions:

1. What is the metaverse for you? Refer to at least three words about what it means.

In this question, Table 31, the participants reveal that for them metaverse concept is something from the past, is not a new concept (N = 13, 100%), is viewed as socialization and evolution (N = 9, 69.2%), and something virtual (N = 7, 53.8%). There is an awareness of the development and history of the metaverse concept and the importance of the socialization and virtual reality themes as features/characteristics that need to be present.

Table 31. Metaverse—What is the metaverse for you? Refer to at least three words about what it means.

Categories	Total	%
Past	13	100
Socialization	9	69.2
Evolution	9	69.2
Virtual	7	53.8
Creation	6	46.2
Immersion	3	23.1
Build	3	23.1
Monitorization	2	15.4
Threat	1	7.7
Risk	1	7.7
Innovation	1	7.7

2. What do you think about the metaverse? What do you think the metaverse is for?

As for this question, the metaverse is seen as an old concept (N = 13, 100%, Table 32), as already among us, promotes socialization and technological evolution (N = 9, 69.2%, Table 32), and it also supports virtual reality (N = 7, 53.8%, Table 32). The metaverse concept is seen as a socialization promoter through virtual reality technology.

Table 32. Metaverse—What do you think about the metaverse? What do you think the metaverse is for?

Categories	Total	%
Old concept	13	100
Promotes Socialization	9	69.2
Technological evolution	9	69.2
Virtual reality	7	53.8
Creates characters	4	30.8
Allows immersion	3	23.1
Allows people to make things virtually	3	23.1
Monitorization of the virtual world	2	15.4
Creates a new reality	2	15.4
Creates new worlds	1	7.7

3. Have you ever been immersed in the metaverse? What made you feel/think?

Almost all participants have never been immersed in the metaverse (N = 10, 76.9%, Table 33). As for the participants that have been immersed in fun (N = 3, 100%, Table 34) and the feeling of being even more immersed in the game (N = 2, 66.7%, Table 34), where the main thoughts they had about their experience. This can lead us to the awareness about the metaverse definition or even how it can be experienced. It is unclear or generates a sense of confusion.

Table 33. Metaverse—Have you ever been immersed in the metaverse?

Categories	Total	%
Yes	3	23.1
No	10	76.9

Table 34. Metaverse—What made you feel/think?

Categories	Total	%
More fun	3	100
More immersion	2	66.7

4. For which population do you think the metaverse is more directed? (Adults, teens, children, or seniors/elderly?)

In this question, we tried to understand the main population N for which the metaverse was aiming, Table 35, and we could see that the participants did not have a clear response, and even a N/A was mentioned. Nevertheless, of the confusion, adults and adolescents were the main population referred (N = 9, 69.2%). At this point, there is significant confusion about the metaverse concept, even inn the population to which it is aiming.

Table 35. Metaverse—For which population do you think the metaverse is more directed? (Adults, teens, children, or seniors/elderly?).

Categories	Total	%
Adults	9	69.2
Adolescent	9	69.2
N/A	5	38.5
Children	4	30.8

5. How is the metaverse present in your daily life?

In this question, we could see that most participants responded that this concept is present in their daily lives (N = 8, 61.5%, Table 36). Once again, we can see confusion or no awareness about the metaverse compared with the previous question. However, we can see that the participants are consciously or unconsciously aware of its presence in their daily lives.

Table 36. Metaverse—How is the metaverse present in your daily life?

Categories	Total	%
Yes	8	61.5
No	5	38.5

6. Do you think the metaverse is a virtual reality? Why?

For this question, we saw the unanimous response of the metaverse being a virtual reality, Table 37, and some even added that this concept is the creator of virtual worlds, so it is responsible for virtual reality (Table 38). It is transparent for these participants that virtual reality is a central component of the metaverse concept.

Table 37. Animation—Metaverse—Do you think the metaverse is a virtual reality?

Categories	Total	%
Yes	13	100
No	0	0

Table 38. Metaverse—Why?

Categories	Total	%
Creates virtual worlds	5	38.5

7. What do you think/feel about how the Metaverse relates to our social reality?

When understanding if the metaverse is related to our social reality, most participants answered yes (N = 9, 69.2%, Table 39), explaining that they considered it a social tool (N = 10, 76.9%, Table 40). The metaverse concept is understood as a social tool that promotes socialization.

Table 39. Metaverse—What do you think/feel about how the metaverse relates to our social reality?

Categories	Total	%
Yes	9	69.2
No	6	46.2

Table 40. Metaverse—What do you think/feel about how the metaverse relates to our social reality?

Categories	Total	%
Social tool	10	76.9
Not a direct impact	1	7.7

8. What do you think about the possibility of social reality being an important factor in interacting with the metaverse?

As for this question, in Table 41, we see that social reality is essential when considering the interaction with the metaverse (N = 9, 69.2%). We can see the importance of socialization in the metaverse concept.

Table 41. Metaverse—What do you think about the possibility of social reality being an important factor in interacting with the metaverse?

Categories	Total	%
Yes	9	69.2
No	6	46.2

9. Is a game a Metaverse?

As for this question, most participants see the Metaverse as a game (N = 9, 69.2%, Table 42). The Metaverse concept is seen as a game, and these results clearly show us the relation between this concept and the technology evolution through the gaming world.

Table 42. Metaverse—Is a game a metaverse?

Categories	Total	%
Yes	9	69.2
No	4	30.8

4. Discussion

Our findings gave us actual results regarding the Metaverse virtual reality and gaming concepts and the relation between these three concepts, contributing to understanding of how gamers perceive and represent the metaverse.

Our findings allow us to identify: how the Metaverse is being represented and characterized, which technologies stimulate the immersion experience, and the main dimensions that influence the acceptance of the metaverse concept. We also understood the perceptions of the relationship between the metaverse and virtual reality regarding socialization and wellbeing and the relationship between these concepts and gaming in a gamer's life. Finally, we determined the social representations of gaming.

Regarding our first objective, how the metaverse is being represented and characterized, we found that this concept is not new for the gamer's perceptions. Technological evolution has developed it, and it is portrayed as a social tool and a virtual reality promoter. It was also possible to understand confusion or lack of knowledge regarding the definition of the metaverse. However, central concepts such as virtual reality and gaming relations were identified, showing the awareness of their association with this concept.

These results are according to the concept's definition and categorizations since it unites socially immersive virtual realities with video games [16] and will transform social networks [35]. It is also considered an environment that merges physical and digital reality [36], and it can promote digital engagement, and mixes gaming, social networking, and virtual reality [37].

According to the results and our second objective, the technologies that stimulate the immersion experience may vary. Still, the gamer's perception shows us that a simple headphone can be crucial for immersion. It is also possible to see awareness of the technology as a keyboard, VR googles, or a monitor that leads to the understanding that the price or more evolved technology does not mean immersion. This leads us to the knowledge that the metaverse is available through different devices [37] with other characteristics.

Third, the main dimensions influencing the acceptance of the metaverse are the gaming world and virtual reality. And this is no surprise because the metaverse relies on a digital universe that mixes online gaming [34] or other gaming worlds [33]. Wellbeing, such as fun and relaxation, are precise dimensions that allow gamers to accept this concept. In a previous study, it was verified that the perceived pleasure is a relevant concept for accepting the metaverse [6].

These also lead to the fourth objective, understanding the perception of the metaverse and virtual reality regarding socialization and wellbeing. Our results show this by the participants when they refer to the metaverse as a socialization concept and socialization promoter (Tables 31 and 32) and by clearly stating that the metaverse creates more fun (Table 34), therefore, a supporter of wellbeing. In terms of the association of the metaverse and virtual reality, the participants stand out by affirming that metaverse is a virtual reality, which states a confusion or lack of knowledge regarding each concept definition, but most importantly, they made the two concepts as one and so they see these concepts as promoters of socialization and wellbeing.

Regarding the perceptions of a gamer's daily life regarding the metaverse, virtual reality, and gaming concepts, it was demonstrated that the daily lives of gamers are continuing to be impacted by the metaverse and virtual reality through the gaming world, because of their predisposition to accept digital transformation into their lives [4].

Looking at objective six, understanding the impact of representation on the gaming concept, the gamers have mentioned social representation regarding the metaverse, virtual reality, and the gaming world with no exception. They all promote individual or combined social communication. In the gaming world, because players enjoy playing with others [14], most video games are played with others [13] and allow bonding [15].

As for our last objective, to understand the perceived role of animation regarding the metaverse, virtual reality, and gaming concepts, we can see their uniqueness and straight relation. Animation, which allows a game to be possible, brings us portals between fantasy and reality, and reality and the social [61]. Animation and its colossal power to transform reality [6] joins virtual reality, providing the participant's experiences and an immersion environment in different forms [32]. In this sense, the gaming world has become the concept that allows the metaverse to emerge.

With our findings, it is understood that the metaverse concept is still to create its own boundaries or complete definitions. However, we can see that this concept relies on virtual reality, and games continue this evolution. This concept is characterized as a promoter of wellbeing, fun, relaxation, and socialization that can be achieved with more immersive experiences provided by technology or gaming characteristics.

In the near future, we consider it essential to continue exploring these concepts' relations and definitions using other methodologies, such as quantitative methods—developing case studies with different types of users/gamers (as long as the metaverse and metaworlds are more widespread in several contexts and daily practices).

5. Research Limitations

The number of focus group interviews made—more focus groups realize more that the data obtained could be considered significant. The fact that it was an online focus group meant that discussions could have reduced the nonverbal communication. However, in our study, we used software to record the video of the interviews, and all the participants were asked to use their cameras—after signing an informed consent, agreeing to participate in the study.

Another limitation could be the large or small number of questions depending on the perspective taken. Many questions become more exhaustive for the participants and, therefore, caused a lack of participation because of the time it takes. Fewer questions can probably promote better participation, but they may not cover all the themes. According to the participants' discussion, it also gives us more time for others that may arise. Nevertheless, the questions previously accorded are not the only ones that can be made depending on the discussion, and further questions can arise.

It is also important to mention that this study only has Portuguese gamers, and the findings could differ (or not) with a diverse population or nationality.

Finally, we have to refer to the knowledge, lack, or confusion regarding the definition of the concepts amongst the participants, which may vary according to other participants.

6. Conclusions

Since 1992, when Neal Stephenson proposed this concept, the metaverse has been gaining a space and relevance in our reality. It is something that, for some, is considered an old concept, perhaps because of its history or dependence on existing concepts such as gaming and virtual reality, and for others is considered something new, perhaps due to the novelty or greater attention that authors or companies have given it.

This concept has gained awareness even by the possible users or active users. However, it lacks an agreed definition by authors or even lacks boundaries since it is still evolving. This creates confusion between what is the metaverse and what is not by their users. Our findings demonstrated this vulnerability of the concept.

This exploratory study is of great importance because it allows us to access the perceptions of Portuguese gamers about this concept, showing that confusion and lack of boundaries percept exist between them. It is also important because, in the scientific world, a lot has been said regarding the metaverse concept. However, there is a lack of investigations focusing on what common people understand regarding this concept. It is also important because it can give the gaming and technology industry and scientific studies more knowledge about tendencies according to the common knowledge that will lead to how these concepts will evolve. After all, all these concepts evolve according to the needs and likes of the people.

Focusing on our research question, "How is the metaverse being percept and represented by gamers?", we verify that they represent it as something technological and social promoting, achieved by games through virtual reality experiences.

We can write a possible definition for this concept based on the participants' answers: The metaverse concept has been around for a long time because it is considered a game that allows immersive experiences through virtual reality technology, and the style and aesthetics of the animation provided. It is also an essential means of socialization and communication, at an individual level with its representations or a community level with general terms. It is also an essential promoter of the wellbeing of its users.

The metaverse still has much to be explored. Still, it already showed us the power of new means of communication through social networks, becoming a social realm where the power of communication is exercised, implemented, and has no limits. The only limit is the human ability to dream or to create things. So, this concept is also making its path in social media, becoming a form of mass self-communication [1].

Looking at the initial idea from Neal Stephenson (1992) until the present, we can see a clear evolution from a conceptual picture to a more eligible or tangible concept. It has gained some definition and importance on fields such as virtual reality and gaming, as well as being considered a new means of communication. Nevertheless, it still has a lot of objective boundaries and limits to explore.

Perhaps the metaverse will be something like the OASIS world in the Ready Player One movie in 2018, where we can be whatever we want, experience different realities in pursuing something different, fantastic, or a dream, hoping to be immersed in these new realms for some time believing that reality is a real thing.

Author Contributions: Conceptualization, M.C. and A.O.; methodology, M.C. and A.O.; validation, A.O.; investigation M.C.; resources, M.C.; data curation, M.C.; writing—original draft preparation, M.C., and A.O.; writing—review and editing, M.C. and A.O. and supervision A.O. All authors have read and agreed to the published version of the manuscript.

Funding: This research received no external funding.

Institutional Review Board Statement: Not applicable.

Informed Consent Statement: Informed consent was obtained from all subjects involved in the study.

Data Availability Statement: Not applicable.

Acknowledgments: Not applicable.

Conflicts of Interest: The authors declare no conflict of interest.

References

1. Castells, M. *Communication Power*; Oxford University Press: London, UK, 2009.
2. Chalmers, D.J. *Reality+: Virtual Worlds and the Problems of Philosophy*; Norton: New York, NY, USA, 2022.
3. Hamit, F. *Virtual Reality and the Exploration of Cyberspace*; SAMS Publishing: Carmel, IN, USA, 1993.
4. Kemeç, A. From Reality to Virtuality: Re-discussing Cities with the Concept of the Metaverse. *Int. J. Manag. Account.* **2022**, *4*, 12–20. [CrossRef]
5. Abbate, S.; Centobelli, P.; Cerchione, R.; Oropallo, E.; Riccio, E. A first bibliometric literature review on Metaverse. In Proceedings of the 2022 IEEE Technology and Engineering Management Conference (TEMSCON EUROPE), Izmir, Turkey, 25–29 April 2022; pp. 254–260. [CrossRef]
6. Cruz, M.; Oliveira, A.; Pinheiro, A. Flowing through Virtual Animated Worlds—Perceptions of the Metaverse. In Proceedings of the 2022 Euro-Asia Conference on Frontiers of Computer Science and Information Technology (FCSIT), Beijing, China, 16–18 December 2022; pp. 241–245. [CrossRef]
7. Miller, T. Gaming for Beginners. *Games Cult.* **2006**, *1*, 5–12. [CrossRef]
8. Burrows, G. *Your Life in the Metaverse*; Really Interesting Books: Torino, Italy, 2022.
9. Marczewski, A. *Even Ninja Monkeys Like to Play: Gamification, Game Thinking & Motivational Design*; Gamified UK: Addlestone, UK, 2015.
10. Sicart, M. *Play Matters, reprint ed.*; MIT Press: Cambridge, MA, USA; London, UK, 2017.
11. Madigan, J. *Getting Gamers: The Psychology of Video Games and Their Impact on the People Who Play Them, Reprint edição*; New Publisher: Lanham, MD, USA; London, UK, 2021.
12. Ross, E. *Filmish*; Self Made Hero: London, UK, 2015.
13. Isbister, K. *How Games Move Us (Playful Thinking): Emotion by Design*; reprint ed.; MIT Press: Cambridge, MA, USA; London, UK, 2017.
14. Mandryk, R.L.; Inkpen, K.M. Physiological Indicators for the Evaluation of Co-located Collaborative Play. In Proceedings of the CSCW04: Computer Supported Cooperative Work, Chicago, IL, USA, 6–10 November 2004; pp. 6–10. [CrossRef]
15. Macaranas, A.; Venolia, G.; Inkpen, K.; Tang, J. Sharing Experiences over Video: Watching Video Programs together at a Distance. In Proceedings of the Human-Computer Interaction–INTERACT 2013: 14th IFIP TC 13 International Conference, Cape Town, South Africa, 2–6 September 2013; Springer: Berlin/Heidelberg, Germany, 2013; pp. 73–90. [CrossRef]
16. Stenros, J.; Paavilainen, J.; Mäyrä, F. The Many Faces of Sociability and Social Play in Games. In Proceedings of the MindTrek '09: Academic MindTrek 2009, Tampere, Finland, 30 September–2 October 2009; pp. 82–89. [CrossRef]
17. Yoh, M.-S. The reality of virtual reality. In Proceedings of the Seventh International Conference on Virtual Systems and Multimedia, Berkeley, CA, USA, 25–27 October 2001; pp. 666–674. [CrossRef]
18. Heim, M. *Virtual Realism*; Oxford University Press: Oxford, UK, 2000.

19. Steuer, J. Defining Virtual Reality: Dimensions Determining Telepresence. *J. Commun.* **1992**, *42*, 73–93. [CrossRef]
20. Pan, Z.; Cheok, A.D.; Yang, H.; Zhu, J.; Shi, J. Virtual reality and mixed reality for virtual learning environments. *Comput. Graph.* **2006**, *30*, 20–28. [CrossRef]
21. Sherman, W.R.; Craig, A.B. *Understanding Virtual Reality: Interface, Application, and Design*; Morgan Kaufmann: Burlington, MA, USA, 2019.
22. Jian, S.; Chen, X.; Yan, J. From Online Games to "Metaverse": The Expanding Impact of Virtual Reality in Daily Life. In *Culture and Computing*; Rauterberg, M., Ed.; Lecture Notes in Computer Science; Springer International Publishing: Cham, Swizterland, 2022; pp. 34–43. [CrossRef]
23. Moran, A.; Gadepally, V.; Hubbell, M.; Kepner, J. Improving Big Data visual analytics with interactive virtual reality. In Proceedings of the 2015 IEEE High Performance Extreme Computing Conference (HPEC), Waltham, MA, USA, 15–17 September 2015; pp. 1–6. [CrossRef]
24. Zheng, J.; Chan, K.; Gibson, I. Virtual reality. *IEEE Potentials* **1998**, *17*, 20–23. [CrossRef]
25. Sanchez-Vives, M.V.; Slater, M. From presence to consciousness through virtual reality. *Nat. Rev. Neurosci.* **2005**, *6*, 332–339. [CrossRef] [PubMed]
26. Júnior, A.L. *A Arte da Animação*; Senac: Lisboa, Portugal, 2005.
27. Burke, T.; Burke, K. *Saturday Morning Fever*; St. Martin's Griffin: New York, NY, USA, 1999. Available online: http://archive.org/details/saturdaymorningf00burk (accessed on 20 October 2022).
28. Selby, A. *Animation*; Portfolio: London, UK, 2013.
29. Denis, S. *O Cinema de Animação*; Edições Texto&Grafia: São Paulo, Brazil, 2007.
30. Bush, A.J.; Hair, J.F., Jr.; Bush, R.P. A Content Analysis of Animation in Television Advertising. *J. Advert.* **1983**, *12*, 20–41. [CrossRef]
31. Ball, M. *THE METAVERSE: And How it Will Revolutionize Everything*; W W NORTON & CO: New York, NY, USA, 2022.
32. Alang, N. Opinion | Facebook Wants to Move to "The Metaverse"—Here's What That Is, and Why You Should Be Worried', thestar.com, 23 October 2021. Available online: https://www.thestar.com/business/opinion/2021/10/23/facebook-wants-to-move-to-the-metaverse-heres-what-that-is-and-why-you-should-be-worried.html (accessed on 5 February 2023).
33. Damar, M. Metaverse Shape of Your Life for Future: A bibliometric snapshot. *J. Metaverse* **2021**, *1*, 1–8.
34. Mitchell, A.; Murphy, J.; Owens, D.; Khazanchi, D.; Zigurs, I. Avatars, People, and Virtual Worlds: Foundations for Research in Metaverses. *JAIS* **2009**, *10*, 90–117. [CrossRef]
35. Hendaoui, A.; Limayem, M.; Thompson, C.W. 3D Social Virtual Worlds: Research Issues and Challenges. *IEEE Internet Comput.* **2008**, *12*, 88–92. [CrossRef]
36. Mystakidis, S. Metaverse. *Encyclopedia* **2022**, *2*, 486–497. [CrossRef]
37. Ramesh, U.V.; Harini, A.; Gowri, C.S.D.; Durga, K.V.; Druvitha, P.; Kumar, K.S. Metaverse: Future of the Internet. *Int. J. Res.* **2022**, *3*, 93–97.
38. Silverman, D. *Interpreting Qualitative Data*, 6th ed.; SAGE Publications Ltd.: Thousand Oaks, CA, USA, 2019.
39. Silverman, D. *Qualitative Research*, 5th ed.; SAGE Publications Ltd.: Thousand Oaks, CA, USA, 2021.
40. Acocella, I.; Cataldi, S. *Using Focus Groups: Theory, Methodology, Practice*; Sage: London, UK, 2021.
41. Morgan, D.L. *Sucessful Focus Group*; Sage: London, UK, 1993.
42. Blumer, H. *Symbolic Interactionism: Perspective and Method*; University of California Press: Berkeley, CA, USA; Los Angeles, CA, USA; London, UK, 2009.
43. Bloor, M.; Frankland, J.; Thomas, M.; Robson, K. *Focus Groups in Social Research*; Sage: London, UK, 2002.
44. Krueger, R.A. *Focus Group*; Sage: London, UK, 1994.
45. Kitzinger, J.; Barbour, R.S. Introduction: The challenge and Promise of Focus Groups. In *Developing Focus Group Research: Politics, Theory and Practice*; Sage: London, UK, 1999; pp. 1–20. [CrossRef]
46. Lunt, P.; Livingstone, S. Rethinking the Focus Group in Media and Communications Research. *J. Commun.* **1996**, *46*, 79–98. [CrossRef]
47. Zenari, V. Barbour, R. (2007). Doing Focus Groups; London: SAGE Publications. 174 pp. ISBN 978-0-7619-4978-7. *Can. J. Action Res.* **2014**, *15*, 65–66. [CrossRef]
48. Flick, U. *An Introduction to Qualitative Research*, 7th ed.; SAGE Publications Ltd.: Thousand Oaks, CA, USA, 2022.
49. Stewart, D.W.; Shamdasani, P. Online Focus Groups. *J. Advert.* **2017**, *46*, 48–60. [CrossRef]
50. Lobe, B. Best Practices for Synchronous Online Focus Groups. In *A New Era in Focus Group Research: Challenges, Innovation and Practice*; Barbour, R.S., Morgan, D.L., Eds.; Palgrave Macmillan: London, UK, 2017; pp. 227–250. [CrossRef]
51. Liamputtong, P. *Focus Group Methodology: Principles and Practice*; Sage: London, UK, 2011. [CrossRef]
52. Joinson, A.N. Self-disclosure in computer-mediated communication: The role of self-awareness and visual anonymity. *Eur. J. Soc. Psychol.* **2001**, *31*, 177–192. [CrossRef]
53. Matthews, K.L.; Baird, M.; Duchesne, G. Using Online Meeting Software to Facilitate Geographically Dispersed Focus Groups for Health Workforce Research. *Qual. Health Res.* **2018**, *28*, 1621–1628. [CrossRef]
54. Patton, M.Q. *Qualitative Evaluation and Research Methods*; SAGE Publications: London, UK, 1990.
55. Silverman, D. *Doing Qualitative Research*, 6th ed.; SAGE Publications Ltd.: Thousand Oaks, CA, USA, 2022.

56. Kriukow, J. Sample Size in Qualitative Research—Qualitative Researcher Dr Kriukow. Available online: https://drkriukow.com/sample-size-in-qualitative-research/ (accessed on 29 June 2023).
57. Sample Size in Qualitative Research, (23 April 2019). Available online: https://www.youtube.com/watch?v=2JeGo3r21vw (accessed on 29 June 2023).
58. Gobo, G. The SAGE Handbook of Social Research Methods. In *The SAGE Handbook of Social Research Methods*; SAGE Publications Ltd.: London, UK, 2008; pp. 193–213. [CrossRef]
59. Guest, G.; Namey, E.; McKenna, K. How Many Focus Groups Are Enough? Building an Evidence Base for Nonprobability Sample Sizes. *Field Methods* **2016**, *29*, 3–22. [CrossRef]
60. Hennink, M.M.; Kaiser, B.; Weber, M.B. What Influences Saturation? Estimating Sample Sizes in Focus Group Research. *Qual. Health Res.* **2019**, *29*, 1483–1496. [CrossRef] [PubMed]
61. Cruz, M.; Oliveira, A.; Esmerado, J. Animation and adults: Between the virtual and social reality. In Proceedings of the Sistemas e Tecnologias de Informação/Information Systems and Technologies—Atas da 12a Conferência Ibérica de Sistemas e Tecnologias de Informação/2017 12th Iberian Conference on Information Systems and Technologies (CISTI), Lisbon, Portugal, 21–24 June 2017; Rocha, Á., Alturas, B., Costa, C., Reis, L.P., Eds.; pp. 55–60. [CrossRef]

applied sciences

MDPI

Article

Predicting Adherence to Home-Based Cardiac Rehabilitation with Data-Driven Methods

Dimitris Filos [1,*], Jomme Claes [2], Véronique Cornelissen [2], Evangelia Kouidi [3] and Ioanna Chouvarda [1,*]

1 Laboratory of Computing, Medical Informatics and Biomedical Imaging Technologies, Aristotle University of Thessaloniki, 54124 Thessaloniki, Greece
2 Department of Rehabilitation Sciences, University of Leuven, 3000 Leuven, Belgium; jomme.claes@kuleuven.be (J.C.); veronique.cornelissen@kuleuven.be (V.C.)
3 Laboratory of Sports Medicine, Department of Physical Education and Sport Science, Aristotle University of Thessaloniki, 54124 Thessaloniki, Greece; kouidi@phed.auth.gr
* Correspondence: dimfilos@auth.gr (D.F.); ioannach@auth.gr (I.C.)

Abstract: Cardiac rehabilitation (CR) focuses on the improvement of health or the prevention of further disease progression after an event. Despite the documented benefits of CR programs, the participation remains suboptimal. Home-based CR programs have been proposed to improve uptake and adherence. The goal of this study was to apply an end-to-end methodology including machine learning techniques to predict the 6-month adherence of cardiovascular disease (CVD) patients to a home-based telemonitoring CR program, combining patients' clinical information with their actual program participation during a short familiarization phase. Fifty CVD patients participated in such a program for 6 months, enabling personalized guidance during a phase III CR study. Clinical, fitness, and psychological data were measured at baseline, whereas actual adherence, in terms of weekly exercise session duration and patient heart rate, was measured using wearables. Hierarchical clustering was used to identify different groups based on (1) patients' clinical baseline characteristics, (2) exercise adherence during the familiarization phase, and (3) the whole program adherence, whereas the output of the clustering was determined using repetitive decision trees (DTs) and random forest (RF) techniques to predict long-term adherence. Finally, for each cluster of patients, network analysis was applied to discover correlations of their characteristics that link to adherence. Based on baseline characteristics, patients were clustered into three groups, with differences in behavior and risk factors, whereas adherent, non-adherent, and transient adherent patients were identified during the familiarization phase. Regarding the prediction of long-term adherence, the most common DT showed higher performance compared with RF (precision: 80.2 ± 19.5% and 71.8 ± 25.8%, recall: 94.5 ± 14.5% and 71.8 ± 25.8% for DT and RF accordingly). The analysis of the DT rules and the analysis of the feature importance of the RF model highlighted the significance of non-adherence during the familiarization phase, as well as that of the baseline characteristics to predict future adherence. Network analysis revealed different relationships in different clusters of patients and the interplay between their behavioral characteristics. In conclusion, the main novelty of this study is the application of machine learning techniques combining patient characteristics before the start of the home-based CR programs with data during a short familiarization phase, which can predict long-term adherence with high accuracy. The data used in this study are available through connected health technologies and standard measurements in CR; thus, the proposed methodology can be generalized to other telerehabilitation programs and help healthcare providers to improve patient-tailored enrolment strategies and resource allocation.

Keywords: adherence; cardiac rehabilitation; machine learning; prediction; exercise; home-based; familiarization phase; telemonitoring

Citation: Filos, D.; Claes, J.; Cornelissen, V.; Kouidi, E.; Chouvarda, I. Predicting Adherence to Home-Based Cardiac Rehabilitation with Data-Driven Methods. *Appl. Sci.* **2023**, *13*, 6120. https://doi.org/10.3390/app13106120

Academic Editors: Marley M.B.R. Vellasco and Luigi Bibbò

Received: 7 April 2023
Revised: 15 May 2023
Accepted: 15 May 2023
Published: 16 May 2023

1. Introduction

Cardiovascular diseases (CVDs) constitute one of the major health problems in Europe, accounting for about 45% of all causes of death, and with a continuously increasing prevalence [1]. This high incidence and prevalence of CVD leads to a high personal health burden and places a huge burden on society, with EUR 210 billion/year spent on the management of CVD [2]. Considerable differences in prevalence are observed between European countries, mainly associated with the prevalence of several risk factors, such as smoking, obesity, diabetes, and physical inactivity.

Physical activity has been recognized to have a beneficial effect on the prevention of CVD. Therefore, exercise training is a central part of secondary prevention programs, referred to as "cardiac rehabilitation" (CR) [3]. Based on the clinical guidelines [3], moderate exercise for at least 150 min per week and behavioral changes towards a less sedentary lifestyle can reduce cardiovascular risk factors. The WHO [4] defines adherence as the extent to which a person's behavior (e.g., lifestyle changes) corresponds with current recommendations. Adherence to physical activity can be quantified in several ways [5]. In general, adherence to lifestyle changes has been recognized as a crucial component towards better management of patients with chronic disease, but this goal is rarely achieved [6,7]. However, despite the beneficial effects of CR, participation rates remain low, with less than 40% of eligible patients attending CR programs [8,9]. Low socioeconomic status, age, gender, the proximity to a CR center, and behavioral aspects such as lack of motivation and reduced self-efficacy have been identified [9] as the main barriers to CR participation.

In order to overcome the aforementioned barriers and increase both uptake and adherence to CR, home-based telerehabilitation services have been developed, considering the advances in technology and the Internet of things (IoT) [10]. Indeed, telerehabilitation programs have proven to be a safe and effective approach to managing heart failure (HF) patients [11]. In a meta-analysis by Claes [12], it was found that center-based and home-based CR had equal effects on exercise capacity, while others found equal effects on quality of life (QoL) and cost-effectiveness [13].

One major advantage of modern telerehabilitation services is the personalized guidance that they offer, which is facilitated by the availability of low-cost and unobtrusive devices that integrate various sensors that are useful for the quantification of exercise response [11]. For example, accelerometry data can be used to evaluate the volume of exercise, heart rate sensors are able to capture exercise intensity, and geolocation services allow for the estimation of walking distance. However, the plethora of available devices also leads to a large heterogeneity in intervention design, ranging from motivational messages [14] to telephone counseling [15] or personalized real-time adaptation of exercise sessions [16].

However, the problem of non-adherence is also apparent in home-based or self-management interventions [17], where significant variations in the levels of adherence have been reported compared to center-based CR programs. Several RCTs [18] and meta-analyses [19,20] have reported that patient-centered approaches show an improvement in patient adherence to CR programs. However, most of these studies were observational and used subjective information and self-reports to quantify adherence [21].

Both patient-related factors and intervention design could be addressed to increase adherence [22]. In a systematic review, it was found that both the program characteristics and personal factors, including health and cognition status, influence adherence to exercise programs [23]. Essery et al. [21] presented a list of factors that are associated with adherence to home-based physical therapies, where it was reported that the perception of health status, self-motivation, or current physical activity level presents a strong positive association with adherence, while daily stress has a strong negative association with it. On the other hand, the incorporation of data-driven or rule-based models can guide decisions, leading to improved adherence [24].

It would be beneficial to integrate objective patient information from a short period of time to predict long-term adherence to exercise and, thus, proceed with appropriate targeted modifications and better use of resources. In [25] the Discontinuation Prediction

Score (DiPS) was introduced, which compares each week's average steps with those of the first week of the program. It can be used to score the probability of dropping out from exercise programs during the week. The prediction model used objectively collected physical activity data from 210 physically inactive women aged 25 to 69 years, and it applied logistic regression and support-vector machines to predict the DiPS. As found, the adherence rate decreased as the program progressed, whereas daily steps at the start of the program and the steps measured during the previous week were significant predictors of DiPS. In a study performed by [26], three different clusters of participants were created based on basic individual characteristics and training data collected during the first three months of the application's use. Deep learning techniques were applied for the prediction of adherence to exercise during the fourth month of the program. Finally, [27] applied data-characteristics-based long short-term memory (DC-LSTM) recurrent neural networks (RNNs) to predict outdoor physical activity, taking into account patient profiles and environmental characteristics, such as weather, temperature, and humidity. However, in all of these studies, the focus was on the short-term prediction. It would be beneficial to identify the patients who are likely to be non-adherent at an early stage of the program, so as to modify the motivation strategies and to use the resources efficiently. In a previous study performed by our research group, adherence to a short familiarization period for home-based CR was combined with clinical characteristics to predict future adherence [28]. A support-vector machine (SVM) classifier was trained using the most significant features. However, in that study, only those patients who could clearly be considered to be adherent or non-adherent during the familiarization phase were included. This resulted in the exclusion of a considerable number of patients who were moderately adherent, hindering the generalization of the method and results.

In this paper, we hypothesize that a predictive model based on machine learning techniques, which integrates (i) patient clinical characteristics, (ii) data from self-reports, and (iii) objective physical activity information gathered during a short familiarization phase, can predict longer-term adherence to a home-based CR program for CVD patients. Therefore, the specific aims of this study were as follows: (1) to cluster patients into distinct groups based on the adherence to the system during a 6-week familiarization period, (2) to investigate significant differences between the groups during the aforementioned period, and (3) to implement a model that could predict the use of the system during a 6-month CR program. Following a data-driven approach, while adherence prediction was considered to be a discrete problem (N classes), the number of classes was not predefined but, rather, identified during the analysis pipeline via clustering. Finally, the predictive model needed to be explainable so that it could be used by the clinical experts to better support patients in adhering to home-based CR or to search for other CR alternatives if predicted adherence to home-based CR was low.

2. Materials and Methods

The graphical overview of the proposed methodology is depicted in Figure 1. Each part of the figure is described in detail in the following section. In brief, the implementation of the predictive model was based on data collected from patients with CVD. Different types of data are available, including clinical data and actual usage of the system based on smartwatches. Unsupervised learning methods, such as hierarchical and spectral clustering, were used, and the patients were grouped into different groups. Machine learning techniques were applied in order to predict long-term adherence to telerehabilitation programs. Finally, network analysis was performed in order to identify relationships between the features.

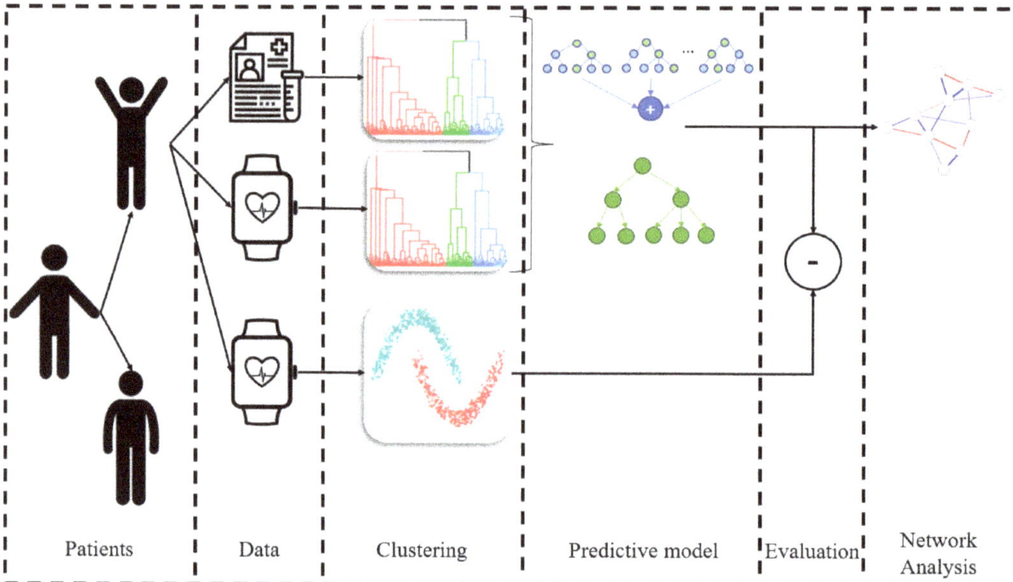

Figure 1. Graphical overview of the proposed approach. Each part of the graph is described in detail in the following sections.

2.1. Data Description

This study uses data that were collected during the PATHway-I trial [16]—a single-blinded randomized control trial (RCT) involving 120 patients that were randomized into a usual care group and an intervention group, on a 1:1 basis. Given the scope of the present study, only the patients from the intervention group were included in this analysis.

In brief, the Physical Activity Towards Health (PATHway) was a home-based CR platform that aimed to empower patients towards self-management of their CVD [16]. It combined gamified approaches (ExerClass/ExerGames), e-coaching, and outdoor activities such as jogging or bicycling, to promote an active and healthy lifestyle according to standard clinical guidelines [29]. Clinical evaluation performed before the start of the CR program assisted clinical experts to set personalized goals and exercise intensities for the patients. Heart rate (HR), captured by smartwatches using Microsoft Band (which measures HR accurately [30]), along with subjective information from questionnaires, allowed for the continuous monitoring and adaptation of the program based on patient performance and preferences, in both the short- and longer-term horizons. In brief, the short-term horizon aimed to guide the patient during the ExerClass/ExerGame sessions to exercise within the personalized beneficial HR zone. This was followed by the provision of a variety of aerobic or resistance exercises of different levels of intensity or difficulty and targeting different body parts. On the other hand, the customization of the exercise program on a weekly basis aimed to improve patients' exercise adherence to the program. A decision support system (DSS) integrated this patient information with clinical guidelines, and experts' knowledge was developed to achieve this goal [24]. Finally, a notification module was included, aiming to provide tailored messages to the patients to maintain their engagement with the PATHway system [31].

Patients randomized to the intervention group participated in a familiarization phase to become acquainted with the home-based CR intervention. During the first 4 weeks, the patient was guided by experts on how to use the PATHway system. To evaluate the adherence to the exercise program, observation of patient behavior without additional supervision was valuable in evaluating adherence to the exercise program. In this respect, an additional 2-week period was considered, where the patient used the system without supervision by an expert. Thus, the total duration of the familiarization phase was 6 weeks, and it represented approximately 20% of the whole program's duration (Figure 2). Patients with a median duration of exercise sessions per week equal to zero were considered to be absent from the program and were excluded from further analysis.

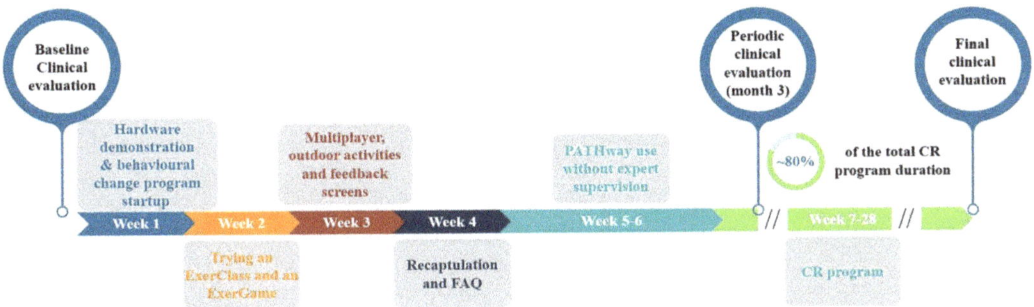

Figure 2. Timeline for the intervention study's structure.

2.1.1. Data from Baseline and Periodic Clinical Evaluation

A plethora of data were collected during baseline and at 3 months and 6 months after the start of the intervention. The data were categorized into three main categories:

1. *Cardiovascular Risk Profile*: These markers were collected through blood sampling and anthropometric measurements. The Framingham cardiovascular risk score was calculated as described in [32].
2. *Health-Related Physical Fitness*: These data represent the findings from a maximally graded cardiopulmonary exercise test (CPET) on a bicycle, along with muscle strength testing including maximal isometric and isokinetic quadriceps strength, handgrip strength, and a 30 s sit-to-stand test.
3. *Psychological wellbeing and intervention effectiveness*: This subjective information was collected using standardized questionnaires assessing QoL [33], physical activity behavior [34–36], smoking, alcohol consumption [37], diet [38], stress [39], medication adherence [40], mental wellbeing [41], social support [42], self-efficacy [43], and perceived health status [44,45].

In total, 59 features were measured at baseline and 6-month follow-up, while 52 of these features were collected at 3-month follow-up. A detailed overview of the collected data has been published previously [16,46].

2.1.2. Exercise Session Data

During the execution of the exercise session, the duration of the session was captured either automatically in the case of ExerClass/ExerGames or synchronized later when the patient exercised outdoors. Independent of the type of session (ExerClass/ExerGame or outdoor activity), the heart rate of each patient was captured by the smartwatch, with a sampling frequency of 1 Hz. These data were used to quantify patient performance and adherence to the exercise program.

Exercise Adherence Metric

The adherence to the system was assessed in terms of the mean duration of exercise sessions performed each week. In more detail, the adherence to the exercise program in week i was measured as follows:

$$adher[i] = SessDuration[i]/Nsessions[i] \quad (1)$$

In Equation (1), SessDuration is the total duration of the exercise session performed during week I, while Nsessions is the total number of sessions for that week. SessDuration was measured automatically in the case of indoor activity with the PATHway system, while in the case of outdoor activity the patient started and ended the recording of the session. Since it could be possible that a patient forgot to stop the recording, the maximum value for SessDuration [i] was set to be equal to 120 min. In addition, sessions with a duration of less than 10 min were also excluded from the analysis, as they were characterized as invalid activities [46].

Exercise Performance Metric

According to [29], a patient must exercise above a minimal HR threshold to achieve health benefits, which is defined as 40% of the maximum HR measured during a cardiopulmonary exercise test (CPET). Thus, HRlower is defined as follows:

$$HRlower = 0.4 * HRpeak \tag{2}$$

where $HRpeak$ is the maximum HR measured during baseline CPET. To quantify patient performance, the $HRtime$ was estimated as the percentage of time that the HR was greater than $HRlower$.

In addition, the $HRmean$ for the kth session was calculated as follows:

$$HRmean[k] = \frac{1}{n}\sum_{i=1}^{n} HRsig(i) \tag{3}$$

where n is the total number of samples of the $HRsig$ signal during the session, and $HRnorm$ was measured as follows:

$$HRnorm = (HRmean/HRpeak) * 100 \tag{4}$$

This reflects the percentage of the mean session HR with respect to the maximum possible value. These metrics provide averaged values of the subject's HR and, therefore, are not significantly affected by any artifacts or low signal accuracy that may occur due to the exercise.

2.2. *Investigation of Different Patient Clusters at Baseline*

The patients that attended the home-based CR programs presented different profiles with regard to their exercise behavior or their clinical characteristics. Thus, the first step towards implementing a model that could predict future adherence to the program was to categorize the patients into different clusters. In this study, the clustering was based on (1) the characteristics collected before the start of the program, (2) the adherence to the program during the familiarization phase, and (3) the adherence to the whole 6-month exercise program.

2.2.1. Clustering Baseline Profiles

Hierarchical clustering was used to categorize the patients into different groups based on their baseline characteristics (Table 1). Hierarchical clustering is an algorithm that groups objects with similar characteristics into a tree-like hierarchy [47]. The main advantage of hierarchical clustering is that it is easy to interpret, as the dendrograms provide visual information on the observations and the clusters to which they belong at each level of detail. In the present study, the number of clusters was selected based on the one that maximized the silhouette value [48].

Table 1. Statistically significant differences between the Present and Absent groups during baseline, and differences between the start and the end of the CR program.

	Present	Absent	*p*-Value
		Baseline	
BARSE	67.361 ± 22.5	53.93 ± 16.6	0.043
Sedentary time (min)	752.53 ± 98.3	677.89 ± 55.1	0.016
Light activity time (min/day)	559.88 ± 80.87	620.78 ± 50.54	0.035
		Baseline–6 months	
BMI (kg/m^2)	0.037 ± 1.08	1.21 ± 1.84	0.022
Waist circumference (cm)	−2.06 ± 5.25	2.77 ± 4.24	0.014
Triglycerides (mmol/L)	−0.029 ± 0.67	0.48 ± 0.72	0.028
pLoad (Watt)	−0.122 ± 25.4	−14.44 ± 18.1	0.028

BARSE = barriers self-efficacy scale; BMI = body mass index; pLoad = peak load achieved during CPET.

2.2.2. Clustering Familiarization Adherence Behavior

The clustering of the patients was based on the mean duration of exercise sessions performed each week (*adher*) during the 6 weeks of the familiarization phase. In this respect, for each patient, the *adher* value for each of the 6 weeks was computed, and hierarchical clustering was applied. Maximum silhouette values were used to identify the optimal number of clusters.

2.2.3. Clustering whole-Program Adherence Behavior

The adherence for the whole 28-week period of the program was based on *adher*, which was calculated for the period after the familiarization phase; thus, 22 weeks were used to cluster the patients. However, the fact that the number of features was comparable to the number of patients included in the study (approximately 1:2) made the hierarchical clustering inefficient, as this method is prone to outliers [47]. For this reason, spectral clustering was applied to categorize the patients into different groups [49]. A self-tuning kernel [50] was used, and the number of diffusion iterations was set to 18.

2.3. *Predictive Modeling for Whole-Program Adherence Prediction*

A decision classification tree was built to predict the adherence to the exercise program. Decision trees are unsupervised learning algorithms that are often used in multilabel classification [51]. The main advantage of their use, apart from their good performance, is their interpretability, as they allow for the visualization of the model in terms of rules. The data used for the model's development were (1) the clusters of patients that were created based on the baseline characteristics, and (2) the clusters related to the adherence to the exercise program during the familiarization phase.

Because of the small sample size, we ran the model 100 times with different combinations of training and test datasets. Each time, the whole dataset was split into training and testing subsets, at a 9:1 ratio.

The minimum number of observations that should exist in each node of the tree to attempt a split was set to 4, and 10 cross-validations were carried out. For the implementation of the model, the "rpart" R package was used [52]

For each of the 100 models, the performance of the classification was measured using precision (*Prec*), recall (*Rec*), and accuracy (*ACC*), which were defined as follows:

$$Prec = \frac{TP}{TP + FP} \tag{5}$$

$$Rec = \frac{TP}{TP + FN} \tag{6}$$

$$ACC = \frac{TP + TN}{TP + TN + FP + FN} \tag{7}$$

where TP, TN, FP, and FN are the true positive, true negative, false positive, and false negative, respectively. The adherent group was selected to be the positive group. The frequency of each model was calculated, and the mean performance metrics were extracted.

However, one of the main drawbacks of decision trees is instability, especially in cases where the sample size is small; thus, minor changes in the training dataset can lead to modifications in the tree. Therefore, a random forest (RF) technique was applied, which is more stable and robust. An RF uses voting techniques to aggregate tree-structured classifiers into a single classifier [53]. A 10-fold cross-validation was applied, and 100 runs of the RF were used to extract the most important features and the performance metrics $Prec$, Rec, and ACC.

2.4. Statistical Differences between the Groups

The Kruskal–Wallis non-parametric statistical test was used to investigate the existence of significant differences among the groups of patients, as well as to identify any significant differences between different time periods, since this test is more robust when the sample size is small [54]. In this case, the analysis was based on the computation of the differences between the two time periods. In all cases, the probability threshold was set to 0.05, to consider statistically significant differences.

Spearman's rank correlation coefficient ρ was used to estimate the rank association between the variables, and it was computed as follows:

$$\rho = \frac{cov(R(x), R(Y))}{\sigma_{R(X)}\sigma_{R(Y)}} \tag{8}$$

where $R(X_i)$ and $R(Y_i)$ are the ranks of the variables X_i and Y_i, respectively, cov is the covariance, and $\sigma_{R(X)}$ and $\sigma_{R(Y)}$ are the standard deviation of $R(X)$ and $R(Y)$, respectively. This measure is non-parametric and is recommended when the data do not necessarily come from a normal distribution.

2.5. Network Analysis Per Group

Network research aims to understand how a process works and identify the system components as well as the statistical relations between them, with the former being represented as the nodes of the system and the latter as links between the nodes [55]. Following this systems medicine approach [56], psychological networks have been widely used in recent years to conceptualize the interplay of different components of human behavior [57].

In this study, a network analysis was performed to identify the network structure for each group of patients based on their baseline characteristics, their adherence during the familiarization phase, and their adherence to the whole program. The data previously used for the creation of the clusters related to the baseline characteristics and the adherence during the familiarization phase were also used to create the networks. For the network analysis of adherence to the whole exercise program, both types of data were considered. However, in all cases, only features that presented statistically significant differences between the clusters using the Kruskal–Wallis test were used for the creation of the networks. In addition, for a more accurate estimation of the networks, the number of nodes had to be less than the number of members of the group. Therefore, the features were ordered based on the p-values calculated using the Kruskal–Wallis test, and only the most significant were included in the analysis.

The network analysis was implemented in R, using the "glasso" package [58] based on [59] for LASSO regularization. In more detail, the Gaussian graphical model (GGM) [60] was estimated using "glasso" and EBIC model selection, since it has been found that this combination works well in retrieving the correct network structure [61]. To assess the importance of the nodes in the network structure, three measures were used: *node strength* and *closeness* quantify how well a node is directly or indirectly connected to others, respectively, while *betweenness* quantifies the node's importance in the average path between two other nodes [57].

Regarding the metrics that were captured during the session (*adher*, *HRnorm*, and *HRtime*), temporal networks were created using the "graphicalVAR" package [62]. The number of LASSO tuning parameters that were tested was set to 50.

3. Results

3.1. Absent Versus Present Patients during Familiarization

From the 50 patients that were included in the intervention group (after the exclusion of the patients who dropped out), 9 of them were considered to be absent (*Absent* group) from the exercise program, since they exercised very sparsely, i.e., their median weekly duration of exercise sessions during the familiarization phase, as well as in the following weeks, was zero minutes. Therefore, they were excluded from further analysis; thus, 41 patients were included in the *Present* group.

It was found that *Absent* had a lower score on the BARSE questionnaire, which measures the subjects' perceived capabilities to exercise three times per week for at least 40 min over the next two months [35]. In addition, the *Absent* patients had a lower sedentary time and a higher light activity time during baseline testing (Table 1). These findings suggest that *Absent* patients were feeling capable of engaging in enough physical activity by themselves, and they considered that they did not need the telerehabilitation system to become more active.

While the *Absent* patients were not further studied in the next sections, it is worth noting their differences with the *Present* group regarding their clinical characteristics after the 6-month intervention period. It was found that *Present* patients reduced their waist circumference, while their BMI, triglyceride levels, and peak load during the CPET remained stable. In contrast, the *Absent* patients had increased BMI, waist circumference, and triglyceride levels, and a reduced peak load during CPET. These findings suggest that exercise had a slightly positive effect on patients who participated in the CR program.

Finally, based on the observation of the exercise behavior in terms of the number of sessions performed as well as their duration, it was found that the patients who were characterized as absent during the familiarization phase continued to remain inactive during the rest of the program (Figure 3). The statistical analysis of the mean duration of the sessions each week revealed the existence of statistically significant differences between the groups—mainly during the first half of the 6-month program.

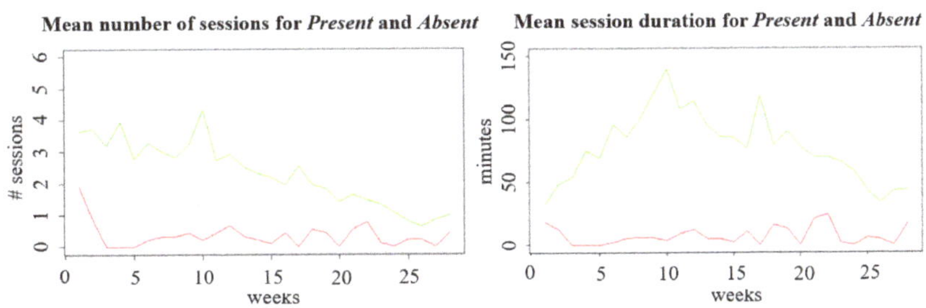

Figure 3. Evolution of the number of sessions (**left**) and the mean session duration (**right**) for the present (green) and absent (red) patients. Regarding the mean session duration (**right**), statistically significant differences were found for weeks 1 to 11, 13, 17, 20, and 24. The character # means number of sessions.

3.2. Patient Profile Clusters

The hierarchical clustering resulted in the creation of different clusters of *Present* patients considering their baseline characteristics and their exercise behavior during the familiarization period. More details are provided in the following sections.

3.2.1. Clusters Based on Clinical Baseline Characteristics

Three clusters of patients were found to maximize the silhouette value, using hierarchical clustering analysis on the baseline characteristics. Cluster 1 included 5 patients, while 15 and 21 patients were included in Clusters 2 and 3, respectively. The use of the Kruskal–Wallis test revealed statistically significant differences between the three clusters (Table 2).

Table 2. Baseline clinical characteristics that presented statistically significant differences between the three groups of patients ($p < 0.05$). The values are presented as the mean value ± standard deviation.

	Cluster 1	Cluster 2	Cluster 3
	Low-Risk & Active	**High-Risk & Sedentary**	**High-Risk & Fit**
Glucose (mmol/L)	4.71 ± 0.5	6.04 ± 1.81	5.81 ± 1.04
Risk score (%)	6.16 ± 5.9	18.65 ± 10.43	16.79 ± 10.035
BARSE	81.23 ± 11.1	75.13 ± 17.63	58.43 ± 24.39
PSS	13 ± 7.5	7.73 ± 5.34	12.48 ± 6.129
PACE	4.5 ± 1.7	4.5 ± 1.85	3.12 ± 1.387
Illness perception	38.2 ± 13.74	24.13 ± 12.69	34.1 ± 13.37
SF-36 mental	78.19 ± 15.14	83.36 ± 14.65	74.18 ± 14.17
EE (kcal)	1576 ± 639.62	1115.4 ± 187.27	1583.62 ± 395.35
MVPA (min)	229.4 ± 46.39	77.2 ± 29.46	132.43 ± 41.3
Steps (n)	16720 ± 767.8	8994.93 ± 903.62	13,173.14 ± 1475.88
30 s STS (n)	23 ± 3.24	16.53 ± 4.29	19.29 ± 4.69
Sedentary time (min)	655.6 ± 35.84	840.93 ± 67.96	712.48 ± 76.99
Quadriceps isokinetic (J)	1636.38 ± 314.61	1885.51 ± 849.03	2378.82 ± 576.13
Quadriceps isometric (Nm)	107.2 ± 26.33	142.4 ± 51.32	156.79 ± 38.1

BARSE = barriers self-efficacy scale; PSS = perceived stress scale; PACE = physical activity questionnaire; SF-36 = short-form 36; EE = energy expenditure; MVPA = moderate-to-vigorous physical activity; STS = sit-to-stand.

As shown in Table 2, Cluster 1 included patients with lower cardiovascular risk compared to the patients from the other clusters. Those patients were confident that they could exercise regularly (BARSE), and this was reflected in a higher daily number of steps and lower sedentary time. The opposite behavior was observed in the patients included in Cluster 2. Those patients were more sedentary and less physically active, as reflected by lower daily levels of MVPA and steps. In addition, they had the lowest PSS scores and the highest BARSE scores, glucose levels, and cardiovascular risk. Finally, the third and largest cluster included patients who were active, as they achieved the recommended guidelines for daily steps and MVPA, and their muscular strength was the highest compared with the other groups. However, these patients were less confident that they could exercise regularly, and they had the lowest scores in the PACE survey, which captures the attainment of physical activity guidelines. For these reasons, Cluster 1 is referred to as "Low-Risk", Cluster 2 as "High-Risk", and Cluster 3 as "Average-Baseline".

3.2.2. Clusters of Patient Adherence during Familiarization

Three clusters were identified based on the hierarchical clustering, with 12, 24, and 5 patients to be included in each cluster. The observation and the statistical analysis of the mean *adher* values revealed information regarding the exercise behavior of the patients in each group. As shown in Figure 4, during the first two weeks, the patients from all of the clusters presented similar behavior as they attended the demonstration sessions, and they performed one ExerClass or ExerGame.

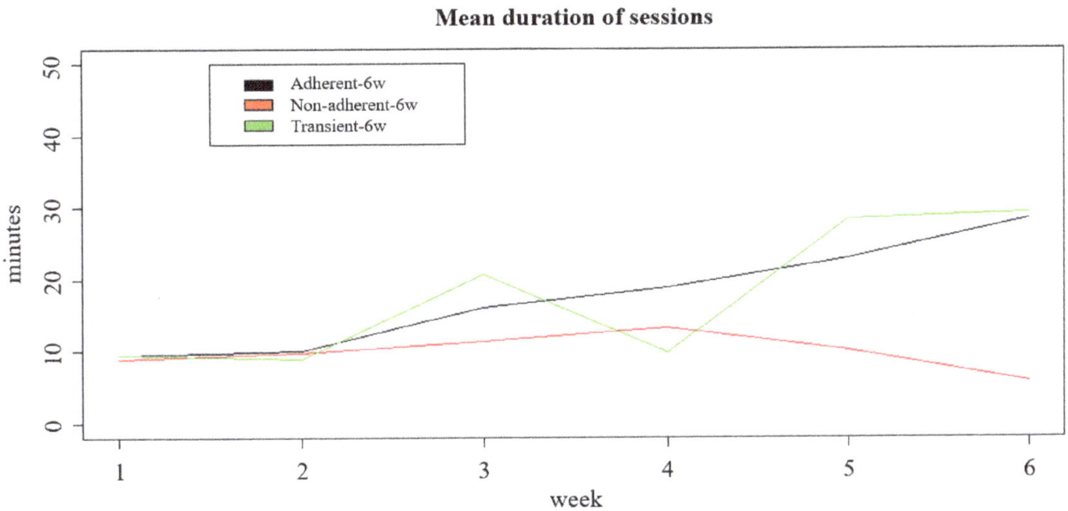

Figure 4. Evolution of mean *adher* values for the patients included in each cluster.

Slight differences are observed for the following 2 weeks, where the demonstration of the systems was performed. However, the observation of the *p*-values after the application of the Kruskal–Wallis test also revealed a continuous decrease, with the differences being statistically significant in the last two weeks of the familiarization phase, where the patients used the system at their homes, without any supervision (Table 3). Patients from Cluster 1 presented a continuous and gradual increase in their adherence, while patients from Cluster 2—which was the largest cluster—had a low adherence that decreased even further during the last 2 weeks. Finally, a small cluster of patients presented fluctuations regarding their time spent exercising (Figure 4). For this reason, and for simplicity, Cluster 1 was named "adherent-6w", Cluster 2 "non-adherent-6w", and Cluster 3 "transient-6w".

Table 3. Mean session duration for all of the patients in each group for weeks 1 to 6 of the familiarization phase. The values are presented in minutes as the mean ± standard deviation.

Week	Cluster 1 Adherent-6w	Cluster 2 Non-Adherent-6w	Cluster 3 Transient-6w	*p*-Value
1	9.43± 1.6	8.94 ± 2.4	9.4 ± 1.3	0.87
2	10.07 ± 5.7	9.69 ± 7.3	8.93 ± 13.4	0.72
3	16 ± 7.9	11.27 ± 8.6	20.6 ± 19	0.35
4	18.75 ± 11.2	13.16 ± 9	9.78 ± 16.3	0.99
5	22.88 ± 9.8	10 ± 9	28.3 ± 16.8	**0.00054**
6	28.28 ± 12.6	5.67 ± 7.3	29.16 ± 2.4	**<0.0001**

The evolution of the performance metrics during the familiarization phase for the three clusters is depicted in Figure 5a,b. As observed, all patients, independent of their adherence to the exercise program, spent more than 60% of their time with an HR above the lower HR threshold, and the mean HR during the session was 80% of the maximum HR. Although the non-adherent-6w patients had lower *HRtime* values in most of the weeks, there were no statistically significant differences between the clusters (Table 4). These results suggest that when the patients exercised, they performed moderate-to-vigorous activity, and they performed similarly, independent of how frequently they participated in the rehabilitation program.

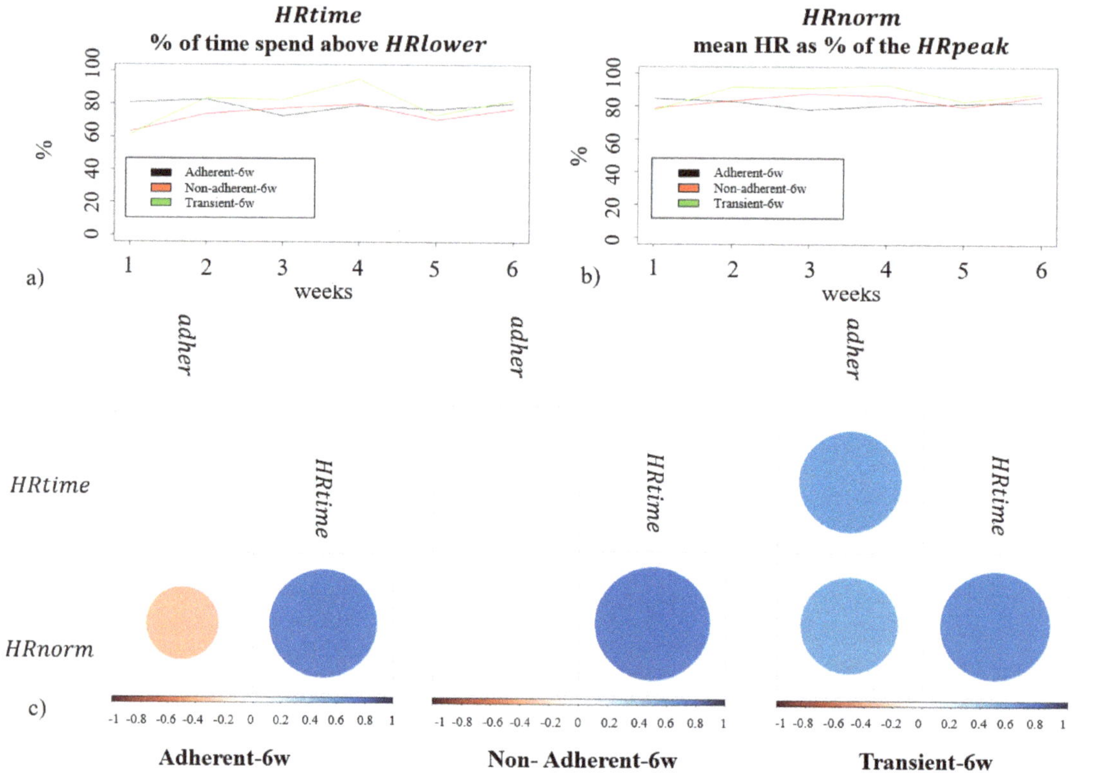

Figure 5. On the upper part, *HRtime* (**a**) and *HRnorm* (**b**) during the familiarization period are depicted for the three clusters. On the bottom (**c**), the Spearman's correlation for those variables with *adher* is provided; the bigger and darker the circle, the greater the correlation. Blue and red denote positive and negative correlation, respectively.

Table 4. Performance metrics for the 3 session adherence clusters.

	% Time Spent above HRlower				*% HRnorm*			
Week	Adherent-6w	Non-Adherent-6w	Transient-6w	*p*-Value	Adherent-6w	Non-Adherent-6w	Transient-6w	*p*-Value
1	81.01 ± 15.5	63.44 ± 25.6	61.41 ± 37.8	0.171	84.62 ± 12.78	78.91 ± 15.69	77.74 ± 18.22	0.455
2	82.74 ± 18.4	74.12 ± 18	83.8 ± 20.9	0.256	83.1 ± 11.92	83.71 ± 15.99	91.83 ± 11.51	0.5
3	72.72 ± 30.2	77.71 ± 14.7	82.87 ± 21.3	0.838	78.03 ± 14.65	87.93 ± 14.34	91.42 ± 19.63	0.161
4	79.38 ± 24.1	80.31 ± 14.7	95.37 ± 0.9	0.181	80.76 ± 12.32	86.67 ± 14.49	93.18 ± 19.94	0.508
5	76.9 ± 27.7	70.77 ± 24.4	73.6 ± 25.3	0.492	81.77 ± 14.59	79.98 ± 14.28	83.44 ± 13.24	0.959
6	80.7 ± 28	77.44 ± 10.4	82.81 ± 15.8	0.36	82.72 ± 16.5	86.63 ± 14.44	88.22 ± 13.83	0.88

Finally, from the observation of the correlation matrices in Figure 5c, we can conclude there was a strong negative correlation between the adherence and the mean HR during the session in the Adherent-6w group (as a percentage of the maximum HR), while for Transient-6w patients the correlation was strongly positive, and for the non-adherent-6w group the correlation was tight. Taking Figure 5b into account as well, where Adherent-6w present lower performance compared with Transient-6w patients, this finding suggests that adherence did not necessarily lead to better performance during exercise and that, generally, the patients tended to exercise in beneficial HR zones (Figure 5a).

3.3. Program Adherence Clusters

The spectral clustering that was based on *adher* for the period after the familiarization phase (week 6) resulted in the formulation of two clusters. Figure 6 depicts the *adher* over the whole intervention period (32 weeks). The first cluster included 24 patients and represented those individuals that were adherent to the exercise program, while the second cluster consisted of non-adherent patients (17 members). As depicted in Figure 6, even for the "Adherent" cluster, a slight decrease in exercise duration was observed during the last 4 weeks of the program.

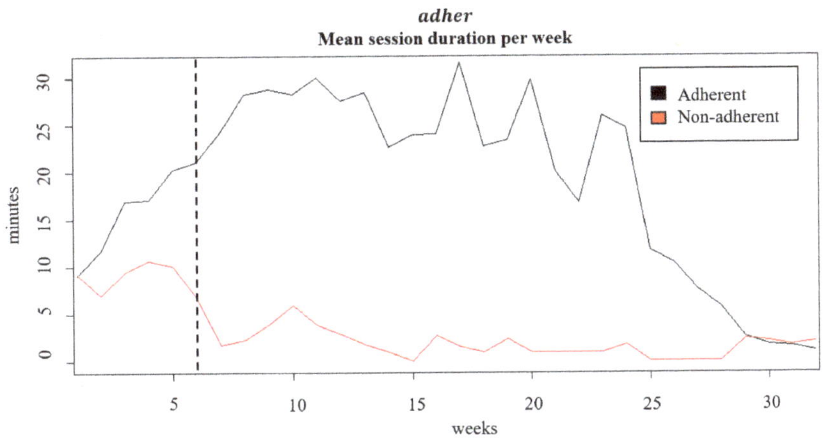

Figure 6. Evolution of the mean *adher* value (mean weekly session duration) for the two clusters based on the spectral clustering. The dotted line reflects the end of the familiarization phase.

3.4. Predicting Program Adherence

Figure 7 provides a visual overview of the distribution of patients into different clusters based on the analysis performed. As depicted, the majority of the patients who remained non-adherent during the whole program's duration were also non-adherent during the familiarization phase. On the other hand, patients who were adherent during the familiarization phase tended to also be adherent for the whole program. One additional interesting finding is that the active patients with low cardiovascular risk during baseline did not adhere to the exercise program.

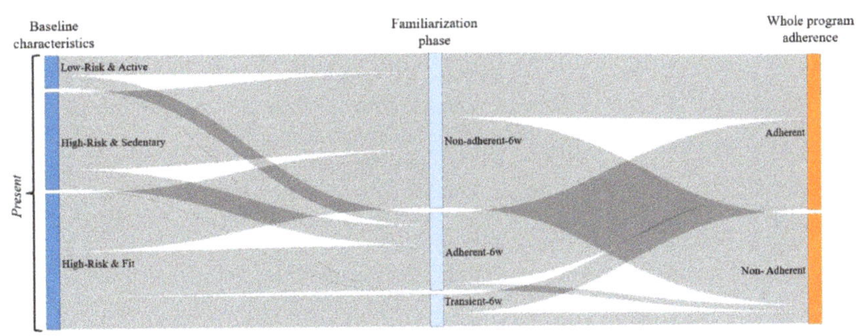

Figure 7. Sankey diagram regarding the different clusters of the analysis for the Present cluster. The Absent patients (n = 9) were not included in the analysis.

A dendrogram was created to predict future adherence to a home-based CR program according to the clinical data at baseline and the adherence to a short familiarization phase. Based on multiple train/test splits and model building with cross-validation in each run, the most frequent models—representing 92% of the total number of models—are depicted in Figure 8. As observed, model "a" (left) was the most frequent model, and it had the highest performance (accuracy = 82.3 ± 14.7%, precision = 80.2 ± 19.5%, and recall = 94.5 ± 14.5%).

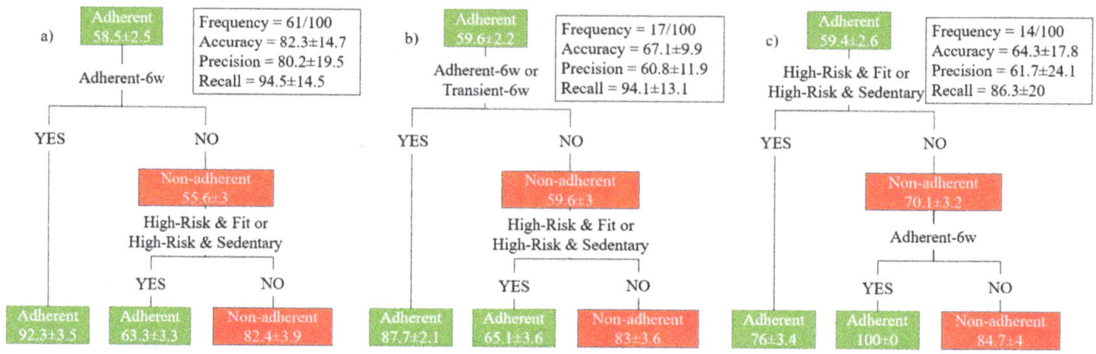

Figure 8. The three most frequent models that were created after splitting the dataset 100 times into different training and testing datasets. Model (**a**) was created 61 times, while the frequency for model (**b**,**c**) was 17 and 14, respectively. The performance metrics for each model is shown in the figure, too. The models are represented as dendrograms with rules. In each node of the tree, the most common class is depicted, along with the respective probability (mean ± std).

The rules of the model with the highest performance (Figure 8a) were as follows:

1. A patient that is recruited for a home- and exercise-based rehabilitation program has a 58.5 ± 2.5% probability to be adherent without any additional knowledge.
2. If the patient is adherent during the familiarization phase, then the probability of being adherent for the whole program reaches 92.3 ± 3.5%.
3. For a patient that is non-adherent or has a transient exercise behavior in the familiarization phase, the possibility to be non-adherent for the rest of the program is 55.6 ± 3%.
    a. If those patients are of high risk, based on the baseline characteristics, then the probability of being non-adherent increases to 82.4 ± 3.9%.
    b. If those patients are of low risk or are included in the average-baseline cluster, then the probability of being adherent is 63.3 ± 3.3%.

Model "b" (middle) is very similar to model "a", where the continuation of adherence (second rule) also includes the transient adherence during the familiarization phase in the same branch, and the third rule is also the same, with very similar probabilities. The third model uses rules similar to model "a", but it considers the baseline clusters first and then the adherence during the familiarization.

This instability of the decision tree classification was reduced by the use of the RF classification technique. Four features were identified in all of the RF runs as being significant for the classification of adherence. Figure 9 depicts the mean importance of the features that were used in each of the 100 runs of the classifier. The performance of the RF model (accuracy = 73.4 ± 17.5%, precision = 71.8 ± 25.8%, and recall = 87.7 ± 24%) was lower compared with the most frequent decision tree model (model "a"), but the RF model was more robust, revealing the importance of transient-6w users for the prediction of adherence to the whole program.

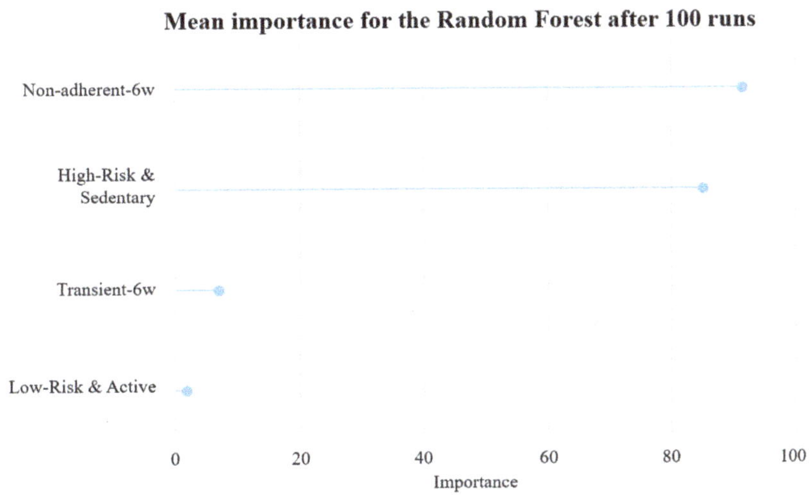

Figure 9. The mean importance for the features that were used in each of the 100 runs of the RF classification.

3.5. Network Analysis and Detection of Structure in Patient Profiles

Network analysis focused on the comparison of the bigger clusters for each type of analysis, i.e., the two clusters that included the most members. For baseline characteristics, the clusters with the high-risk and sedentary patients and the high-risk and fit patients were compared. The nodes on the graphs represent the features that were statistically significant between all three groups. As shown in Figure 10 (upper), the structure of the networks differed. In the cluster with the high-risk and fit patients, a stronger interplay among the characteristics was observed. The centrality measures denoted that the effect of each node was stronger for most of the features. Although a strictly causal relation was not defined, this structure may suggest that it is possible to drive changes in some factors and see effects in others, much more than in the high-risk and sedentary group. The main differences between the groups were as follows:

- In the high-risk and fit group, the risk was correlated with glucose and SBP, while in the high-risk and sedentary group, the risk was correlated with the level of MVPA.
- In the average group, STS and SBP were positively correlated, while in the high-risk and sedentary group they were negatively correlated.
- In the high-risk and fit group, the main connections included peak HR–MVPA–STS–SBP (physical/cardiovascular condition), while in the X group a glucose–SBP–STS link prevailed.

Better interpretable results of the network analysis are provided by the comparison of the clusters that were created based on the *adher* during the familiarization period. In this case, the comparison focused on the adherent and non-adherent clusters, and each node denotes a week. As depicted in Figure 11 (upper), for the adherent group, there were positive relationships with *adher*. In the non-adherent cluster, there was a break of the positive relationship between week 4 and week 5.

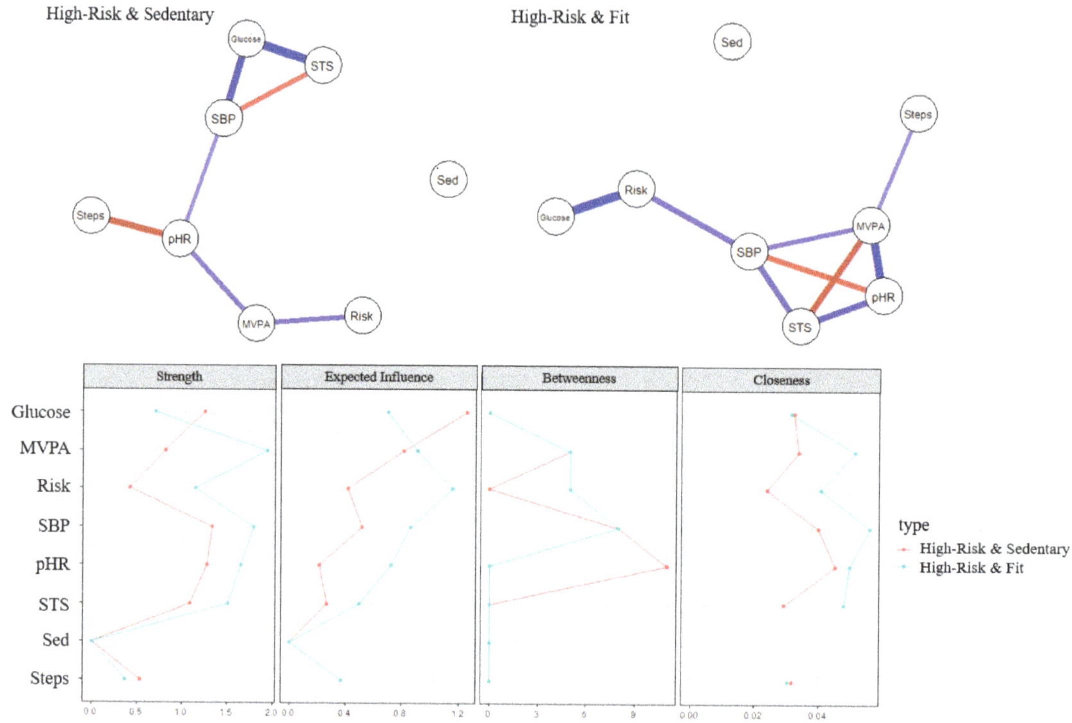

Figure 10. Networks of the two most popular clusters, based on the baseline clinical characteristics (**upper**). The centrality measures are depicted on the bottom (**bottom**).

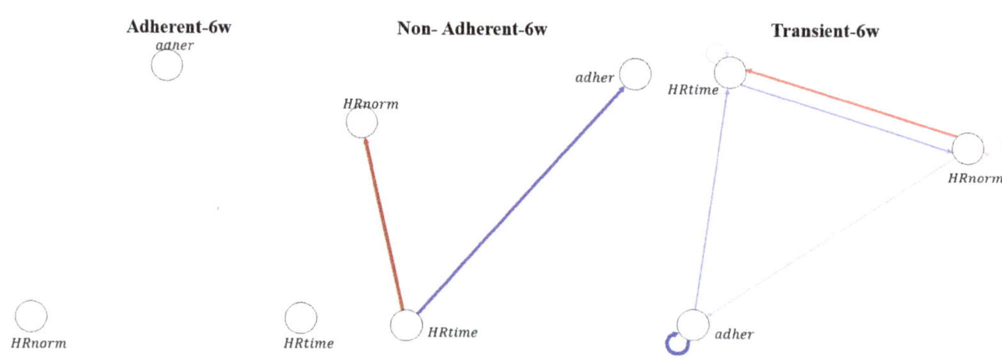

Figure 11. Temporal network for the three clusters created using the adherence during the familiarization phase. In the Adherent-6w group (left), there seems to exist no connection between the adherence and the HR metrics representing the performance during the session. The respective graphs for the non-adherent and the transient users are depicted in the middle and on the right, respectively.

The temporal graphs suggest a causal relationship between exercise HR performance and the next week's adherence. In the transient adherence group, (a) adherence was positively affected by previous adherence, and good *HRnorm*, i.e., performance, (b) adherence improved next week's *HRtime*. In the non-adherent group, *HRtime* positively affected *adher*. These links did not exist in the adherent group, in which the adherence behavior was not affected by the performance within the session. This means that there may be space for adjustments in the exercise sessions, to improve performance and influence adherence.

Finally, regarding the analysis of the graphs for the two clusters that were created based on adherence to the whole exercise program, the 10 most significant features were considered. Those features included adherence to weeks 2–6 of the familiarization phase, as well as five features based on the baseline characteristics. The network structure for both the adherent and non-adherent groups is depicted in Figure 12. As observed, weight and pVO2 were important and influential nodes in the non-adherent group, whereas in the adherence group, the adherence in weeks 2–6 remained correlated.

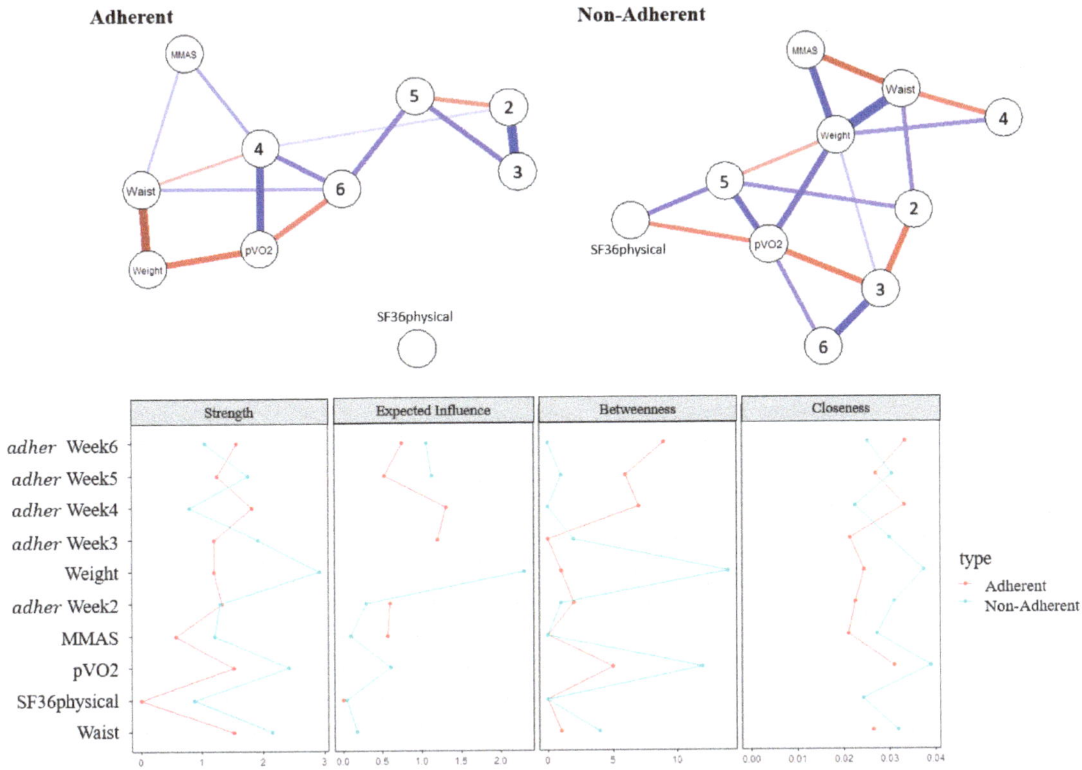

Figure 12. Networks for the adherent and non-adherent clusters include data from both the adherence to the familiarization phase and the baseline clinical characteristics. The numbers inside the nodes (**upper**) represent the variable adher during each week. The different measures for the importance of each node is depicted (**bottom**).

4. Discussion

Although the beneficial effects of CR have been thoroughly described in several studies, the uptake and adherence to center-based or home-based CR remains suboptimal. The limited adherence to CR programs leads to implications for patients' clinical status and the effective use of resources.

This study proposes an approach to predict long-term exercise adherence in a home-based CR setting, based on readily available baseline data before the start of a CR program. These data include clinical information, behavioral characteristics, and cardiovascular fitness, as well as HR and exercise duration during a familiarization phase of the intervention.

The methodology is based on the combination of unsupervised and supervised machine learning techniques in order to predict, from the initial stages of the CR programs, those patients who are more likely to be adherent during a 6-month period. In more detail, the unsupervised methods aim to identify different patients' profiles based on clinical and behavioral characteristics, whereas supervised techniques use these profiles to make the prediction. Based on the bibliography, this is the first data-driven end-to-end method that is able to predict long-term adherence in such programs, using data that are commonly collected during CR programs.

Initially, clustering was chosen as an unsupervised method to show the group characteristics at baseline and the adherence behavior in a limited familiarization period, without imposing a binary problem. The baseline data led to the formation of three patient groups, suggesting (1) a low-risk and active group of patients, (2) high-risk sedentary patients, and (3) a considerable number of patients who were of high cardiovascular risk but were also fit and motivated. The exercise familiarization showed three adherence behaviors (high adherence, low adherence, and transient adherence), while the exercise sessions after the familiarization phase led to two clusters: adherent and non-adherent. These two clusters were the targets for prediction, while the clusters based on the baseline data and the familiarization phase served as inputs for the prediction model.

Two types of models were tested: (1) decision trees, and (2) RF. The first type is more interpretable but also unstable, while the second type offers both robustness and explainability. Regarding the decision trees, the most common model produced after 100 runs with 10-fold cross-validation achieved both high precision and high recall (80.2 ± 19.5% and 94.4 ± 14.5%, respectively), and the rules were simple and explainable. As shown in Figure 8a, only approximately 60% of the target patients were adherent. However, if a patient was adherent during the familiarization phase, the long-term adherence rates reached 90%. For the rest of the patients, their clinical profiles can help the clinical experts to identify the non-adherent ones. A similar conclusion can also be reached by the observation of Figure 8b,c.

On the other hand, the RF model had lower performance (precision = 71.8 ± 25.8% and recall = 87.7 ± 24%), but it also revealed the importance of non-adherence during the familiarization phase and the high-risk and sedentary profile for the prediction of the whole-program adherence.

Previous studies focused on groups of patients that presented clear exercise behavior in terms of adherence, while they excluded patients with intermediate behaviors from the analysis [28], thereby somewhat limiting the generalizability of the model. In the present study, the transient adherence and initial clinical profile were found to be important for the prediction in both the RF model and the decision tree one (Figures 8b and 9, respectively). However, the validation of the models using an external dataset is a necessary next step.

While the decision tree model predicted that those who were adherent in the familiarization phase would continue to be adherent, it also shed light on the other cases, where the combination of adherence profile and clinical baseline seemed to play a role in subsequent adherence. For example, the patients with high cardiovascular risk seemed to be more susceptible to support and improved adherence, while patients with a low cardiovascular risk might need different handling, as they were predicted to continue being non-adherent, potentially because they had already established a physically active lifestyle and, perhaps, did not have the motivation to follow a specific program.

This is an important point that recognizes and sheds some light on the gray zone profiles or behaviors, which is also supported by the network analysis. Different network structures of baseline characteristics showed more correlated features in the high-risk and fit group of patients, and potentially more room for intervention. Temporal analysis at familiarization showed an interplay between HR performance and adherence in the transient and non-adherent groups, with adherence influenced by *HRtime* or *HRnorm*, which may also suggest further room for improvement and personalization of sessions. In the present study, exercise intensity was not a factor predicting adherence; however, in the temporal graph analysis a temporal link between HR and subsequent session duration was noted.

The role of both the familiarization phase and patient self-confidence is closely linked to understanding the program and self-motivation of patients. This has also been highlighted by [63], who mentioned family support to help keep patients engaged in a home-based CR program and suggested educating both patients and families to improve adherence to home-based CR programs. In addition, several previous works have identified factors that affect either short-term or long-term adherence to home-based CR programs, such as self-motivation, physical activity levels, or perception of self-status [9,21], and they propose patient-centered strategies to improve adherence to the exercise programs [18,64].

On the other hand, few works have attempted to make a predictive model in a data-driven manner to increase the chances of a match between patient and CR program. Recently, predictive models using machine learning techniques have been proposed [26]. However, those studies are only able to perform short-term predictions, while our model provides a longer-term adherence prediction.

A major advantage of the methodology presented in the present article was that the models were based on variables that are easily collected. In addition, the present study does not disregard the patients with intermediate behavior, such as transient adherence, to make future predictions, making our approach more generalizable compared with previous studies [28].

Addressing adherence to lifestyle changes, including exercise training, is significant and incredibly difficult, since participation rates in CR programs depend on several factors. Understanding those factors and predicting patients' behavior, such as exercise compliance, is important in clinical practice; thus, the clinical implications of our work could be substantial. Identifying areas for improvement in the interventions can increase adherence and the effectiveness of home-based CR; this, in turn, can lead to a better health status and quality of life for patients with CVD. In addition, since home-based CR methods have also proven to be more cost-effective, this could also help alleviate the financial stress placed on healthcare systems by the management of CVD patients [65]. Second, being able to predict adherence to home-based CR could contribute to better allocation of resources. Tang [66] showed that patient characteristics influence the choice of a certain type of CR delivery mode. The clinician could use this information to advise for or against home-based CR for a specific patient, increasing the likelihood of a match between patient and CR program.

The main limitation of the present study is the fact that the results were based on a small dataset (41 patients) collected as part of an RCT described in [16]. However, the data used for the predictive models and patient clustering are typically collected before a patient is recruited into a CR program, increasing the generalizability of the method and making it feasible to increase the sample size and allow for external validation of the models. However, this method needs to be validated using larger datasets, and this is one of the future directions of our study.

An additional limitation is that in the present study, adherence was mainly associated with the use of a home-based CR platform. However, the use of technology during exercise may not fully cover or represent adherence to the desired health behavior. As observed in Figure 6, patients in the adherent group presented a decrease in their adherence over time. This finding could be explained by the fact that these patients were becoming more confident in their physical activity behavior and might choose to exercise on their own, without the constant need to be stimulated by a home-based system. Finally, information related to the age and the sex of the patients was not available during the analysis, and their inclusion could lead to different clusters based on patients' baseline characteristics. This lack of information is a limitation of our study.

The results of the present study highlighted the importance of patients' characteristics and behavior in the familiarization phase for predicting adherence to home-based CR programs. Considering that CR programs are effective in improving patients' functional capacity, psychosocial status, and quality of life, technology should be leveraged for the widespread implementation of CR programs in patients with CVD or other chronic diseases.

Author Contributions: I.C. conceived the idea and formulated the research goals. I.C. and D.F. designed and developed the methodology and implemented the computer code and the algorithms. J.C. and D.F. preprocessed the data. D.F. and I.C. coordinated the writing of all drafts of the manuscript. J.C., E.K. and V.C. provided knowledge in the field of cardiac rehabilitation and performed the critical review of the manuscript. All authors contributed to the submitted versions of the manuscript. All authors have read and agreed to the published version of the manuscript.

Funding: The authors received no financial support for the research, authorship, and/or publication of this article.

Institutional Review Board Statement: All procedures performed in studies involving human participants were in accordance with the ethical standards of the institutional and/or national research committee and with the 1964 Helsinki Declaration and its later amendments or comparable ethical standards. The study protocol was approved by the ethics committees of UZ Leuven/KU Leuven (Belgium; S59023), the Research Ethics Committees of Mater Misericordiae University Hospital and Beaumont University Hospital in Dublin, Ireland (1/378/1846), and the ethics committee of Dublin City University (DCU; REC2016/123), Ireland.

Informed Consent Statement: Informed consent was obtained from all individual participants included in the study.

Data Availability Statement: Data sharing is not applicable to this article.

Acknowledgments: We would like to thank the PATHway consortium for their cooperation in completing the PATHway trial and for providing the data necessary to make this work possible. We would also like to thank Elisavet Koutsiana for her support in cleaning the data. More information about the PATHway trial can be found at: https://cordis.europa.eu/project/id/643491 (accessed on 16 May 2013).

Conflicts of Interest: The authors declare no potential conflict of interest with respect to the research, authorship, and/or publication of this article.

References

1. Timmis, A.; Townsend, N.; Gale, C.P.; Torbica, A.; Lettino, M.; Petersen, S.E.; Mossialos, E.A.; Maggioni, A.P.; Kazakiewicz, D.; May, H.T.; et al. European society of cardiology: Cardiovascular disease statistics 2019. *Eur. Heart J.* **2020**, *41*, 12–85. [CrossRef] [PubMed]
2. Wilkins, E.; Wilson, L.; Wickramasinghe, K.; Bhatnagar, P.; Leal, J.; Luengo-Fernandez, R.; Burns, R.; Rayner, M.; Townsend, N. *European Cardiovascular Disease Statistics 2017*; European Heart Network: Brussels, Belgium, 2017.
3. Piepoli, M.F.; Hoes, A.W.; Agewall, S.; Albus, C.; Brotons, C.; Catapano, A.L.; Cooney, M.T.; Corrà, U.; Cosyns, B.; Deaton, C.; et al. 2016 European Guidelines on cardiovascular disease prevention in clinical practice. *Eur. Heart J.* **2016**, *37*, 2315–2381. [CrossRef] [PubMed]
4. WHO. *Adherence to Long-Term Therapies: Evidence for Action*; WHO: Geneva, Switzerland, 2003.
5. Livitckaia, K.; Koutkias, V.; Maglaveras, N.; Kouidi, E.; Van Gils, M.; Chouvarda, I. Adherence to physical activity in patients with heart disease: Types, settings and evaluation instruments. In Proceedings of the International Conference on Biomedical and Health Informatics, Thessaloniki, Greece, 18–21 November 2017; pp. 255–259.
6. Naderi, S.H.; Bestwick, J.P.; Wald, D.S. Adherence to drugs that prevent cardiovascular disease: Meta-analysis on 376,162 patients. *Am. J. Med.* **2012**, *125*, 882–887.e1. [CrossRef] [PubMed]
7. Bjarnason-Wehrens, B.; McGee, H.; Zwisler, A.D.; Piepoli, M.F.; Benzer, W.; Schmid, J.P.; Dendale, P.; Pogosova, N.G.V.; Zdrenghea, D.; Niebauer, J.; et al. Cardiac rehabilitation in Europe: Results from the European Cardiac Rehabilitation Inventory Survey. *Eur. J. Prev. Cardiol.* **2010**, *17*, 410–418. [CrossRef]
8. Kotseva, K.; De Backer, G.; De Bacquer, D.; Rydén, L.; Hoes, A.; Grobbee, D.; Maggioni, A.; Marques-Vidal, P.; Jennings, C.; Abreu, A.; et al. Lifestyle and impact on cardiovascular risk factor control in coronary patients across 27 countries: Results from the European Society of Cardiology ESC-EORP EUROASPIRE V registry. *Eur. J. Prev. Cardiol.* **2019**, *26*, 824–835. [CrossRef]
9. Chindhy, S.; Taub, P.R.; Lavie, C.J.J.; Shen, J. Current Challenges in Cardiac Rehabilitation: Strategies to Overcome Social Factors and Attendance Barriers. *Expert Rev. Cardiovasc. Ther.* **2020**, *18*, 777–789. [CrossRef]
10. Rose, K.; Eldridge, S.; Chapin, L. The Internet of Things (IoT): An Overview. *Int. J. Eng. Res. Appl.* **2015**, *5*, 71–82.
11. Cavalheiro, A.H.; Silva Cardoso, J.; Rocha, A.; Moreira, E.; Azevedo, L.F. Effectiveness of Tele-rehabilitation Programs in Heart Failure: A Systematic Review and Meta-analysis. *Health Serv. Insights* **2021**, *14*, 1–10. [CrossRef]

12. Claes, J.; Buys, R.; Budts, W.; Smart, N.; Cornelissen, V.A. Longer-term effects of home-based exercise interventions on exercise capacity and physical activity in coronary artery disease patients: A systematic review and meta-analysis. *Eur. J. Prev. Cardiol.* **2017**, *24*, 244–256. [CrossRef]
13. Rawstorn, J.C.; Gant, N.; Direito, A.; Beckmann, C.; Maddison, R. Telehealth exercise-based cardiac rehabilitation: A systematic review and meta-analysis. *Heart* **2016**, *102*, 1183–1192. [CrossRef]
14. Frederix, I.; Hansen, D.; Coninx, K.; Vandervoort, P.; Vandijck, D.; Hens, N.; Van Craenenbroeck, E.; Van Driessche, N.; Dendale, P. Medium-term effectiveness of a comprehensive internet-based and patient-specific telerehabilitation program with text messaging support for cardiac patients: Randomized controlled trial. *J. Med. Internet Res.* **2015**, *17*, e185. [CrossRef]
15. Pinto, B.M.; Goldstein, M.G.; Papandonatos, G.D.; Farrell, N.; Tilkemeier, P.; Marcus, B.H.; Todaro, J.F. Maintenance of exercise after phase II cardiac rehabilitation: A randomized controlled trial. *Am. J. Prev. Med.* **2011**, *41*, 274–283. [CrossRef]
16. Claes, J.; Buys, R.; Woods, C.; Briggs, A.; Geue, C.; Aitken, M.; Moyna, N.; Moran, K.; McCaffrey, N.; Chouvarda, I.; et al. PATHway I: Design and rationale for the investigation of the feasibility, clinical effectiveness and cost-effectiveness of a technology-enabled cardiac rehabilitation platform. *BMJ Open* **2017**, *7*, e016781. [CrossRef]
17. Anderson, L.; Sharp, G.A.; Norton, R.J.; Dalal, H.; Dean, S.G.; Jolly, K.; Cowie, A.; Zawada, A.; Taylor, R.S. Home-based versus centre-based cardiac rehabilitation. *Cochrane Database Syst. Rev.* **2017**, *6*. [CrossRef]
18. Pfaeffli Dale, L.; Whittaker, R.; Dixon, R.; Stewart, R.; Jiang, Y.; Carter, K.; Maddison, R. Acceptability of a Mobile Health Exercise-Based Cardiac Rehabilitation Intervention. *J. Cardiopulm. Rehabil. Prev.* **2015**, *35*, 312–319. [CrossRef]
19. Hannan, A.L.; Harders, M.P.; Hing, W.; Climstein, M.; Coombes, J.S.; Furness, J. Impact of wearable physical activity monitoring devices with exercise prescription or advice in the maintenance phase of cardiac rehabilitation: Systematic review and meta-analysis. *BMC Sports Sci. Med. Rehabil.* **2019**, *11*, 14. [CrossRef]
20. Hamilton, S.J.; Mills, B.; Birch, E.M.; Thompson, S.C. Smartphones in the secondary prevention of cardiovascular disease: A systematic review. *BMC Cardiovasc. Disord.* **2018**, *18*, 25. [CrossRef]
21. Essery, R.; Geraghty, A.W.A.; Kirby, S.; Yardley, L. Predictors of adherence to home-based physical therapies: A systematic review. *Disabil. Rehabil.* **2017**, *39*, 519–534. [CrossRef]
22. Beinart, N.A.; Goodchild, C.E.; Weinman, J.A.; Ayis, S.; Godfrey, E.L. Individual and intervention-related factors associated with adherence to home exercise in chronic low back pain: A systematic review. *Spine J.* **2013**, *13*, 1940–1950. [CrossRef]
23. Picorelli, A.M.A.; Pereira, L.S.M.; Pereira, D.S.; Felício, D.; Sherrington, C. Adherence to exercise programs for older people is influenced by program characteristics and personal factors: A systematic review. *J. Physiother.* **2014**, *60*, 151–156. [CrossRef]
24. Triantafyllidis, A.; Filos, D.; Buys, R.; Claes, J.; Cornelissen, V.; Kouidi, E.; Chatzitofis, A.; Zarpalas, D.; Daras, P.; Walsh, D.; et al. Computerized decision support for beneficial home-based exercise rehabilitation in patients with cardiovascular disease. *Comput. Methods Programs Biomed.* **2018**, *162*, 1–10. [CrossRef] [PubMed]
25. Zhou, M.; Fukuoka, Y.; Goldberg, K.; Vittinghoff, E.; Aswani, A. Applying machine learning to predict future adherence to physical activity programs. *BMC Med. Inform. Decis. Mak.* **2019**, *19*, 169. [CrossRef] [PubMed]
26. Bastidas, O.J.; Zahia, S.; Fuente-Vidal, A.; Férez, N.S.; Noguera, O.R.; Montane, J.; Garcia-Zapirain, B. Predicting physical exercise adherence in fitness apps using a deep learning approach. *Int. J. Environ. Res. Public Health* **2021**, *18*, 10769. [CrossRef] [PubMed]
27. Kim, J.C.; Chung, K. Prediction model of user physical activity using data characteristics-based long short-term memory recurrent neural networks. *KSII Trans. Internet Inf. Syst.* **2019**, *13*, 2060–2077. [CrossRef]
28. Claes, J.; Filos, D.; Cornelissen, V.; Chouvarda, I. Prediction of the Adherence to a Home-Based Cardiac Rehabilitation Program. In Proceedings of the Annual International Conference of the IEEE Engineering in Medicine and Biology Society (EMBS), Berlin, Germany, 23–27 July 2019.
29. ACSM. *ACSM's Guidelines for Exercise Testing and Prescription*; ACSM: Indianapolis, IN, USA, 2013; Volume 9, ISBN 978-1-6091-3955-1.
30. Shcherbina, A.; Mikael Mattsson, C.; Waggott, D.; Salisbury, H.; Christle, J.W.; Hastie, T.; Wheeler, M.T.; Ashley, E.A. Accuracy in wrist-worn, sensor-based measurements of heart rate and energy expenditure in a diverse cohort. *J. Pers. Med.* **2017**, *7*, 3. [CrossRef]
31. Walsh, D.M.J.; Kieran, M.; Cornelissen, V.; Buys, R.; Claes, J.; Zampognaro, P.; Melillo, F.; Maglaveras, N.; Chouvarda, I.; Triantafyllidis, A.; et al. The development and codesign of the PATHway intervention: A theory-driven eHealth platform for the self-management of cardiovascular disease. *Transl. Behav. Med.* **2019**, *9*, 76–98. [CrossRef]
32. Wilson, P.W.F.; D'Agostino, R.B.; Levy, D.; Belanger, A.M.; Silbershatz, H.; Kannel, W.B. Prediction of coronary heart disease using risk factor categories. *Circulation* **1998**, *97*, 1837–1847. [CrossRef]
33. Cruz, L.N.; Camey, S.A.; Fleck, M.P.; Polanczyk, C.A. World Health Organization quality of life instrument-brief and Short Form-36 in patients with coronary artery disease: Do they measure similar quality of life concepts? *Psychol. Health Med.* **2009**, *14*, 619–628. [CrossRef]
34. Hardie Murphy, M.; Rowe, D.A.; Belton, S.; Woods, C.B. Validity of a two-item physical activity questionnaire for assessing attainment of physical activity guidelines in youth. *BMC Public Health* **2015**, *15*, 1080. [CrossRef]
35. McAuley, E. The role of efficacy cognitions in the prediction of exercise behavior in middle-aged adults. *J. Behav. Med.* **1992**, *15*, 65–88. [CrossRef]
36. Sniehotta, F.F.; Schwarzer, R.; Scholz, U.; Schuz, B. Action planning and coping planning for long-term lifestyle change theory and.pdf. *Eur. J. Soc. Psychol.* **2005**, *35*, 565–579. [CrossRef]

37. Lawford, B.R.; Barnes, M.; Connor, J.P.; Heslop, K.; Nyst, P.; Young, R.M.D. Alcohol use disorders identification test (AUDIT) scores are elevated in antipsychotic-induced hyperprolactinaemia. *J. Psychopharmacol.* **2012**, *26*, 324–329. [CrossRef]
38. Martínez-González, M.A.; García-Arellano, A.; Toledo, E.; Salas-Salvadó, J.; Buil-Cosiales, P.; Corella, D.; Covas, M.I.; Schröder, H.; Arós, F.; Gómez-Gracia, E.; et al. A 14-item mediterranean diet assessment tool and obesity indexes among high-risk subjects: The PREDIMED trial. *PLoS ONE* **2012**, *7*, e43134. [CrossRef]
39. Cohen, S.; Kamarck, T.; Mermelstein, R. A Global Measure of Perceived Stress. *J. Health Soc. Behav.* **1983**, *24*, 385–396. [CrossRef]
40. Morisky, D.E.; Ang, A.; Krousel-Wood, M.; Ward, H.J. Predictive validity of a medication adherence measure in an outpatient setting. *J. Clin. Hypertens.* **2008**, *10*, 348–354. [CrossRef]
41. Ng Fat, L.; Scholes, S.; Boniface, S.; Mindell, J.; Stewart-Brown, S. Evaluating and establishing national norms for mental wellbeing using the short Warwick–Edinburgh Mental Well-being Scale (SWEMWBS): Findings from the Health Survey for England. *Qual. Life Res.* **2017**, *26*, 1129–1144. [CrossRef]
42. Vaglio, J.; Conard, M.; Poston, W.S.; O'Keefe, J.; Haddock, C.K.; House, J.; Spertus, J.A. Testing the performance of the ENRICHD Social Support Instrument in cardiac patients. *Health Qual. Life Outcomes* **2004**, *2*, 24. [CrossRef]
43. Shields, C.A.; Brawley, L.R. Preferring proxy-agency: Impact on self-efficacy for exercise. *J. Health Psychol.* **2006**, *11*, 904–914. [CrossRef]
44. Razykov, I.; Ziegelstein, R.C.; Whooley, M.A.; Thombs, B.D. The PHQ-9 versus the PHQ-8—Is item 9 useful for assessing suicide risk in coronary artery disease patients? Data from the Heart and Soul Study. *J. Psychosom. Res.* **2012**, *73*, 163–168. [CrossRef]
45. Broadbent, E.; Petrie, K.J.; Main, J.; Weinman, J. The Brief Illness Perception Questionnaire. *J. Psychosom. Res.* **2006**, *60*, 631–637. [CrossRef]
46. Claes, J.; Cornelissen, V.; McDermott, C.; Moyna, N.; Pattyn, N.; Cornelis, N.; Gallagher, A.; McCormack, C.; Newton, H.; Gillain, A.; et al. Feasibility, Acceptability, and Clinical Effectiveness of a Technology-Enabled Cardiac Rehabilitation Platform (Physical Activity Toward Health-I): Randomized Controlled Trial. *J. Med. Internet Res.* **2020**, *22*, e14221. [CrossRef]
47. Nielsen, F. Hierarchical Clustering. In *Introduction to HPC with MPI for Data Science*; Springer International Publishing: Cham, Switzerland, 2016; pp. 195–211. ISBN 9789811305535.
48. Rousseeuw, P.J. Silhouettes: A graphical aid to the interpretation and validation of cluster analysis. *J. Comput. Appl. Math.* **1987**, *20*, 53–65. [CrossRef]
49. John, C.R.; Watson, D.; Barnes, M.R.; Pitzalis, C.; Lewis, M.J. Spectrum: Fast density-aware spectral clustering for single and multi-omic data. *Bioinformatics* **2020**, *36*, 1159–1166. [CrossRef]
50. Lihi, Z.-M.; Perona, P. Self-Tuning Spectral Clustering. In *Advances in Neural Information Processing Systems*; Saul, L., Weiss, Y., Bottou, L., Eds.; MIT Press: Cambridge, MA, USA, 2004; Volume 17.
51. Vens, C.; Struyf, J.; Schietgat, L.; Džeroski, S.; Blockeel, H. Decision trees for hierarchical multi-label classification. *Mach. Learn.* **2008**, *73*, 185–214. [CrossRef]
52. Therneau, T.; Atkinson, B. *rpart: Recursive Partitioning and Regression Trees*; Scientific Research Publishing: Wuhan, China, 2019.
53. Mahdi Abdulkareem, N.; Mohsin Abdulazeez, A. Machine Learning Classification Based on Radom Forest Algorithm: A Review. *Int. J. Sci. Bus.* **2021**, *5*, 128–142. [CrossRef]
54. Kruskal, W.H.; Wallis, W.A. Use of Ranks in One-Criterion Variance Analysis. *J. Am. Stat. Assoc.* **1952**, *47*, 583–621. [CrossRef]
55. Borsboom, D.; Deserno, M.K.; Rhemtulla, M.; Epskamp, S.; Fried, E.I.; McNally, R.J.; Robinaugh, D.J.; Perugini, M.; Dalege, J.; Costantini, G.; et al. Network analysis of multivariate data in psychological science. *Nat. Rev. Methods Prim.* **2021**, *1*, 58. [CrossRef]
56. Zanin, M.; Aitya, N.A.A.; Basilio, J.; Baumbach, J.; Benis, A.; Behera, C.K.; Bucholc, M.; Castiglione, F.; Chouvarda, I.; Comte, B.; et al. An Early Stage Researcher's Primer on Systems Medicine Terminology. *Netw. Syst. Med.* **2021**, *4*, 2–50. [CrossRef] [PubMed]
57. Epskamp, S.; Borsboom, D.; Fried, E.I. Estimating psychological networks and their accuracy: A tutorial paper. *Behav. Res. Methods* **2018**, *50*, 195–212. [CrossRef]
58. Friedman, J.; Hastie, T.; Tibshirani, R. glasso: Graphical Lasso: Estimation of Gaussian Graphical Models. 2019. Available online: https://CRAN.R-project.org/package=glasso (accessed on 6 April 2023).
59. Friedman, J.; Hastie, T.; Tibshirani, R. Sparse inverse covariance estimation with the graphical lasso. *Biostatistics* **2008**, *9*, 432–441. [CrossRef]
60. Epskamp, S.; Waldorp, L.J.; Mõttus, R.; Borsboom, D. The Gaussian Graphical Model in Cross-Sectional and Time-Series Data. *Multivar. Behav. Res.* **2018**, *53*, 453–480. [CrossRef]
61. Epskamp, S. Brief Report on Estimating Regularized Gaussian Networks from Continuous and Ordinal Data. *arXiv* **2016**, arXiv:1606.05771.
62. Epskamp, S. graphicalVAR: Graphical VAR for Experience Sampling Data. 2021. Available online: https://cran.r-project.org/web/packages/graphicalVAR/graphicalVAR.pdf (accessed on 6 April 2023).
63. Ge, C.; Ma, J.; Xu, Y.; Shi, Y.J.; Zhao, C.H.; Gao, L.; Bai, J.; Wang, Y.; Sun, Z.J.; Guo, J.; et al. Predictors of adherence to home-based cardiac rehabilitation program among coronary artery disease outpatients in China. *J. Geriatr. Cardiol.* **2019**, *16*, 749–755. [CrossRef]
64. Shaw, J.F.; Pilon, S.; Vierula, M.; McIsaac, D.I. Predictors of adherence to prescribed exercise programs for older adults with medical or surgical indications for exercise: A systematic review. *Syst. Rev.* **2022**, *11*, 80. [CrossRef] [PubMed]

65. Heindl, B.; Ramirez, L.; Joseph, L.; Clarkson, S.; Thomas, R.; Bittner, V. Hybrid cardiac rehabilitation—The state of the science and the way forward. *Prog. Cardiovasc. Dis.* **2022**, *70*, 175–182. [CrossRef]
66. Tang, L.H.; Harrison, A.; Skou, S.T.; Taylor, R.S.; Dalal, H.; Doherty, P. Are patient characteristics and modes of delivery associated with completion of cardiac rehabilitation? A national registry analysis. *Int. J. Cardiol.* **2022**, *361*, 7–13. [CrossRef]

applied sciences

MDPI

Article

Human Activity Recognition by the Image Type Encoding Method of 3-Axial Sensor Data

Changmin Kim [1] and Woobeom Lee [2,*]

[1] AI Software Education Institute, Soonchunhyang University, Asan 31538, Republic of Korea; changingstart@gmail.com
[2] Department of Information Communication Software Engineering, Sangji University, Wonju 26339, Republic of Korea
* Correspondence: beomlee@sangji.ac.kr

Abstract: HAR technology uses computer and machine vision to analyze human activity and gestures by processing sensor data. The 3-axis acceleration and gyro sensor data are particularly effective in measuring human activity as they can calculate movement speed, direction, and angle. Our paper emphasizes the importance of developing a method to expand the recognition range of human activity due to the many types of activities and similar movements that can result in misrecognition. The proposed method uses 3-axis acceleration and gyro sensor data to visually define human activity patterns and improve recognition accuracy, particularly for similar activities. The method involves converting the sensor data into an image format, removing noise using time series features, generating visual patterns of waveforms, and standardizing geometric patterns. The resulting data (1D, 2D, and 3D) can simultaneously process each type by extracting pattern features using parallel convolution layers and performing classification by applying two fully connected layers in parallel to the merged data from the output data of three convolution layers. The proposed neural network model achieved 98.1% accuracy and recognized 18 types of activities, three times more than previous studies, with a shallower layer structure due to the enhanced input data features.

Keywords: human activity recognition (HAR); 3-axial sensor; image type encoding method; WISDM dataset; CNN

Citation: Kim, C.; Lee, W. Human Activity Recognition by the Image Type Encoding Method of 3-Axial Sensor Data. *Appl. Sci.* **2023**, *13*, 4961. https://doi.org/10.3390/app13084961

Academic Editors: Luigi Bibbò and Marley M.B.R. Vellasco

Received: 10 March 2023
Revised: 7 April 2023
Accepted: 10 April 2023
Published: 14 April 2023

1. Introduction

Currently, smartphones are one of the essential items in daily life [1]. Smartphones integrate various sensors such as accelerometers, gyroscopes, light sensors, and temperature sensors, making them versatile for a wide range of services such as device control and monitoring. They are also used as wearable devices for analyzing physical activity [2–5]. For this analysis, data from 3-axis accelerometers and gyroscopes are commonly used, as they provide useful information on speed, direction, and angles of human movement. This data is crucial for human activity recognition (HAR), a technology that learns and infers advanced knowledge necessary for physical activity recognition based on raw sensor data. HAR can be effectively utilized in everyday life [6].

HAR is being pursued through various measurement methods and related services and research. Tian et al. [7] attempted HAR using a single-band wearable accelerometer and proposed an ensemble-based filter feature selection method that enhanced the strength of a single accelerometer and improved accuracy by removing overlap and unnecessary attributes. Kang et al. [8] proposed a hybrid deep learning model that uses both sensor data from accelerometers and skeleton data from images. Anguita et al. [9] collected sensor data by attaching smartphones to people's waists to differentiate various human activities and performed activity recognition using support vector machines. Sengul et al. [10] distinguished four common activities in daily life using accelerometer and gyroscope data to predict injuries caused by falls in the elderly. Moreover, many previous studies have focused on segmentation algorithms for accelerometer time series data [11], random undersampling, random oversampling, ensemble learning methods [12], and so on.

However, human physical activities can be divided into various types (walking, running, hiking, drinking water, sitting, etc.), and they also include similar activities (drinking water vs. eating, etc.) as well as types with clear differences (lying down vs. climbing stairs, etc.). Additionally, 3-axial sensor data can be prone to errors due to noise and uncertainty (sensor shaking, functional impairment, etc.), and the data size is smaller than that of video data, making it difficult to train. Therefore, various explored to obtain stable 3-axial sensor data, and there is considerable interest in visualization research for encoding sensor data into images without loss [13–16].

Therefore, this paper proposes a method to improve the accuracy of HAR by utilizing the 3-axial data (accelerometer and gyroscope sensor data) of a smartphone to visualize 2D and 3D. In addition, it recognizes 18 human physical activities through a single device (smartphone) instead of attaching multiple devices. Partial activity patterns of a single body movement were obtained through time series data grouped at regular intervals, and they were visualized in 2D and 3D image streaming formats. By clearly differentiating between similar human physical activities through this process, an improved HAR is proposed.

Section 2 of this study describes the body activity recognition technology using sensors. Section 3 introduces the proposed method of encoding the raw sensor data into an image form. Section 4 comparatively analyzes the performances of the previously studied neural network learning model and the proposed model. In the final section, we present our conclusions.

2. Related Research

Defining human actions as a single motion or external form is difficult because even if two motions may appear identical, they may result in different outcomes depending on subsequent movements. Therefore, time series data that captures the changes in data over time is used more frequently than a single data point for recognizing human actions [17,18]. Sensors are the most effective devices for gathering such data [12,19,20]. Currently, deep-learning-based models associated with sensor data can automatically extract and classify the characteristics of time series data, enabling accurate behavioral recognition.

In [21], a CNN with local loss was proposed for HAR. The experimental results showed that the local loss performed better than the global loss for the baseline architecture, and various human activities could be identified despite the low number of parameters. However, this study only showed high performance in recognizing six activities (walking, jogging, walking upstairs, walking downstairs, sitting, and standing) with 98.6% accuracy. The present study proposes a method to recognize 18 different types of actions, enabling more diverse biometrics.

A lightweight deep learning model for HAR was proposed in [22]. This model was developed using long short-term memory (LSTM) and recurrent neural network (RNN) and showed high performance, achieving an accuracy of 95.78% for recognizing 18 types of activities on the WISDM dataset. However, due to their recurrent structures, LSTM and RNN models require longer training and inference times compared to general CNN-based models. To address this issue, we utilized only convolutional layers (1D, 2D, and 3D convolutional layers) in a parallel structure, allowing us to analyze and observe a small dataset from various perspectives.

Ignatov et al. [23] studied an independent deep-learning-based approach for the classification of human actions. In addition to the simple statistical feature of preserving the global shape of time series data, they proposed a CNN model for extracting local characteristics. This study segmented the collected accelerometer sensor data into various sizes to determine the most effective segmentation size and evaluated the performance of each segmentation. In our study, we used the duration of the actions to set the size of the segmented data and performed activity classification using this configuration.

In [24], to capture various activities for HAR, mobile devices with built-in perceptual extraction networks were attached to users, and the data collected from these devices were used for the initial training. The trained weight values were transferred to the server through the communication network. The transferred data were compared with the trained weight values from other devices to determine the optimal weight value, and the final weight value was delivered to each device for re-training. The method proposed by [24] allows for the simultaneous collection and training of multiple activity data, and strong performance can be achieved by comprehensively determining the weights of individually trained models. However, comprehensive weight determination can emphasize strong performance, but it may also reduce accuracy when classifying similar activities for precise analysis. In consideration of this, we proposed a method to enhance the original sensor data, which enabled the classification of 18 distinct activities.

Previous studies on HAR have utilized various methods such as using RNN-based models to learn temporal changes or hybrid models that mix CNNs. Although HAR using CNN models has also been studied, it does not perform as well as RNN or hybrid models (refer to Chapter 6). However, RNN-based models can be limited in real-life usage due to long training and inference times, and hybrid models have complex structures that make it difficult to understand the learning process. Additionally, since human physical activity is diverse and there are many similar movements, there is a high possibility that features may be lost during the operation process of the layers in deep model structures, and it is difficult to wear many wearable devices due to discomfort. To address these issues, we propose a HAR method based on a wearable device using a single smartphone.

To effectively collect human physical activity from wearable devices, we expand (encode) high-dimensional 3-axis sensor data. This generates new features of human physical activity that could not be detected in one-dimensional data and removes fine noise from the sensor. In other words, by defining high-dimensional features such as directionality and spatiality in one-dimensional data, we propose new information about features of human physical activity. These new features enable the recognition of more diverse types of human physical activity and the discovery of unique features among similar types of human physical activity. Additionally, to effectively learn from the increased input data, we connect convolutional layers in parallel to enable parallel computation and complement the missing information in the encoding and learning processes using various dimensional data (1D data (3-axis sensor), 2D data (image), and 3D data (video image)). The encoding process is described in detail in Section 3.

3. Image Type Encoding Method of the 3-Axial Sensor Data

Accelerometer and gyroscope sensors that measure the velocity, momentum change, etc., of an object can detect the active state of an object, due to which both these devices are used extensively. The (x, y, and z) 3-axial data values from these sensors are arranged into a time series structure to recognize human activities using the properties of data changes according to time. However, in the case of similar human activities, the recognition accuracy decreases due to the small data dimension, which limits the expression of the characteristics. Therefore, the 3-axial raw data gathered through the accelerometer and gyroscope from this study were encoded into 2D and 3D images that express time properties. The image data were trained together with the 1D raw data to increase the precision and accuracy in order to perform high-dimensional HAR.

3.1. Three-Axial Acceleration and Gyroscope Data Analysis of the WISDM Dataset

The 3-axial accelerometer and gyroscope sensor data used in this study are from the "WISDM smartphone and smartwatch activity and biometrics" database published by Weiss [25]. This database consists of data gathered at 50 ms intervals for 18 daily activities from smartphones placed in the pockets of 51 subjects for three minutes. Table 1 summarizes the 18 measured activities, which are largely distinguished into basic activities related to walking (A), hand-based activities (B), and dining activities (C).

Table 1. Smartphone acceleration and gyroscope data from the WISDM database.

Label	Activity	No. of Columns		No. of Merged Columns	No. of Data	Grouping Type
		Accel	Gyro			
0	Walking	279,817	203,919	152,114	51	A
1	Jogging	268,409	200,252	154,020	49	A
2	Stairs	255,645	197,857	160,430	50	A
3	Sitting	264,592	202,370	180,315	51	A
4	Standing	269,604	202,351	165,068	51	A
5	Typing	246,356	194,540	166,646	49	B
6	Brushing teeth	269,609	202,622	168,771	51	B
7	Eating soup	270,756	202,408	164,177	51	C
8	Eating chips	261,360	197,905	160,237	50	C
9	Eating pasta	249,793	197,844	170,598	50	C
10	Drinking	285,190	202,395	149,138	51	C
11	Eating sandwich	265,781	197,915	164,635	51	C
12	Kicking	278,766	202,625	150,651	51	A
13	Catching	272,219	198,756	146,675	50	B
14	Dribbling	272,730	202,331	150,333	51	B
15	Writing	260,497	197,894	175,638	51	B
16	Clapping	268,065	202,330	165,304	51	B
17	Folding clothes	265,214	202,321	164,006	51	B

In Table 1, activity A is based on lower body movements, while most activities in B involve both lower and upper body movements, and C includes activities such as eating or drinking. Each activity's data includes a minimum of 194,540 raw data points or more, and the accelerometer and gyroscope data were merged based on the measurement time (Table 1, no. of merged columns). Since the WISDM database comprises similar activity groups and a small amount of data from 49 to 51 (number of subjects), in this study, we augmented the training dataset by segmenting the data into time units.

3.2. Walking-Activity-Based Data Argumentation

Among the 18 activities of the WISDM dataset, the "Walking" activity in the given time unit was the easiest to analyze. "Walking" is among the most common human activities, and a healthy person can normally walk 4.5 km/h, and approximately 8 km can be covered in 10,000 steps [26–30]. This shows that about 800 ms is required for a movement of 1 m. In addition, it can be inferred that about 6,400,000 ms (=1 h 46 m 40 s) is required for an 8 km walk, which amounts to 10,000 steps. The time required for one step, denoted as T_w, corresponds to about 640 ms of time. Therefore, this study sets the data segment size (*DSS*) as shown in Equation (1) for the raw sensor data of the WISDM generated at 50 ms intervals based on T_w, which equals one human step.

$$DSS = \frac{T_w}{T_R} + bias \tag{1}$$

where, T_w: one step time; T_R: sampling time of the WISDM dataset.

In Equation (1), $T_R = 50$ ms indicates the interval of data collection of the WISDM dataset, and $T_w = 640$ ms indicates the time consumed per step taken. The *DSS* was set to 15 with a bias value of 2.2. One input pattern for neural network training corresponds to 15 raw sensor data points, and the raw WISDM dataset segments the data repetitively by moving by one each. Ultimately, 910 physical activity data points were increased to 2,896,476 as a result of using the data segmentation method proposed in this study. These data were divided into training data and test data in a ratio of 8:2 (2,317,180 data points in the training set and 579,296 in the test set).

3.3. Brightness Intensity Distribution Pattern Transformation

Image type expansion was performed for the increased data obtained through raw sensor data segmentation. The accelerometer and gyroscope sensor data segmented into identical sizes can express 2D image patterns using the raw values that correspond to the amplitude of the continuous data, and these pattern data can be used to analyze physical activities.

Figure 1 shows an example of the raw accelerometer sensor data expressed as a brightness value. The raw time series data in Figure 1a are mapped to a brightness value and visualized according to that value. In the case of transforming each point A–E of the time series graph into a brightness value, the brightness intensity distribution pattern (BIDP) for each physical activity data can be obtained, as shown in Figure 2b.

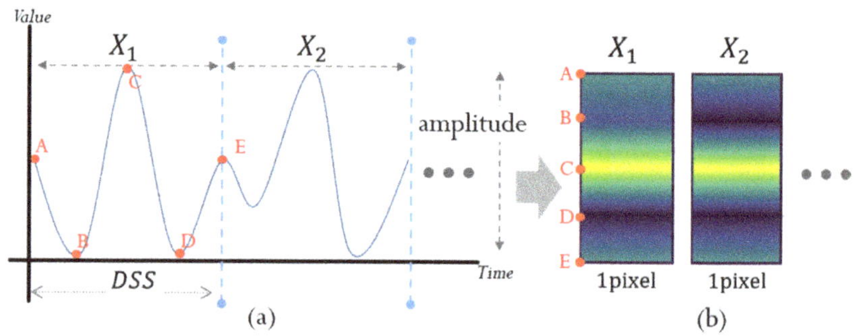

Figure 1. Brightness distribution transformation of raw sensor data: (**a**) raw data graph, and (**b**) brightness intensity distribution pattern ($BIDP$).

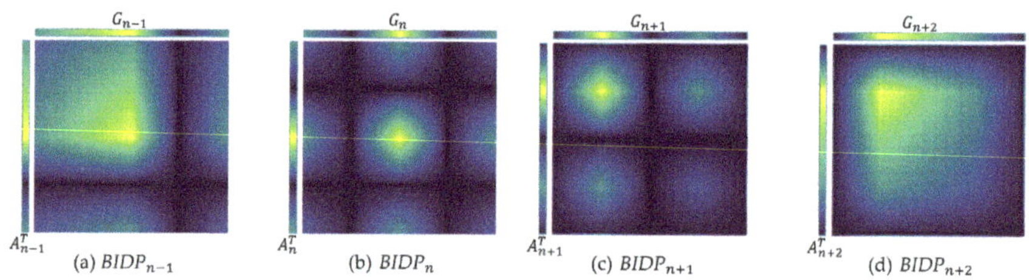

Figure 2. Example of $BIDP$ visualization.

Each point is expressed as a distinct brightness value according to the measured value. In the case of transformation into a 256-grayscale image, a brightness value of 128 is assigned to point A as it is located at the center between the maximum and minimum amplitudes. Point B, which has the minimum amplitude, is assigned a brightness value of 0, while point C, which has the maximum amplitude, is assigned a brightness value of 255. Points D and E are assigned brightness values of 0 and 128, respectively.

First, to represent the consistent pattern of physical activity in an image format, the BIDP was transformed into a $DSS \times DSS$ matrix by applying Equation (2) after expressing the raw data from the accelerometer and gyroscope sensors as brightness values in a $1 \times DSS$ matrix.

$$BIDP = A^T G = \begin{bmatrix} a_1 \\ \vdots \\ a_{DSS} \end{bmatrix} \begin{bmatrix} g_1 & \cdots & g_{DSS} \end{bmatrix} = \begin{bmatrix} a_1 g_1 & \cdots & a_1 g_{DSS} \\ \vdots & \ddots & \vdots \\ a_{DSS} g_1 & \cdots & a_{DSS} g_{DSS} \end{bmatrix} \quad (2)$$

where, $A = \begin{bmatrix} a_1 & a_2 & a_3 & \ldots & a_{DSS} \end{bmatrix}$, $G = \begin{bmatrix} g_1 & g_2 & g_3 & \cdots & g_{DSS} \end{bmatrix}$.

In Equation (2), A and G represent the $1 \times DSS$ size $BDIP$ matrices of the accelerometer and gyroscope sensors that correspond to one DSS, respectively. They are transformed into images of $DSS \times DSS$ size by taking the dot product with the transposed matrix of matrix A, denoted as A^T.

Figure 2 shows the results of the $BIDP$ dimension expansion over time. The spatial characteristics of physical activities can be obtained by discerning brightness intensity within patterns, which can be observed based on the raw sensor values. Figure 2a shows a strong area of brightness distributed at the beginning of the $BIDP$, and the resulting image is characterized by an emphasized space at the upper left corner. Figure 2b shows a dot pattern with a strong brightness area distributed between light brightness intensities, which is emphasized at the center. Figure 2c also shows a dot pattern, but the strong brightness area is emphasized at the upper left corner instead of the center. Figure 2d is similar to Figure 2a, but the location of the brightness area differs. In short, distinct spatial characteristics can be obtained depending on the location of the strong brightness intensities, which can be used to emphasize the properties of the sensor data.

However, Figure 2 shows experimental results that did not consider the 3-axial nature of the raw data. The raw accelerometer data, which comprises three axes, does not exhibit a standardized form as shown in Figure 3. Therefore, this study serializes the 3-axial sensor data to apply Equation (2) above and express the spatial characteristics of physical activities in a more accurate form.

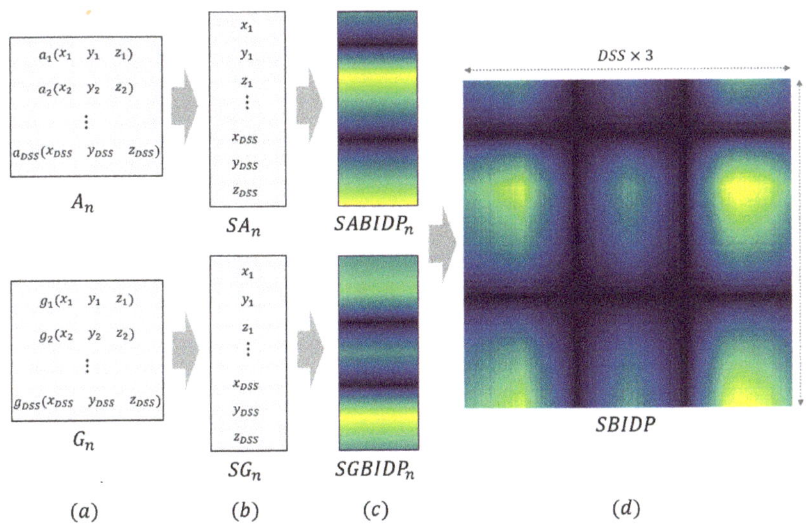

Figure 3. Example of BIDP visualization by 3-axial raw data serialization: (**a**) A_n: acceleration dataset; G_n: gyro dataset; (**b**) SA_n: serialized acceleration data; SG_n: serialized gyro data; (**c**) $SABIDP_n$: $BIDP$ of serialized acceleration data; $SGBDP_n$: $BIDP$ of serialized gyro data; (**d**) $SBIDP_n$: serialized $BIDP$.

Serializing the 3-axial sensor data, as shown in Figure 3, differentiates the sensor values for each axis and expresses a more complex geometric spatial pattern. A_n and G_n in Figure 3 represent the 3-axial dataset of the accelerometer and gyroscope sensors with DSS size, respectively, while SA_n and SG_n represent each component of the 3-axial dataset serialized into linear form. Applying Equation (2) generates a $SBIDP_n$ of size $(DSS \times 3) \times (DSS \times 3)$. The generated $SBIDP_n$ exhibits greater geometric spatial patterns than Figure 2, which uses 1-axial data. This is clearly evident in the dimensional expansion using actual 3-axial data. The generated $SBIDP_n$ exhibits greater geometric spatial patterns than Figure 2, which uses 1-axial data. This is clearly evident in the dimensional expansion using actual 3-axial data.

Figure 4 shows an example of *SBIDP* for the 18 types of physical activities presented by the WISDM dataset using the actual 3-axial raw accelerometer and gyroscope data. All physical activities show dot patterns while some linear patterns can be seen in the inner part due to the effect of the color space caused by the different ranges of brightness. The line patterns inside the image represent information expressed from the different strength values of each axis, which can be recognized as the spatial characteristics of the physical activities. These characteristics are emphasized to a greater extent depending on the magnitude of the differences in the strength values.

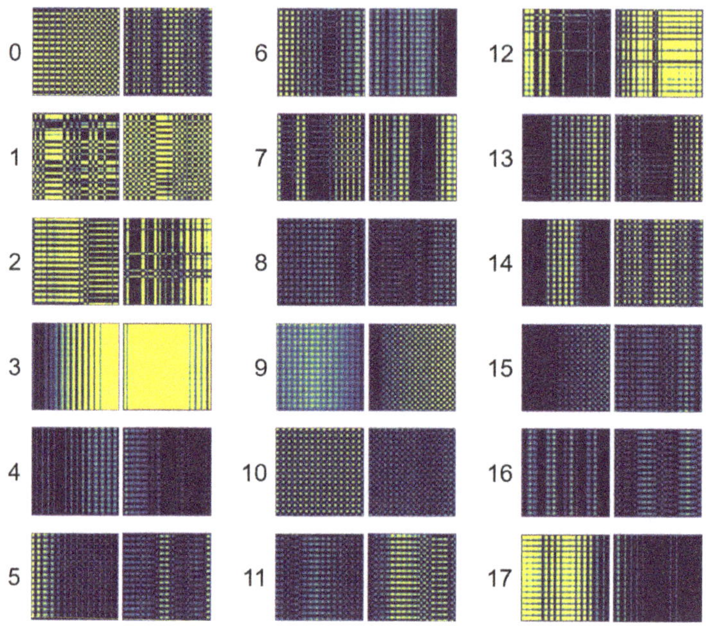

Figure 4. *SBIDP* example of 18 activities in the WISDM dataset.

Figure 5 shows the magnified *SBIDP* results for physical activity labels 3, 7, and 17 from Figure 4. While all patterns may appear rectangular or magnified, different patterns are expressed based on brightness. Therefore, these patterns are used as classification features for physical activities.

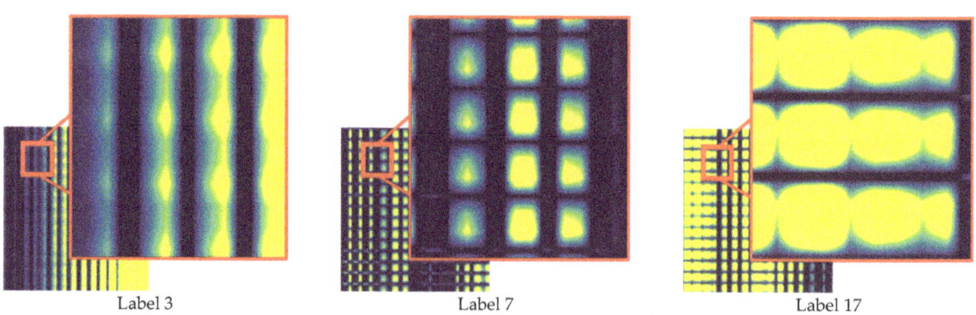

Figure 5. Example of the magnified *SBIDP* of some samples in Figure 4.

3.4. 2 Step SBIDP Enhancement Method

The $SBIDP$ generated through image encoding of raw sensor data expresses physical activity characteristics as spatially diverse brightness, patterns, and shapes, as shown in Figure 6. Figure 6 shows the change in the continuous $BIDP$ images for three physical activity data points according to the change in T. Labels 3, 7, and 17 have overall strong brightness and take the form of vertical grid patterns, but their detailed characteristics differ, as seen in their magnifications in Figure 5. In addition, while the physical activity performed in label 3 of Figure 6 remains the same, the vertical pattern gradually becomes stronger over time. However, the detailed pattern of label 3 in Figure 5 does not change. Similar results were obtained for physical activity in labels 7 and 17. They exhibited stronger grid patterns compared to label 3, as illustrated in Figure 5, which shows the varying levels of brightness in different areas upon magnification. However, utilizing these robust grid pattern features without any modifications as input for training a neural network model may negatively impact its ability to accurately recognize physical activities.

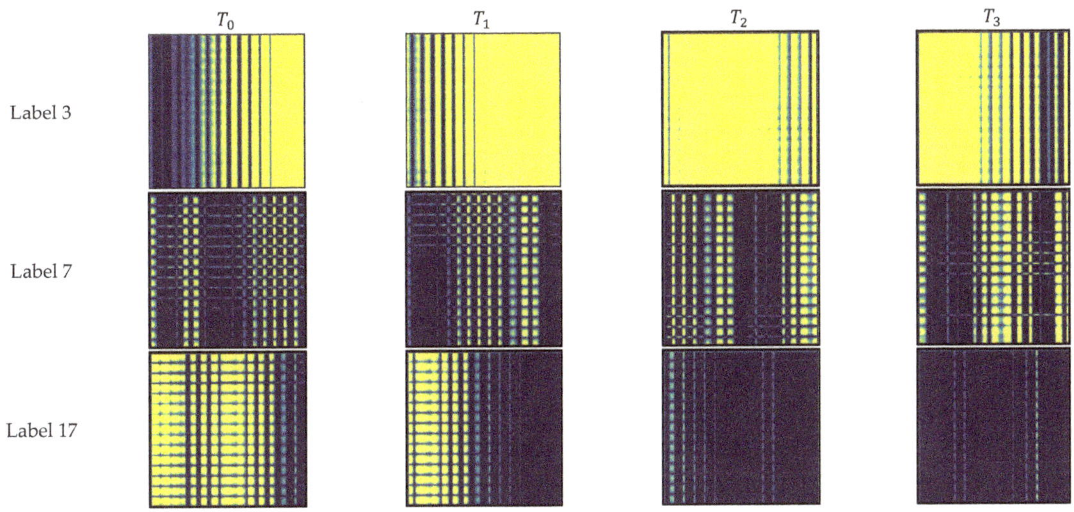

Figure 6. Examples of sequential $SBIDP$.

Therefore, in this study, to transform the detailed characteristics of the grid pattern into one large pattern, component values of the raw accelerometer sensor value matrix $A[\cdot]$ and of the gyroscopic sensor value matrix $G[\cdot]$ were arranged to generate $SBIDP$. This, as a primary pre-processing step for neural network input, generates $BIDP_{E1}$ with strengthened spatial characteristic information. Figure 7 is an example of $BIDP_{E1}$ generated using the arranged sensor data matrix, and as can be seen, there are clearer and more defined gradation spatial characteristics compared with the grid pattern of each label in Figure 6. However, due to varying brightness values, the resulting pattern took on a curved shape. The angular features of this curve were utilized to represent changes in physical activity data, and Equation (3) was employed to generate $BIDP_{E2}$ with further improved spatial characteristics as a secondary step.

$$BIDP_{E2} = \sum_{i=0}^{3} BIDP_{E1}\left(\frac{\pi}{2} \times i\right) \quad (3)$$

where $BDIP_{E1}(\theta)$: θ *rotated* $BIDP_{E1}$.

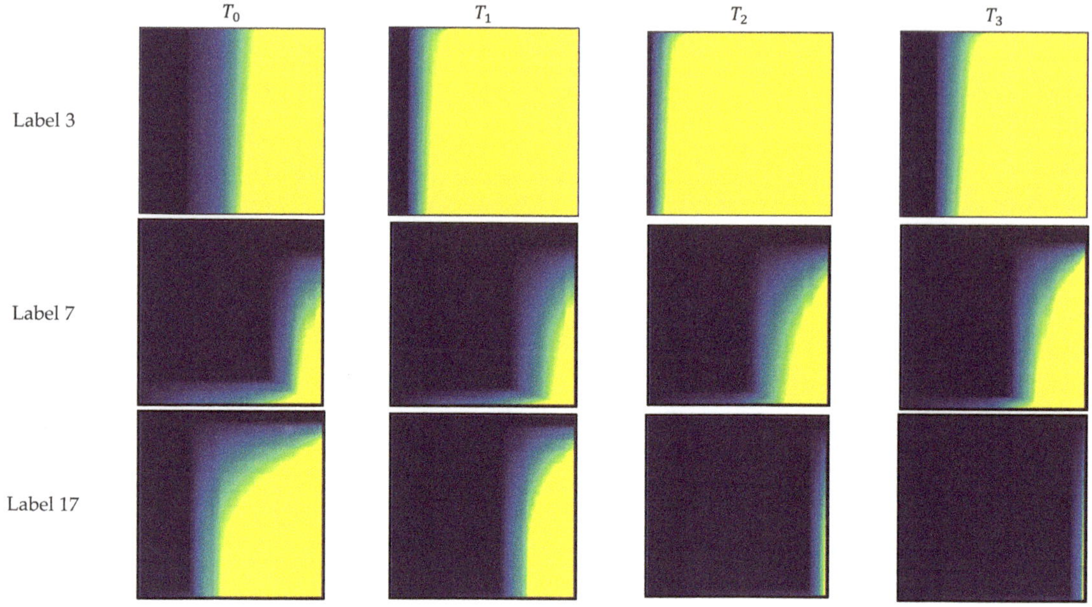

Figure 7. $BIDP_{E1}$ examples of 1st enhanced $SBIDP$ by sorting elements of the $A[\cdot]$ and $G[\cdot]$ matrices.

$\sum$ in Equation (3) denotes the image sum (OR) operation, and it refers to the image OR of the arranged $BIDP_{E1}$ rotated by 90°, 180°, and 280°. Figure 8 illustrates the outcomes of $BIDP_{E2}$ after the secondary enhancement of spatial characteristics, wherein label 3 is represented as an angled propeller and label 17 as a curved propeller. Figure 9 displays the resulting $BIDP_{E2}$ for all 18 physical activities in the WISDM dataset.

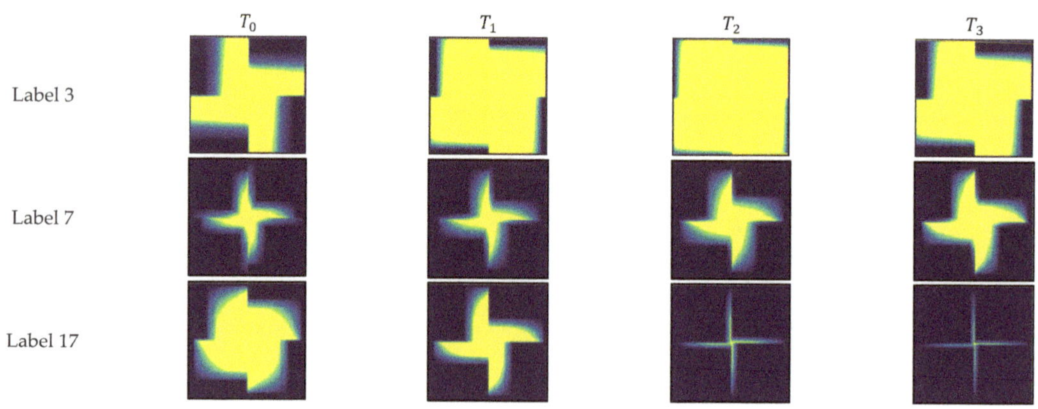

Figure 8. $BIDP_{E2}$ examples of 2nd enhanced $BIDP_{E1}$.

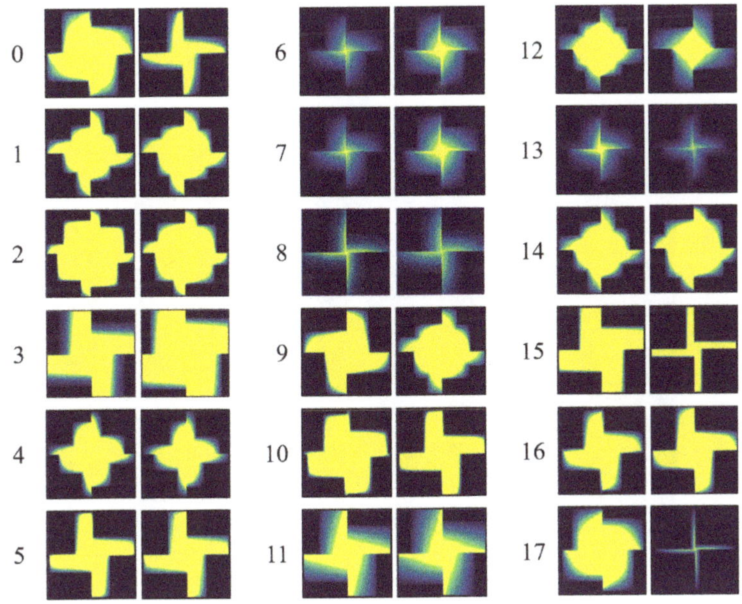

Figure 9. $BIDP_{E2}$ example of 18 activities in the WISDM dataset.

4. Three-Dimensional Visualization Method of BIDP

The $BIDP_{E2}$ produced by the secondary process of enhancing spatial characteristics is transformed into an image with various shapes based on the finely expressed brightness value. To express this characteristic in detail, this section visualizes this image into a 3D image with depth information, as shown in Figure 10. In general, raw sensor data as time series data contain the recognition of the features of the physical activity of humans according to time. In this study, to spatially express the time series feature of these raw data, one physical activity record segmented as DSS was divided into three equal parts for encoding into the form of a 3D image, as shown in Figure 10.

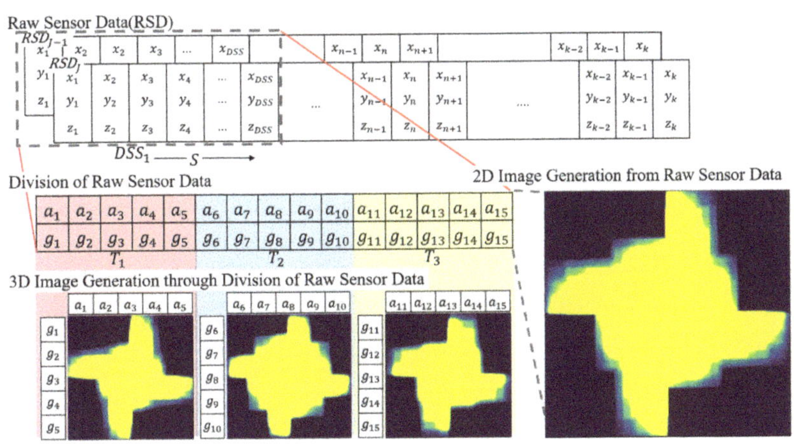

Figure 10. 3D Visualization processing concept from $BIDP$ of raw sensor data (J is no. of datasets).

Figure 11 presents an example of $BIDP_{3D}$ for the 18 physical activities of the WISDM dataset, which were generated using the processing steps shown in Figure 10. $BIDP$ refers to the 2D image, and $BIDP_{3D}(t_1)$, $BIDP_{3D}(t_2)$, and $BIDP_{3D}(t_3)$ each represent one of the three even parts of a segmented physical activity, as a set of continuous 2D images, showing 3-channel spatial characteristics with time properties.

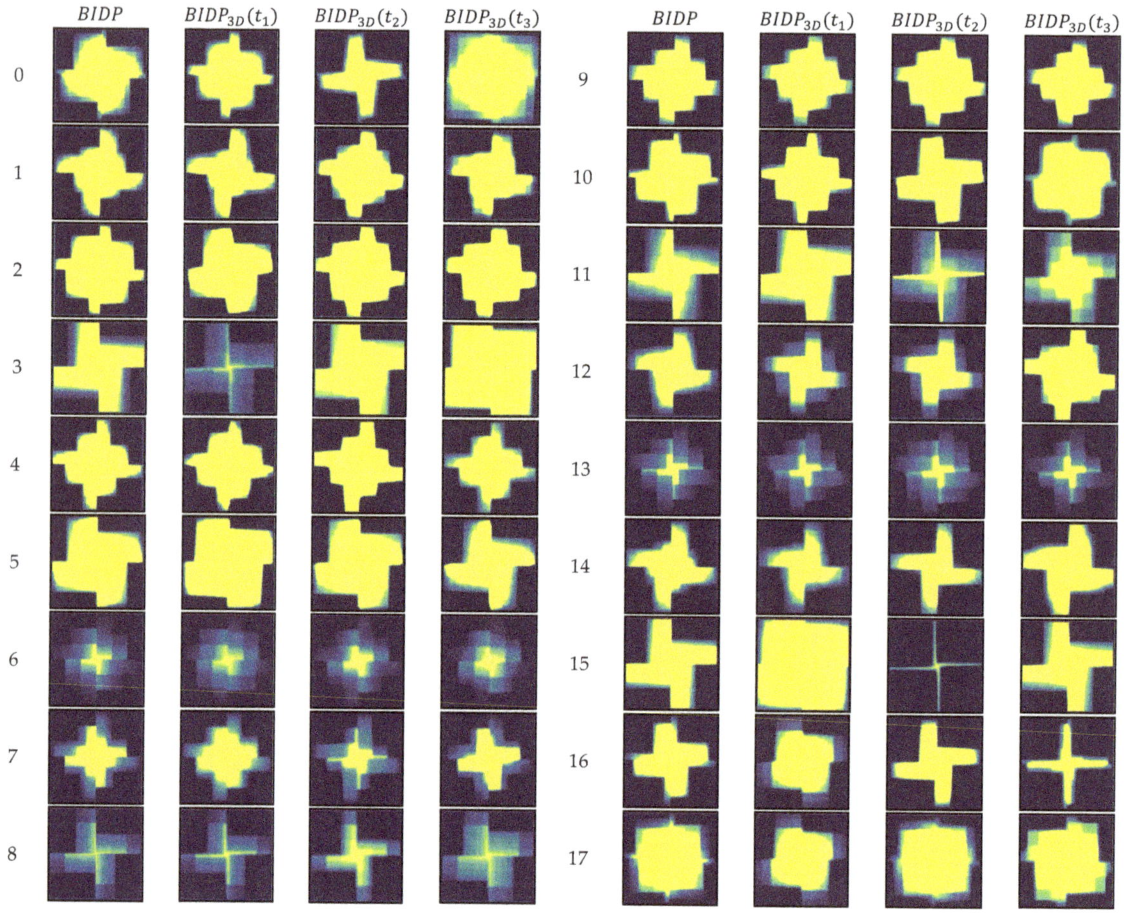

Figure 11. $BIDP_{3D}$ examples of 18 activities in the WISDM Dataset.

5. Proposed CNN Architecture for Learning Activity Data

For the simultaneous training of 1D raw sensor data (RSD), 2D $BIDP$, and 3D $BIDP_{3D}$ data, 1D, 2D, and 3D convolutional layers are used. The 1D convolutional layer convolves the sequence data and is well-suited for training long sequences, such as text. The 2D convolutional layer can extract the feature map for the spatial and directional information of image data, while the 3D convolutional layer extracts the feature map for the spatial and directional changes over time. Figure 12 shows the CNN model structure for training 1D RSD and the expanded 2D $BIDP$ and 3D $BIDP_{3D}$ data.

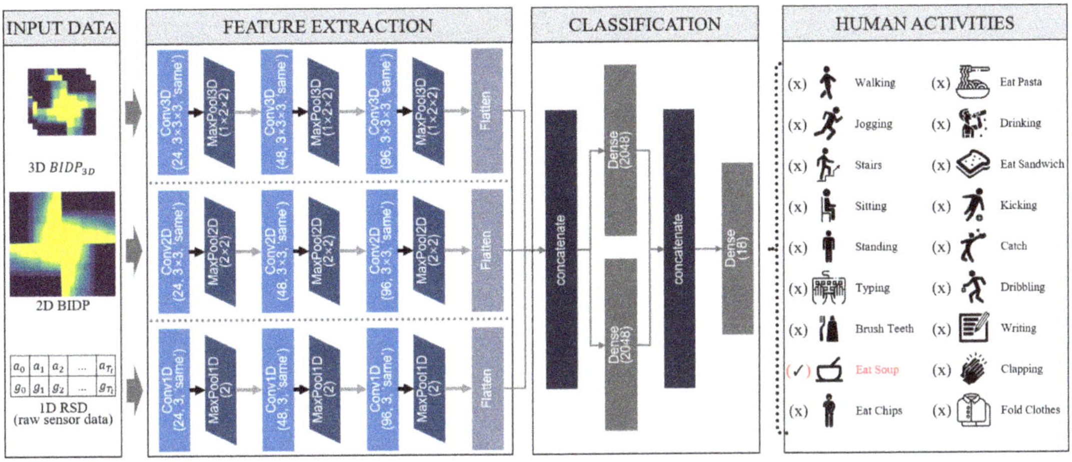

Figure 12. A Proposed multi-dimensional convolutional neural network.

As shown in Figure 12, the feature extraction part consists of three convolutional layers, and the max-pooling layer (1D, 2D, and 3D) is used for subsampling. The number of kernels in each convolutional layer is 24, 48, and 96, and the filter size is (3), (3 × 3), and (3 × 3 × 3). All layers have "same" padding, and "ReLU" is used as the activation function. The max-pooling layer was set to (2), (2 × 2), and (1 × 2 × 2) to reduce the feature map size by 50%, and the resulting feature map was flattened into 1D. Classification using two dense layers was performed in parallel, after merging the feature maps extracted through the convolutional layer of each dimension. Each dense layer has 2,048 nodes, and "ReLU" is used as the activation function. The results from the dense layers were merged again using the concatenate function and used as the input to the output layer.

The model parameters mentioned in this study were set using the "keras_tuner" of the open-source Keras library. The system used for the experiments was a Windows 10 64-bit environment with an i7-6700 CPU, 48 GB of RAM, and two NVIDIA GeForce RTX 3060 GPUs with 12 GB of memory each.

6. Performance Evaluation

6.1. Training Result

The training results for the images generated using RSD and the original data with the learning model shown in Figure 12 demonstrate identical accuracy and loss, as shown in Table 2 and Figure 13. The accuracy of the training data in Table 2 was 99.6%, and the loss was approximately 0.0134. The model completed training at 90 epochs because there was no significant difference in loss after the 73rd epoch, as shown in Figure 13.

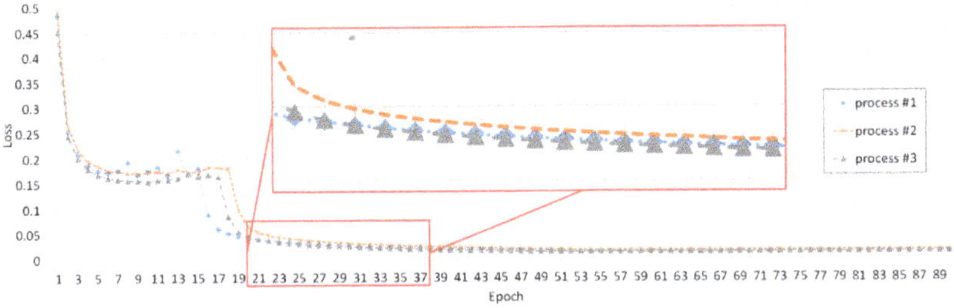

Figure 13. Loss of training data.

Table 2. Accuracy and loss from training model.

	Our Model
Accuracy	99.52%
Loss	0.0134

6.2. Performance Evaluation Result

Table 3 shows the precision, recall, and F1 scores of the proposed model for each class using validation data. The model achieved a performance of 90% or above for all 18 physical activity classes, but classes 12, 13, 14, and 17 showed low performance. This was due to the fact that physical activities such as climbing stairs, kicking, catching, dribbling, and folding clothes, which are expressed as slight left and right or up and down movements, and have similar activity data, were included in classes 2, 12, 13, 14, and 17, as presented in the confusion matrix in Figure 14.

Table 3. Performance evaluation of expanded data.

Class	Precision	Recall	F1 Score
0	99.0%	99.0%	99.0%
1	99.0%	99.0%	99.0%
2	97.0%	97.0%	97.0%
3	99.0%	99.0%	99.0%
4	99.0%	99.0%	99.0%
5	100.0%	100.0%	100.0%
6	100.0%	100.0%	100.0%
7	99.0%	99.0%	99.0%
8	99.0%	99.0%	99.0%
9	99.0%	99.0%	99.0%
10	99.0%	99.0%	99.0%
11	99.0%	99.0%	99.0%
12	91.0%	93.0%	92.0%
13	94.0%	93.0%	94.0%
14	96.0%	96.0%	96.0%
15	100.0%	100.0%	100.0%
16	99.0%	99.0%	99.0%
17	97.0%	98.0%	97.0%

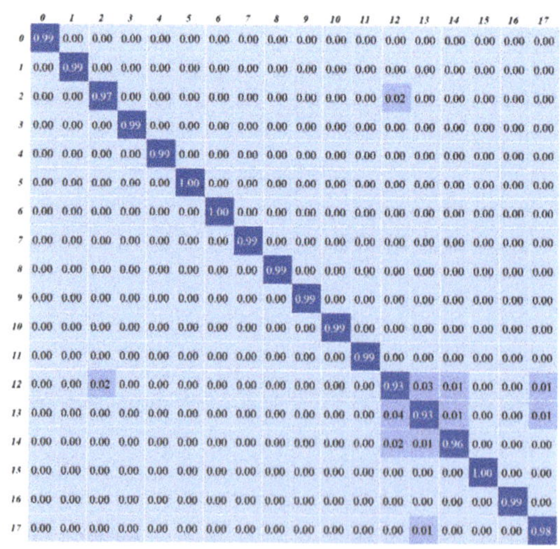

Figure 14. Confusion matrix of validation data (%).

6.3. Performance Evaluation Comparison by Using the WISDM Dataset

This section compares the performance of the proposed model and that of a well-known neural network model with those of previous studies. Table 4 compares the HAR performance with that of the previous RNN-based model using the WISDM dataset. The proposed method shows a value of 98.15%, which is higher than the corresponding results of previous studies. However, the proposed method showed a slightly lower performance compared with the structure that serially connected numerous models (CNN-GRU-LSTM); however, the proposed algorithm has a relatively simple and shallow layer structure as a parallel convolutional layer, as shown in Figure 12.

Table 4. Evaluation of the proposed model compared with models based on RNN.

Ref.	Model	F1 Score (%)	Accuracy (%)
[31]	Tri-PSRNN	96.62	94.76
[31]	PSDRNN	94.01	93.06
[32]	LSTM-CNN	-	95.85
[33]	LSTM-RNN	95.40	96.40
[34]	Single-input CNN-GRU model A	92.42	92.03
[34]	Single-input CNN-GRU model B	94.50	94.71
[34]	Single-input CNN-GRU model C	92.55	92.37
[34]	Multi-input CNN-LSTM	95.55	95.45
[34]	Multi-input CNN-GRU	97.22	97.21
[35]	CNN-GRU-LSTM	98.52	98.51
-	Proposed model	98.00	98.15

The use of RNN-based models for HAR can lead to performance degradation due to the issues of exploding and vanishing gradients in back-propagation. Although LSTM and GRU techniques have been introduced to address these issues, the sequential nature of vector inputs allows for the processing of only one sequential data at a time, making it difficult to take advantage of the parallel processing capabilities of GPUs. As a result, training and inference models may experience somewhat slower speeds. However, the algorithm proposed in this paper uses CNN-based methods to overcome these shortcomings. With a relatively simple image encoding method, it can perform HAR with dimensional concepts (such as space and direction) in the CNN model, allowing for the extraction of features that were not previously detectable in time series data.

Table 5 compares the proposed method with CNN-based models, including CNN models that use input data that have been expanded into multidimensional data. The proposed method achieved higher performance than previous CNN-based models. In addition, the HAR data were composed in the form of a time series. Thus, the RNN model that used the data change according to time showed a higher performance than the CNN-based models. However, the method proposed in this study uses only a convolutional layer and shows results similar to those of the RNN-based models. This implies that 18 physical activities can be classified even with a relatively simpler eight-layer model.

When examining the structure of the comparison models in Table 5, the large-scale models (Inception-V3 with 313 layers, EfficientNet B0 with 233 layers, and Xception with 126 layers) showed an accuracy of 90.27%, while the small-scale models (Multichannel CNN-GRU with 9 layers, CNN with an attention mechanism with 6 layers, CNN with 6 layers) showed a higher accuracy of 95.38% compared to the large-scale models. We attribute this performance to the loss of feature points between classes due to deep-layer operations on the input data. When visualizing time series data in a typical way, such as generating waveform-based visual data such as graphs or histograms, the feature information that can be obtained from the waveform information is limited, and all features will eventually be integrated unless there are clear feature points. This is because the entire waveform can contain similar features. To prove this, we designed a shallow-layer neural model and chose a parallel input structure and method of expanding the dimension of input data to mimic deep feature information even in shallow layers. Through this, we were able to recognize many categories of classes with a shallow structure compared to the comparison model.

Table 5. Evaluation of the proposed model in comparison with models based on CNN.

Ref.	Model	No. of Activities	Layer	F1 Score (%)	Accuracy (%)
[36]	Baseline	6	10	-	89.55
[37]	VGG16	6	23	-	89.32
[38]	Inception-V3	6	313	-	91.54
[39]	Xception	6	126	-	90.17
[40]	EfficientNet B0	6	233	-	89.11
[23]	CNN	6	6	-	93.32
[41]	Multichannel CNN-GRU	6	9	96.39	96.41
[42]	U-Net	6	11	96.50	96.40
[43]	CNN with an attention mechanism	6	6	-	96.40
-	Proposed Model	18	8	98.00	98.15

7. Conclusions

This paper proposes an image encoding method using 3-axial sensor data of acceleration and gyro and a human activity recognition (HAR) model based on it. By visualizing the raw sensor data from the WISDM dataset, strong visual features of the data waveform could be extracted, which improved recognition accuracy and categories. To augment the 1D raw sensor data, we divided it into time intervals calculated based on the "walking" activity, which is one of the fundamental human activities, and normalized the representation range of the segmented 1D sensor data to values between 0 and 255. This enabled clustering of the finely represented sensor data into a larger range, making it possible to remove noise caused by fine changes, such as shaking. The data with the modified representation range creates a 2D image through the matrix dot product of the acceleration and gyro data, and this image includes areas of strong brightness and weak brightness depending on the position of the data waveform. However, this can show overly geometric patterns, which can actually degrade the performance of the model. Therefore, a second processing step is used to generate a standardized visual image.

The standardized visual image shows a propeller shape with different curves and brightness areas of the wings depending on the sensor data waveform, creating visual feature differences in similar types of human activities. Moreover, due to the clear input data, the hierarchical structure of the HAR model could be simplified to a relatively shallow eight layers compared to previous studies. In addition, it was possible to recognize 18 categories of human activity, which is three times higher than in previous HAR studies, and achieve a high accuracy of 98.15%.

Our proposed algorithm is a method for detecting various types of human body activities on a single device. Through this, we were able to recognize 18 categories of body activities. In future research, additional experiments are needed to recognize more types of body activities, and comparison and analysis with previous studies that use dimension expansion concepts such as image encoding will be necessary. Additionally, analysis of the correlation between increased computational load due to data expansion and changes in encoding images based on data waveforms will be needed.

If we design a self-big-data-measurement device for detecting human body activities and collecting the measured data, we can expect its usefulness in the development of customized healthcare services based on lifelogging.

Author Contributions: Writing—original draft, C.K.; Writing—review & editing, W.L. All authors have read and agreed to the published version of the manuscript.

Funding: This research was supported by Sangji University Research Fund, 2020. This research was supported by "Regional Innovation Strategy (RIS)" through the National Research Foundation of Korea (NRF) funded by the Ministry of Education (MOE) (2022RIS-005).

Conflicts of Interest: The authors declare no conflict of interest.

References

1. Keusch, F.; Wenz, A.; Conrad, F. Do You Have Your Smartphone with You? Behavioral Barriers for Measuring Everyday Activities with Smartphone Sensors. *Comput. Hum. Behav.* **2022**, *127*, 107054. [CrossRef]
2. Yang, P.; Yang, C.; Lanfranchi, V.; Ciravegna, F. Activity Graph based Convolutional Neural Network for Physical Activity Recognition using Acceleration and Gyroscope Data. *IEEE Trans. Ind. Inform.* **2022**, *18*, 6619–6630. [CrossRef]
3. Alrazzak, U.; Alhalabi, B. A survey on human activity recognition using accelerometer sensor. In Proceedings of the Joint 8th International Conference on Informatics, Electronics & Vision (ICIEV) and 2019 3rd International Conference on Imaging, Vision & Pattern Recognition (icIVPR), Spokane, WA, USA, 30 May–2 June 2019; pp. 152–159.
4. Huang, J.; Kaewunruen, S.; Ning, J. AI-based quantification of fitness activities using smartphones. *Sustainability* **2022**, *14*, 1–19. [CrossRef]
5. Ehatisham-ul-Haq, M.; Murtaza, F.; Azam, M.A.; Amin, Y. Daily Living Activity Recognition In-The-Wild: Modeling and Inferring Activity-Aware Human Contexts. *Electronics* **2022**, *11*, 1–24. [CrossRef]
6. Wang, J.; Chen, Y.; Hao, S.; Peng, X.; Lisha, H. Deep Learning for Sensor-based Activity Recognition: A Survey. *Pattern Recognit. Lett.* **2017**, *119*, 3–11. [CrossRef]
7. Tian, Y.; Zhang, J.; Wang, J.; Geng, Y.; Wang, X. Robust human activity recognition using single accelerometer via wavelet energy spectrum features and ensemble feature selection. *Syst. Sci. Control. Eng.* **2020**, *8*, 83–96. [CrossRef]
8. Kang, J.; Shin, J.; Shin, J.; Lee, D.; Choi, A. Robust Human Activity Recognition by Integrating Image and Accelerometer Sensor Data Using Deep Fusion Network. *Sensors* **2022**, *22*, 174. [CrossRef]
9. Anguita, D.; Ghio, A.; Oneto, L.; Parra, X.; Reyes-Ortiz, J.L. Human Activity Recognition on Smartphones Using a Multiclass Hardware-Friendly Support Vector Machine. *Adv. Nonlinear Speech Process.* **2012**, *7657*, 216–223.
10. Sengül, G.; Karakaya, M.; Misra, S.; Abayomi-Alli, O.O.; Damaševi ˇ cius, R. Deep learning based fall detection using smartwatches for healthcare applications. *Biomed. Signal Process. Control* **2022**, *71*, 103242. [CrossRef]
11. Ignatov, A.D.; Strijov, V.V. Human activity recognition using quasiperiodic time series collected from a single tri-axial accelerometer. *Multimed. Tools Appl.* **2016**, *75*, 7257–7270. [CrossRef]
12. Gupta, A.; Semwal, V.B. Multiple task human gait analysis and identification: Ensemble learning approach. In *Emotion and Information Processing*; A Practical Approach; Springer: Cham, Switzerland, 2020; pp. 185–197. [CrossRef]
13. Barra, S.; Carta, S.M.; Corriga, A.; Podda, A.S.; Reforgiato Recupero, D. Deep Learning and Time Series-to-Image Encoding for Financial Forecasting. *IEEE/CAA J. Autom. Sin.* **2020**, *7*, 683. [CrossRef]
14. Ahmad, Z.; Khan, N. Inertial Sensor Data to Image Encoding for Human Action Recognition. *IEEE Sens. J.* **2021**, *9*, 10978–10988. [CrossRef]
15. Wang, D.; Wang, T.; Florescu, I. Is Image Encoding Beneficial for Deep Learning in Finance? *IEEE Internet Things J.* **2020**, *9*, 5617–5628. [CrossRef]
16. Estebsari, A.; Rajabi, R. Single residential load forecasting using deep learning and image encoding techniques. *Electronics* **2020**, *9*, 68. [CrossRef]
17. Bulling, A.; Blanke, U.; Schiele, B. A tutorial on human activity recognition using body-worn inertial sensors. *ACM Comput. Surv.* **2014**, *46*, 1–33. [CrossRef]
18. Sadouk, L. CNN approaches for time series classification. In *Time Series Analysis-Data, Methods, and Applications*; IntechOpen: London, UK, 2019; pp. 1–23.
19. Vishwakarma, D.K.; Dhiman, C. A unified model for human activity recognition using spatial distribution of gradients and difference of Gaussian kernel. *Vis. Comput.* **2019**, *35*, 1595–1613. [CrossRef]
20. Semwal, V.B.; Nandi, G.C. Generation of joint trajectories using hybrid automate-based model: A rocking block-based approach. *IEEE Sens. J.* **2016**, *16*, 5805–5816. [CrossRef]
21. Teng, Q.; Wang, K.; Zhang, L.; He, J. The layer-wise training convolutional neural networks using local loss for sensor based human activity recognition. *IEEE Sens. J.* **2020**, *20*, 7265–7274. [CrossRef]
22. Agarwal, P.; Alam, M. A Lightweight Deep Learning Model for Human Activity Recognition on Edge Devices. *arXiv* **2019**, arXiv:1909.12917. Available online: https://arxiv.org/abs/1909.12917 (accessed on 8 July 2020).
23. Ignatov, A. Real-time human activity recognition from accelerometer data using Convolutional Neural Networks. *Appl. Soft Comput.* **2018**, *62*, 915–922. [CrossRef]
24. Xiao, Z.; Xu, X.; Xing, H.; Song, F.; Wang, X.; Zhao, B. A federated learning system with enhanced feature extraction for human activity recognition. *Knowl. Based Syst.* **2021**, *229*, 107338. [CrossRef]
25. Weiss, G.M. Wisdm smartphone and smartwatch activity and biometrics dataset. In *UCI Machine Learning Repository: WISDM Smartphone and Smartwatch Activity and Biometrics Dataset Data Set*; 2019; Available online: https://archive.ics.uci.edu/ml/machine-learning-databases/00507/WISDM-dataset-description.pdf (accessed on 8 July 2021).

26. Chen, L.J.; Stubbs, B.; Chien, I.C.; Lan, T.H.; Chung, M.S.; Lee, H.L.; Ku, P.W. Associations between daily steps and cognitive function among inpatients with schizophrenia. *BMC Psychiatry* **2022**, *22*, 87. [CrossRef] [PubMed]
27. Yuenyongchaiwat, K.; Pipatsitipong, D.; Sangprasert, P. Increasing walking steps daily can reduce blood pressure and diabetes in overweight participants. *Diabetol. Int.* **2018**, *9*, 75–79. [CrossRef] [PubMed]
28. Nagovitsyn, R.S.; Osipov, A.Y.; Ratmanskaya, T.I.; Loginov, D.V.; Prikhodov, D.S. The Program for Monitoring Students' Walking and Running according to the System "10,000 Steps a Day" During the Spread of COVID-19. In Proceedings of the Winter Conferences of Sports Science, Costa Blanca Sports Science Events Alicante, Alicante, Spain, 22–23 March 2021.
29. Willis, W.T.; Ganley, K.J.; Herman, R.M. Fuel oxidation during human walking. *Metabolism* **2005**, *54*, 793–799. [CrossRef]
30. Hallam, K.T.; Bilsborough, S.; De Courten, M. "Happy feet": Evaluating the benefits of a 100-day 10,000 step challenge on mental health and wellbeing. *BMC Psychiatry* **2018**, *18*, 19. [CrossRef]
31. Li, X.; Wang, Y.; Zhang, B.; Ma, J. PSDRNN: An efficient and effective HAR scheme based on feature extraction and deep learning. *IEEE Trans. Ind. Inform.* **2020**, *16*, 6703–6713. [CrossRef]
32. Xia, K.; Huang, J.; Wang, H. LSTM-CNN architecture for human activity recognition. *IEEE Access* **2020**, *8*, 56855–56866. [CrossRef]
33. Pienaar, S.W.; Malekian, R. Human Activity Recognition using LSTM-RNN Deep Neural Network Architecture. In Proceedings of the 2019 IEEE 2nd Wireless Africa Conference (WAC), Pretoria, South Africa, 18–20 August 2019; pp. 1–5.
34. Dua, N.; Singh, S.N.; Semwal, V.B. Multi-input CNN-GRU based human activity recognition using wearable sensors. *Computing* **2021**, *103*, 1461–1478. [CrossRef]
35. Verma, U.; Tyagi, P.; Kaur, M. Single Input Single Head CNN-GRU-LSTM Architecture for Recognition of Human Activities. *Indones. J. Electr. Eng. Inform* **2022**, *10*, 410–420. [CrossRef]
36. Li, F.; Shirahama, K.; Nisar, M.; Köping, L.; Grzegorzek, M. Comparison of Feature Learning Methods for Human Activity Recognition Using Wearable Sensors. *Sensors* **2018**, *18*, 679. [CrossRef]
37. Simonyan, K.; Zisserman, A. Very Deep Convolutional Networks for Large-Scale Image Recognition. *arXiv* arXiv:1409.1556, 2014.
38. Szegedy, C.; Vanhoucke, V.; Ioffe, S.; Shlens, J.; Wojna, Z. Rethinking the Inception Architecture for Computer Vision. In Proceedings of the IEEE Computer Society Conference on Computer Vision and Pattern Recognition, Las Vegas, NV, USA, 27 June–28 July 2016; Volume 1, pp. 2818–2826.
39. Chollet, F. Xception: Deep Learning with Depthwise Separable Convolutions. In Proceedings of the 2017 IEEE Conference on Computer Vision and Pattern Recognition (CVPR), Honolulu, HI, USA, 21–26 July 2017; pp. 1800–1807.
40. Tan, M.; Le, Q.V. EfficientNet: Rethinking Model Scaling for Convolutional Neural Networks. *Proc. Mach. Learn. Res.* **2019**, *97*, 6105–6114.
41. Lu, L.; Zhang, C.; Cao, K.; Deng, T.; Yang, Q. A multichannel CNN-GRU model for human activity recognition. *IEEE Access* **2022**, *10*, 66797–66810. [CrossRef]
42. Zhang, Y.; Zhang, Z.; Zhang, Y.; Bao, J.; Zhang, Y.; Deng, H. Human Activity Recognition Based on Motion Sensor Using U-Net. *IEEE Access* **2019**, *7*, 75213–75226. [CrossRef]
43. Zhang, H.; Xiao, Z.; Wang, J.; Li, F.; Szczerbicki, E. A novel IoT-perceptive human activity recognition (HAR) approach using multihead convolutional attention. *IEEE Internet Things J.* **2019**, *7*, 1072–1080. [CrossRef]

applied sciences

MDPI

Article

Leg-Joint Angle Estimation from a Single Inertial Sensor Attached to Various Lower-Body Links during Walking Motion †

Tsige Tadesse Alemayoh, Jae Hoon Lee * and Shingo Okamoto

Department of Mechanical Engineering, Graduate School of Science and Engineering, Ehime University, Bunkyo-cho 3, Matsuyama 790-8577, Japan
* Correspondence: jhlee@ehime-u.ac.jp; Tel./Fax: +81-89-927-9709

† This paper is an extended version of our previously published paper: Alemayoh, T.T.; Lee, J.H.; Okamoto, S. LocoESIS: Deep-Learning-Based Leg-Joint Angle Estimation from a Single Pelvis Inertial Sensor. In Proceedings of the 2022 9th IEEE RAS/EMBS International Conference for Biomedical Robotics and Biomechatronics (BioRob), Seoul, Republic of Korea, 21–24 August 2022, pp. 1–7. https://doi.org/10.1109/BioRob52689.2022.9925420.

Abstract: Gait analysis is important in a variety of applications such as animation, healthcare, and virtual reality. So far, high-cost experimental setups employing special cameras, markers, and multiple wearable sensors have been used for indoor human pose-tracking and gait-analysis purposes. Since locomotive activities such as walking are rhythmic and exhibit a kinematically constrained motion, fewer wearable sensors can be employed for gait and pose analysis. One of the core parts of gait analysis and pose-tracking is lower-limb-joint angle estimation. Therefore, this study proposes a neural network-based lower-limb-joint angle-estimation method from a single inertial sensor unit. As proof of concept, four different neural-network models were investigated, including bidirectional long short-term memory (BLSTM), convolutional neural network, wavelet neural network, and unidirectional LSTM. Not only could the selected network affect the estimation results, but also the sensor placement. Hence, the waist, thigh, shank, and foot were selected as candidate inertial sensor positions. From these inertial sensors, two sets of lower-limb-joint angles were estimated. One set contains only four sagittal-plane leg-joint angles, while the second includes six sagittal-plane leg-joint angles and two coronal-plane leg-joint angles. After the assessment of different combinations of networks and datasets, the BLSTM network with either shank or thigh inertial datasets performed well for both joint-angle sets. Hence, the shank and thigh parts are the better candidates for a single inertial sensor-based leg-joint estimation. Consequently, a mean absolute error (MAE) of 3.65° and 5.32° for the four-joint-angle set and the eight-joint-angle set were obtained, respectively. Additionally, the actual leg motion was compared to a computer-generated simulation of the predicted leg joints, which proved the possibility of estimating leg-joint angles during walking with a single inertial sensor unit.

Keywords: joint-angle estimation; human motion analysis; deep learning; inertial sensors

Citation: Alemayoh, T.T.; Lee, J.H.; Okamoto, S. Leg-Joint Angle Estimation from a Single Inertial Sensor Attached to Various Lower-Body Links during Walking Motion. *Appl. Sci.* **2023**, *13*, 4794. https://doi.org/10.3390/app13084794

Academic Editors: Marley M.B.R. Vellasco and Luigi Bibbò

Received: 3 March 2023
Revised: 5 April 2023
Accepted: 7 April 2023
Published: 11 April 2023

1. Introduction

Locomotion is a universal behavior that animals and humans use to efficiently translocate and navigate between places. Particularly in humans, the central pattern generator, a complex network located in the spinal cord, is responsible for the generation of rhythmic motor behaviors such as walking. The brain stem and motor cortex supply this network with inputs and motor commands, while the various joints, muscles, and skin provide it with sensory feedback. This network then produces different patterns of bipedal gait [1]. Furthermore, musculoskeletal/neurological disorders and the overall health status of a person can affect their gait, hence producing a unique walking pattern (gait) [2].

Gait analysis is highly demanded in the medical field, which is mainly adopted for precise patient monitoring, pathological gait treatment assessment, movement abnormality identification, and surgical outcome evaluation [3]. Its importance in the health area has been discussed in various studies. These studies cover areas such as knee and hip osteoarthritis [4], falling risk [5], spinal damage-level determination [6], Parkinson's disease diagnosis [7], and facilitating interactive rehabilitation and predictive diagnostics [8,9]. Moreover, it can also be crucial in sports and robotics applications [10], virtual reality, and character animation applications [11]. Gaits are interpreted by first quantifying them using representative parameters that are easier to understand. These parameters mainly fall into two categories, either spatiotemporal (e.g., speed and stride/step length), kinematic (e.g., hip extension/flexion), or kinetic (e.g., moments and ground reaction forces) parameters [3]. In this paper, the focus is the estimation of the kinematic parameters for the lower half of the body. Leg joints are the key source of degrees of freedom for walking locomotion. Hence, accurately computing the joint angles is vital in understanding human gaits during walking. To do so, the type of sensor employed for data acquisition plays a key role in the accuracy of joint-angle computation. Hence, several data-collection techniques have been investigated over the past few years. Generally, they can be categorized as wearable and nonwearable sensor systems.

Nonwearable sensor methods mostly employ a 3D motion capture system using special markers attached to the bodies of subjects. The 3D human pose is captured in a specialized indoor setting, such as laboratories and studios, using a high level of position accuracy optical motion capture systems [12]. These methods have long been considered the industry standard methods. Another type of nonwearable system which is a pressure-sensing carpet was proposed by the Massachusetts Institute of Technology. It is used to estimate the 3D human pose using the pressure data acquired from the tactile carpet. The system includes a carpet of 36 ft^2 areas with 9216 sensors, readout circuits, and two cameras [13]. Moreover, vision-based methods by [14–16] developed a 3D reconstruction of a human pose from 2D still images and movies while [17] computed walking speed and stride length from a Kinect camera depth data. Despite their excellent performance, nonwearable systems only operate inside controlled laboratory settings, which makes them difficult for physiotherapists and sports scientists who are looking to bridge the lab-to-field gap. On top of that, such systems are expensive and demand longer setup time and substantial skill.

These limitations are currently being eased owing to the technological advancement of wearable sensor miniaturization. Inertial measurement units (IMUs), electromyography, and other wearable sensors have opened the way for practical indoor/outdoor motion capture systems for long-term use. The continuous digitization progress and the high demand for motion analysis in various fields such as rehabilitation centers have made inertial sensors to be the center of the topic over the last few years. Even though they enable us to assess movements in a real-world setting with easier portability, wearable sensors are not yet a standard practice in motion analysis because of a lack of examination related to accuracy and reliability. However, recent works by [18,19] performed an investigation on the reliability and validity of the commercially available inertial sensors called Xsens inertial sensors. They evaluated them for different activities including walking, squatting, and jumping. As a result, they concluded reliability and validity were fair to excellent in the sagittal plane for hip, knee, and ankle joint angles and the system can be used by a clinician to quantify leg-joint angles. For their convenient accompanying software, these inertial sensors were used in this study as well. However, many of the inertial capture systems vary in terms of sensor quantity, sensor positioning, and estimation method [20–22]. The study by [20] adopted an extended Kalman filter method for lower-limb segment position and orientation estimation from two (fixed only to the feet) and three (attached to the pelvis and the feet) sensor sets. For the three-sensor set, they achieved an overall root mean square error (RMSE) of 5.0 $\pm$ 1.0, 8.2 $\pm$ 2.2, and 5.9 $\pm$ 1.6 for the hip, knee, and ankle, respectively. A study by [21] developed a microcontroller with two inertial sensors mounted to the thigh and the shank for the computation of the knee joint angle. Their system claimed to have achieved an RMSE of 0.04° with a mean average percentage error of

2.95% compared to a Vicon motion capture system. Similarly, [22] used one inertial sensor fixed to the thigh to target the knee joint angle and two inertial sensors fixed to the shank and thigh to target the ankle joint angles during walking. They have achieved an MAE of $1.69 \pm 1.43^\circ$, $1.29 \pm 1.0^\circ$, and $0.82 \pm 0.69^\circ$ for the knee, talocrural joint, and subtalar joint, respectively. In the existing systems, there is a lack of information on how many inertial sensors are enough to correctly estimate the lower-limb-joint angles during walking locomotion. Certainly, multiple inertial sensors would make the subject uncomfortable and the system complex and thus expensive to run. Therefore, any method which employs a reduced sensor quantity while not sacrificing the performance of the system is favorable. Additionally, considering the fact that each person has a unique gait makes it challenging for implementing gait-analysis systems for any random subject. However, a walking motion is comprised of cyclic leg motions where the bone segments move in a correlated way with each other. Hence, the walking motion can be mapped or reconstructed from the motion of a single bone segment. The nonlinear relation that exists among the bone segments could be possibly approximated by neural networks.

Various algorithms have been used to estimate human poses. However, with the ability to reconstruct human poses from fewer sensor quantities and the ability to generalize across subjects, neural networks have been the center of attention in recent years. This has been demonstrated by our previous study, where we investigated the estimating leg joints from only one IMU sensor fixed onto the pelvis of a subject using a neural network [23]. Another data-driven technique by [24] gathered data from five people with one IMU sensor unit fixed on the shank of the right leg to train a recurrent neural network (RNN) that approximates the gaits of construction workers. They made a special rectangular wooden frame to perform data measurement experimentation. Then subjects were instructed to walk on top of it while carrying all the computing equipment. Similarly, [25] also used a shank-mounted single IMU sensor to estimate the sagittal-plane lower-limb-joint angles. Their data collection was performed by instructing subjects to walk in a straight line of a 5-m distance inside a laboratory.

The existing methods explained above proved one or two sensors can be enough to estimate the leg-joint angles with good accuracy. This is possible due to the periodicity and kinematically constrained biomechanical walking of humans. Reduced sensor quantity not only helps reduce the complexity but also contributes to a more natural gait performed by subjects. Despite increased research in this field, there is a paucity of information investigating the most suitable single IMU placement for leg-joint estimation. As the need for portable and simple wearable sensors for motion analysis is growing, identifying the best possible sensor-fixing body locations is the critical part. The position of the fixed single inertial sensor highly affects the estimation result of the neural networks. There is no consensus regarding the position of the sensors on the body as previous studies fix inertial sensors on the pelvis [20,23], thigh [21,22], shank [21,22,24,25], and foot [20]. Hence, in this study, the placement of a single sensor on different parts of the body for joint-angle estimation of both legs will be investigated by employing various neural-network algorithms. This is essential to understand the optimal inertial sensor placement on the lower half of the body when reduced inertial sensors are needed for lower-body motion analysis. This study will contribute to healthcare physiotherapists and motion analysts in the sports field. The most dominant sensor positions in many of the existing studies will be the potential candidates for the inertial sensor placement to estimate two lower-limb-joint angle sets. These include the pelvis, thigh, shank, and foot. According to [26], CNN is a better candidate for only prediction tasks while LSTM is desired for sagittal-plane joint-angle prediction and real-time joint-angle estimation over multilayer perceptron networks. Hence, four neural networks including convolution-based ones and LSTM networks were selected. These include a unidirectional LSTM, a bidirectional long short-term memory (BLSTM), a convolutional neural network (CNN), and a wavelet neural network (WNN). For the neural-network training, walking data were collected from 16 subjects. The data measurement was performed in an outdoor setting where subjects were told to walk freely and naturally. This study was accomplished with easier mounting labor and significantly lower sensor setup cost.

Therefore, the main contributions of this research are: (i) the use of a single IMU sensor to estimate the lower-limb joint rotation angles from data collected outdoors; (ii) the investigation of an optimal body position for a single inertial sensor placement to estimate the lower-limb-joint angles; (iii) to show the promising future of reduced wearable sensors in addressing gait analysis and pose estimation problems; and (iv) to give physiotherapists and sports scientists insight regarding how good a single inertial sensor can be in estimating lower-limb-joint angles in an outdoor setting. Therefore, this could be further extended for daily activity pose-tracking which could be crucial in rehabilitation and assistive robot applications.

2. Data Acquisition

2.1. IMU Sensor

The sensors used in this study are called MTw Awinda (hereafter referred to as Awinda sensors), manufactured by Movella Inc., which is headquartered in Henderson, NV, USA. These sensors are wireless and easy to integrate small microelectromechanical system inertial sensors that are convenient for real-time human motion tracking. Awinda sensors ensure accurate and well-synchronized data among all connected sensors, which is vital in human pose estimation. The sensors are accompanied by a free software named MT Manager, which has the functionality of recording and exporting raw inertial data and orientation data of each sensor.

Since IMU sensors suffer from drifting errors and environmental magnetism, validating and evaluating their performance is a necessary step before their usage. A study by [27] compared the Awinda sensor system and an 8-camera Qualisys optical motion capture system for walking and static poses. The minimum and maximum average root mean square error (RMSE) results for 18 lower-limb joints were 3.2° and 10.1° for walking and 3.7° and 8.0° for the static pose, respectively. Additionally, the effectiveness of the Awinda sensor system was evaluated in a study by [28] in comparison to the Optotrak motion capture system using three activities namely walking, descending stairs, and ascending stairs. Resultantly, a mean estimation error of the joint angles ranged from a minimum of 1.38° to a maximum of 6.69°. However, since experiment environments affect the performance of the Awinda inertial sensors, the sensors were tested in our optical motion capture indoor experiment. In particular, verifying the performance of the Awinda inertial sensors' orientation is the main goal as their orientation is used to compute the joint angles. To do so, five-minute data were collected using a rectangular rigid frame with markers and an Awinda sensor mounted on it. Resultantly, the orientation deviation of the Awinda sensor system from the Optotrack motion capture system was 1.45°, 1.66°, and 0.67° corresponding to the x, y, and z axes. On top of the lower results, our data-collection experiments were conducted for a shorter period, 10 min, to avoid any possible long-term error. However, more importantly, our actual data-collection experimentation was carried out in a barely magnetized outdoor space. The magnetization of the site was verified by the magnetic norm of the sensors as recommended by the manufacturer, which hardly varies. This is because there are no big man-made structures in the outdoor experimental site. Therefore, the Awinda sensor system data are sufficient to rely on for this study's experimental and analytical needs.

2.2. Data Measurement

To compute the ground-truth joint-angle values of the lower limb, seven individual Awinda sensors were mounted to the lower half of each subject's body. As depicted in Figure 1, one sensor unit per each lower-body bone segment was fixed. The bone segments include the pelvis, the thighs, the shanks, and the upper parts of the feet. To reduce the effect of skin motion artifacts, sensors are mounted in places with less skin movement.

These include the pelvis bone at the height of the anterior superior iliac spine, the middle of the lateral thighs, the upper parts of the tibiae, and the front upper parts of the feet.

Figure 1. A subject wearing seven Awinda sensors during data acquisition.

Here the objective is to estimate the leg kinematics (joint angles, particularly) from any of the sensors fixed to the body as summarized in Figure 2. As the right leg is dominant for most people, the three sensors on the right leg in addition to the waist sensor were investigated and compared in this study. A study by [29] suggested that human locomotor muscle synergies are decoded from slow cortical waves of the brain. They claimed to have formulated a relationship between brain signals and leg kinematics. However, in this study, a noninvasive method with only a single sensor is used to mimic the function of spinal cord signals during locomotion. This is possible because the movement of our leg is manifested in our pelvis motion, presuming the subject always maintains contact with the ground. The pelvis moves forward/backward and sideways during normal walking. Due to maintaining continuous ground contact, the leg motion directly drives the trunk body depending on the speed and direction. This creates a repetitive rhythmic motion. This makes it easier to estimate the repetitive poses of the lower half of the body from various bone segments' inertial data. As an example, Figure 3, shows the inertial data of the pelvis for a single gait leg pose.

After sensor synchronization, sensor calibration was performed before every experiment by orienting the sensors in one direction on a level surface. Next, sensors were carefully attached to subjects by Velcro tape straps in a similar direction as recommended by the manufacturer. Then, subjects were instructed so that they walk naturally, in any direction, by switching their paces to slow, normal, or fast at their convenience. Hence, diverse data were collected during our experimentation from the 16 subjects. The Awinda station, which is connected directly to an LG Gram 11th Gen Intel® Core™ i7 computer, receives the synchronized data from the seven sensors via a wireless transmission. The Awinda station antenna supports wireless communication up to 50 m range in an outdoor area. This made the data-collection process a lot easier. The data collection was made at a sampling rate of 100 Hz for approximately 10 min per subject. Sixteen subjects comprised 13 males and 3 females; an age group of 28 $\pm$ 7.2 years old; a weight group of 63.3 $\pm$ 12.2 [Kg]; and a height group of 169.3 $\pm$ 8.1 [cm]. In this study, the data were collected from walking activity only. The experiment was carried out in a level, open space field which does not have any structures that could pose magnetic interference to the sensor. A Google map of the experimental site is shown in Figure 4.

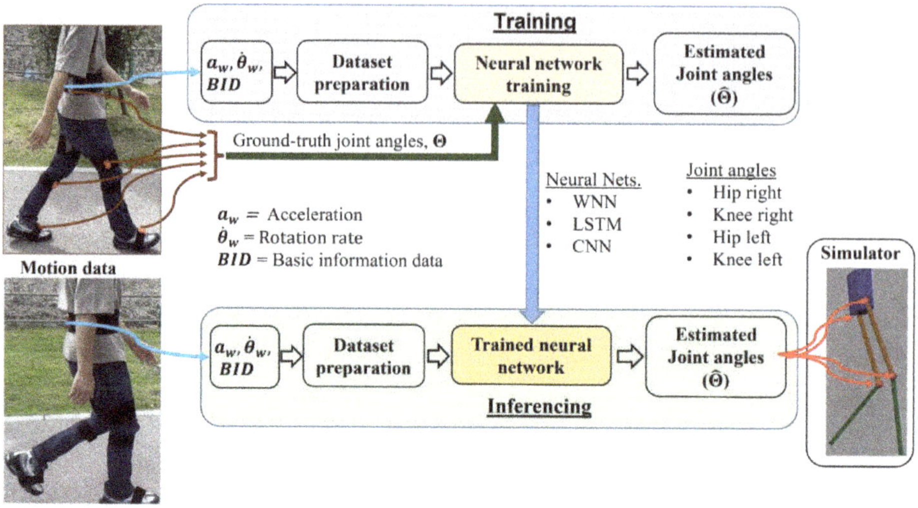

Figure 2. Summarized diagram of the developed system. Adapted with permission from Ref. [23]. 2022, IEEE.

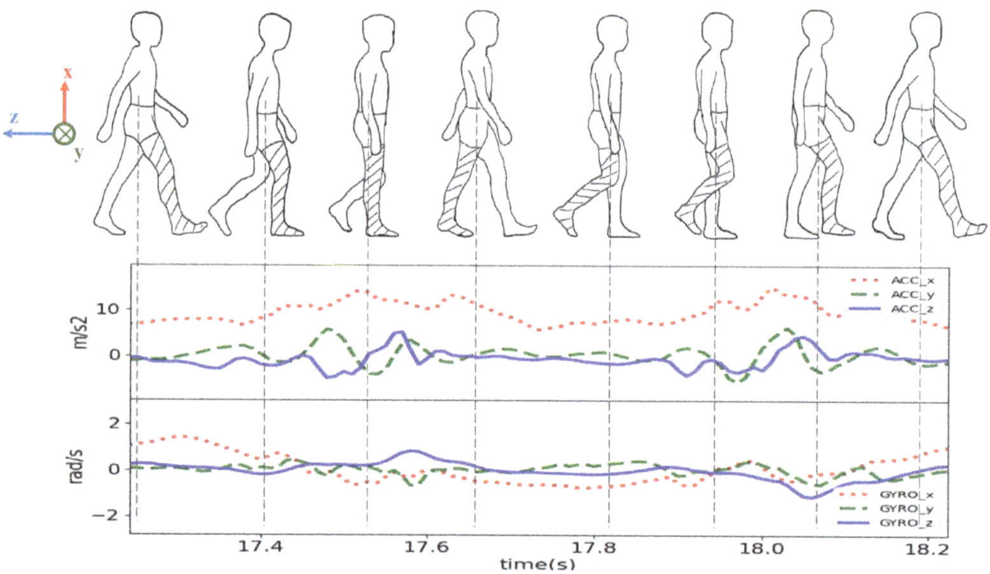

Figure 3. Pelvis inertial data of a single gait cycle. Red (x-axis), green (y-axis), and blue (z-axis).

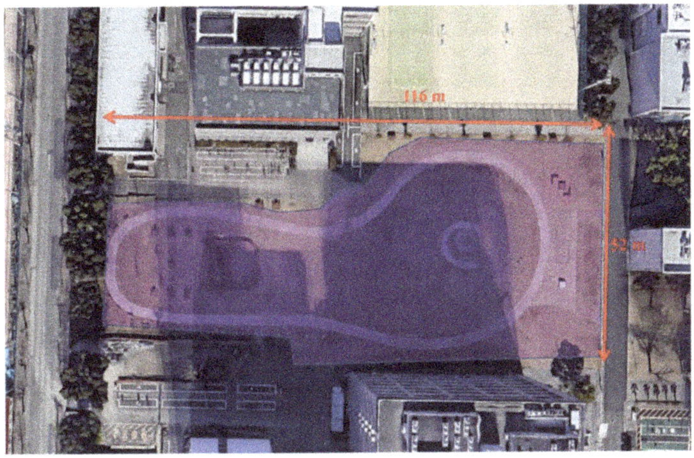

Figure 4. Experimental area (Google Maps).

2.3. Data Preparation

The first step of dataset preparation is the ground-truth joint-angle computation. The MT Manager software exports the collected raw motion data from the seven sensors as a text file. However, only three quantities, a 3-axis accelerometer, a 3-axis gyroscope, and a quaternion orientation, were extracted. The MT Manager software calculates each sensor's orientation in both Euler angles and unit quaternions and outputs it with reference to a global coordinate system. After the raw data are exported and saved as a text file, the next step is to compute the leg-joint angles which will be used as target values during the supervised neural-network training. The joint-angle calculation, dataset preparation, training, and inferencing steps were computed and programmed on the PyCharm IDE using Python 3.7.

Since each sensor is firmly attached to each bone segment of the body, it is assumed that the sensor's orientation corresponds to the orientation of the associated body segment. The orientation difference between the distal and proximal segments then defines the joint rotation angle that connects them. This is mathematically expressed in Equation (1). All attached sensors are aligned to face the same direction.

In other words, if a subject stands upright, making his shank and thigh perpendicular to the flat ground, the extension/flexion angle of the knee and hip will be 0°.

$$q^{dis\_prox} = {}^{*}q^{dis} \otimes q^{prox}. \tag{1}$$

where q^{dis_prox} denotes the distal and proximal bone segments orientation difference, q^{dis} is the distal bone segment orientation, and q^{prox} is the proximal bone segment orientation. Both the later quantities are measured in reference to the global frame. The '⊗' symbol denotes quaternion multiplication while '*' indicates quaternion complex conjugate. For instance, the rotation angle of the knee joint is computed from the orientations of the distal (thigh) and the proximal (shank) bone segments. This is illustrated in Figure 5. Subsequently, the quaternion result from Equation (1) was transformed to Euler angles format from which relevant Euler angles corresponding to the extension/flexion of hip and knee joints were taken as the ground-truth values. The size of the computed joint angles is the same in size as the original raw data collected.

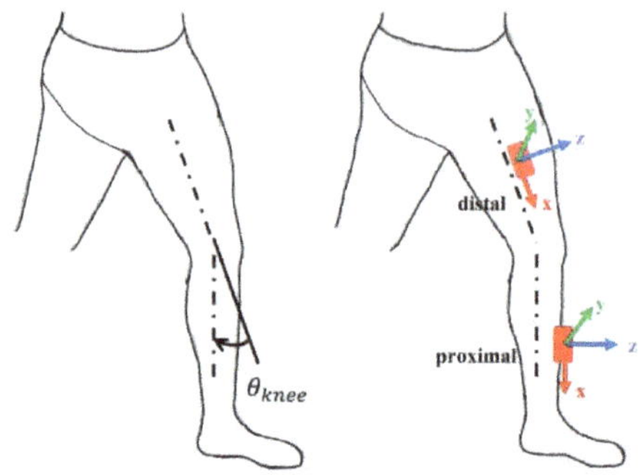

Figure 5. The computation of knee joint angles from proximal and distal inertial sensors.

Two sets of target leg-joint angles were investigated. The first set is comprised of four joint angles, namely the extension/flexion joint angles of both the hip and knee of both legs. The second set contains the ankle dorsiflexion/plantarflexion and hip abduction and adduction joint angles of both legs in addition to the first leg-joint angle set. From the collected data, the rotation of hip, knee, and ankle joints ranges from −40° (flexion) to 20° (extension) and 0° (extension) to 80° (flexion), and −18° (dorsiflexion) to 40° (plantarflexion), respectively.

Datasets preparation is the second step during the data preparation stage. Datasets are the input arrays for neural networks during deep learning. These are created by cutting the raw time-series data into smaller-sized data pieces. To prepare the datasets, a sampling window of 100 samples-wide (equivalent to 1 s) with an overlap of 80% was employed to cut the time-series raw data as shown in Figure 6. The resultant dataset becomes an array of size 100 × 6 inertial data. This method was implemented on all the inertial data of the pelvis, thigh, shank, and foot. The target labels for the neural networks are the joint angles that correspond to the last frame of the shifting window. The target joint angles which correspond to the input inertial datasets are shown with the vertical lines in Figure 6. The target (label) joint-angle data were then organized into 4 × 1 and 8 × 1 arrays for both sets.

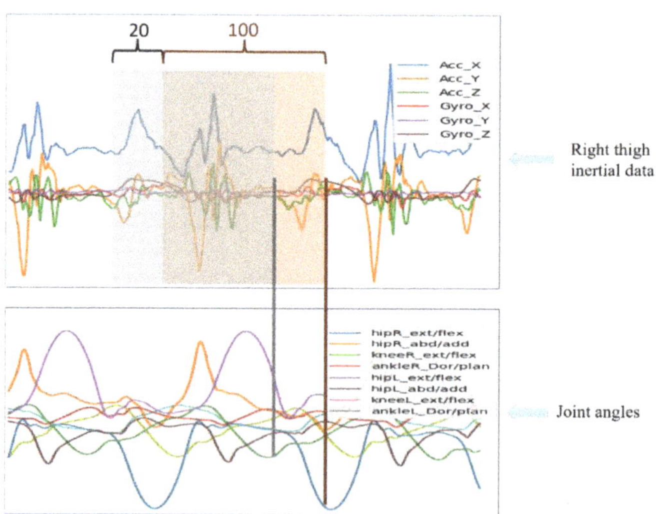

Figure 6. Dataset preparation using a sampling window.

result is shown in Table 4. The MAE values of the personal dataset indicated in the table are obtained by averaging the MAE of all subjects. The dataset division for this training was 74%, 16%, and 10% for training, validation, and testing, respectively. As indicated in Table 4, the errors for the individual dataset are noticeably lower than the general (whole) dataset errors. This might be adopted in applications that call for a more accurate personalized joint-angle prediction.

Table 4. MAE (in °) of the trained BLSTM network for personal and general pelvis datasets. Adapted with permission from Ref. [23]. 2022, IEEE.

Dataset	hpR_x	knR_x	hpL_x	knL_x
General	5.76	6.01	6.81	6.16
Personal	2.65	3.79	2.73	3.30

4.4. Evaluation with Unseen Dataset

Lastly, the trained BLSTM model was evaluated by the unencountered testing dataset. The graphs in Figure 9 show the testing dataset's predicted and actual joint angles. The testing was performed offline, where test data collected as part of the data collection was restructured into datasets and fed to the trained BLSTM model for prediction. The figures show some bias errors, which is to be expected given that each subject has a unique gait. However, this is a highly promising result for input data solely from a single IMU. Furthermore, a MATLAB Simulink® skeleton model was also created to visualize the estimated joint angles from the testing dataset. Figure 10 shows the comparison of the actual and simulated versions of the predicted four joint angles set. Both successive images were captured from a camera video and a simulated video. The video of the subject was taken during the data collection using a camera. Where the video of the skeleton was generated using a MATLAB built-in video recorder function. The subject was instructed to make momentary stops during the walking which we use later to synchronize both videos. An excellent pose estimation was achieved from only a single inertial sensor on the shank as can be referred from the figure.

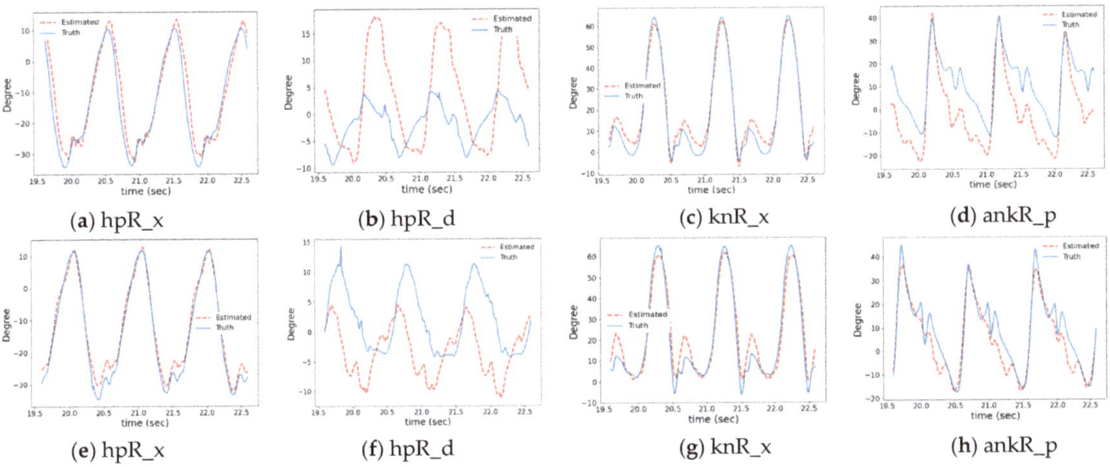

(a) hpR_x (b) hpR_d (c) knR_x (d) ankR_p

(e) hpR_x (f) hpR_d (g) knR_x (h) ankR_p

Figure 9. Ground-truth vs. estimated joint angles from a shank IMU using the trained BLSTM model. (**a**) right hip ext/flex angle; (**b**) right hip abd/add; (**c**) right knee ext/flex angle; (**d**) right ankle dorsi/plant; (**e**) left hip ext/flex angle; (**f**) left hip abd/add; (**g**) left knee ext/flex angle; (**h**) left ankle dorsi/plant.

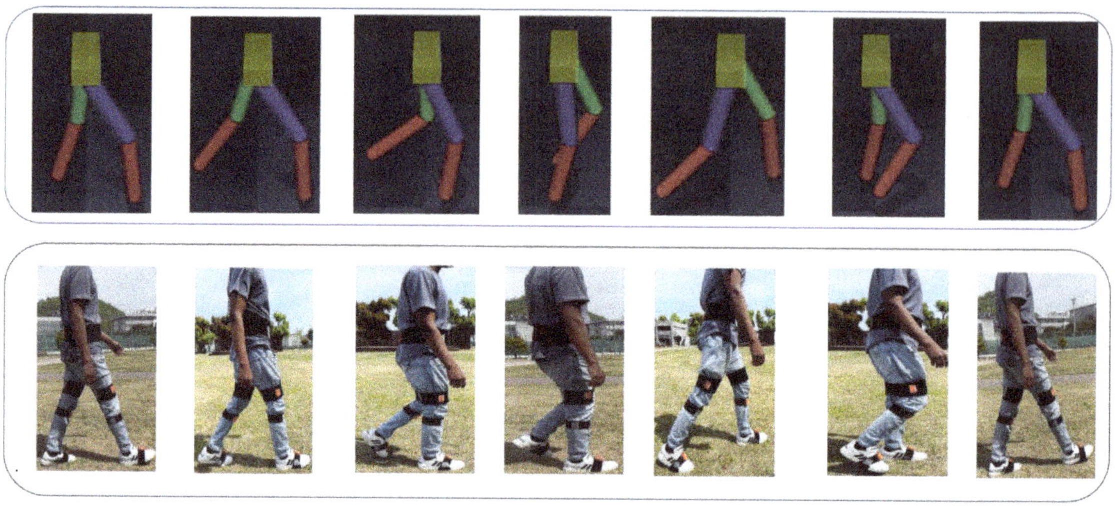

Figure 10. Actual and predicted leg-joint comparison (for the four joint angles) through a graphical simulation.

Furthermore, the model was evaluated using a cross-validation method. Table 5 shows the result of a 10-fold cross-validation over the testing dataset. The rows represent the MAE of the best model and the average of the MAE values of the 10 models of the cross-validator by joint angle. The best model was selected as the model with the smaller overall mean value of the joint-angle MAEs. The overall mean value of a model was calculated by taking the average of the MAE values of each joint. As a result, the overall mean value of the joint-angle MAEs ranges from 4.46° to 5.13° which indicates a similar result was obtained from the different dataset arrangement. Moreover, the results show a similar trend to Table 3 where the errors for the ankle joints and hip adduction/abduction are larger.

Table 5. Average MAE (in °) of the 10-fold cross-validation result over the testing dataset.

Quantity	hpR_x	hpR_d [a]	knR_x	ankR_p [b]	hpL_x	hpL_d [c]	knL_x	ankL_p [d]
MAE of the best model	2.69	4.54	3.82	7.02	2.62	5.23	4.24	5.52
Average of all models	3.31	4.19	4.44	7.77	2.55	5.13	4.86	5.94

[a] right hip adduction/abduction, [b] right ankle dorsiflexion/plantarflexion, [c] left hip adduction/abduction, [d] left ankle dorsiflexion/plantarflexion.

To have an idea of how well our method can handle other datasets, an assessment with open-source datasets is essential. However, there are no relevant open-source datasets collected similar to ours. For reference, the results of the studies by the authors in [24,25] are mentioned here, even though both studies employed different data-collection techniques and estimation methodologies. The authors in [24] gathered their data by giving their subjects instructions to walk on a wooden frame along a predetermined path. They claimed that for their 5 subjects, they were able to achieve a mean joint-angle error range of 5.35° to 12.3°. The data-collection process by the authors in [25] was carried out in a 5 m-long indoor area. They have achieved a root mean square error range of 7.49° to 8.14° (using all features) and 6.19° to 7.0° (using selected features).

4.5. Discussion

The neural-network models have resulted in a promising result in estimating, particularly the sagittal-plane lower-limb-joint angles. The results could have been improved if the data collection was made only for a straight walk on perfectly level ground. However, the outdoor ground had a gentle slope and subjects were taking turns at different angles. Hence, for more instructed straight walking in medical environments, the system could potentially be used to give insight into the kinematics of the lower half of the body. In particular, in a lower-limb exoskeleton robot where the robot needs to identify the patient's walking intention so that it applies a mechanical force to assist the walking movement. In addition, the before and after walking status of patients who underwent leg-joint surgery, and their progress can be tracked with this system. The main advantage of this system is its portability and reduced sensor complexity which could be used in different scenarios without too much effort.

Even though promising results were obtained for the sagittal-plane joint angles with SID, the model has difficulty estimating ankle joint angles and coronal-plane lower-body joint angles. One reason for the difficulty of coronal-plane joint angles is that during walking our legs barely move along the coronal plane resulting in smaller angle values that are prone to noise. On the other hand, the ground-truth value of the ankle joints is affected by the foot–ground impact during heel strike which resulted in higher error. This could be improved by introducing other low-level sensors on the foot. Another general limitation of deep learning methods is the lack of explainability and interpretability. This could cause unreliable results of machine-learning methods. To be used in real-world applications, machine-learning methods must be easier to understand for unskilled personnel as well. Some studies have started the work of addressing this issue for an easier understanding of machine-learning methods. The authors in [35] employed various methods, including Local Interpretable Model-agnostic Explanations, to explain and interpret the decision-making of machine-learning methods. This could make machine-learning methods less challenging when used by less-experienced clinicians. Hence in the future, the interpretability of the system will be addressed by adopting different techniques such as the black-box explainers which will be then followed by system reliability and validity evaluation by hiring inexperienced physiotherapists and skilled people to operate the system. Eventually, the study will be extended to rehabilitation and eldercare applications. However, for more depth analysis in these fields, the addition of sensors such as insole sensors, full gait parameterization, and visualization will be implemented which will give physiotherapists a clear understanding of a patient's walking conditions.

5. Conclusions

The gait-analysis research area is expanding quickly due to its fast-growing demand in areas such as health services and robotics. Due to the rapid advancement in sensing technology and artificial intelligence, gait analysis has become possible using only a few wearable sensors. However, there is less consensus on the sensor quantity and placement for better lower-leg pose estimation. Therefore, in this study, the placement of a single inertial sensor on the lower half of the body for the leg-joint angle estimation using neural networks was investigated. Four neural-network models were compared using walking-motion data collection from 16 multiracial subjects. Among the neural networks, BLSTM networks performed better with MAE ranging from 3.02° to 4.33° for the four dominant sagittal-plane leg-joint angles. The results were improved with the increment of sensors and the introduction of biometric information. From the investigation of single senor placement, it was found that the shank or thigh is the optimal position for leg-joint angle estimation. Both achieve similar results with an overall average error of 3.84° and 3.65° for the thigh and shank, respectively. Others positions such as the pelvis would not be close enough to capture whole-leg kinematics from the hip to the toe. Furthermore, it was confirmed from the estimation results that a single inertial sensor can be enough to estimate the extension/flexion angles of the hip and knee joints. However, it was challenging to accurately estimate the coronal-plane joint angles of the lower limb and ankle joints owing to the inherent small lateral movement during walking foot–ground impact during heal strike.

Hence, adding low-dimensional sensors, such as pressure sensors, could potentially improve the obtained result. However, this study has achieved a promising result that could serve as a springboard for the further extension of the study to other human activities. If a robust estimation mechanism for various human activities is developed, it can be implemented to solve real-world issues, particularly in healthcare services, assistive robotics, and collaborative robotics.

Author Contributions: Conceptualization, J.H.L.; Data curation, T.T.A.; Formal analysis, T.T.A.; Investigation, T.T.A. and J.H.L.; Methodology, T.T.A. and J.H.L.; Project administration, J.H.L.; Software, T.T.A.; Supervision, J.H.L. and S.O.; Validation, J.H.L. and S.O.; Writing—original draft, T.T.A.; Writing—review and editing, J.H.L. and S.O. All authors have read and agreed to the published version of the manuscript.

Funding: This research was funded by JSPS KAKENHI, Grant Number JP22K04012.

Institutional Review Board Statement: Not applicable.

Informed Consent Statement: Informed consent was obtained from all subjects involved in the study.

Data Availability Statement: Partial resources of this research can be found here. https://github.com/tsgtdss583/JointAngleEstimation, accessed on 23 February 2023.

Conflicts of Interest: The authors declare no conflict of interest.

References

1. Nielsen, J.B. How we Walk: Central Control of Muscle Activity during Human Walking. *Neuroscience* **2003**, *9*, 195–204. [CrossRef] [PubMed]
2. Horst, F.; Mildner, M.; Schöllhorn, W. One-year persistence of individual gait patterns identified in a follow-up study—A call for individualised diagnose and therapy. *Gait Posture* **2017**, *58*, 476–480. [CrossRef]
3. Shull, P.B.; Jirattigalachote, W.; Hunt, M.A.; Cutkosky, M.R.; Delp, S.L. Quantified self and human movement: A review on the clinical impact of wearable sensing and feedback for gait analysis and intervention. *Gait Posture* **2014**, *40*, 11–19. [CrossRef] [PubMed]
4. Ornetti, P.; Maillefert, J.-F.; Laroche, D.; Morisset, C.; Dougados, M.; Gossec, L. Gait analysis as a quantifiable outcome measure in hip or knee osteoarthritis: A systematic review. *Jt. Bone Spine* **2010**, *77*, 421–425. [CrossRef]
5. Hausdorff, J.M.; Rios, D.A.; Edelberg, H.K. Gait variability and fall risk in community living older adults: A 1-year pro-spective study. *Arch. Phys. Med. Rehabil.* **2001**, *82*, 1050–1056. [CrossRef]
6. Glowinski, S.; Łosi, K.; Kowia, P.; Wa, M.; Bryndal, A.; Grochulska, A. Inertial sensors as a tool for diagnosing discopathy lumbosacral pathologic gait: A preliminary research. *Diagnostics* **2020**, *10*, 342. [CrossRef] [PubMed]
7. Rovini, E.; Maremmani, C.; Cavallo, F. A Wearable System to Objectify Assessment of Motor Tasks for Supporting Parkinson's Disease Diagnosis. *Sensors* **2020**, *20*, 2630. [CrossRef]
8. Lloréns, R.; Gil-Gómez, J.A.; Alcañiz, M.; Colomer, C.; Noé, E. Improvement in balance using a virtual reality-based stepping exercise: A randomized controlled trial involving individuals with chronic stroke. *Clin. Rehabil. Mar.* **2015**, *29*, 261–268. [CrossRef]
9. Shull, P.; Lurie, K.; Shin, M.; Besier, T.; Cutkosky, M. Haptic gait retraining for knee osteoarthritis treatment. In Proceedings of the 2010 IEEE Haptics Symposium, Waltham, MA, USA, 25–26 March 2010; pp. 409–416. [CrossRef]
10. Maurice, P.; Malaisé, A.; Amiot, C.; Paris, N.; Richard, G.-J.; Rochel, O.; Ivaldi, S. Human movement and ergonomics: An industry-oriented dataset for collaborative robotics. *Int. J. Robot. Res.* **2019**, *38*, 1529–1537. [CrossRef]
11. Ke, S.-R.; Zhu, L.; Hwang, J.-N.; Pai, H.-I.; Lan, K.-M.; Liao, C.-P. Real-Time 3D Human Pose Estimation from Monocular View with Applications to Event Detection and Video Gaming. In Proceedings of the 2010 7th IEEE International Conference on Advanced Video and Signal Based Surveillance, Boston, MA, USA, 29 August–1 September 2010; pp. 489–496. [CrossRef]
12. Merriaux, P.; Dupuis, Y.; Boutteau, R.; Vasseur, P.; Savatier, X. A Study of Vicon System Positioning Performance. *Sensors* **2017**, *17*, 1591. [CrossRef]
13. Luo, Y.; Li, Y.; Foshey, M.; Shou, W.; Sharma, P.; Palacios, T.; Torralba, A.; Matusik, W. Intelligent Carpet: Inferring 3D Human Pose from Tactile Signals. In Proceedings of the 2021 IEEE/CVF Conference on Computer Vision and Pattern Recognition (CVPR), Nashville, TN, USA, 20–25 June 2021; pp. 11250–11260.
14. Yang, W.; Ouyang, W.; Li, H.; Wang, X. End-to-End Learning of Deformable Mixture of Parts and Deep Convolutional Neural Networks for Human Pose Estimation. In Proceedings of the 2016 IEEE Conference on Computer Vision and Pattern Recognition (CVPR), Las Vegas, NV, USA, 27–30 June 2016; pp. 3073–3082. [CrossRef]

15. Newell, A.; Yang, K.; Deng, J. Stacked hourglass networks for human pose estimation. In *European Conference on Computer Vision*; Springer: Cham, Switzerland, 2016; pp. 483–499.
16. Sun, X.; Xiao, B.; Wei, F.; Liang, S.; Wei, Y. Integral human pose regression. In Proceedings of the European Conference on Computer Vision (ECCV), Munich, Germany, 8–14 September 2018; pp. 529–545.
17. Stone, E.E.; Skubic, M. Unobtrusive, Continuous, In-Home Gait Measurement Using the Microsoft Kinect. *IEEE Trans. Biomed. Eng.* **2013**, *60*, 2925–2932. [CrossRef]
18. Al-Amri, M.; Nicholas, K.; Button, K.; Sparkes, V.; Sheeran, L.; Davies, J.L. Inertial Measurement Units for Clinical Movement Analysis: Reliability and Concurrent Validity. *Sensors* **2018**, *18*, 719. [CrossRef]
19. Cudejko, T.; Button, K.; Al-Amri, M. Validity and reliability of accelerations and orientations measured using wearable sensors during functional activities. *Sci. Rep.* **2022**, *12*, 14619. [CrossRef] [PubMed]
20. Sy, L.; Lovell, N.; Redmond, S. Estimating Lower Limb Kinematics Using a Lie Group Constrained Extended Kalman Filter with a Reduced Wearable IMU Count and Distance Measurements. *Sensors* **2020**, *20*, 6829. [CrossRef]
21. de Almeida, T.F.; Morya, E.; Rodrigues, A.C.; de Azevedo Dantas, A.F.O. Development of a Low-Cost Open-Source Measurement System for Joint Angle Estimation. *Sensors* **2021**, *21*, 6477. [CrossRef] [PubMed]
22. Lee, T.; Kim, I.; Lee, S.-H. Estimation of the Continuous Walking Angle of Knee and Ankle (Talocrural Joint, Subtalar Joint) of a Lower-Limb Exoskeleton Robot Using a Neural Network. *Sensors* **2021**, *21*, 2807. [CrossRef] [PubMed]
23. Alemayoh, T.T.; Lee, J.H.; Okamoto, S. LocoESIS: Deep-Learning-Based Leg-Joint Angle Estimation from a Single Pelvis Inertial Sensor. In Proceedings of the 2022 9th IEEE RAS/EMBS International Conference for Biomedical Robotics and Biomechatronics (BioRob), Seoul, Republic of Korea, 21–24 August 2022; pp. 1–7. [CrossRef]
24. Chen, S.; Bangaru, S.S.; Yigit, T.; Trkov, M.; Wang, C.; Yi, J. Real-Time Walking Gait Estimation for Construction Workers Using a Single Wearable Inertial Measurement Unit (IMU). In Proceedings of the 2021 IEEE/ASME International Conference on Advanced Intelligent Mechatronics (AIM), Delft, The Netherlands, 12–16 July 2021; pp. 753–758. [CrossRef]
25. Sung, J.; Han, S.; Park, H.; Cho, H.-M.; Hwang, S.; Park, J.W.; Youn, I. Prediction of Lower Extremity Multi-Joint Angles during Overground Walking by Using a Single IMU with a Low Frequency Based on an LSTM Recurrent Neural Network. *Sensors* **2022**, *22*, 53. [CrossRef] [PubMed]
26. Mundt, M.; Johnson, W.; Potthast, W.; Markert, B.; Mian, A.; Alderson, J. A Comparison of Three Neural Network Approaches for Estimating Joint Angles and Moments from Inertial Measurement Units. *Sensors* **2021**, *21*, 4535. [CrossRef]
27. Schepers, M.; Giuberti, M.; Bellusci, G. Xsens MVN: Consistent Tracking of Human Motion Using Inertial Sensing. *Xsens Technol.* **2018**, *1*, 1–8. [CrossRef]
28. Zhang, J.-T.; Novak, A.; Brouwer, B.; Li, Q. Concurrent validation of Xsens MVN measurement of lower limb joint angular kinematics. *Physiol. Meas.* **2013**, *34*, N63–N69. [CrossRef]
29. Yokoyama, H.; Kaneko, N.; Ogawa, T.; Kawashima, N.; Watanabe, K.; Nakazawa, K. Cortical Correlates of Locomotor Muscle Synergy Activation in Humans: An Electroencephalographic Decoding Study. *iScience* **2019**, *15*, 623–639. [CrossRef]
30. Hochreiter, S.; Schmidhuber, J. Long short-term memory. *Neural Comput.* **1997**, *9*, 1735–1780. [CrossRef] [PubMed]
31. Elsworth, S.; Guttel, S. Time Series Forecasting Using LSTM Networks: A Symbolic Approach. *arXiv* **2020**, arXiv:2003.05672.
32. Graves, A.; Schmidhuber, J. Framewise phoneme classification with bidirectional LSTM and other neural network architectures. *Neural Netw. Off. J. Int. Neural Netw. Soc.* **2005**, *18*, 602–610. [CrossRef] [PubMed]
33. Liu, J. Convolutional Neural Network-Based Human Movement Recognition Algorithm in Sports Analysis. *Front. Psychol.* **2021**, *12*, 663359. [CrossRef]
34. Alemayoh, T.; Lee, J.; Okamoto, S. New Sensor Data Structuring for Deeper Feature Extraction in Human Activity Recognition. *Sensors* **2021**, *21*, 2814. [CrossRef] [PubMed]
35. Khare, S.K.; Acharya, U.R. An explainable and interpretable model for attention deficit hyperactivity disorder in children using EEG signals. *Comput. Biol. Med.* **2023**, *155*, 106676. [CrossRef]

applied sciences

Article

Device Orientation Independent Human Activity Recognition Model for Patient Monitoring Based on Triaxial Acceleration

Sara Caramaschi [1,2,*,†], Gabriele B. Papini [3,4,†] and Enrico G. Caiani [1,5,†]

1 Department of Electronics, Information and Bioengineering, Politecnico di Milano, 20133 Milan, Italy
2 Department of Computer Science and Media Technology, Internet of Things and People, Malmö University, 211 19 Malmö, Sweden
3 Department of Patient Care & Monitoring, Philips Research, 5656 AE Eindhoven, The Netherlands
4 Department of Electrical Engineering, Eindhoven University of Technology, 5612 AZ Eindhoven, The Netherlands
5 Istituto Auxologico Italiano, IRCCS, S. Luca Hospital, 20149 Milan, Italy
* Correspondence: sara1.caramaschi@mail.polimi.it
† These authors contributed equally to this work.

Abstract: Tracking a person's activities is relevant in a variety of contexts, from health and group-specific assessments, such as elderly care, to fitness tracking and human–computer interaction. In a clinical context, sensor-based activity tracking could help monitor patients' progress or deterioration during their hospitalization time. However, during routine hospital care, devices could face displacements in their position and orientation caused by incorrect device application, patients' physical peculiarities, or patients' day-to-day free movement. These aspects can significantly reduce algorithms' performances. In this work, we investigated how shifts in orientation could impact Human Activity Recognition (HAR) classification. To reach this purpose, we propose an HAR model based on a single three-axis accelerometer that can be located anywhere on the participant's trunk, capable of recognizing activities from multiple movement patterns, and, thanks to data augmentation, can deal with device displacement. Developed models were trained and validated using acceleration measurements acquired in fifteen participants, and tested on twenty-four participants, of which twenty were from a different study protocol for external validation. The obtained results highlight the impact of changes in device orientation on a HAR algorithm and the potential of simple wearable sensor data augmentation for tackling this challenge. When applying small rotations (<20 degrees), the error of the baseline non-augmented model steeply increased. On the contrary, even when considering rotations ranging from 0 to 180 along the frontal axis, our model reached a f1-score of 0.85 ± 0.11 against a baseline model f1-score equal to 0.49 ± 0.12.

Keywords: device displacement; acceleration; wearable devices; data augmentation; patient monitoring; human activity recognition

Citation: Caramaschi, S.; Papini, G.B.; Caiani, E.G. Device Orientation Independent Human Activity Recognition Model for Patient Monitoring Based on Triaxial Acceleration. *Appl. Sci.* **2023**, *13*, 4175. https://doi.org/10.3390/app13074175

Academic Editors: Marley M.B.R. Vellasco and Luigi Bibbò

Received: 16 February 2023
Revised: 19 March 2023
Accepted: 21 March 2023
Published: 24 March 2023

1. Introduction

The goal of Human Activity Recognition (HAR) is to classify the movement of a person into a pre-defined activity set. This information is used in multiple contexts, ranging from fitness tracking, health assessment and elderly care, to human–robot interaction [1–4]. In a clinical context, HAR can be used to outline the patients activities during hospitalization to improve, or enable, recovery/deterioration monitoring [5]; additionally, HAR allows for the contextualization of electrocardiographic patterns [6,7]. As the study from Brown et al. [8] stated, a low amount of dynamic activities may cause negative consequences in hospitalized patients; therefore, it appears relevant to recognize and quantify their activities to timely assist them. Wearable sensor technologies can support clinicians by providing tools for continuous measurement acquisition; however, the positioning of these devices is critical.

Once worn or applied to the body, sensor displacement can occur caused by wrong positioning, or by physical peculiarities of the patient such as gender, height, weight, and age [9]. Additionally, within a single position and if free of moving, the wearable device could have continuous unexpected movements, mostly of small entity [10]. HAR algorithms are mainly data-driven, meaning that poor results are expected upon random movements.

Most HAR approaches rely on machine learning (ML) techniques based on feature-based models or raw-data models. Among the commonly applied algorithms, it is possible to find Hidden Markov Models, Support Vector Machines (SVM), k-Nearest Neighbor, and Random Forest. In addition to ML techniques, Deep Neural Networks (DNN)-based algorithms are also used in the HAR context, considering a trade-off between model simplicity and interpretability, as mentioned by the review from Zhang et al. [11].

In a previous work on HAR from our team, Fridriksdottir et al. [12] described a DNN based on three-axial accelerometer to recognize hospitalized patients' activity and compared its results with those obtained with a feature-based SVM algorithm, where the best performance was achieved by the DNN approach (accuracy of 94.5% and f1-score of 94.6% against 83.35% and 85.07%, respectively, with SVM). This study was based on a single device, body-taped to the patient's chest to avoid its displacement. This way, the body positions range that could have been recognized was narrowed down to a limited set.

Other researchers used a combination of an initial position classifier with a subsequent position-dependent HAR algorithm. This concept relies on the assumption that HAR can be obtained from sensors applied on different body locations: Saeedi et al. [13] considered seven different locations (i.e., both ankles, wrists, left thigh, right arm, and waist), while Sztyler et al. [14] included the chest, forearm, head, shin, thigh, upper arm, and waist. In [10], different correction methods for sensor displacement were proposed, including both a feature-based approach and an ML classifier in an attempt to make the HAR model position independent. The proposed method was developed for a multi-sensor scenario.

As these studies showed, it is challenging to obtain representative data from multiple positions and their possible displacements. For example, pending devices (pendants) make the task difficult because of the countless movement combinations that could occur. In this context, we hypothesized that data augmentation techniques could help in synthesizing different sensors' configurations to artificially explore a wide range of possible scenarios.

Nowadays, data augmentation is standard practice when dealing with ML applied to images, to obtain additional information for the ML models and to avoid overfitting [15]. Typically applied image-augmentation techniques include geometric transformations, filtering, mixing images, random erasing, and feature space augmentation [16]. Wearable sensor data augmentation represents a less common approach field; however, it was shown to positively affect time-series based computation and to provide potential improvements in data-driven tasks such as HAR. The review from Zhang et al. [11] states that high quality data augmentation techniques are necessary for the growth of HAR research. Augmentation of wearable sensors data was firstly addressed by Ohashi et al. [17], proposing an augmentation strategy that considers the physical constraints of the arms applied to a multi-sensor scenario, including an accelerometer, a gyroscope, and an electromyography sensor. Steven et al. [18] proposed an ensemble data augmentation to the spectral feature space to improve activity recognition performances among only three classes (sitting, standing, and walking), reaching an accuracy of 88.87%. The study by Um et al. [19] proposed a method to classify the motor state of Parkinson's Disease patients by using data augmentation, where applying measurements rotation improved the performance compared to other techniques. Wang et al. [20] stated how HAR sensor data annotation represents a challenging task. To tackle it, they applied resampling augmentation of accelerometer data within a contrastive learning framework. This newly proposed approach learns representations by contrasting positive pairs, corresponding to the same sample augmentations, against negative pairs, or unrelated separated samples, helpful when few training data are available [21,22].

Device orientation is an important determinant when a three-axial acceleration solution for HAR is considered. Accordingly, the aim of this research was to investigate the impact of changes in sensor orientation on a deep-learning (DL) HAR algorithm targeted on patient-like activities, such as slow and aided walking and wheelchair. Ultimately, we propose an orientation-independent HAR model that leverages data augmentation, and that is trained with acceleration measurements recorded from five sensor locations on the participant's trunk.

2. Materials and Methods

2.1. Dataset

Two datasets were considered in this research. The first was represented by the Wearing Position Study (WPS) acquired within Philips Research laboratories (2022). It contains three-axis acceleration measurements from nineteen healthy volunteers, ten males and nine females, while the second is the Simulated Hospital Study (SHS) acquired within Philips Research laboratories (2019). The SHS includes ten male and ten female healthy volunteers. Table 1 shows the age, weight, height, and BMI median and first and third quartiles of both WPS and SHS participants. Before starting the test, each participant was explained the protocol and afterwards was asked to signed an informed consent, obtained from all participants involved. Both studies, according to the regulations in the Netherlands, were waived as non-medical research, and therefore, approval by an IRB institution was not needed. The Internal Committee for Biomedical Experiments at Philips approved both studies. Each study was characterized by a specific protocol of activities to be followed (see Table 2) by the participants. The protocol was performed under the guidance and observation of two researchers, who annotated the start and end time for each activity. Self-paced activities (i.e., self-paced walking and self-push wheelchair) were acquired along a 30-meter corridor without obstacles.

In the WPS study, five GENEActiv (GA) accelerometers [23] were used. Two were applied on the skin of the participant on the left lower rib (GA lower rib) and on the chest (GA chest) using body tape, while the other three were applied on a rigid support that simulates the position of a patient monitor device, with two of them pending from the neck (GA front and GA side) and the third one placed inside the pocket of a clinical gown (GA gown). In the SHS study, the sensors' setting included the GA front only. Figure 1 shows examples of a patient monitoring device usage in two different positions, front and side. The sampling frequency of all accelerometers was set to 100 Hz with a dynamic range of ± 8 g ($1g = 9.8\ \mathrm{m/s^2}$).

Once data acquisition was completed, signals were synchronized to the annotations based on the performed activities and synchronization patterns (i.e., three jumps at the beginning and end of the session). Signals were down-sampled to 16 Hz and split into windows of 6 s, with 4.5 s of overlap. No other preprocessing operation was applied; the development and testing of the models used raw acceleration data as input.

Table 1. Median, first (Q1) and third (Q3) quartiles of the Wearing Position Study (WPS, left side) and Simulated Hospital Study population (SHS, right side) characteristics: age, weight, height, and Body Mass Index (BMI).

	Age	**Weight [kg]**	**Height [cm]**	**BMI [kg/m^2]**	**Age**	**Weight [kg]**	**Height [cm]**	**BMI [kg/m^2]**
Median	41.5	71.5	174.5	23.05	44.5	75.0	175.0	25.34
Q1	25.8	61.2	167.8	21.32	32.8	68.5	166.5	23.77
Q3	53.3	79.5	184.8	25.12	54.3	86.5	182.0	26.28

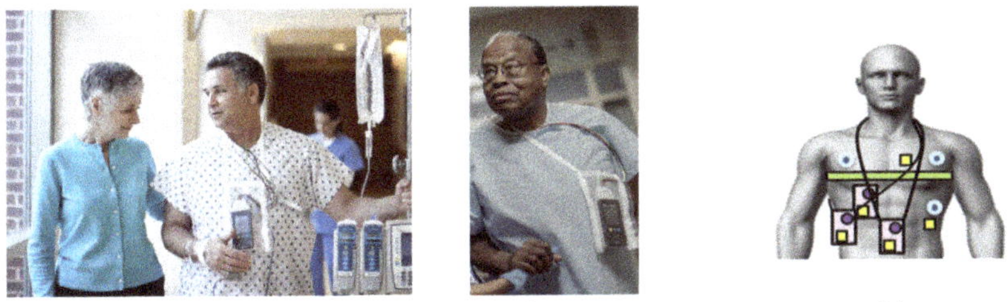

(a) (b) (c)

Figure 1. Patient monitoring device placement in the front (**a**) and side (**b**) positions [24,25]. (**c**) The sensor settings for the Wearing Position Study data collection. Yellow squares are GENEActive sensors: two in contact with the skin, two pending from the neck and one in the clinical gown pocket.

Table 2. Wearing Position Study and Simulated Hospital Study activities reported in chronological order.

Activity	Duration	Activity	Duration
Jump 3x (sync) **	Self-paced		
Lying in bed **	3 min	Physioterapy on chair **	2 min
Left side **	30 s	Patient transport in wheelchair **	1 min
Right side **	30 s	Wheelchair self-push	Self-paced
Reclined **	30 s	Crutches **	Self-paced
Upright **	30 s	Anterior walker **	Self-paced
Sitting edge of the bed **	30 s	IV pole **	Self-paced
Standing **	30 s	4-wheel rollator **	Self-paced
0.6 km/h **	2 min	Walk slow *	Self-paced
0.8 km/h **	2 min	Walk normal *	Self-paced
1.0 km/h **	2 min	Walk fast *	Self-paced
1.5 km/h **	2 min	Intermittent walking *	Self-paced
2.0 km/h **	2 min	Shuffling *	Self-paced
3.0 km/h **	2 min	Upstairs one leg first **	Self-paced
4.0 km/h **	2 min	Downstairs one leg first **	Self-paced
4.0 km/h inclined *	2 min	Stairs ascent **	Self-paced
Washing hands **	1 min	Stairs descent **	Self-paced
Reading **	1 min	Jump 3x (sync) **	Self-paced

*: Activities performed only in the Wearing Position Study (WPS); **: Activities performed in the Wearing Position Study and in the Simulated Hospital Study (SHS).

2.2. Model Architecture

The implemented HAR model architecture is shown in Figure 2 and represents a modified version of the DNN proposed by Fridriksdottir et al. [12]. The main difference with the previous model consists of the substitution of the Long Short Time Memory layer with a convolutional layer: this change in architecture was introduced to simplify the model and it did not generate results significantly different from the previous DNN. The model input consists of the X-, Y-, and Z- acceleration segments of shape *(number of segments, 96, 3)*. The model includes four 1D convolutional layers interspersed with four batch normalization layers. Moreover, two max-pooling and dropout layers were added to reduce overfitting risks. After the fourth batch normalization layer, a flattening layer was added to reshape the data and to provide input for the final dense layer that computes the prediction probabilities of five classes, by means of a softmax activation function [26].

The model uses categorical cross entropy as loss function, and the 'Adam' optimizer [27], considering a batch size of 100 samples. The 'Balanced Batch Generator' function was used to fit the model: it is a Keras [28] function that allows creating balanced batches during model training by specifying the desired sampler, where in this case a random sampler was applied.

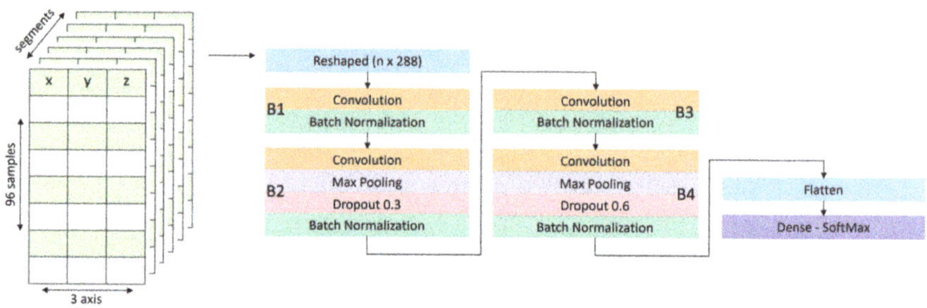

Figure 2. Convolutional Neural Network model architecture composed of an input layer, four blocks including multiple layers (B1, B2, B3, B4), flattening and ending softmax layer.

2.3. Data Augmentation

Data augmentation was used to synthesize different points of view relevant to the same data [29]. A rotational matrix was applied to the original acceleration measurements as in the Equation:

$$\begin{bmatrix} acc'_x \\ acc'_y \\ acc'_z \end{bmatrix} = R_x R_y R_z \begin{bmatrix} acc_x \\ acc_y \\ acc_z \end{bmatrix} \quad (1)$$

In particular, (acc_x, acc_y, acc_z) are the original values and (acc'_x, acc'_y, acc'_z) are the computed acceleration values associated with the applied rotation. The chosen rotation angle is α, in degrees units. The rotational matrixes are defined for each axis and correspond to R_x, R_y, R_z:

$$R_x = \begin{bmatrix} 1 & 0 & 0 \\ 0 & \cos(\alpha) & -\sin(\alpha) \\ 0 & \sin(\alpha) & \cos(\alpha) \end{bmatrix} \quad (2)$$

$$R_y = \begin{bmatrix} \cos(\alpha) & 0 & \sin(\alpha) \\ 0 & 1 & 0 \\ -\sin(\alpha) & 0 & \cos(\alpha) \end{bmatrix} \quad (3)$$

$$R_z = \begin{bmatrix} \cos(\alpha) & -\sin(\alpha) & 0 \\ \sin(\alpha) & \cos(\alpha) & 0 \\ 0 & 0 & 1 \end{bmatrix} \quad (4)$$

2.3.1. Augmentation Setting for Training Data

The number and range of rotations applied to the accelerometer signals might affect the success of data augmentation. Therefore, we initially tested which rotation pattern resulted in the largest performance improvement for our model during cross-validation. Two augmentation training datasets were considered: the first set consisted of seven rotations between 0 and 90 degrees, while the second set consisted of seven rotations between 0 and 180 degrees. Rotations were applied separately along the frontal and sagittal axis of the human body. The frontal axis splits the body into a dorsal and ventral parts, while the sagittal axis splits the body into an upper and lower halves. To compare the two augmented sets, tests were made for rotations from 0 to 360 degrees with a step of 5 degrees.

Based on this preliminary analysis, the final augmentation settings for the training set of the augmented model consisted of ten rotations from 0 to 180, with a 20 degree step on the frontal and sagittal axis separately. While all the original acceleration signals were considered in the training data, only a randomly selected portion (11.1%) of these signals was kept when applying a single rotation. The baseline model was trained using the data collected by the five upper body sensors in the WPS dataset, including a total of 73,683 segments (windows of 6 s overlapped by 4.5 s). The resulting training size of the augmented model was three times the size of the baseline training set.

2.3.2. Augmentation Setting of Testing Data

The models were evaluated through three different test sets shown in Figure 3 and reported below:

- Original: this test set did not have any data augmentation.
- Real-life test set: double-axis small rotations along the frontal and sagittal axis (respectively X- and Z-axis). In particular: [[5, 5], [5, 2], [2, 5], [10, 10], [10, 5], [5, 10], [15, 15], [15, 10], [10, 15]], unit of measurement in degrees.
- Fully-rotated test set: fifty-six rotations between 0 and 360 degrees applied along the frontal, longitudinal, and sagittal axis (respectively, X-,Y-, and Z-axis) separately.

Table 3 describes the selected participants and sensors used for training and testing of both the baseline and augmented HAR models. Fifteen participants of the WPS were considered when cross-validating the model: ten for training, two for validation, and three for testing. The participants in the cross-validation procedure were randomly split and performance for each fold was observed to see if there were any discrepancies between the splits. On the other hand, four random participants of the WPS and all twenty participants of the SHS were kept separated and considered only in the final testing as a holdout set (i.e., external validation).

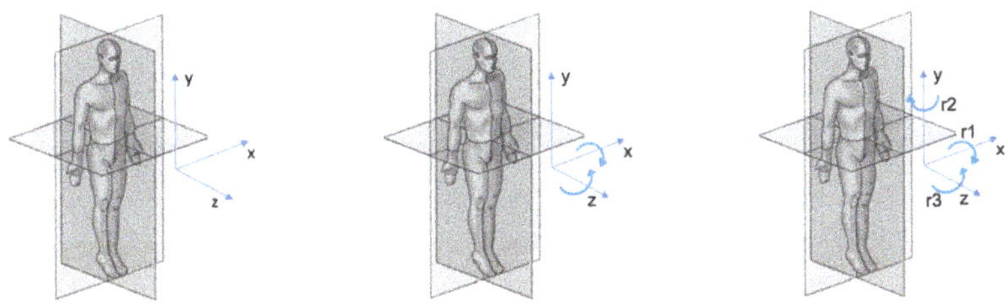

(a) (b) (c)

Figure 3. Augmented test set visualization. (**a**) The original sensor orientation compared to the standing human body. (**b**) The applied rotations of the real-life test set along the frontal and sagittal axis. (**c**) The three non-simultaneous rotations applied along the frontal, longitudinal, and sagittal axis (r1, r2, r3) with the fully-rotated test set.

Table 3. Train and test settings for the baseline and the augmented model computation. The baseline model training did not undergo data augmentation. The two models were tested in the same way by means of three test sets.

Train/Test	Participants	Rotations	Rotation Axis	Sensors' Location
Train baseline model	WPS—15 participants	-	-	Front, side, gown, chest, left lower rib
Train augmented model	WPS—15 participants	0 to 180 deg. step 20	Frontal (X-axis), sagittal (Z-axis)	Front, side, gown, chest, left lower rib
Test holdout	WPS—4 holdout participants	Test sets: Original, real-life, fully-rotated test sets		Front, side, gown
	SHS—20 participants			Front

3. Evaluation of the Orientation Impact Model and HAR Performance

A five-fold cross-validation [30] was used to train both the baseline and the augmented models. The cross-validation performance was used to determine the augmentation approach (i.e., the range of rotations), and the effect of the rotation on the baseline model.

Each cross-validation fold used the WPS data of ten participants for training the model, the data of two participants for early stopping, and the data of three participants to assess the model performance.

The activity labels of the two holdout sets were estimated by a majority-voting ensemble of the results of the five models obtained during cross-validation for baseline and augmented models. The results of the original test sets were averaged over the considered participants. The real-life and fully-rotated test sets' results were averaged on the applied external rotations and the considered f1-score was computed by micro-averaging obtained predictions. The performance metrics that evaluated each class were the f1-score, precision, recall, and specificity. Additionally, the Cohen's Kappa (Kappa-score) was considered: it represents an inter-rater agreement coefficient between two raters, as a function of the probability that the two raters are in perfect agreement [31]. For statistical analysis, first the Shapiro–Wilk [32] test was used to verify the normality of f1-score values. Then, the Wilcoxon signed-rank and the t-test were applied to establish differences within performance distributions. The Wilcoxon test is non-parametric, and therefore, does not require normality of the observed data [33].

4. Results

4.1. Rotation Impact on the Baseline Model

The baseline model was tested by using data augmentation, in particular, by applying rotations, from 0 to 180 degrees, on the frontal, longitudinal, and sagittal axis. Performances between the five cross-validation splits were observed. In particular, a minimum Kappa-score value of 0.87 and a maximal Kappa-score value of 0.92 were obtained when testing the baseline model with the original test set. Thus, it could be concluded that the model performance was not dependent on which recordings were included in the training set. Figure 4 reports the percentage of wrong classifications according to multiple axis and groups of activities. It is noticeable how the Y-axis, parallel to the participant's frontal plane and parallel to the Earth's gravity acceleration, was the least impacted axis by orientation changes. Moreover, because of the nature of the proposed activities, the static ones (Lying in bed, Left side, Passive wheelchair, Right side, Reading, Reclined, Sitting on the edge of the bed, Standing, Upright, Washing hands/brushing teeth) were the least affected compared to the dynamic ones.

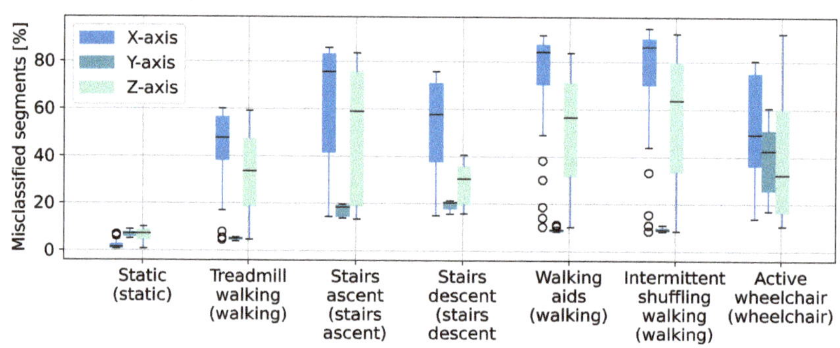

Figure 4. Percentage of misclassified segments when testing the baseline model with rotations from 0 to 180 degrees applied to each axis separately. Misclassified segments correspond to the amount of false negative predictions for the specific label

Figure 5 shows the percentage of misclassified segments of selected groups of activities when rotations were applied along the frontal, longitudinal, and sagittal axis (respectively, X-, Y-, and Z-axis) separately; the performance is shown for each applied rotation from 0 to 180 degrees (0, 5, 10, 20, 25, 30, 40, . . . , 180 degrees). Two groups of activities are reported: treadmill walking and static activities. As previously observed, major differences were noticeable in relation to the type of activity being considered and the axis to which the rotation was applied. It is relevant to highlight that, within dynamic activities, the error percentage increased rapidly even for low values of applied rotations. Activity distribution from the WPS and SHS data, divided according to the label of our interest, were as follows: stairs ascent 5.2%, stairs descent 4.9%, static 25.2%, walking 62.5%, wheelchair 2.3%.

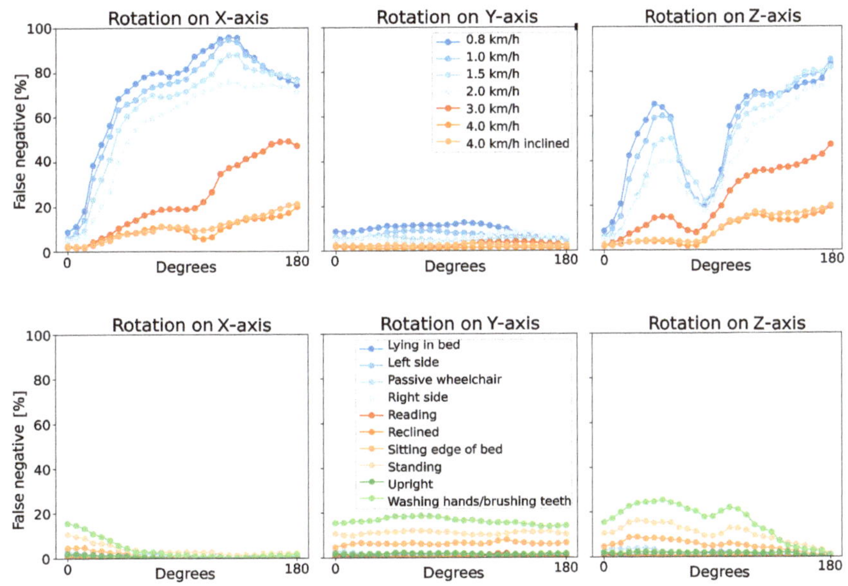

Figure 5. Top panels show false negative percentage profiles of treadmill walking activities; bottom panels report false negative percentage profiles of static activities. Rotations on the X-, Y-, and Z-axis correspond to rotations applied along the frontal, longitudinal, and sagittal axis, respectively.

4.2. Augmentation Approach

The performance of models trained with two augmented training sets was observed to determine which one would suit best. In particular, the comparison between the two ranges of rotation was computed from 0 to 360 degrees, every five degrees, and results were presented for each 90 degree range. As shown in Figure 6, the model trained with a range of rotations that span from 0 to 180 had better results over three quarters out of four, in terms of Kappa score.

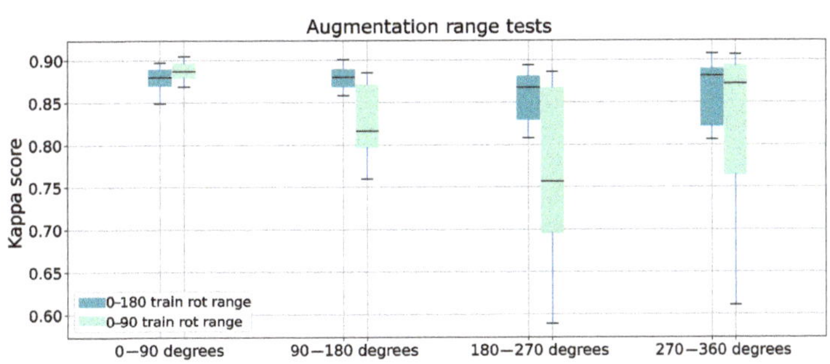

Figure 6. Performances comparison of Kappa score between two differently augmented models.

4.3. Holdout Data Results—External Validation

When rotations were applied on a single or double axis, the baseline model significantly increased the errors when classifying what activity the participant was doing, thus decreasing the performance. The augmented model maintained high performance even when rotations were applied. This consideration was confirmed from testing outcomes on both WPS holdout and SHS data, as external validation. Figure 7 reports the obtained results for the baseline and the augmented model according to the three augmented test sets in terms of f1-score and Kappa-score. Appendix A reports detailed numerical results, such as the median and interquartile range referring to Figure 7 and single class results according to each model, each testing set, and considered participants.

Statistical analysis was conducted on the f1-score and Kappa-score of the two models. For all data (cross-validated participants, WPS holdout participants, and SHS external validation), no significant difference was observed related to the original test set. The paired t-test was applied to test real-life test set performances, obtaining a p-value smaller than 0.01 for both holdout source sets. The Wilcoxon-rank test was used for the fully-rotated test set, showing a p-value < 0.01 for each axis of the WPS holdout data. The SHS p-values were below 0.01 for both the frontal and sagittal axis (X- and Z-axis), while for rotations applied along the longitudinal axis (Y-axis), no significant difference was shown.

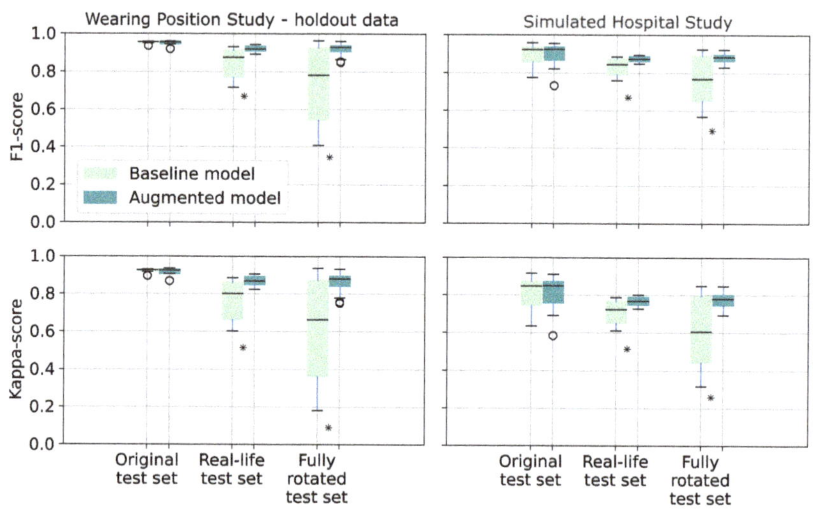

Figure 7. F1-score (top panels) and Kappa-score (bottom panels) of the baseline and the augmented model for the three test sets: Original, real-life and fully rotated test sets. *: test sets obtained statistically different results for the baseline and augmented model with a p-value < 0.01.

Additionally, Figure 8 highlights the covered area of false negative percentage profile related to treadmill walking activities. The green area belongs to the baseline model and it is generally wider than the one of the augmented model. Low-speed treadmill activities (⩽2.0 km/h) majorly contributed to the upper part of the green area. On the contrary, high-speed treadmill activities (>2.0 km/h) had generally fewer false negatives (lower part of the green area). This behavior was less visible in the profiles of the augmented model.

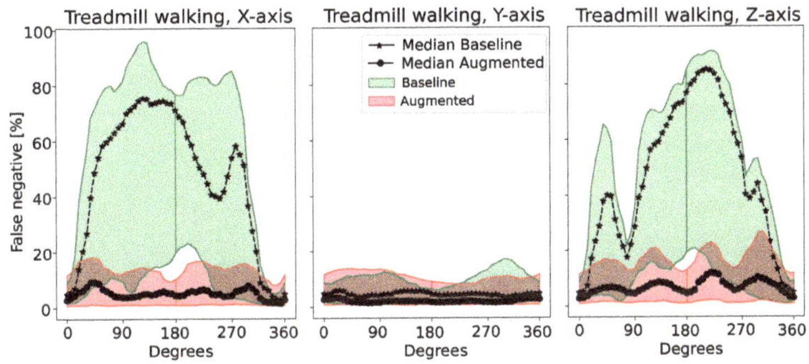

Figure 8. False negative percentage profiles of treadmill activities (i.e., walking class) for rotations applied to each axis separately for baseline and augmented models. The top line corresponds to the maximum profile for that rotation; the bottom line corresponds to the minimum profile for that rotation; the black dotted lines correspond to the profile median value.

5. Discussion

The context of HAR is broad and with multiple fields of application, making it hard, sometimes, to compare studies due to the diversity in the selected activities, environment conditions, target population, and chosen metrics [34].

Our study was focused on simulated activities that may characterize a hospitalized patient wearing a device with freedom of movement (i.e., pendants or inside a pocket), localized in the upper part of the patient's body. Thanks to data augmentation, the HAR model was able to learn additional configurations not provided by the initial dataset. As Figure 8 shows, the false negative percentage red area covered by the augmented model was significantly smaller compared to the green area belonging to the baseline model. Additionally, the red area kept the error profile low and stable while the applied rotations increased.

To choose the augmented rotation ranges to be applied to the training data, performances obtained from two different sets, shown in Figure 6, were evaluated: despite the seven rotations between 0 and 180 degrees being sparse, they allowed the model to better learn device configurations characterized by higher applied rotations. In light of these considerations, a rotation range from 0 to 180 degrees was chosen for training data augmentation.

To the best of our knowledge, few research studies addressed data augmentation of acceleration signals; therefore, expanding this research field and its potential applications could be of relevant interest in this knowledge domain. The study by Ohashi et al. [17] addressed data augmentation according to a specific physical constraint; in particular, it allows sensor movement only on a certain trajectory dictated by the arm's degrees of freedom. In contrast, our applied augmentation does not follow physical constraints. In fact, it includes rotations that could easily happen when using sensors pending from the body in patient monitoring devices (i.e., the Portrait^{TM} Mobile, by GE Healthcare [35], or the IntelliVue MX40 by Philips [36]), such as for example: the up-side down flipping of the device (i.e., 180 degrees on the frontal axis), inclined device due to body shape (i.e., small rotations along the frontal axis), and inclined device due to asymmetric position of the pending rigid support (small rotations along sagittal axis).

Collecting data spanning from many orientation configurations is highly time- and computationally expensive; from this perspective, data augmentation could represent an optimal approach to deal with this aspect and to increase overall performance. In Table 4, the main augmentation-related studies found in the literature are reported, along with the considered sensors and their positions, the applied augmentations, and the identified activities within the proposed framework.

Table 4. Description of the most relevant studies related to wearable sensor data augmentation in the context of HAR. Each study is described by its sensors' positioning, applied augmentation, type of sensor, and recognized activities.

Author	Sensors' Position	Applied Augmentation	Augmented Sensors	Recognized Activities
[17]	Forearm	Rotations around X-axis	Accelerometer Gyroscope EMG *	Holding, Twisting, Folding
[18]	Left wrist	Averaging, combining, shuffling	Spectral features of accelerometer and gyroscope	Sitting, Standing, Walking
[19]	Wrist	Rotation, Permutation, Time-warping, Magnitude-warping	Accelerometer	Motor state of Parkinson sbj: Bradyiknesia, Dyskinesia
[20]	Mobile phone pockets	Resampling for contrastive learning	Accelerometer Gyroscope Magnetometer	UCI-HAR [37], MotionSense [38], USC-HAD [39]
Proposed model	Body trunk	Rotations around the three axis separately	Accelerometer	Stairs up, Stairs down, Static, Walking, Wheelchair

*: augmented sensors that undergo different kind of augmentation than the one reported in the table.

In accordance with the literature, our initial results confirmed that device displacement might cause significant performance loss when using sensor orientation-dependent models. The error rate steeply rises even with small rotations (i.e., 5 degrees applied to the frontal axis $\approx$ 10%; 10 degrees applied to the frontal axis $\approx$ 20% for 0.8 km/h from Figure 5). False negative percentages of static activities did not increase when rotations were applied (i.e., 5 and 10 degrees applied to the frontal axis $\approx$ 5% for "Sitting edge of the bed" from Figure 5). As a result of the stable acceleration pattern, the model was able to recognize and classify this behavior as static activity. On the other hand, treadmill-related activity results showed an error rise as the applied rotation increased over the frontal and sagittal axis (X- and Z-axis). This trend was probably due to the nature of the different treadmill walking activities. In particular, high-speed walking activities had a low error profile. This activity type showed high peaks during the heel-strike and toe-off gait phases, allowing the model to predict it more easily. However, even for high-speed walking activities, their error percentage increased when larger rotations were applied ($\approx$90 degree on the frontal axis). A possible reason for this could be that large rotations along the frontal and sagittal axis (X- and Z-axis) implied switching the acceleration component parallel to gravity that usually carries most part of the information. Figure 9 shows an example of walking activities of 0.8 km/h and 4.0 km/h and their corresponding applied rotations of twenty and sixty degrees. It was visible how slower walking had a smaller acceleration range. On the other hand, faster walking acceleration range had more dynamism and the information spanned a wider acceleration range.

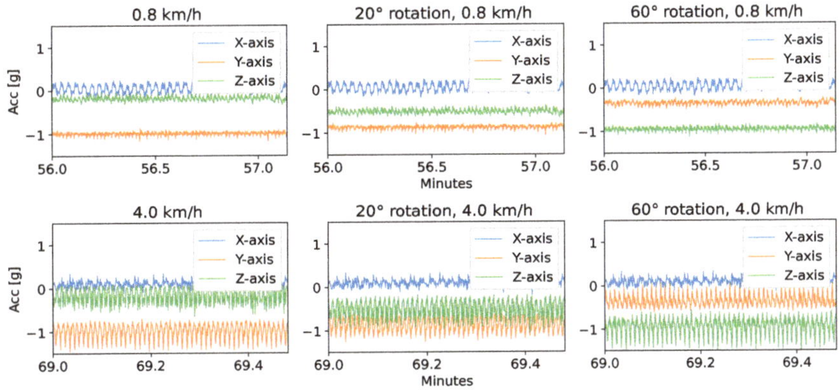

Figure 9. Walking activities of 0.8 km/h (top) and 4.0 km/h (bottom) and the corresponding applied rotations of twenty and sixty degrees ($g = 9.81$ km/s^2).

As shown in Figure 4, the static activities were the least affected by rotations on all orientation axes, probably due to their low acceleration values. Considering the models' performance differences among activities, another possible approach could be a tailored augmentation to the activity itself. Future work might consider transformations applied only to the classes that are majorly influenced by rotation, i.e., the classes with a high dynamic range, in terms, for example, of acceleration magnitude. This way, redundancy would be avoided and data would be augmented more efficiently.

Limitations and Future Work

Among the five prediction classes, further processing could be applied to the "wheelchair" class. As a matter of fact, it was easy to misclassify it with static or walking activities, due to acceleration pattern similarities. Our performance showed a low precision for the original test set and a high value for recall of the wheelchair class (0.41 ± 0.23 precision, 0.92 ± 0.12 recall for SHS participants, original test set). Frequently, slow walking activities were wrongly classified as wheelchair. A possible future improvement to "wheelchair" precision could be to apply post-processing steps to the predicted "wheelchair" class. For example, contextualizing the single "wheelchair" segment with the surrounding ones (i.e., within a certain number of consecutive "walking" segments, if "wheelchair" is detected, that prediction will likely be wrong, and therefore, post-processed as "walking"). Further steps could also consider prediction contextualization for all classes, either through post-processing or by adding specific layers to the deep-learning model (i.e., recurrent layer). Additionally, future studies should collect an higher amount of "wheelchair", "stairs ascent", and "stairs descent" data, given the imbalance of such data classes used in these studies.

Our application used accelerometer sensors; however, multiple studies have combined together different sensor modalities belonging to Inertial Measurement Unit technology, involving measurements of accelerometer, gyroscope, and sometimes, magnetometer data. Jiang et al. [40] proposed a method that merges accelerometer and gyroscope data into an activity image. They used CNN power and obtained outstanding accuracy performances related to three different public datasets. Using these sensors could be helpful, respectively, for different types of activities. For example, stairs ascending and descending performances could be improved using gyroscope or barometer data, while more dynamic activities, such as walking, rely on acceleration data. In most circumstances, acceleration measurements primary lead the activity classification, while gyroscope data have a secondary support role [41]. In spite of the fact that more signals and sensors could be integrated, we focused our research on a single triaxial accelerometer-based solution. This approach has the advantage of being easily applicable to any device that contains an accelerometer, without the need to re-design its components. Additionally, it maintains low power consumption.

The used model architecture, CNN, lies within the most common DNN-based approaches [11]. Despite many advantages and progresses made through DNN-based models, multiple challenges still apply to these techniques, such as their explainability and generalization capabilities compared with models built on extracted features from the respective knowledge domain [42]. Considering the SHS study, within the context of a patient-monitoring solution, using DL capabilities proved to be effective and promising [12]. Through this study, we examined how rotations could impact DL algorithms and how data augmentation address for this aspect. This challenge might be found also for other ML approaches that are orientation-dependent (e.g., orientation dependent features, three-axis acceleration). Future work should focus on comparing the augmented DL approach with other techniques, such as HMM, or feature-based models [43,44].

The good performances of the augmented model obtained during cross-validation were confirmed by the holdout data results. This indicates that our model can well generalize using unseen data, i.e., participants. However, holdout data belong to the same study (WPS) or to a similarly acquired one (SHS) compared to training data, and while the participants were different between the sets, the activities performed were similar. This might have partially biased the performance of the classification algorithms that still needs to be confirmed in a real-life scenario. Despite this, the SHS was a different research study compared to the WPS and added additional holdout data. Moreover, many activities of the protocols were self-paced, meaning that each participant could choose their own walking speed (i.e., slow, fast, normal walk, and the aided-walking activities), and thus, adding data variability. Studies that include acceleration measurements whose source is a clinical population would help better define the generalization capabilities of the model.

6. Conclusions

This research investigated the effects of device displacement on a DNN-based HAR model performance and proposed an orientation-independent HAR model. Further relevant steps might relate to model testing on a real clinical population and to wearable sensor data augmentation using other approaches, such as activity-tailored augmentation.

By applying HAR to wearable devices, it is possible to monitor and classify the activities performed by a patient. Device displacement is among the biggest challenges related to wearable sensors. A primary analysis showed how displacement, even of small entity, could negatively impact HAR algorithm performance. Ultimately, we developed an orientation-independent model that classified five pre-defined activities within a range of actions likely to happen in a clinical environment. Through this research, a possible solution was proposed for device displacement in HAR, and new challenges were highlighted to broaden this field and get closer to better activity monitoring solutions for clinicians and patients.

Author Contributions: Conceptualization, S.C., G.B.P. and E.G.C.; methodology, S.C., G.B.P. and E.G.C.; software, S.C. and G.B.P.; validation, S.C. and G.B.P.; formal analysis, S.C., G.B.P. and E.G.C.; investigation, S.C. and G.B.P.; resources, S.C. and G.B.P.; data curation, S.C. and G.B.P.; writing—original draft preparation, S.C.; writing—review and editing, S.C., G.B.P. and E.G.C.; visualization, S.C.; supervision, G.B.P. and E.G.C.; project administration, G.B.P. All authors have read and agreed to the published version of the manuscript.

Funding: This research received no external funding.

Institutional Review Board Statement: Ethical review and approval were waived for this study, due to its consideration as non-medical research, and therefore, approval by an IRB institution was not needed. The Internal Committee for Biomedical Experiments at Philips approved the collection of data used in this research.

Informed Consent Statement: Informed consent was obtained from all subjects involved in the study.

Data Availability Statement: Restrictions apply to the availability of these data.

Acknowledgments: We acknowledge Lieke Cox's support during data acquisition.

Conflicts of Interest: Gabriele B. Papini is a Philips employee.

Appendix A

Here, we report numerical performances related to the baseline and augmented model in particular, as referred to in Figure 4 (Table A1) and Figure 7 (Table A2) .

Table A1. Median and IQR of false negative percentages according to different activity groups.

	X-Axis	Y-Axis	Z-Axis
Static (static)	1.43 (1.58)	7.14 (1.45)	7.11 (4.19)
Treadmill walking (walking)	47.69 (18.02)	5.01 (0.62)	33.71 (28.74)
Stairs ascent (stairs ascent)	75.67 (41.21)	18.34 (4.6)	58.99 (56.78)
Stairs descent (stairs descent)	57.71 (32.85)	20.32 (2.78)	30.69 (16.24)
Walking aids (walking)	84.13 (16.58)	8.9 (0.75)	56.65 (39.47)
Intermittent shuffling(walking)	86.38 (19.42)	9.09 (1.0)	63.63 (46.32)
Active wheelchair(wheelchair)	49.33 (38.33)	42.62 (25.06)	32.41 (43.6)

Table A2. Median and IQR of f1-score and Kappa-score according to the two holdout sets and three test sets.

	Test Set	Mdl	Original	Real-Life	Fully-Rotated
f1-Score	**WPS Holdout**	**Base.**	0.96 (0.01)	0.80 (0.15)	0.78 (0.38)
		Aug.	0.96 (0.02)	0.92 (0.03)	0.92 (0.03)
	SHS	**Base.**	0.92 (0.08)	0.84 (0.09)	0.77 (0.24)
		Aug.	0.92 (0.07)	0.87 (0.03)	0.88 (0.03)
Kappa-score	**WPS Holdout**	**Base.**	0.93 (0.01)	0.80 (0.20)	0.66 (0.51)
		Aug.	0.92 (0.02)	0.87 (0.04)	0.88 (0.05)
	SHS	**Base.**	0.85 (0.13)	0.72 (0.12)	0.61 (0.35)
		Aug.	0.85 (0.11)	0.77 (0.04)	0.78 (0.05)

Following the numerical results of the baseline and augmented models of holdout data, each of the three proposed test sets were divided in subsections.

Appendix A.1. Original Test Set Results for Individual Classes

Table A3 reports the results of the original test set referring to the WPS holdout participants. Table A4 reports the same results but referring to the SHS participants.

Table A3. Single class results of baseline and augmented model for the original test set. Considered data: WPS holdout participants.

Mdl	Metric	Stairs Ascent	Stairs Descent	Static	Walking	Wheelchair
Base.	**precision**	0.89 ± 0.03	0.99 ± 0.01	0.98 ± 0.01	0.97 ± 0.01	0.70 ± 0.13
	recall	0.88 ± 0.02	0.86 ± 0.06	0.96 ± 0.03	0.97 ± 0.02	0.93 ± 0.06
	f1-score	0.89 ± 0.02	0.92 ± 0.04	0.97 ± 0.01	0.97 ± 0.01	0.79 ± 0.1
	specificity	0.99 ± 0.0	1.00 ± 0.0	0.99 ± 0.0	0.95 ± 0.02	0.99 ± 0.01
Aug.	**precision**	0.88 ± 0.09	0.94 ± 0.05	0.9 ± 0.07	0.97 ± 0.01	0.41 ± 0.23
	recall	0.89 ± 0.09	0.88 ± 0.12	0.94 ± 0.04	0.89 ± 0.09	0.92 ± 0.12
	f1-score	0.88 ± 0.06	0.90 ± 0.08	0.92 ± 0.03	0.92 ± 0.05	0.53 ± 0.23
	specificity	1.00 ± 0.0	1.00 ± 0.0	0.99 ± 0.0	0.93 ± 0.02	0.98 ± 0.01

Table A4. Single class results of baseline and augmented model for the original test set. Considered data: SHS participants.

Mdl	Metric	Stairs Ascent	Stairs Descent	Static	Walking	Wheelchair
Base.	precision	0.83 ± 0.09	0.94 ± 0.05	0.92 ± 0.06	0.97 ± 0.01	0.39 ± 0.21
	recall	0.92 ± 0.07	0.88 ± 0.12	0.92 ± 0.04	0.89 ± 0.09	0.91 ± 0.15
	f1-score	0.87 ± 0.06	0.90 ± 0.07	0.92 ± 0.03	0.92 ± 0.05	0.51 ± 0.23
	specificity	0.99 ± 0.01	1.0 ± 0.0	0.97 ± 0.02	0.94 ± 0.02	0.95 ± 0.06
Aug.	precision	0.88 ± 0.09	0.94 ± 0.05	0.90 ± 0.07	0.97 ± 0.01	0.41 ± 0.23
	recall	0.89 ± 0.09	0.88 ± 0.12	0.94 ± 0.04	0.89 ± 0.09	0.92 ± 0.12
	f1-score	0.88 ± 0.06	0.90 ± 0.08	0.92 ± 0.03	0.92 ± 0.05	0.53 ± 0.23
	specificity	1.0 ± 0.01	1.0 ± 0.0	0.96 ± 0.03	0.94 ± 0.03	0.95 ± 0.06

Appendix A.2. Real-Life Test Set Results for Individual Classes

Table A5 reports the results of the real-life test set referring to the WPS holdout participants. Table A6 reports the same results but referring to the SHS participants.

Table A5. Single class results of the baseline and augmented model for the real-life test set. Considered data: WPS holdout participants.

Mdl	Metric	Stairs Ascent	Stairs Descent	Static	Walking	Wheelchair
Base.	precision	0.88 ± 0.02	0.98 ± 0.01	0.97 ± 0.01	0.96 ± 0.01	0.23 ± 0.12
	recall	0.87 ± 0.03	0.84 ± 0.03	0.96 ± 0.0	0.79 ± 0.12	0.88 ± 0.03
	f1-score	0.87 ± 0.02	0.9 ± 0.02	0.97 ± 0.0	0.86 ± 0.08	0.35 ± 0.15
	specificity	0.99 ± 0.0	1.0 ± 0.0	0.99 ± 0.0	0.95 ± 0.0	0.88 ± 0.08
Aug.	precision	0.94 ± 0.0	0.99 ± 0.0	0.98 ± 0.0	0.95 ± 0.0	0.41 ± 0.09
	recall	0.81 ± 0.01	0.83 ± 0.01	0.98 ± 0.0	0.92 ± 0.03	0.93 ± 0.0
	f1-score	0.87 ± 0.01	0.90 ± 0.01	0.98 ± 0.0	0.94 ± 0.02	0.56 ± 0.09
	specificity	1.0 ± 0.0	1.0 ± 0.0	0.99 ± 0.0	0.93 ± 0.0	0.96 ± 0.02

Table A6. Single class results of the baseline and augmented model for the real-life test set. Considered data: SHS participants.

Mdl	Metric	Stairs Ascent	Stairs Descent	Static	Walking	Wheelchair
Base.	precision	0.80 ± 0.02	0.95 ± 0.02	0.92 ± 0.01	0.97 ± 0.0	0.13 ± 0.04
	recall	0.91 ± 0.01	0.84 ± 0.02	0.93 ± 0.0	0.79 ± 0.06	0.93 ± 0.01
	f1-score	0.85 ± 0.01	0.89 ± 0.02	0.92 ± 0.0	0.87 ± 0.04	0.23 ± 0.07
	specificity	0.99 ± 0.0	1.0 ± 0.0	0.97 ± 0.0	0.95 ± 0.01	0.88 ± 0.05
Aug.	precision	0.84 ± 0.01	0.93 ± 0.0	0.91 ± 0.0	0.97 ± 0.0	0.18 ± 0.03
	recall	0.88 ± 0.01	0.83 ± 0.02	0.94 ± 0.0	0.85 ± 0.02	0.93 ± 0.01
	f1-score	0.86 ± 0.01	0.88 ± 0.01	0.92 ± 0.0	0.90 ± 0.01	0.30 ± 0.04
	specificity	0.99 ± 0.0	1.0 ± 0.0	0.97 ± 0.0	0.94 ± 0.0	0.92 ± 0.02

Appendix A.3. Fully-Rotated Test Set Results for Individual Classes

Table A7 reports the results for the baseline and augmented models of the fully-rotated test sets referring to the WPS holdout participants. Table A8 reports the same results but referring to the SHS participants.

Table A7. Single class results of baseline and augmented model for the fully-rotated test set on every axis. Considered data: WPS holdout participants.

Mdl	Ax	Metric	Stairs Ascent	Stairs Descent	Static	Walking	Wheelchair
Base.	X	precision	0.34 ± 0.32	0.40 ± 0.34	0.99 ± 0.01	0.53 ± 0.23	0.43 ± 0.29
		recall	0.66 ± 0.23	0.56 ± 0.31	0.58 ± 0.23	0.91 ± 0.06	0.33 ± 0.29
		f1-score	0.37 ± 0.3	0.39 ± 0.3	0.70 ± 0.16	0.65 ± 0.17	0.32 ± 0.27
		specificity	0.99 ± 0.02	0.97 ± 0.06	0.69 ± 0.21	0.93 ± 0.05	0.92 ± 0.1
	Y	precision	0.84 ± 0.03	0.79 ± 0.05	0.95 ± 0.01	0.96 ± 0.02	0.66 ± 0.17
		recall	0.85 ± 0.04	0.97 ± 0.01	0.95 ± 0.02	0.96 ± 0.01	0.55 ± 0.2
		f1-score	0.84 ± 0.03	0.87 ± 0.03	0.95 ± 0.01	0.96 ± 0.01	0.57 ± 0.13
		specificity	0.99 ± 0.0	1.0 ± 0.0	0.99 ± 0.01	0.94 ± 0.01	0.98 ± 0.02
	Z	precision	0.43 ± 0.32	0.65 ± 0.21	0.98 ± 0.02	0.57 ± 0.23	0.48 ± 0.3
		recall	0.61 ± 0.2	0.59 ± 0.24	0.73 ± 0.26	0.95 ± 0.03	0.19 ± 0.15
		f1-score	0.46 ± 0.28	0.58 ± 0.19	0.81 ± 0.19	0.69 ± 0.18	0.23 ± 0.18
		specificity	0.98 ± 0.01	0.95 ± 0.05	0.79 ± 0.26	0.95 ± 0.04	0.90 ± 0.09
Aug.	X	precision	0.74 ± 0.07	0.71 ± 0.13	0.98 ± 0.01	0.95 ± 0.02	0.91 ± 0.04
		recall	0.91 ± 0.03	0.96 ± 0.03	0.96 ± 0.03	0.93 ± 0.02	0.59 ± 0.17
		f1-score	0.82 ± 0.05	0.81 ± 0.1	0.97 ± 0.01	0.94 ± 0.02	0.70 ± 0.12
		specificity	0.99 ± 0.0	1.0 ± 0.0	0.99 ± 0.01	0.90 ± 0.03	0.98 ± 0.02
	Y	precision	0.75 ± 0.04	0.81 ± 0.02	0.96 ± 0.0	0.97 ± 0.01	0.89 ± 0.04
		recall	0.92 ± 0.02	0.97 ± 0.02	0.98 ± 0.0	0.94 ± 0.01	0.64 ± 0.13
		f1-score	0.83 ± 0.03	0.88 ± 0.02	0.97 ± 0.0	0.96 ± 0.01	0.74 ± 0.07
		specificity	0.99 ± 0.0	1.0 ± 0.0	0.99 ± 0.01	0.94 ± 0.01	0.98 ± 0.02
	Z	precision	0.70 ± 0.08	0.79 ± 0.06	0.97 ± 0.01	0.92 ± 0.03	0.93 ± 0.02
		recall	0.93 ± 0.02	0.96 ± 0.02	0.98 ± 0.01	0.93 ± 0.02	0.42 ± 0.09
		f1-score	0.79 ± 0.06	0.86 ± 0.04	0.97 ± 0.0	0.93 ± 0.02	0.57 ± 0.08
		specificity	0.98 ± 0.01	0.95 ± 0.05	0.79 ± 0.26	0.95 ± 0.04	0.90 ± 0.09

Table A8. Single class results of baseline and augmented model for the fully-rotated test set on every axis. Considered data: SHS participants.

Mdl	Ax	Metric	Stairs Ascent	Stairs Descent	Static	Walking	Wheelchair
Base.	X	precision	0.40 ± 0.30	0.40 ± 0.31	0.98 ± 0.03	0.64 ± 0.13	0.40 ± 0.32
		recall	0.53 ± 0.24	0.49 ± 0.30	0.61 ± 0.17	0.96 ± 0.03	0.17 ± 0.17
		f1-score	0.41 ± 0.26	0.40 ± 0.28	0.73 ± 0.11	0.76 ± 0.09	0.20 ± 0.18
		specificity	0.99 ± 0.02	0.99 ± 0.02	0.75 ± 0.14	0.94 ± 0.04	0.94 ± 0.07
	Y	precision	0.89 ± 0.02	0.81 ± 0.02	0.91 ± 0.01	0.90 ± 0.02	0.70 ± 0.24
		recall	0.80 ± 0.03	0.93 ± 0.02	0.90 ± 0.02	0.96 ± 0.01	0.24 ± 0.09
		f1-score	0.84 ± 0.02	0.87 ± 0.02	0.91 ± 0.01	0.93 ± 0.01	0.34 ± 0.09
		specificity	0.99 ± 0.0	1.0 ± 0.0	0.97 ± 0.01	0.92 ± 0.01	0.96 ± 0.02
	Z	precision	0.44 ± 0.36	0.68 ± 0.17	0.96 ± 0.04	0.63 ± 0.13	0.65 ± 0.31
		recall	0.56 ± 0.16	0.62 ± 0.25	0.72 ± 0.21	0.98 ± 0.01	0.15 ± 0.10
		f1-score	0.42 ± 0.28	0.61 ± 0.17	0.80 ± 0.14	0.76 ± 0.09	0.18 ± 0.08
		specificity	0.99 ± 0.01	0.98 ± 0.03	0.82 ± 0.19	0.97 ± 0.02	0.89 ± 0.09
Aug.	X	precision	0.80 ± 0.05	0.72 ± 0.11	0.94 ± 0.02	0.86 ± 0.03	0.86 ± 0.08
		recall	0.81 ± 0.08	0.84 ± 0.07	0.88 ± 0.04	0.96 ± 0.01	0.24 ± 0.10
		f1-score	0.80 ± 0.06	0.77 ± 0.09	0.91 ± 0.02	0.91 ± 0.02	0.37 ± 0.10
		specificity	0.99 ± 0.0	1.0 ± 0.0	0.95 ± 0.02	0.93 ± 0.01	0.94 ± 0.03
	Y	precision	0.84 ± 0.03	0.81 ± 0.02	0.92 ± 0.01	0.90 ± 0.02	0.81 ± 0.09
		recall	0.88 ± 0.02	0.91 ± 0.02	0.90 ± 0.01	0.96 ± 0.0	0.26 ± 0.04
		f1-score	0.86 ± 0.02	0.86 ± 0.02	0.91 ± 0.01	0.93 ± 0.01	0.38 ± 0.04
		specificity	1.0 ± 0.0	1.0 ± 0.0	0.96 ± 0.0	0.92 ± 0.01	0.96 ± 0.01
	Z	precision	0.79 ± 0.05	0.80 ± 0.05	0.93 ± 0.01	0.85 ± 0.02	0.92 ± 0.01
		recall	0.86 ± 0.04	0.89 ± 0.04	0.89 ± 0.02	0.96 ± 0.0	0.19 ± 0.03
		f1-score	0.82 ± 0.04	0.84 ± 0.03	0.91 ± 0.01	0.90 ± 0.02	0.31 ± 0.04
		specificity	1.0 ± 0.0	1.0 ± 0.0	0.96 ± 0.01	0.93 ± 0.01	0.93 ± 0.01

References

1. Fu, B.; Kirchbuchner, F.; Kuijper, A.; Braun, A.; Vaithyalingam Gangatharan, D. Fitness activity recognition on smartphones using doppler measurements. *Informatics* **2018**, *5*, 24. [CrossRef]
2. Cheng, W.Y.; Scotland, A.; Lipsmeier, F.; Kilchenmann, T.; Jin, L.; Schjodt-Eriksen, J.; Wolf, D.; Zhang-Schaerer, Y.P.; Garcia, I.F.; Siebourg-Polster, J.; et al. Human activity recognition from sensor-based large-scale continuous monitoring of Parkinson's disease patients. In Proceedings of the 2017 IEEE/ACM International Conference on Connected Health: Applications, Systems and Engineering Technologies (CHASE), Philadelphia, PA, USA, 17–19 July 2017; pp. 249–250.
3. Dang, L.M.; Min, K.; Wang, H.; Piran, M.J.; Lee, C.H.; Moon, H. Sensor-based and vision-based human activity recognition: A comprehensive survey. *Pattern Recognit.* **2020**, *108*, 107561. [CrossRef]
4. Roitberg, A.; Perzylo, A.; Somani, N.; Giuliani, M.; Rickert, M.; Knoll, A. Human activity recognition in the context of industrial human–robot interaction. In Proceedings of the Signal and Information Processing Association Annual Summit and Conference (APSIPA), 2014 Asia-Pacific, Siem Reap, Cambodia, 9–12 December 2014; pp. 1–10.
5. Schrader, L.; Vargas Toro, A.; Konietzny, S.; Rüping, S.; Schäpers, B.; Steinböck, M.; Krewer, C.; Müller, F.; Güttler, J.; Bock, T. Advanced sensing and human activity recognition in early intervention and rehabilitation of elderly people. *J. Popul. Ageing* **2020**, *13*, 139–165. [CrossRef]
6. Altini, M.; Casale, P.; Penders, J.; Amft, O. Cardiorespiratory fitness estimation in free-living using wearable sensors. *Artif. Intell. Med.* **2016**, *68*, 37–46. [CrossRef] [PubMed]
7. Chaari, M.; Abid, M.; Ouakrim, Y.; Lahami, M.; Mezghani, N. A Mobile Application for Physical Activity Recognition Using Acceleration Data from Wearable Sensors for Cardiac Rehabilitation. 2020. Available online: https://r-libre.teluq.ca/1936/1/HEALTHINF_2020_84_CR.pdf (accessed on 20 March 2023).
8. Brown, C.J.; Friedkin, R.J.; Inouye, S.K. Prevalence and outcomes of low mobility in hospitalized older patients. *J. Am. Geriatr. Soc.* **2004**, *52*, 1263–1270. [CrossRef]
9. Jiang, W.; Miao, C.; Ma, F.; Yao, S.; Wang, Y.; Yuan, Y.; Xue, H.; Song, C.; Ma, X.; Koutsonikolas, D.; et al. Towards environment independent device free human activity recognition. In Proceedings of the 24th Annual International Conference on Mobile Computing and Networking, New Delhi, India, 29 October–2 November 2018; pp. 289–304.
10. Kunze, K.; Lukowicz, P. Sensor placement variations in wearable activity recognition. *IEEE Pervasive Comput.* **2014**, *13*, 32–41. [CrossRef]
11. Zhang, S.; Li, Y.; Zhang, S.; Shahabi, F.; Xia, S.; Deng, Y.; Alshurafa, N. Deep learning in human activity recognition with wearable sensors: A review on advances. *Sensors* **2022**, *22*, 1476. [CrossRef]
12. Fridriksdottir, E.; Bonomi, A.G. Accelerometer-based human activity recognition for patient monitoring using a deep neural network. *Sensors* **2020**, *20*, 6424. [CrossRef]
13. Saeedi, R.; Purath, J.; Venkatasubramanian, K.; Ghasemzadeh, H. Toward seamless wearable sensing: Automatic on-body sensor localization for physical activity monitoring. In Proceedings of the 2014 36th Annual International Conference of the IEEE Engineering in Medicine and Biology Society, Chicago, IL, USA, 26–30 August 2014; pp. 5385–5388.
14. Sztyler, T.; Stuckenschmidt, H. On-body localization of wearable devices: An investigation of position-aware activity recognition. In Proceedings of the 2016 IEEE International Conference on Pervasive Computing and Communications (PerCom), Sydney, Australia, 14–19 March 2016; pp. 1–9.
15. Inoue, H. Data augmentation by pairing samples for images classification. *arXiv* **2018**, arXiv:1801.02929.
16. Shorten, C.; Khoshgoftaar, T.M. A survey on image data augmentation for deep learning. *J. Big Data* **2019**, *6*, 60. [CrossRef]
17. Ohashi, H.; Al-Nasser, M.; Ahmed, S.; Akiyama, T.; Sato, T.; Nguyen, P.; Nakamura, K.; Dengel, A. Augmenting wearable sensor data with physical constraint for DNN-based human-action recognition. In Proceedings of the ICML 2017 Times Series Workshop, Sydney, NSW, Australia, 6–11 August 2017; pp. 6–11.
18. Steven Eyobu, O.; Han, D.S. Feature representation and data augmentation for human activity classification based on wearable IMU sensor data using a deep LSTM neural network. *Sensors* **2018**, *18*, 2892. [CrossRef] [PubMed]
19. Um, T.T.; Pfister, F.M.; Pichler, D.; Endo, S.; Lang, M.; Hirche, S.; Fietzek, U.; Kulić, D. Data augmentation of wearable sensor data for parkinson's disease monitoring using convolutional neural networks. In Proceedings of the 19th ACM International Conference on Multimodal Interaction, Glasgow, UK, 13–17 November 2017; pp. 216–220.
20. Wang, J.; Zhu, T.; Gan, J.; Ning, H.; Wan, Y. Sensor data augmentation with resampling for contrastive learning in human activity recognition. *arXiv* **2021**, arXiv:2109.02054.
21. Chen, T.; Kornblith, S.; Norouzi, M.; Hinton, G. A simple framework for contrastive learning of visual representations. In Proceedings of the International Conference on Machine Learning (PMLR), Virtual, 13–18 July 2020; pp. 1597–1607.
22. Zimmermann, R.S.; Sharma, Y.; Schneider, S.; Bethge, M.; Brendel, W. Contrastive learning inverts the data generating process. In Proceedings of the International Conference on Machine Learning (PMLR), Virtual, 18–24 July 2021; pp. 12979–12990.
23. GeneActiv. Available online: https://activinsights.com/technology/geneactiv/ (accessed on 20 March 2023).
24. IntelliVue MX40front, Philips Healthcare. Available online: https://www.usa.philips.com/healthcare/product/HC865350/intellivue-mx40-patient-wearable-monitor (accessed on 20 March 2023).
25. IntelliVue MX40side, Philips Healthcare. Available online: https://www.documents.philips.com/assets/20170523/b349908a9e374f02a157a77c016a06b7.pdf?_ga=2.3824953.803133925.1663919802-56406853.1639166097 (accessed on 20 March 2023).
26. Sharma, S.; Sharma, S.; Athaiya, A. Activation functions in neural networks. *Towards Data Sci.* **2017**, *6*, 310–316. [CrossRef]

27. Kingma, D.P.; Ba, J. Adam: A method for stochastic optimization. *arXiv* **2014**, arXiv:1412.6980.
28. Chollet, F. Keras. 2015. Available online: https://keras.io (accessed on 20 March 2023).
29. Van Dyk, D.A.; Meng, X.L. The art of data augmentation. *J. Comput. Graph. Stat.* **2001**, *10*, 1–50. [CrossRef]
30. Refaeilzadeh, P.; Tang, L.; Liu, H. Cross-validation. *Encycl. Database Syst.* **2009**, *5*, 532–538.
31. Cohen, J. A coefficient of agreement for nominal scales. *Educ. Psychol. Meas.* **1960**, *20*, 37–46. [CrossRef]
32. Shapiro, S.S.; Wilk, M.B. An analysis of variance test for normality (complete samples). *Biometrika* **1965**, *52*, 591–611. [CrossRef]
33. Nahm, F.S. Nonparametric statistical tests for the continuous data: the basic concept and the practical use. *Korean J. Anesthesiol.* **2016**, *69*, 8–14. [CrossRef]
34. Barshan, B.; Yurtman, A. Classifying daily and sports activities invariantly to the positioning of wearable motion sensor units. *IEEE Internet Things J.* **2020**, *7*, 4801–4815. [CrossRef]
35. Portrait Mobile, GE Healthcare. Available online: https://www.gehealthcare.it/products/patient-monitoring/portrait-mobile (accessed on 20 March 2023).
36. IntelliVue MX40, Philips Healthcare. Available online: https://www.philips.dk/healthcare/product/HC865351/philips-intellivue-mx40-patient-wearable-monitor-2-4-ghz-smart-hopping (accessed on 20 March 2023).
37. Anguita, D.; Ghio, A.; Oneto, L.; Parra Perez, X.; Reyes Ortiz, J.L. A public domain dataset for human activity recognition using smartphones. In Proceedings of the 21th International European Symposium on Artificial Neural Networks, Computational Intelligence and Machine Learning, Bruges, Belgium, 24–26 April 2013; pp. 437–442.
38. Malekzadeh, M.; Clegg, R.G.; Cavallaro, A.; Haddadi, H. Protecting sensory data against sensitive inferences. In Proceedings of the 1st Workshop on Privacy by Design in Distributed Systems, Porto, Portugal, 23 April 2018; pp. 1–6.
39. Zhang, M.; Sawchuk, A.A. USC-HAD: A daily activity dataset for ubiquitous activity recognition using wearable sensors. In Proceedings of the 2012 ACM Conference on Ubiquitous Computing, Pittsburgh, PA, USA, 5–8 September 2012; pp. 1036–1043.
40. Jiang, W.; Yin, Z. Human activity recognition using wearable sensors by deep convolutional neural networks. In Proceedings of the 23rd ACM International Conference on Multimedia, Brisbane, Australia, 26–30 October 2015; pp. 1307–1310.
41. Wang, Z.; Yang, Z.; Dong, T. A review of wearable technologies for elderly care that can accurately track indoor position, recognize physical activities and monitor vital signs in real time. *Sensors* **2017**, *17*, 341. [CrossRef] [PubMed]
42. Bento, N.; Rebelo, J.; Barandas, M.; Carreiro, A.V.; Campagner, A.; Cabitza, F.; Gamboa, H. Comparing Handcrafted Features and Deep Neural Representations for Domain Generalization in Human Activity Recognition. *Sensors* **2022**, *22*, 7324. [PubMed]
43. Xue, T.; Liu, H. Hidden Markov Model and its application in human activity recognition and fall detection: A review. In *Communications, Signal Processing, and Systems*; Liang, Q., Wang, W., Liu, X., Na, Z., Zhang, B., Eds.; Singapore: Springer Singapore, 2022; pp. 863–869.
44. Liu, H.; Schultz, I.T. Biosignal Processing and Activity Modeling for Multimodal Human Activity Recognition. Ph.D. Thesis, Universität Bremen, Bremen, Germany, 2021.

applied sciences

MDPI

Article

Emotional Health Detection in HAR: New Approach Using Ensemble SNN

Luigi Bibbo' [1,*], Francesco Cotroneo [2] and Marley Vellasco [3]

1 Department of Information Infrastructure and Sustainable Energy, University Mediterranea of Reggio Calabria, Via dell'Università, 25, 89126 Reggio Calabria, Italy
2 Nophys S.r.l.s., Via Maddaloni 74, 00177 Roma, Italy
3 Department of Electrical Engineering, Pontifical Catholic University of Rio de Janeiro (PUC-Rio), Rua Marquês de São Vicente, 225, Rio de Janeiro 22451-000, Brazil
* Correspondence: luigi.bibbo@unirc.it

Abstract: Computer recognition of human activity is an important area of research in computer vision. Human activity recognition (HAR) involves identifying human activities in real-life contexts and plays an important role in interpersonal interaction. Artificial intelligence usually identifies activities by analyzing data collected using different sources. These can be wearable sensors, MEMS devices embedded in smartphones, cameras, or CCTV systems. As part of HAR, computer vision technology can be applied to the recognition of the emotional state through facial expressions using facial positions such as the nose, eyes, and lips. Human facial expressions change with different health states. Our application is oriented toward the detection of the emotional health of subjects using a self-normalizing neural network (SNN) in cascade with an ensemble layer. We identify the subjects' emotional states through which the medical staff can derive useful indications of the patient's state of health.

Keywords: HAR; face emotion recognition; face detection; computer vision; deep learning; SNN; ensemble; vectorflow

Citation: Bibbo', L.; Cotroneo, F.; Vellasco, M. Emotional Health Detection in HAR: New Approach Using Ensemble SNN. *Appl. Sci.* **2023**, *13*, 3259. https://doi.org/10.3390/app13053259

Academic Editor: Yu-Dong Zhang

Received: 7 February 2023
Revised: 21 February 2023
Accepted: 28 February 2023
Published: 3 March 2023

1. Introduction

Human activity recognition (HAR) designates the complex of human action, which can be decomposed into human-to-human interaction, human-to-object events, and gestures [1]. Its objective is to detect data relating to the activities usually carried out by the elderly or those in need of care using sensors or observing a sequence of actions from videos or images. An applicable technique is facial expression recognition (FER) [2,3]. Human beings interact with each other through gestures and emotions [4]; therefore, facial expressions are a way to obtain emotional information [5] and can reflect a person's psychophysical state [6,7].

Thanks to various technological innovations, the emotion recognition and detection (EDR) has found widespread applications in different sectors and, according to some estimates, will have its highest growth rate in the coming years. During the pandemic, EDR technology was used by some companies to assess the state of satisfaction of workers who had been employed in smart working activities. Through computer vision algorithms, recognizing the emotions and moods of workers through their facial expressions, it was possible to assess the stress level to which they were subjected. Another sector in which it has found applications is learning and education. EDR technology has been used to assess the learning level of students by providing helpful guidance to educators to adopt the proper corrections to improve the learning process. Another sector in which EDR technology finds applications is healthcare. Thanks to the creation of smart homes and IoT technologies, patients can be provided with efficient healthcare without resorting to hospital admissions. A large amount of data can be acquired through computer vision and sensors, which, when processed and analyzed, provide valuable indications to healthcare personnel and doctors to improve care and provide adequate services. This is aimed at improving the lifestyle of people in need of assistance.

The recognition of facial emotions is important because, from the analysis of the face, it is possible to detect the state of health of the subject, such as anxiety, depression, stress, or malaise, making a facial diagnosis possible. It is a beneficial technique in caring for the elderly; through the information provided, medical personnel can evaluate the type of intervention to reduce the state of the discomfort of the subjects. Some manifestations of the face can be associated with the first pathological symptoms facilitating the prevention of diseases that can degenerate. The eyes, in particular, can report physical and mental changes. This technique has ancient roots, in particular in traditional Chinese medicine (TCM), in which doctors performed a diagnosis of a disease by looking at facial features. They believed that pathological changes of internal organs reflected directly on the face allowed them to determine a diagnosis. Each anatomical part of the face reflected the state of functioning of each organ; for example, the cheeks were associated with the lungs, the lips with the digestive system and stomach, and the eyebrows with the nervous and respiratory systems. This technique, called "facial diagnosis," requires considerable experience in order to perform an accurate diagnosis. In modern times, the difficulty of obtaining a medical examination due to economic conditions and the scarce availability of medical resources for those who live in underdeveloped geographical areas has stimulated research to develop techniques and diagnoses using artificial intelligence. Finally, thanks to the technological evolution of deep learning, it has been found that computer-assisted facial diagnosis has low error rates [8].

While being a helpful tool, the use of deep learning in facial recognition presents some problems on which researchers work to improve efficiency. The main challenges must be addressed: accuracy, security, and privacy.

Accuracy is an essential aspect of the recognition process. The detected face may have lighting problems, poor image quality, low resolution, a blurred face, or different types of occlusions: systematic (hair, masks, clothes, and make-up) and temporary (hands covering the face or pose variations). These factors create errors in the faceprint feedback with faces in the database. Using a large amount of training data and 3D imagery improves accuracy.

Security refers to the risk of using facial recognition for identity theft or illicit purposes. Efficient ML and DL security systems already present in systems can provide adequate protection against illegal use.

Additionally, regarding privacy, the use of facial images must comply with the laws on processing personal data.

In interpreting images in the biomedical field, specific studies have been presented on improving the efficiency of deep learning. Below are some of the most significant examples.

Zhao et al. [9] developed an interesting method of deep learning in bioimaging called VoxelEmbed. Their work was finalized in the realization of an innovative multistream approach that facilitates embedding pixels with 3D contextual information. This solution arose from the need to meet the need for tools for the analysis of the dynamics of living cells. The segmentation and tracking of cell instances based on pixel incorporation have proven helpful for studying cellular dynamics. This method was validated through tests on four 3D datasets of the Cell Tracking Challenge.

Meanwhile, Zheng et al. [10] proposed a system to optimize the feature boundary of deep CNN through a two-step training method: a pre-training step and implicit regularization. Regularization is the process of enhancing the generalization ability of a CNN in order to train complex models while maintaining lower overfitting. It has a primary role in the tuning parameters of deep CNN. In the pre-training step, the authors trained the model to obtain the image representation for anomaly detection. Based on the anomaly detection results, the implicit regularization step re-trained the network to regularize the feature boundary and obtain the convergence. The implicit regularization can be considered as an implicit model ensemble. It can be regarded as the training process of a different network that shares weights with different training samples; it can be viewed as a combination of a wide number of similar CNNs trained with different datasets.

Finally, Yao et al. [11] presented interesting findings relating to overcoming the problem of training self-supervised machine learning algorithms using massive data of biomedical images from databases or specialized journals. However, the images from such sources consist of a considerably large amount of compound figures with subplots.

In their work, these authors developed a framework (SimCFS) for separating compound figures using weak classification annotations. In particular, they proposed a system to separate the compound figures with lateral loss. The training stage contains these steps. SimCFS only requires single images from different categories. The pseudo compound figures are generated from the augmentation simulator (SimCFS-AUG). Then, a detection network (SimCFS-DET) is trained to perform compound figure separation. In the testing stage, they used only the trained SimCFS-DET for separating the images.

For evaluating the performance of different compound figure separation strategies, they used one compound figure dataset (called Glomeruli-2000) consisting of 917 training and 917 testing real figure plots from the American Journal of Kidney Diseases (AJKD).

The proposed method SimCFS-DET was then compared with the most used methods for separating compound figures showing better performance. ImageCLEF2016 was used as the dataset, containing 8397 figures, of which 6783 were for training and 1614 for testing. The system ultimately allows efficient distribution to new image classes.

In this work, a facial emotion recognition system based on an innovative approach of an SNN ensemble network is designed to support the work of medical staff in the diagnostic evaluation of the type of detectable malaise. The work after the introduction containing the importance of FER is articulated as follows: Section 2 presents the related works, Section 3 presents the analysis of the problem, Section 4 provides the methodology, Section 5 sets out the dataset and model design, Section 6 presents the results and discussion, and finally, Section 7 provides the conclusions.

2. Related Works

In recent years, many applications of emotion recognition have been developed using single modalities, multiple modalities, static images, and videos; here are some examples.

Jin et al. [12] proposed a system for identifying specific diseases using the deep transfer learning technique from facial recognition to facial diagnosis. With this technique, they solved the problem of the difficulty of finding images for facial diagnosis. They developed a suitable system for detecting and screening diseases using a small dataset. The study was aimed at identifying the following diseases:

- Thalassemia: a genetic blood disorder caused by abnormal hemoglobin production, which is a hereditary disease.
- Hyperthyroidism: an endocrine disease caused by excessive amounts of thyroid hormones T3 and T4.
- Down syndrome: a genetic disorder caused by trisomy of chromosome 21.
- Leprosy: an infectious disease also known as Hansen's disease, caused by the bacterium Mycobacterium leprae.

The methodology adopted was deep transfer learning (DTL), which transfers knowledge from a pre-trained deep neural network for facial verification and recognition. Starting from the recognition and verification of the face, the authors moved on to facial diagnosis.

Since these domains have the same feature space and related activities, it was possible to use a small dataset for deep transfer learning from facial recognition to facial diagnosis. The implementation of the model was based on MatLab's MatConvNet. The NVIDIA CUDA toolkit and CuDNN library were used for GPU acceleration.

The model was built through a fine-tuning phase of a pre-trained VGG-Face CNN and using pre-trained CNN as a feature extractor for the smaller dataset. The VGG-Face dataset contained 2.6 million images.

The model was tested on two cases of facial diagnosis. One was the detection of beta-thalassemia, which was a binary classification activity. The other was detecting four diseases, such as beta-thalassemia, hyperthyroidism, Down syndrome, and leprosy, a multi-class classification activity. Only 140 images from the dataset were used to detect a single disease, of which 70 were for facial images specific for beta-thalassemia and 70 for healthy subjects. Of the 70 of each type, 40 were used for training and 30 for testing. Comparing the results obtained with the VGG-Face model with those of traditional machine learning methods (AlexNet and ResNet50), it was found that its accuracy, being greater than 95%, is much better than that of the others. In further evaluating the algorithm, the authors performed a multi-class classification. In this case, 350 images from the dataset were used (70 for each face). Two hundred images are used for the training process (40 images for each face). One hundred and fifty images (30 images for each face) were used for the testing process. Although the classification process was more complex, the model had excellent accuracy for beta-thalassemia, Down syndrome, and leprosy. It had low accuracy for hyperthyroidism. The performance obtained was better than that of traditional machine learning methods. The accuracy was 93%.

Therefore, CNN as a feature extractor has been proven to be a suitable deep transfer learning method when using a small dataset for facial analysis.

Jin et al. [13] introduced an innovative deep-learning model to improve facial recognition. Many factors, such as lighting, variation of head pose, and lack of information about the spatial characteristics of the face, influence the accuracy of facial recognition. The latter can be overcome with the use of RGB-D sensors. In practice, images of RGB-D faces are challenging to find. Therefore, in the face of these color and depth problems connected to RGB sensors, these authors developed a model to obtain more accurate facial recognition based on deep learning. The proposed solution allowed for obtaining depth maps from images of 2D faces in place of those obtainable with a depth sensor. In particular, they designed a neural network model called "D+GAN" (Depth plus Generative Adversarial network), with which they performed multi-conditional translation from image to image with facial attributes. Compared to the normal two-component GANs generator and discriminator, this network had the advantage of generating high-quality face depth maps by making greater use of facial attribute information and determining sex, age, and race categories. The facial recognition process was divided into the following phases:

- Capturing RGB face images.
- Image preprocessing to remove the image background from the face evenly.
- Generating face depth maps
- Merging images using the unsampled Shearlet transform (NSST).
- Using different tools for face recognition.

The Bosphorus 3D Face Database and the CASUA 3D Face Database were used to train the model, and the BU-3DFe Database was used for testing.

To evaluate the quality of the depth maps obtained, face depth maps were created for each of the previous datasets using different techniques:

➢ Monodepth2
➢ DenseDepth Method (KTTI)
➢ DenseDepth (NYUDepth)
➢ DenseDepth (NYUDepthV2)
➢ 3DMorphable Model (3DMMI)
➢ Pix2Pix
➢ CycleGAN

and compared with D+GAN.

Numerous experiments were carried out to validate the model. The authors compared the eight depth maps obtained with the techniques cited for each dataset used. The results showed that the outputs generated by D+GAN show more detailed depth information for all three datasets. Even in the correlation graphs of the various output images, there was a higher quality for the depth maps generated by 3DMM, Pix2Pix, Cycle GAN, and D+GAN.

For a quantitative analysis of the face depth maps generated by the different models, SSIM, RMSE (root-mean-squared error), and PSNR (peak-signal-to-noise ratio) were used. SSIM is a parameter used for assessing the structural similarity of images. It is used to evaluate the quality of the processed image compared to the reference one. Additionally, from a quantitative point of view, these three indices for D+GAN depth maps were the best.

The four models, PCA, ICA, Facenet, and InsightFace, were used as face recognition methods. ENTL, Yale, UMIST, AR, and ERET were used as datasets. From the experiments, it was found that for each dataset of the five used, the best results were obtained when operating with the pseudo-RGB-D facial recognition modes compared to the RGB mode. The best result was obtained when combining the FaceNet model with the ORL database.

Ghosh et al. [14] developed an innovative model of recognition of human emotions using analyses of both physiological and textual characteristics considering heart rate [15] and blood pressure, or changes in pupil size or even textual analysis. Their study analyzed five emotions: anger, sadness, joy, disgust, and fear. The model was built taking into account two physiological characteristics: facial muscle movements and HRV combined with textual analysis. Heart rate variability (HRV) is the oscillation of heart rate over a series of consecutive heartbeats. This study's novelty lay in the analysis of the combination of these characteristics with the classification of emotions obtained by applying a deep learning model based on RNN (Recurrent Neural Network). The methodological approach used to collect the characteristics corresponding to each of the five classes of emotions mentioned above involved showing 500 subjects belonging to different cultural backgrounds and age groups a series of photograms of various films to arouse emotions, which were the object of the study. The data on HRV were captured using a wearable device containing various biometric sensors such as a heart rate monitor, blood pressure measurement sensor, and body temperature sensor. The parameters measured were heart rate, systolic blood pressure, and diastolic blood pressure concerning the above categories of emotions.

Sixty-eight reference points have been identified on facial images to extract features from facial muscle movement. The positions of these points vary according to different emotions. The characteristics associated with the different landmarks of the face make it possible to distinguish the five different emotions. Only 47 landmarks were used in this study. Considering that each facial reference point is identified by x and y coordinates, a 94-dimensional characteristic vector was derived for each emotional category for each person. For textual analysis, ISEAR public datasets were used [16]. This dataset consists of several blogs written by different subjects in a specific emotional state. Each blog is associated with a label for emotional class. The datasets were associated with the five emotions: anger, sadness, joy, disgust, and fear. The ISEAR dataset consists of 7666 samples, but 1400 samples were used for each of the five emotional categories above. Using the word-emotion lexicon of the National Research Council (NRC), Canada, tokens related to each emotional category were extracted. Features were studied using long short-term memory (LSTM) and bidirectional long short-term memory (BLSTM) variants of the RNN classifier. The experimental results showed a classification accuracy of 98.5% in the case of BLSTM and 95.1% for LSTM.

Dahua et al. [17], for the recognition of emotions, used a multimodal model that, compared to the single-mode model, used complementary information that improved classification accuracy. They merged the features extracted from electroencephalography (EEG) to detect emotions continuously with those derived from facial expressions. To arouse emotions in the subjects, films and excerpts from the SEED dataset (SJTU Emotion EEG Dataset) [18] representing types of negative, neutral, and positive emotions were screened, and simultaneously EEG signals and facial expressions were recorded separately. Ten subjects participated in the experiment. Six sessions of movie clips representing a combination of the three classes of emotions were presented to each subject. Before each visualization session, the subjects were required to stay relaxed for 10 s to obtain the baseline to capture the change in emotion. The length of each clip is about 200 s. A 30 s break was provided between one film and another. Ten observers, specialists in psychology, were employed to carry out the continuous annotation of the response of the facial expression of the subjects. For this phase, the DARMA program was used, which allowed continuous evaluations of valence and excitement to be collected when viewing audio and video files.

With the help of a joystick, the observers performed the continuous annotation of emotions. The EEG data were sampled ussing the Emotive EPOC headset equipped with 14 acquisition channels. The ECG signals were preprocessed to delete artifacts by applying the 4–47 Hz bandpass filter and the spatial filter based on independent component analysis (ICA). The PSD (PhotoShop Document) features were extracted using the short-term Fourier transform (STFT). The PSD features are correlated with emotions in different bands, such as theta bands (4–7 Hz), alpha bands (8–12 Hz), beta bands (13–30 Hz), and gamma bands (30–47 Hz). The 56 features (14 channels $\times$ 4 frequency bands) were used to represent the EEG signals. After this phase, feature selection was performed to simplify the model and to improve performance by reducing irrelevant or redundant features. The authors applied t-distributed stochastic neighbor embedding (t-SNE), a nonlinear feature selection algorithm that was very efficient in computer vision. The valence predictions of EEG were obtained by support vector regression (SVR). Facial geometric features were extracted using the facial reference point localization model for facial expression. In particular, the inclination of the forehead, the extension of the opening of the eyes, the extension of the mouth, and the inclination of a corner of the mouth were chosen as facial features. These features were extracted by considering the coordinates of 29 landmarks in the eye and mouth. SVR was also applied for facial predictions. Both features were merged. Long short-term memory networks (LSTM) were utilized to accomplish the decision-level fusion and capture the temporal dynamics of emotions. To verify the validity of their classification method, the authors compared their t-SNE feature selection method with principal component analysis (PCA) with different dimensions. The results showed that the precision of EEG-based emotion recognition improves with decreasing feature dimensions. Both methods demonstrated the validity of the recognition system.

Moreover, t-SNE achieved more significant improvement than PCA. The best performances achieved by t-SNE and PCA were 0.534 ± 0.028 and 0.464 ± 0.032, respectively, when the dimension of the mapped feature was 15. The results of continuous emotion recognition showed that the fusion of two modalities provided better results than EEG and facial expressions separately. For the results of a single modality, facial expressions were better than EEG. The experimental results found that three steps of LSTM yielded the best CCC (concordance correlation coefficient) of 0.625 ± 0.029.

The possibility of using wireless devices and networks has stimulated research in the design of innovative models capable of recognizing human activities through the collection of physiological, environmental, and position data to obtain valuable information on the state of health of people, to develop intervention strategies to improve living conditions. In addition, the development of machine learning algorithms makes it possible to deduce human emotions from sensory data that can facilitate the identification of mental situations in need of help.

In this context, Kanjo et al. [19] proposed a model that is based on the detection of emotions in motion and in real-life environments, different from other models in which emotions are detected in laboratory environments and with samples in which emotions are stimulated by audiovisual means or by asking participants to perform activities designed to induce emotional states. The experience was developed with the following:

- The use of multimodal sensors: physiological, environmental, and position data collected in a global template representing the signal's dynamics together with the temporal relationships of each mode.
- The application of different deep learning models to extract emotions automatically.
- Collecting data in real situations from subjects wearing a bracelet and a smartphone.

- In classifying emotions, the characteristics of the three types of signals are examined individually and combined.

The authors used the EnvBodySens dataset, already tested in a previous work [20], which collected data from 40 participants who walked on specific paths. The data were obtained for heart rate (HR), galvanic skin response (SGR), body temperature, motion data (accelerometer and gyroscope), environmental data such as noise levels, UV, atmospheric pressure and location data, GPS locations, and self-reported emotion levels recorded on Android phones (Nexus), wirelessly connected to Microsoft Wrist Band 2 [21]. The self-reported data referred to the responses given by the participants about the sensations they experienced while walking based on a predefined scale of emotions. The data collected included 550,432 sensor data frames and 5345 self-report responses. The signals were preprocessed and subsequently inputted into a hybrid model of a convolutional neural network and long short-term memory recurrent neural network (CNN-LSTM). The results showed that deep learning algorithms effectively classify human emotions when using many sensor inputs. The average accuracy was 95%. In addition, tests carried out using MLP, CNN, and CNN-LSTM models showed that with the hybrid model, the accuracy of emotional states increased by more than 20% compared to a traditional MLP model.

The application developed by Suraj et al. [22] was part of the research aimed at the automatic detection of emotions, using deep learning algorithms, to detect pain or discomfort to help medical personnel immediately activate the most suitable treatments. The solution adopted is based on the use of a CNN network to which images of the face and mouth are transferred. The authors created the model through human face detection, eliminating unwanted components using a webcam. Images underwent a preprocessing step to convert from RGB to grayscale using OpenCV libraries. Histogram equalization was performed to unify and improve image contrast for better edge identification. Next, a cascade Haar classifier was used to recognize the mouth and eyes in each frame. The classification of emotions was performed by the last level of the CNN network (SoftMax).

Experimental results showed that this system can detect normal emotions, pain, and fatigue accuracy of 79.71%.

3. Emotion Recognition Analysis

To offer readers a clear understanding of how emotions can be derived through visual images of the face, we developed an analysis of the theme reported below.

3.1. Detection Technique

The FER is also used in human intention prediction (HIP), which represents an emerging area of research in which the system, through the collected data, predicts human behavior to improve assisted living.

Face recognition in the context of the HAR in healthcare can be applied for:

- Detecting neurodegenerative disorders;
- Detecting states of depression or, in general, identifying subjects who need assistance;
- Observing the condition of patients during medical treatment;
- Detecting psychotic disorders;
- Monitoring anxiety states;
- Detecting pain or stress.

Human behavior can be characterized by analyzing facial expressions through the vision system. The face is the most expressive part of our body; it makes visible every emotional trace, thus making a face the primary source from which to obtain information on emotions.

Abdulsalam et al. analyzed how emotions can be detected [23]. They can be recognized through unimodal social behaviors, such as speech, facial expressions, texts, or gestures; bimodal behaviors, such as speech associated with facial expressions; or multimodal behaviors, such as audio, video, or physiological signals.

As part of our study, we focused on recognizing emotions through facial expression without considering other methodologies that use voice, body movements, or physiological signals.

Ekman was one of the first researchers to study emotions and their relationship with facial expressions; his research demonstrated the universality and discretion of emotions following Darwinian theory [24]. Over the years, he developed a set for the recognition of emotions based on a series of stimuli called POFA (Pictures of Facial Affect) consisting of 110 black and white images. According to Ekman et al. [25], in nature, there are two different categories of emotions, primary or universal emotions, and secondary or complex emotions. The former can also be present in other animals, as Charles Darwin argued in *The Expression of Emotion in Man and Animals*; the latter, however, is present only in human beings. Primary emotions are universal and innate emotions.

On the other hand, secondary emotions are affected by environmental and socio-cultural influences. The primary emotions are also essential: anger, fear, sadness, happiness, disgust, and surprise. Complex emotions include joy, envy, shame, anxiety, boredom, resignation, jealousy, hope, forgiveness, offense, nostalgia, remorse, disappointment, and relief.

In 1992, Ekman expanded his list of basic emotions, adding contempt, embarrassment, guilt, and shame to those already known. For each of the primary emotions, there are characteristic elements of the face that allow one to identify the type of emotions:

Anger, generated by frustration, manifests itself through aggressiveness and can be identified through the following features: a flushed face, hard look, dilated nostrils, clenched jaws, lowered eyebrows, and tight lips. Some of these characteristics are also present in expressions of fear. However, the eyebrows, the forehead movement, and the type of mouth allow us to differentiate the two expressions. In fear, the eyebrows are raised, the eyelids are stretched, and the mouth is open.

Happiness, the manifestation of a mood of satisfaction, is one of the easiest emotions to recognize because a smile appears on the person's face. The lips can be joined in the smile or open, including the teeth and cheeks raised. The more pronounced the smile, the more the cheeks rise.

Disgust is a feeling of repulsion, and its characteristics are: clenched nostrils, raised upper lip, and curled nose. The greater the sense of disgust, the more pronounced the upper lip and the wrinkling of the nose will be.

Sadness is identified through the forehead and eyebrows: the first displays a frown, and for the second, the inner corners are raised. Sometimes sadness can be confused with the emotion of fear.

Surprise, the manifestation of the state of mind in the face of an unexpected event, is a type of brief emotion in which the eyebrows appear curved and raised, the eyes wide, the forehead wrinkled, and the jaw is lowered, causing the lips to open.

Fear, an emotion produced in the face of a dangerous situation, is identified through the following characteristics: raised eyebrows, wide-open eyes, dilated pupils, joined eyebrows, and elongated lips.

There are two methods for studying facial expression: one based on an analytical method through which the mimic components that contribute to the determination of a specific facial expression are identified and the other based on the judgment of the facial expressions manifested. The facial action coding system (FACS) can be used as an analytical method. This system, developed by Ekman and Friesen, constitutes a measurement system to evaluate the movements of facial expressions of emotion. It can be used to identify the internal and emotional state of the subject. Through the analysis of facial micro expressions, which are involuntary and rapid expressions, it is possible to deduce indications of hidden thoughts and emotions of the subject. They appear with a fraction of a second and reveal the subject's genuine emotion.

The system is based on the coding of evaluators based on the presence and extent of facial micromovements, called facial action units (AU), such as the face, eye, and head movements. Face emotion recognition is a technology that belongs to the field of "Affective computing" [26], enabling automatic systems to interpret and recognize human emotions.

It is an interdisciplinary field that exploits computer science, psychology, neuroscience, and cognitive science. It is a technology that reasonably and accurately recognizes emotions from visual, textual, and auditory sources. High-resolution cameras and powerful machine learning capabilities allow artificial intelligence to identify emotion through facial expressions. It is used in various fields of application, as already seen above, including health, to study stress and psychophysical disorders.

3.2. FER Structure

Face emotion recognition (FER) is a technique for the recognition of emotions through the analysis of facial expressions in multimodal form.

FER has increased in the field of perceptual and cognitive sciences and affective computing with the development of artificial intelligence techniques, virtual reality [27], and augmented reality [28,29]. Different inputs are available for the FER, such as electromyography (EMG), electrocardiograms (ECG), electroencephalograms (EEG), and the a camera; the latter is preferable because it provides more information and does not require the use of wearable devices. The technology on which the FER is based uses mathematical algorithms to analyze faces acquired from images or videos to recognize emotions or behaviors through facial features. Recognition systems can use 2D images as input data, but newer approaches employ 3D models or combined 2D–3D models called FER multimodal models [30]. Three-dimensional technology performs better, but due to the high resolution and frame rate, it requires more computational power as the amount of data captured in 3D databases increases.

In addition to traditional approaches [31], deep learning-based algorithms can be applied for extraction, classification, and recognition activities.

FER is divided into the following phases: image acquisition, image processing, face detection, feature extraction, and emotion classification (Figure 1).

Figure 1. Flow chart of facial emotion recognition.

- Image processing is a preliminary phase to eliminate all interfering factors in the input image that can affect classification performance and complicate processing. It consists of locating and extracting the region of the face. It is used to eliminate the background noise through processing filters and to normalize the image's color. For example, one of the most commonly used filters to obtain a sharper image is RIR (Regularized Inverse Auto-Regressive) [32].
- Face detection involves distinguishing faces in an image or video and constructing bounding boxes for faces. One algorithm used for this purpose is the Viola–Jones algorithm, developed initially for object detection. This algorithm examines the minor features of a human face in an image, and if all these features are found, the algorithm predicts that there is a face in that image or a secondary image. Its application requires that requirements such as full-view, frontal, vertical, well-lit, and life-size faces in fixed-resolution images are met. Paul Viola and Michael Jones modified Haar's wavelets to develop so-called Haar-like features. A Haar-like feature considers adjacent rectangular regions in a sensing window, adds pixel intensities in each region and calculates the difference between these sums. This difference is used to categorize subsections of an image.
- Feature extraction is the process of extracting reference points that facilitate the algorithm to recognize the expression. Extraction methods can be different depending on the type of input image. For static images, the extraction method can be based on "geometric features" or "aspects". One commonly used geometric feature model is the active shape model (ASM) [33]. It consists of creating a suggested shape by looking at the image around each point for a better location for the point. Based on this aspect, local feature analysis (LFA) methods use the entire face or specific

measures to extract facial changes. The commonly used methods are local binary pattern (LBP) and Gabor feature extraction. LBP [34] is a texture operator defined as an ordered binary sequence of color depth comparisons between pixel p and pixels belonging to the neighborhood under consideration. To calculate the LPB code, for each generic pixel "p", the 8 "x" neighbors of the center pixel are compared with the pixel p and assigned a value of one if $x \geq p$. Calculating LBP on the entire image means producing a feature vector consisting of a histogram as an output result.

- ➢ Gabor feature extraction applies a series of filters to extract features. They are extracted from sequences of dynamic images and are derived from changes in expressions and the displacement of characteristic points of the face [35].
- ➢ Emotion classification has the task of identifying which emotions correspond to the facial features examined. The following is an overview of the approaches based on traditional methods and those based on deep learning [36]. In facial recognition technology, data separation is crucial, belonging to the same class. A class represents all data from the same subject. Linear discriminant analysis (LDA) and principal component analysis (PCA) are among the most commonly used classifiers. Both aim to separate data into classes. LDA [37] is a method that transforms image vectors into a low-dimensional space maximizing data separation between classes and minimizing dispersion within the classroom. That is, it groups the images of the same class and separates the images of a different class. LDA allows for identifying the aim of an objective evaluation of the visual information present in the features. Similarly, PCA [38] is an algorithm that transforms image vectors by reducing large dimensions into smaller values while preserving as much information as possible and separating data into the classroom. It employs eigenvalues and eigenvectors to reduce dimensionality and projects data samples onto a small space.

Another algorithm used for classification is the K-nearest neighbor algorithm [39]. Classification is performed by comparing the sample with its neighbors. The input consists of the training samples, while the output is the result of the sample belonging to a class. The sample is classified through the class to which its neighbors belong. Based on the value of **K**, the **K** elements closest to the sample to be examined are considered. Based on most elements of a given class, the sample under examination will be assigned to the same class.

Among the algorithms based on supervised learning models are support vector machines (SVMs) [40], which are binary linear classification methods. With the two training datasets, each identified according to the class it belongs to between the two possible classes, the model assigns the new examples to one of them. The algorithm is based on the identification of the separation line between the two classes that maximizes the margin between the classes themselves, where the margin means the minimum distance from the line to the points of the two classes. The so-called support vectors achieve this goal using only a minimal part of the training dataset. Supporting vectors are those datasets that reside on the margin and are used to perform classification.

Finally, random forest is a classifier formed by combining decision trees [41]. The algorithm builds multiple trees based on randomly selected subsets of the training dataset, then aggregates the predictions of each tree to choose the best prediction. Random forest belongs to the class of algorithms called "Ensemble". They work based on a combination of machine learning algorithms to create a predictive model that ensures better performance. There are different methods of aggregation, including bagging and boosting. Bagging consists of sampling the initial dataset N times, training it N times, and choosing the category most frequently for classification. On the other hand, boosting is based on a sequential process in which, at each step, the previous model is improved by correcting errors; each model depends on the previous one and tends to decrease the error.

Deep learning-based FER approaches significantly reduce reliance on models based on physical facial features and other preprocessing techniques, enabling learning directly from input images. The convolutional neural network (CNN) and recurrent neural network (RNN) are the most widely used network models.

3.3. Neural Network

The CNN network is a deep neural network that learns the characteristics of data layer by layer through a nonlinear structure. It consists of a set of several layers that have the function of extracting the characteristics of the input images and a completely connected terminal layer that acts as a classifier. They are suitable for analyzing images in specific datasets and classifying objects within them. Each processing layer contains a convolutional filter, a trigger function (Relu), and a pooling function. At the end of each processing step, an input is generated for the next level. The convolution subjects the images to a series of filters, each of which manages to activate specific characteristics of the images to create the feature map that becomes the input for the next filter. The activation function is intended to introduce a non-linearity into the system using nonlinear functions, and it can cancel negative values obtained in the previous classes. The pooling function obtains images with a particular input resolution. It returns the same number of images with fewer pixels, thus reducing the size of the output matrices and the number of parameters that must be learned from the network. At the end of the convolutional layers is the fully connected level (FC), which aims to identify the classes obtained in the previous levels according to a certain probability. These operations are repeated on multiple levels, and each level learns to classify different characteristics. A fully connected level and classification level are used to provide classification output. Designing a CNN network requires a training phase followed by a testing phase. During the training phase, the images are labeled and transferred to subsequent levels to allow conversion from the original input representation layer to a higher-level and more abstract representation to build the reference feature maps with which the network must compare the output feature maps. Each class represents a possible answer that the system will choose. During the recognition phase, the network follows a classification operation to identify which class the input image belongs to, identifying the one with the highest probability.

RNN is a feed-forward neural network similar to the CNN network. It still has an input layer, hidden intermediate levels, and an output layer. Land connections between nodes form a graph directed along a timeline. While in CNN, neurons of the same level cannot communicate with each other but can only send signals to the next layer, in RNN, neurons can also admit loops. They can be interconnected even to neurons of an earlier level. These networks link backward or to the same level. They can use their internal memory to process any input sequence. The output of a neuron can influence itself in a subsequent time step or affect the neurons of the previous chain, which will interfere with the behavior of the neuron on which the loop closes. RNN networks can process a data timeline, unlike classical feed-forward networks where the data provided are static. A timeline can be thought of as a function sampled over several moments.

Deep learning methods must use extensive datasets to achieve a high recognition rate, and so the algorithms do not work well if a few subjects form the datasets.

3.4. Dataset Used

The public databases used for analyzing emotions are the BU-3DFE and the BU-4DFE.

The BU-3DFE [42] is a 3D facial model database at Binghamton University containing facial images of 100 subjects of different ethnic and racial origins. Each subject was scanned with seven expressions. Except for the neutral expression, each of the six basic expressions (happiness, disgust, fear, anger, surprise, and sadness) includes four intensity levels. Thus, there are a total of 2500 3D facial expression models. Each expression pattern has an image of the corresponding facial texture captured at two views (approximately +45° and −45°). As a result, the database consists of 2500 two-view texture images and 2500 geometric shape models. To analyze facial behavior from static 3D to dynamic 3D space, the BU-3DFE was extended to the BU-4DFE [42]. The new database of high-resolution 3D dynamic facial expressions refers to 101 subjects of different sexes, ages, racial and ethnic origins. Three-dimensional facial expressions were captured at a rate of 25 frames per second. Each sequence of expressions contains approximately 100 frames. Each subject performed the six basic emotions, ending with the neutral expression. The database contains 606 sequences of 3D facial expressions.

Another database used is the Bosphorus [43], which contains 2D and 3D images of 105 subjects, of which a third are professional actors and actresses. The data were collected in the laboratory, and the subjects were instructed to perform the seven basic facial expressions. The scans for the 105 subjects were carried out considering different poses, expressions, and occlusion conditions. The total number of facial scans is 4666. This database contains examples of the unit of action (A.U.) faces defined in the facial action coding system.

Other databases with visual sequences and images are available for studying emotions; some examples are presented below.

The extended Cohn–Kanade Dataset (cK+) [44] contains 593 sequences of 123 subjects. The sequence of images varies in duration from 10 to 60 frames. The images are labeled with seven emotions, including six basic emotions and contempt. All images were taken with a constant background. To avoid mistakes during the training phase, the labels were assigned respecting the coding of FACS emotions.

Another database is the CASME [45], which contains spontaneous microexpressions. Microexpressions are fleeting facial expressions that reveal authentic emotions that people try to hide. From the 1500 facial movements filmed at 60 fps, 195 microexpressions were selected. Samples from the dataset were taken from thirty-five participants. Each clip has a minimum length of 500 ms. The images were labeled based on psychological studies and participants' self-assessments.

Still, the FER-2013 [46] is a widely used dataset containing 28,000 training data, 3500 validation data, and 3500 test data. Land images are stored in a spreadsheet where the pixel values of each image are reported in cells per row. The images were obtained using Google search and then grouped by emotional classes. The images were collected from varying poses, ages, and occlusion.

BAUM [47] is a spontaneous audiovisual facial database of affective and mental states. Video clips were obtained by shooting subjects from a front view using a stereo camera and a semi-profile view using a mono camera. Subjects were shown images and short video clips to evoke emotions and mental states. The target emotions are happiness, anger, sadness, disgust, fear, surprise, boredom, and contempt; mental targets are uncertain (even confused, indecisive), thoughtful, focused, interested (even curious), and annoyed. The database contains 273 clips obtained from 31 subjects (13 females, 18 males) with the age range of subjects being 19–65 years.

4. Methodology

A deep learning architecture is certainly not an innovative approach; in recent years, numerous applications have been developed and shown excellent facial and emotional recognition results. A deep neural architecture represents a practical solution; it allows one to analyze and extract the characteristics of each face to train the network and associate the characteristics of a new image with one of the seven emotions.

The innovation brought by our project is the development of an AI classifier based on a set of classifying neural networks whose outputs are directed to an ensemble layer [48]. In particular, the networks are self-normalizing neural networks (SNN) [49]. We can operate assumptions for which the problem is framed in the detection of phenomenological expressions that:

- They are finite and contained.
- They may have a certain degree of overlap in their manifestation.
- They evolve in a specific time frame, during which common randomness mechanisms govern the type of variation; in other words, the comparison between different temporal evolutions of the same phenomenology has little variability.

- The last stage of this evolution represents more distance between the expected classes (or with less overlap between classes), which can be defined as a maximum characterization event.

The architecture consists of 6 SNNs, each trained to identify the six emotions. The networks are cascaded, and each is dedicated to detecting the presence or absence in the input image of a single specific emotion (among the six present in this study) assigned and associated with it. Each neural network is trained with its images for a specific emotion. Each network will produce two outputs, of which the first identified with EM, through a numerical enhancement (from 0 to 1), will confirm the correspondence of the detected emotion with that assigned to the network, and the second identified with AM, similarly through a numerical enhancement (from 0 to 1), will signal the presence of another emotion than that assigned to the specific network. If, for example, the first network has been trained to detect anger, the eligible cases will be EM1t1 = 1 and AM1t1 = 0 if the emotion is anger, and EM1t1 = 0 AM1t1 = 1 when the emotion detected is "another" different from anger.

These outputs are then transferred to the ensemble layer, which provides an accurate result by analyzing the outputs of the individual networks according to statistical logic. Ensemble is an algorithm that combines several trained models, allowing them to obtain better predictive results than single models.

Wanting to apply this architecture to the time interval during which the face passes from a "resting" stage to the stage "of complete characterization" of a specific emotion, it will be necessary to provide as an input to neural networks three frames obtained from a single specific video. In this case, the ensemble classifier will consist of 18 neural networks, six dedicated to identifying the six emotions for each video frame. Its architecture is represented by the diagram shown in Figure 2.

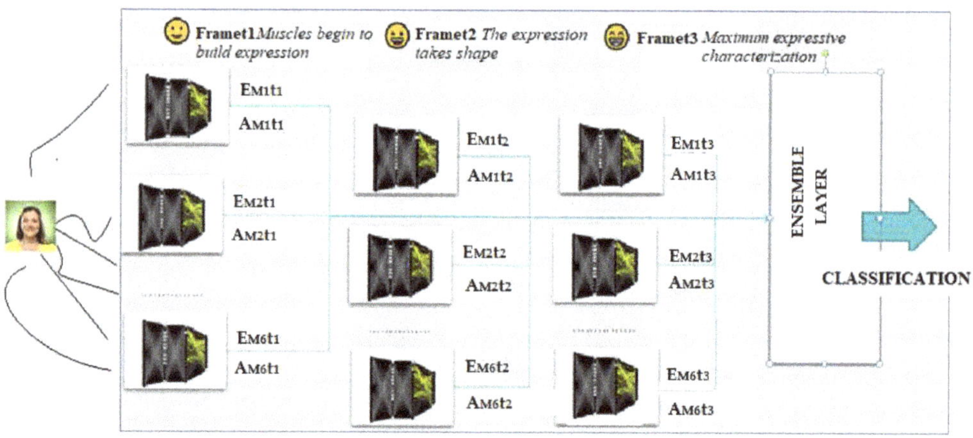

Figure 2. Network architecture.

The system's functioning can be described by assuming that we want to classify a specific emotion that we already know, such as "happiness." With its three frames, this emotion is inputted into the system. Assuming that the M2 network has been trained for this type of emotion, we will obtain that, for Frame 1, EM2t1 will take on a more significant weight value than all the EMit1 of the other five networks. Similarly, when we move on to analyze Frame 2, in which the expression takes shape, the EM2t2 will increase its weight value, resulting in more significance than the EMit2. Finally, with frame three, we will obtain a maximum evaluation of EM2t3 far superior to the other values for EMit3. Finally, the Classification Ensemble module, in analyzing all of the EMitj, determines as a predictive value the classification obtained from EM2t3, considering the temporal variation obtained.

This mode of analysis performed at three different time intervals allows us to evaluate the difference, even on the same individual, between the movements that the face performs during the moments leading to the full manifestation of emotion. It allows us to evaluate whether it is the result of a subconscious reaction to an event ("genuine reaction") or, vice versa, produced by an act of conscious voluntariness ("voluntary fiction").

This approach is challenging to implement since building a training set with the visual traits described above is complex. The extraction from the videos of the three frames that belong to the exact configuration of the muscles of the face relative to the evolution of a specific emotion needs to be revised. For example, extracting frames with only time synchronization in mind could compromise model inference. While the evolution of expressions can be correlated, the timing of expressions can vary significantly from individual to individual.

Therefore, finding such videos at a helpful quantity for training networks is challenging. The hypothesized architecture remains valid, excluding the temporal component, considering that a single image is instantly acquired. Even with this mode, the qualities related to the performance and near observability of inferential states remain preserved. For these reasons, a simpler architecture was applied in this work, as shown in Figure 3.

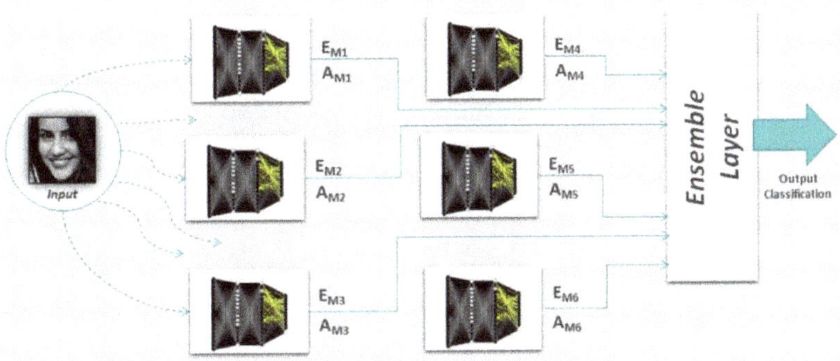

Figure 3. "Single frame" Configuration.

The input images in this configuration can be assimilated to the frame at time t3 of the configuration in Figure 2. The images are supposed to be no longer sequences of movie frames. Instead, the images of the training set are all referable to the stage of the maximum characterization of emotions.

Compared to a single neural network, this configuration has the advantage of implementing a classifier with inferential states that are "almost observable". With this solution, we can overcome the problem that afflicts a specific classifier if it produces an erroneous result. This classifier provides the advantage of being able to intervene when it is affected by development or model errors in the case of unwanted outputs. In the case of using neural networks, it is impossible to identify the "neuron" to be replaced as it is the entire network that has extracted a model that does not conform to the phenomenology to which it was applied. So, with an AI Ensemble classifier, it becomes possible to identify the subnet that gave the output altering the correct functioning of the ensemble module. It is possible to intervene directly in that specific subnet. This peculiarity, in addition to providing elements to understand why and how the error was born, allows for obtaining improvements in all parts of the classifier.

5. Dataset and Model Design

The research activities focused mainly on identifying, studying, and highlighting how the proposed AI ensemble approach can provide different advantages in the FER field. With this in mind, design choices can be characterized as "stress tests."

In particular, a Kaggle dataset was chosen for the training and test sets (Figure 4). The dataset also predicts the "neutral" emotion, which we did not consider.

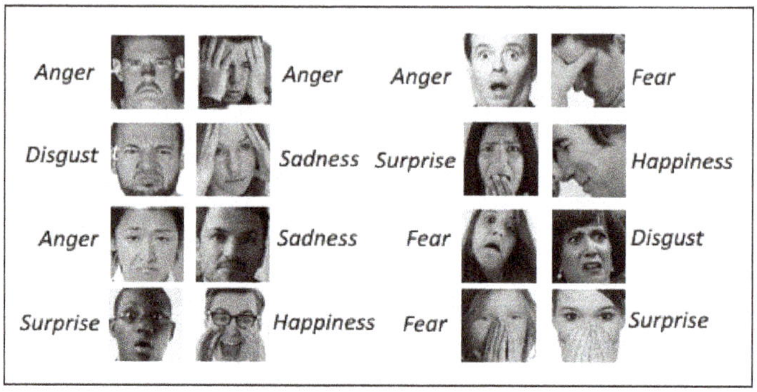

Figure 4. Some emotions from the Kaggle Dataset.

This presents some critical issues:

- Facial expressions, or gestures, are not always the primary characterization of images.
- The numerical distribution of classes is very uneven and, in some cases, limited (Tables 1 and 2).
- The "distance" between the reference classes is not very marked (we collected conflicting opinions of attribution through small surveys aimed at students).

Table 1. Training set.

Training set	Total
L0 (Anger)	3995
L1 (Disgust)	436
L2 (Fear)	4097
L3 (Happines)	7215
L4 (Sad)	4830
L5 (surprise)	3171

Table 2. Testset.

Testset	Total
L0 (Anger)	958
L1 (Disgust)	111
L2 (Fear)	1024
L3 (Happines)	1774
L4 (Sad)	1247
L5 (surprise)	831

The single images are grayscale and have a resolution of 48 × 48 pixels.

The training set has been appropriately relabeled by generating six different training sets from two classes ("reference emotion" and "other emotion").

In this scenario, it seemed helpful and not too expensive in computational terms to use SNNs (self-normalizing neural networks). These are networks robust to noise and disturbances and do not exhibit high variation in their training errors. In deep learning, a widely used technique is batch normalization, which leads to the normalization of neuron activation towards mean zero and unit variance. Each level is normalized and used as an input to the next level. SNNs, on the other hand, are self-normalizing, neural activations that automatically converge towards mean zero and unit variance. This property is ensured by the activation function, which consists of scaled exponential linear units (SELU). This characteristic accelerates convergence in the formation process. SELU learns faster and

6. Results and Discussion

In the experiments, we used a result validation approach through the control network. In Table 3 we reported the results for the six emotions analyzed. Success rates were achieved using the original test dataset and a training dataset reduced by several images to make it more consistent. The percentages refer to each type of image (emotion) in the case of the control neural network, to the single AI NN units, and to the entire model in the Ensemble algorithm.

Table 3. Success Rate.

	Control Network	Sub Network	Ensamble
L0 (Anger)	22%	62%	78%
L1 (Disgust)	10%	18%	22%
L2 (Fear)	82%	94%	95%
L3 (Happiness)	43%	76%	81%
L4 (Sad)	64%	83%	85%
L5 (surprise)	54%	77%	80%

From the analysis of the data, there is a low value for the "Disgust" emotion for all types of networks used, both due to the low number of samples present in the datasets and the difficulty of its identification due to the lack of expressive separability from the "Anger" class.

We also found that network performance improved by moving from the single control network trained for the six types of emotions to those of individual networks built to identify a specific emotion (no false positives were detected). Moreover, finally adding the rules of decision and unification of the ensemble layer, we noticed that the performance of the network improved further. The success rates are almost all around 80%, with a peak of 95% for the "Fear" emotion.

We compared the model's performance with the other proposals in the related work (Table 4). Depending on the specific functionalities of the emotion recognition system, researchers used different methodologies, technologies and databases. In our analysis, we represented different experiences testifying to a varied scenario.

The results obtained show that the algorithm adopted ensures that facial emotion recognition results are compatible from the point of view of accuracy with the state-of-the-art.

The efficiency of the model was based on the type of network used. SNN networks allowed us to create a model with a reduced number of levels compared to existing models. This choice arose from some considerations related to the intrinsic quality of the model (e.g., not requiring any normalization of the input data) and the peculiarities of the dataset used in conjunction with the learning phase. The dataset is, in fact, not very homogeneous in terms of the numerical distribution of classes. Therefore, two of the qualities of SELUs are very valuable: it does not have a vanishing gradient problem, and neurons cannot die, as can happen with RELUs.

Then, the outputs of the individual networks are sent to the Ensemble layer, which has the task of improving the performance of the individual classification systems through the analysis of the results rendered.

We achieved 98.4% accuracy with a learning rate of 0.0001 and 60 epochs, while in the test phase we obtained an accuracy value of 85%, excluding the emotion disgust.

Table 4. Comparison of face emotion recognition systems.

Authors	Purpose	Technologies	Database	Efficiency
Jn et al. [12]	Direct diagnosis of disease	• Deep Transfer • Learning DTL • MatConvNet	VGG-Face	93% accuracy
Jn et al. [13]	Improved facial emotion recognition using pseudo RGB-D	• RGB-D sensor • Depth plus • Generator • Adversarial network	• Bosphorous 3d • Face • CASUA 3d Face • Bu-3DFe	97% SSIM (Similarity index for measuring image quality)
Ghosh et al. [14]	Improved facial emotion recognition using physiological signals	• RNN • HRV sensor	ISEAR	96% accuracy
Dahua et al. [17]	Improved facial emotion recognition using physiological signals	• t-SNE • PCA • SVR • PSD	SEED dataset	0.625 ± 0.029 CCC (Concordance correlation coefficient)
Kanio et al. [19]	Improved facial emotion recognition using MEMS, environmental an physiological signals in real-life environments	• CNN • CNN-LSTM	EnvBodySens	95% accuracy
Suraj et al. [22]	Pain or discomfort recognition in patients monitoring	• CNN • Haar classifier	N.D.	79.71% accuracy
Bibbo' et al.	Face emotion recognition	Ensemble SNN	Kaggle	98.4% accuracy in training and 85% in test

The emotion collection was carried out based on static images. The usefulness of a video would provide spatiotemporal information for expression dynamics captured in a video sequence [51]. The temporal information is accurate, allowing us to perform better. However, it involves significant differences in the characteristics extracted during the duration of the transition and in the specific characteristics of the expressions depending on the subject's physiognomy. Possible approaches to solving this type of problem are costly in terms of computational time and complexity. Therefore, they do not efficiently reduce time redundancies in extracted frames.

The dataset used, which is complex in itself, presents for some classes a limited number of samples. Numerous images are not sufficiently clear, and can lead to misinterpretation. This led us to reduce the number of samples per class to make the entire dataset homogeneous. In order to improve accuracy, the number of samples for each class can be increased in future work.

Therefore, we believe that the proposed solution, due to the reduced computational load and its structural simplicity, can be used in the monitoring of the elderly to support medical staff in the assessment of the health status of patients.

7. Conclusions

In this article, we have developed a facial expression recognition system that can help improve healthcare. Despite the results obtained with technological progress in the development of automatic emotion recognition systems, this technology, as observed from the review of the literature, is not widely used in the health system.

The solution we propose is based on the Ensemble AI model. The methodology applied is part of an ensemble learning area in which the models, in comparison, discriminate two classes, with one referring to the specific emotion for the network for which it was trained and the other regerring to "other emotion" class. The advantages obtained were:

"Almost observable states". It is possible to investigate and highlight which module caused errors. It operates a debugging similar to the case of deterministic algorithms.

"Modularity and parallelism". Individual modules can be trained on different workstations, at different times, without synchronization between parts. This feature allows one to independently develop different configurations and calibrations of the specific module research groups.

"Embedded application". The Vectorflow framework in D language allows the realization of the model even in embedded hardware on many platforms and operating systems.

The results show an increase in performance compared to the control neural network, confirming that the proposed system can recognize emotions with high precision. With this system, doctors and healthcare professionals can constantly monitor, as part of the broader human activity recognition system, the psychophysical conditions of patients, detecting malaise, pain and fatigue and taking appropriate actions as needed.

This solution can be seen as a component of smart healthcare centers.

In the future, we plan to extend the work by investigating the infrastructure on a less complex dataset and analyzing video sequences.

Author Contributions: L.B. and F.C. contributed to conception and design of study. L.B. called the methodology. L.B., M.V. and F.C. investigated. L.B. and F.C. developed the model. L.B. wrote original draft of the manuscript. L.B., M.V. and F.C. contributed to write and editing of the manuscript. All authors have read and agreed to the published version of the manuscript.

Funding: This work is supported by the Italian MIUR Project under GRANT PON Research and Innovation 2014–2020 Project Code C35E19000020001, AIM 1839112-1: Technologies for the living environment.

Institutional Review Board Statement: Not applicable.

Informed Consent Statement: Not applicable.

Data Availability Statement: Public dataset Kaggle.

Conflicts of Interest: The authors declare no conflict of interest.

References

1. Aggarwal, J.K.; Ryoo, M.S. Human activity analysis: A review. *ACM Comput. Surv.* **2011**, *43*, 16. [CrossRef]
2. Li, M.; Xu, H.; Huang, X.; Song, Z.; Liu, X.; Li, X. Facial Expression Recognition with Identity and Emotion Joint Learning. *IEEE Trans. Affect. Comput.* **2018**, *12*, 544–550. [CrossRef]
3. Adjabi, I.; Ouahabi, A.; Benzaoui, A.; Taleb-Ahmed, A. Past, present, and future of face recognition: A review. *Electronics* **2020**, *9*, 1188. [CrossRef]
4. Tan, L.; Zhang, K.; Wang, K.; Zeng, X.; Peng, X.; Qiao, Y. Group emotion recognition with individual facial emotion CNNs and global image based CNNs. In Proceedings of the 19th ACM International Conference on Multimodal Interaction-ICMI, Glasgow, UK, 13–17 November 2017; pp. 549–552.
5. Song, Z. Facial Expression Emotion Recognition Model Integrating Philosophy and Machine Learning Theory. *Front. Psychol.* **2021**, *12*, 759485. [CrossRef] [PubMed]
6. Sun, A.; Li, Y.; Huang, Y.-M.; Li, Q.; Lu, G. Facial expression recognition using optimized active regions. *Hum. Cent. Comput. Inf. Sci.* **2018**, *8*, 33. [CrossRef]
7. De Risi, M.; Di Gennaro, G.; Picardi, A.; Casciato, S.; Grammaldo, L.G.; D'Aniello, A.; Lanni, D.; Meletti, S.; Modugno, N. Facial emotion decoding in patients with Parkinson's disease. *Int. J. Neurosci.* **2018**, *128*, 71–78. [CrossRef]
8. Liu, H.; Mo, Z.-H.; Yang, H.; Zhang, Z.-F.; Hong, D.; Wen, L.; Lin, M.-Y.; Zheng, Y.-Y.; Zhang, Z.-W.; Xu, X.-W.; et al. Automatic Facial Recognition of Williams-Beuren Syndrome Based on Deep Convolutional Neural Networks. *Front. Pediatr.* **2021**, *9*, 648255. [CrossRef]
9. Zhao, M.; Liu, Q.; Jha, A.; Deng, R.; Yao, T.; Mahadevan-Jansen, A.; Tyska, M.J.; Millis, B.A.; Huo, Y. VoxelEmbed: 3D Instance Segmentation and Tracking with Voxel Embedding based Deep Learning. In *Machine Learning in Medical Imaging. MLMI 2021. Lecture Notes in Computer Science*; Lian, C., Cao, X., Rekik, I., Xu, X., Yan, P., Eds.; Springer: Cham, Switzerland, 2021; Volume 12966.

10. Zheng, Q.; Yang, M.; Yang, J.; Zhang, Q.; Zhang, X. Improvement of Generalization Ability of Deep CNN via Implicit Regularization in Two-Stage Training Process. *IEEE Access* **2018**, *6*, 15844–15869. [CrossRef]
11. Yao, T.; Qu, C.; Liu, Q.; Deng, R.; Tian, Y.; Xu, J.; Jha, A.; Bao, S.; Zhao, M.; Fogo, A.B.; et al. Compound Figure Separation of Biomedical Images with Side Loss. In *Deep Generative Models, and Data Augmentation, Labelling, and Imperfections*; Lecture Notes in Computer Science; Springer: Cham, Switzerland, 2021; Volume 13003, pp. 173–183.
12. Jin, B.; Cruz, L.; Gonçalves, N. Deep Facial Diagnosis: Deep Transfer Learning from Face Recognition to Facial Diagnosis. *IEEE Access* **2020**, *8*, 123649–123661. [CrossRef]
13. Jin, B.; Cruz, L.; Gonçalves, N. Pseudo RGB-D Face Recognition. *Sens. J.* **2022**, *22*, 21780–21794. [CrossRef]
14. Ghosh, R.; Sinha, D. Human emotion recognition by analyzing facial expressions, heart rate and blogs using deep learning method. *Innov. Syst. Softw. Eng.* **2022**, *2022*, 1–9. [CrossRef]
15. Ghosh, R.; Sinha, D. Human emotion detection based on questionnaire and text analysis. *Int. J. Work. Organ. Emot.* **2019**, *10*, 66–89. [CrossRef]
16. Available online: https://www.Kaggle.com/shrivastva/isears-dataset (accessed on 4 September 2017).
17. Li, D.; Wang, Z.; Wang, C.; Liu, S.; Chi, W.; Dong, E.; Song, X.; Gao, Q.; Song, Y. The Fusion of Electroencephalography and Facial Expression for Continuous Emotion Recognition. *IEEE Access* **2019**, *7*, 155724–155736. [CrossRef]
18. Liu, J.; Wu, G.; Luo, Y.; Qiu, S.; Yang, S.; Li, W.; Bi, Y. EEG-Based Emotion Classification Using a Deep Neural Network and Sparse Autoencoder. *Front Syst. Neurosci.* **2020**, *14*, 43. [CrossRef]
19. Kanjo, E.; Eman, M.G.; Younis, E.M.; Ang, C.S. Deep learning analysis of mobile physiological, environmental and location sensor data for emotion detection. *Inf. Fusion* **2019**, *49*, 46–56. [CrossRef]
20. Kanjo, E.; Younis, E.M.; Sherkat, N. Towards unravelling the relationship between on-body, environmental and emotion data using sensor information fusion approach. *Inf. Fusion* **2018**, *4*, 18–31. [CrossRef]
21. Microsoft Wrist Band Kernel Description. Available online: https://www.microsoft.com/microsoftband/en-gb (accessed on 4 September 2017).
22. Suraj, A.; Kaushik, A.S.; Bai, K. Patient Monitoring Using Emotion Recognition. *Int. J. Res. Appl. Sci. Eng. Technol.* **2022**, *10*, 46387. [CrossRef]
23. Abdulsalam, W.; Alhamdani, R.S.; Abdullah, M.N. Facial Emotion Recognition: A Survey. *Int. J. Adv. Res. Comput. Eng. Technol.* **2018**, *7*, 771–779.
24. Ekman, P. Facial expression and emotion. *Am. Psychol.* **1993**, *48*, 384–392. [CrossRef]
25. Ekman, P.; Friesen, W.V.; Ellsworth, P. *Emotion in the Human Face: Guidelines for Research and an Integration of Findings*; Elsevier: Amsterdam, The Netherlands, 2013.
26. Daily, S.B.; James, M.T.; Cherry, D.; Porter, J.J., III; Darnell, S.S.; Isaac, J.; Roy, T. Affective Computing: Historical Foundations, Current Applications, and Future Trends. In *Emotions and Affect in Human Factors and Human-Computer Interaction*; Elsevier: Amsterdam, The Netherlands, 2017; pp. 213–231. [CrossRef]
27. Hickson, S.; Dufour, N.; Sud, A.; Kwatra, V.; Essa, I. Eyemotion: Classifying Facial Expressions in V.R. Using Eye-Tracking Cameras. In Proceedings of the IEEE Winter Conference on Applications of Computer Vision (WACV), Waikoloa, HI, USA, 7–11 January 2019; pp. 1626–1635. [CrossRef]
28. Chen, C.H.; Lee, I.J.; Lin, L.Y. Augmented reality-based self-facial modeling to promote the emotional expression and social skills of adolescents with autism spectrum disorders. *Res. Dev. Disabil.* **2015**, *36*, 396–403. [CrossRef]
29. Mehta, D.; Siddiqui, M.F.H.; Javaid, A.Y. Facial Emotion Recognition: A Survey and Real-World User Experiences in Mixed Reality. *Sensors* **2018**, *18*, 416. [CrossRef] [PubMed]
30. Li, H.; Sun, J.; Xu, Z.; Chen, L. Multimodal 2D + 3D facial expression recognition with deep fusion convolutional neural network. *IEEE Trans. Multimed* **2017**, *19*, 2816–2831. [CrossRef]
31. Deshmukh, S.; Patwardhan, M.; Mahajan, A. Survey on real-time facial expression recognition techniques. *IET Biom.* **2016**, *5*, 155–163. [CrossRef]
32. Hadis, M.S.; Akita, J.; Toda, M.; Zaenab, N. The Impact of Preprocessing on Face Recognition using Pseudorandom Pixel Placement. In Proceedings of the 29th International Conference on Systems, Signals and Image Processing (IWSSIP), Sofia, Bulgaria, 1–3 June 2022; pp. 1–5.
33. Lu, H.; Yang, F. Active Shape Model and Its Application to Face Alignment. In *Subspace Methods for Pattern Recognition in Intelligent Environment*; Chen, Y.W., Jain, C.L., Eds.; Springer: Berlin/Heidelberg, Germany, 2014; Volume 552, pp. 1–31. [CrossRef]
34. Tao, Y.; He, Y. Face Recognition Based on LBP Algorithm. In Proceedings of the 2020 International Conference on Computer Network, Electronic and Automation (ICCNEA), Xi'an, China, 25–27 September 2020; pp. 21–25.
35. Abhishree, T.M.; Latha, J.; Manikantan, K.; Ramachandran, S. Face Recognition Using Gabor Filter Based Feature Extraction with Anisotropic Diffusion as a Preprocessing Technique. *Procedia Comput. Sci.* **2015**, *45*, 312–321. [CrossRef]
36. Nonis, F.; Dagnes, N.; Marcolin, F.; Vezzetti, E. 3D Approaches and Challenges in Facial Expression Recognition Algorithms—A Literature Review. *Appl. Sci.* **2019**, *9*, 3904. [CrossRef]
37. Bhattacharyya, S.K.; Rahul, K. Face recognition by linear discriminant analysis. *Int. J. Commun. Netw. Secur.* **2014**, *2*, 1087. [CrossRef]
38. Devi, N.S.; Hemachandran, K. Face Recognition Using Principal Component Analysis. *Int. J. Comput. Sci. Inf. Technol.* **2014**, *5*, 509–520.

39. Wirdiani, N.K.A.; Hridayami, P.; Widiari, N.P.A.; Rismawan, K.D.; Candradinata, P.B.; Jayantha, I.P.D. Face Identification Based on K-Nearest Neighbor. *Sci. J. Inform.* **2019**, *6*, 151–154. [CrossRef]
40. Cadena Moreano, J.A.; La Serna Palomino, N.B.; Llano Casa, A.C. Facial recognition techniques using SVM: A comparative analysis. *Enfoque UTE* **2019**, *10*, 98–111. [CrossRef]
41. Mady, H.; Hilles, S.M.S. Face recognition and detection using Random forest and combination of LBP and HOG features. In Proceedings of the International Conference on Smart Computing and Electronic Enterprise (ICSCEE), Shah Alam, Malaysia, 11–12 July 2018; pp. 1–7. [CrossRef]
42. Yin, L.; Wei, X.; Sun, Y.; Wang, J.; Rosato, M.J. A 3D facial expression database for facial behavior research. In Proceedings of the 7th International Conference on Automatic Face and Gesture Recognition (FGR06), Southampton, UK, 10–12 April 2006; pp. 211–216. [CrossRef]
43. Savran, A.; Alyüz, N.; Dibeklioğlu, H.; Çeliktutan, O.; Gökberk, B.; Sankur, B.; Akarun, L. Bosphorus Database for 3D Face Analysis. In *Biometrics and Identity Management: First European Workshop, BIOID 2008, Roskilde, Denmark, May 7–9, 2008, Revised Selected Papers (Lecture Notes in Computer Science, 5372)*; Schouten, B., Juul, N.C., Drygajlo, A., Tistarelli, M., Eds.; Springer: Berlin/Heidelberg, Germany, 2008; Volume 5372. [CrossRef]
44. Lucey, P.; Cohn, J.F.; Kanade, T.; Saragih, J.; Ambadar, Z.; Matthews, I. The Extended Cohn-Kanade Dataset (CK+): A complete dataset for action unit and emotion-specified expression. In Proceedings of the IEEE Computer Society Conference on Computer Vision and Pattern Recognition—Workshops, San Francisco, CA, USA, 13–18 June 2010; pp. 94–101. [CrossRef]
45. Yan, W.J.; Wu, Q.; Liu, Y.J.; Wang, S.J.; Fu, X. CASME database: A dataset of spontaneous micro-expressions collected from neutralized faces. In Proceedings of the 10th IEEE International Conference and Workshops on Automatic Face and Gesture Recognition (F.G.), Shanghai, China, 22–26 April 2013; pp. 1–7. [CrossRef]
46. Kusuma, G.P.; Lim, J.A.P. Emotion Recognition on FER-2013 Face Images Using Fine-Tuned VGG-16. *Adv. Sci. Technol. Eng. Syst. J.* **2020**, *5*, 315–322. [CrossRef]
47. Zhalehpour, S.; Onder, O.; Akhtar, Z.; Erdem, C.E. BAUM-1: A Spontaneous Audiovisual Face Database of Affective and Mental States. *IEEE Trans. Affect. Comput.* **2017**, *8*, 300–313. [CrossRef]
48. Zheng, H.; Zhang, Y.; Yang, L.; Liang, P.; Zhao, Z.; Wang, C.; Chen, D.Z. A new ensemble learning framework for 3D biomedical image segmentation. In Proceedings of the Thirty-Third AAAI Conference on Artificial Intelligence. *AAAI* **2019**, *33*, 5909–5916. [CrossRef]
49. Klambauer, G.; Unterthiner, T.; Mayr, A.; Hochreiter, S. Self-Normalizing Neural Networks. *arXiv* **2017**, *30*. [CrossRef]
50. Kingma, D.; Ba, J. Adam: A Method for Stochastic Optimization. In Proceedings of the of the 3rd International Conference on Learning Representations (ICLR), San Diego, CA, USA, 7–9 May 2015. [CrossRef]
51. Kaya, H.; Fu Gürpınar, F.; Ali Salah, A. Video-based emotion recognition in the wild using deep transfer learning and score fusion. *Image Vis. Comput.* **2017**, *65*, 66–75. [CrossRef]

applied sciences

MDPI

Article

Association between Body Mass Index and the Use of Digital Platforms to Record Food Intake: Cross-Sectional Analysis

Héctor José Tricás-Vidal [1,2], María Concepción Vidal-Peracho [1,3], María Orosia Lucha-López [1,*], César Hidalgo-García [1,*], Sofía Monti-Ballano [1], Sergio Márquez-Gonzalvo [1] and José Miguel Tricás-Moreno [1]

1 Unidad de Investigación en Fisioterapia, Universidad de Zaragoza, Domingo Miral s/n, 50009 Zaragoza, Spain
2 School of Health Professions, University of Mary Hardin Baylor, 900 College St., Belton, TX 76513, USA
3 Department of Endocrinology and Nutrition, Hospital Royo Villanova, SALUD, Barrio San Gregorio s/n, 50015 Zaragoza, Spain
* Correspondence: orolucha@unizar.es (M.O.L.-L.); hidalgo@unizar.es (C.H.-G.); Tel.: +34-626-480-131 (M.O.L.-L.)

Featured Application: This study informs the healthcare workers implicated in the treatment of obesity about how the use of digital platforms to record food intake is related to the body mass index in a sample of a general population with high internet literacy. These data can be applied to guide the appropriate use of these resources by the population and thus improve the repercussions of their utilization on the user's health.

Abstract: An inadequate diet has been shown to be a cause of obesity. Nowadays, digital resources are replacing traditional methods of recording food consumption. Thus, the objective of this study was to analyze a sample of United States of America (USA) residents to determine if the usage of any meal tracker platform to record food intake was related to an improved body mass index (BMI). An analytical cross-sectional study that included 896 subjects with an Instagram account who enrolled to participate in an anonymous online survey was performed. Any meal tracker platform used to record food intake over the last month was employed by 34.2% of the sample. A total of 85.3% of the participants who had tracked their food intake were women ($p < 0.001$), and 33.3% ($p = 0.018$) had a doctorate degree. Participants who used any meal tracker platform also had higher BMIs (median: 24.9 (Q1: 22.7–Q3: 27.9), $p < 0.001$), invested more hours a week on Instagram looking over nutrition or physical activity (median: 2.0 (Q1: 1.0–Q3: 4.0), $p = 0.028$) and performed more minutes per week of strong physical activity (median: 240.0 (Q1: 135.0–Q3: 450.0), $p = 0.007$). Conclusions: USA residents with an Instagram account who had been using any meal tracker platform to record food intake were predominantly highly educated women. They had higher BMIs despite the fact they were engaged in stronger exercise and invested more hours a week on Instagram looking over nutrition or physical activity.

Keywords: diet records; eHealth; body mass index; internet of things; social media

Citation: Tricás-Vidal, H.J.; Vidal-Peracho, M.C.; Lucha-López, M.O.; Hidalgo-García, C.; Monti-Ballano, S.; Márquez-Gonzalvo, S.; Tricás-Moreno, J.M. Association between Body Mass Index and the Use of Digital Platforms to Record Food Intake: Cross-Sectional Analysis. *Appl. Sci.* **2022**, *12*, 12144. https://doi.org/10.3390/app122312144

Academic Editor: Lapo Governi

Received: 16 November 2022
Accepted: 25 November 2022
Published: 28 November 2022

1. Introduction

In 2016, the prevalence of being overweight in the adult world population was 39% in persons over 18 years old (39% of men and 40% of women). The prevalence of obesity was 13% (11% of men and 15% of women). The prevalence of obesity throughout the world almost tripled between 1975 and 2016 [1]. The prevalence of obesity has been reported at about 20% in the United States of America [2]. Being overweight or obese is related to overall mortality [3] and particular causes of death, including cardiovascular and respiratory diseases and cancer [3]. Being overweight or obese augments the risk of numerous chronic diseases, especially cardiovascular diseases, type 2 diabetes mellitus, and some cancers [4].

Inadequate dietary habits have been shown to cause obesity prevalence among the population [5]. In the age of digital technology, different ways of trying to improve health with innovative technologies have been developed [6]. Health information via social media, with nutrition [7] and fitness counseling [8], wearable devices to track physical activity [9], and applications to record food intake—or even more specific platforms for different types of users, such as patients with food allergies [10], older adults [11] or young children [12]—are frequently used by the population. Thus, nowadays, digital applications or platforms are replacing traditional ways of recording our food intake, such as written food diaries or food frequency questionnaires [13,14].

Some of these applications have been developed for different populations, such as the Irish [15], British [16–18], German [19,20], French [21], Swedish [22], Italian [23], Arabian [24], Canadian [25], Australian [26] or United States of America [27] populations, with the aim of addressing the epidemiological challenges regarding health and weight loss. On the contrary, a large number of smartphone applications have been created by private institutions, with a mainly commercial purpose [28]. Usually, they have not been validated (only around 0.8% of the apps registering food intake have been scientifically evaluated [29]); they have not involved nutrition professionals during their development (only around 0.05% have been created with identifiable professional advice [30]) [31], and they have not been adapted to the different cultural food habits [32]. These apps are developed to be used by the general population, with the main objective of weight management [31]. They have been shown to report acceptable energy intake and fat proportions [33], despite micronutrients being predominantly underrated [33]. For example, MyFitnessPal has been shown to be accurate for calculating total energy intake and fiber [34] but underrated sodium intake [35]. The accuracy of the apps in registering the consumption of saturated and polyunsaturated fatty acids, a relevant aspect of cardiovascular health, has been evaluated as poor [36]. It has been stated that the greater source of error might reside in the estimation of the portion size [37], in the use of non-specific food composition data for each country, and in the modification of a food list by the user [38].

Widely used applications, such as MyFitnessPal, Lose It!, or FatSecret [31], are designed to capture dietary data and even to provide personalized nutritional advice, and the majority are used without professional support [39]. The quality of the information provided by some of these apps (Yazi, FeelEat, and Bonne App) has been evaluated by dieticians and nutritionists, showing high-quality scores, although other widely used applications, such as Lose It!, obtained worse marks [40]. Specificity of the content has been shown as a deficit topic in general, although FeelEat has also been evaluated as being correct in this issue [40]. The experiences that favor the use of apps to track food consumption have been elucidated. Between them, easier and quicker food data annotation, with respect to more conventional methods, the provision of goals, diet recommendations, and the indications of progress [39], are noticeable. When considering personal factors favoring the use of these apps, privacy has been identified as the most remarkable [39]. On the other hand, it has also been stated that the user can become addicted and obsessed [39]. For example, it has been shown that people with high signs of eating disorders use MyFitnessPal more [41]. Dietary tracking with MyFitnessPal has also been linked to an exacerbation of body concern in college women with body dissatisfaction and to changes in feelings (both positive and negative), dietary intake and even increases in weight [42]. Users are worried about the possibility of becoming obsessed, especially those with a poor body image [42]. In young adults, dietary tracking with apps has been associated with a greater presence of irregular weight control behaviors, such as fasting or purging [43].

In summary, the way in which the use of these applications, without professional intervention, influences the maintenance of a healthy weight has not been widely studied, despite the huge number of apps available on the market (it has been reported that there are around 30,000 marketable mobile apps dedicated to a selection of food and/or physical activity) [31]. In order to enhance the evidence about the effects of the use of these apps on the population has been recommended [40]. Thus, the objective of this manuscript is to present an analytical cross-sectional study of United States of America (USA) residents who have an Instagram account and to determine if the usage of any meal tracker platform to record food consumption was related to an improved body mass index (BMI). We hypothesized that using any meal tracker platform to record food intake would improve healthy weight maintenance.

2. Materials and Methods

2.1. Study Design

The study was a cross-sectional analysis and included USA residents enrolled to contribute to an anonymous online survey.

2.2. Setting

The connecting link to the research was sent via email to actual or graduated students from the University of Mary Hardin Baylor, Oakland University, the University of Kentucky, and Queens University of Charlotte. The survey link was also expanded via Facebook and Instagram. The distribution of the link was achieved with a cascade effect. The survey was hosted on the Survey Monkey platform. An opportunity sampling method was performed.

2.3. Participants

In order to estimate the sample size, an infinite population was assumed. The expected proportion used was 71%. Instagram was used in 2021 by around 71% of the United States of America adults [44]. The GRANMO calculator "https://www.imim.es/ofertadeserveis/software-public/granmo/ (accessed on 2 September 2019)" was utilized to compute the sample size [45], with a 0.95 confidence level and desired precision of +/− 3.5 percent units in the population estimation option. A minimal number of 646 participants was obtained.

Finally, the number of registered surveys was 896, taking into consideration the possibility of doubtful or incomplete answers in some of the registers.

The participants were eligible for inclusion if they were older than 18 years and they had an Instagram account. The consideration of users' internet literacy was considered a relevant factor in influencing the capacity of users to track their food intake digitally [46]. The selection of a sample connected to Instagram might favor its homogeneity regarding the user profile according to their literacy level or technological skills [47].

2.4. Ethical Considerations

The University of Zaragoza, via the Academic Commission of the Doctoral Program in Health and Sports Sciences (protocol code: "Impact of Instagram on the lifestyle and physical activity in the United States of America" 2 July 2019), approved the study, which observed the ethical stipulations of the Declaration of Helsinki [48]. The survey was conducted in a way that minimizes possible harm to the environment; it was anonymous, and the information was to be destroyed after the study was completed.

The study did not register questions regarding religion, political views, race, or other aspects that could infringe on research ethics. Before starting the completion of the survey, the subjects dispensed volunteer informed consent.

2.5. Data Sources

In the survey, the participants were questioned about the following:

- Gender: man/woman/others.
- Age, grouped in generations: Generation Z (born 1997–2012); Millennials (born 1981–1996); Generation X (born 1965–1980); Boomers (born 1946–1964) [49].
- Height, measured in feet and inches, and weight, measured in pounds. BMI was determined: BMI = 703 × weight (pounds)/[height (inches)]^2. BMI is considered an index with very high specificity (97%) to detect obesity [50]. Self-reported weight and height online have shown to be a valid method, with moderate to good agreement between measured anthropometric data and those self-reported [51].

- Do you smoke? Yes/No/Occasionally. It has been stated that traditional epidemiological risk factors can be collected with equivalent or superior reliability online compared with conventional methods [52].
- Highest academic degree attained, classified by a doctorate degree; master's degree; bachelor's degree; associate degree; trade/technical/vocational training; some college credit, no degree; high school graduate or the equivalent.
- How long the participants have been regularly on Instagram, classified as less than 1 year, between 1–2.5 years, and more than 2.5 years.
- How many hours per week on Instagram looking over nutrition or physical activity.
- The physical activity executed by the participants was registered with the short form "last 7 days" of the International Physical Activity Questionnaire (IPAQ) [53]. It was self-administered, and vigorous physical activity (minutes per week), moderate physical activity (minutes per week), time spent walking (minutes per week), and time spent sitting (hours per day) were recorded. This questionnaire is considered reliable and valid for noting physical activity information [54].

In order to test the influence of the usage of any meal tracker platform to record food intake regarding BMIs, the participants answered about the usage over the last month of any meal tracker platforms to record their food intake. The answer was classified as: No/Yes.

2.6. Statistical Analyses

Gender, generation, smoking habits, academic degree, and time spent on Instagram were described with percentages in each category. BMI, hours per week on Instagram looking over nutrition or physical activity, vigorous physical activity, moderate physical activity, time spent walking, and time spent sitting were described with the median, 25th percentile (Q1) and 75th percentile (Q3) because they were not normally distributed according to the Kolmogorov–Smirnov test.

A chi-squared test was selected to study the relations of the usage, over the last month, of any meal tracker platforms to record food intake with gender, generation, smoking habits, highest academic degree attained, and time spent on Instagram (the maximum likelihood ratio chi-squared test was used when expected frequencies in some cells were less than 5). The Mann–Whitney U test was adopted to compare BMIs, hours per week spent on Instagram looking over nutrition or physical activity, vigorous physical activity, moderate physical activity, time spent walking, and time spent sitting between the participants who did not use any meal tracker platforms to record their food intake over the last month with those who did. The statistical significance was established at a $p < 0.05$.

SPSS 25.0 for Mac was used for the calculations.

3. Results

Of the 896 who participated, 78.7% were women, 20.6% were men, and 0.7% classified themselves as others. Regarding the generations, 11.5% belonged to Generation Z, 75.6% belonged to the Millennials, 11.4% belonged to Generation X, and 1.6% belonged to the Boomers. A total of 93.5% of the sample did not smoke, 2.3% used to smoke, and 4.1% used to smoke occasionally. Regarding the academic degree attained, 3.7% were high school graduates, 6.1% had some college credit, 0.6% had technical training, 3.2% had an associate degree, 43.2% had a bachelor's degree, 15.1% possessed a master's degree, and 28.1% possessed a doctorate. The majority of the participants (52.3%) regularly consulted Instagram for less than one year, 17.8% regularly consulted Instagram for between 1 and 2.5 years, and 29.9% had more than 2.5 years. They spent a median of 2 h per week (Q1: 1–Q3: 3) on Instagram looking over nutrition or physical activity. In relation to BMI, the median was 24.0 (Q1: 21.8–Q3: 27.2). The median of the total minutes per week performing vigorous physical activity was 240.0 (Q1: 120.0–Q3: 360.0), and performing moderate physical activity was 180.0 (Q1: 90.0–Q3: 360.0). The median of the minutes per week spent walking was 360.0 (Q1: 140.0–Q3: 840.0), and the median of the time spent sitting (hours per day) was 5.0 (Q1: 4.0–Q3: 8.0).

Any meal tracker platform to record food intake over the last month was used by 34.2% (n = 306) of the sample (Table 1). The associations between gender, generation, smoking habits, academic degree, time on Instagram, BMI, hours per week on Instagram looking over nutrition or physical activity, vigorous physical activity, moderate physical activity, time spent walking, and time spent sitting, and the variable usage of any meal tracker platform to record food intake can be seen in Table 1. Gender, academic degree, BMI, hours per week on Instagram looking over nutrition or physical activity, and minutes per week of vigorous physical activity showed a significant dependency on the usage of any meal tracker platform to record food intake. The percentage of women and the percentage of participants with a doctorate were significantly higher in the group that used any meal tracker platform than in the group that did not. Of the participants who had tracked their food intake, 85.3% were women, and 33.3% had a doctorate. The participants who used any meal tracker platform had higher BMIs, invested more hours a week on Instagram looking over nutrition or physical activity, and performed more vigorous physical activity. They had a median BMI of 24.9, invested a median of 2 h a week on Instagram looking over nutrition or physical activity, and performed a median of 240.0 min a week of vigorous exercise.

Table 1. Comparative analysis of the participants depending on the usage of any meal tracker platform to record food intake over the last month.

	Usage of Any Meal Tracker Platform to Record Food Intake over the Last Month		
	No	**Yes**	***p* Value**
Gender (n = 896)			
Man	23.7%	14.7%	<0.001
Woman	75.3%	85.3%	
Other	1.0%	0.0%	
Generation (n = 896)			
Generation Z (born 1997–2012)	11.0%	12.4%	0.057
Millennials (born 1981–1996)	73.9%	78.8%	
Generation X (born 1965–1980)	13.2%	7.8%	
Boomers (born 1946–1964)	1.9%	1.0%	
Smoke (n = 896)			
No	92.9%	94.8%	0.548
Yes	2.5%	2.0%	
Occasionally	4.6%	3.2%	
Degree (n = 896)			
High school graduate. diploma or the equivalent	4.6%	2.0%	0.018
Some college credit. No degree	6.9%	4.6%	
Trade/technical/vocational training	0.8%	0.0%	
Associate degree	3.6%	2.6%	
Bachelor's degree	43.4%	42.8%	
Master's degree	15.3%	14.7%	
Doctorate Degree	25.4%	33.3%	

Table 1. *Cont.*

	Usage of Any Meal Tracker Platform to Record Food Intake over the Last Month		
Time on Instagram (n = 792)			
Less than 1 year	50.8%	55.1%	0.455
Between 1–2.5 years	18.0%	17.5%	
More than 2.5 years	31.2%	27.4%	
	Median (Q1–Q3)	**Median (Q1–Q3)**	
Body Mass Index (n = 896)	23.6 (21.5–26.7)	24.9 (22.7–27.9)	<0.001
Hours per week on Instagram looking over nutrition or physical activity (n = 685)	2.0 (1.0–3.0)	2.0 (1.0–4.0)	0.028
Vigorous physical activity (min per week) (n = 765)	232.5 (120.0–360.0)	240.0 (135.0–450.0)	0.007
Moderate physical activity (min per week) (n = 741)	180.0 (90.0–360.0)	180.0 (90.0–360.0)	0.692
Time spent walking (min per week) (n = 844)	420.0 (140.0–840.0)	315.0 (122.5–840.0)	0.377
Time spent sitting (hours per day) (n = 859)	5.0 (4.0–8.0)	5.0 (4.0–8.0)	0.415

4. Discussion

This study has examined the relationship between the usage of any meal tracker platform to record food intake and gender, generation, smoking habits, academic degree, time on Instagram, BMI, hours per week on Instagram looking over nutrition or physical activity, and physical activity in USA residents that possessed an Instagram account. It was shown that a superior percentage of women and participants with a doctorate tracked their food intake. Moreover, those participants who tracked their food intake had higher BMIs, invested more hours a week on Instagram looking over nutrition or physical activity, and performed more vigorous physical activity. Thus, our outcomes suggest that using any meal tracker platform to record food intake over the last month would not lead to a lower BMI.

Any meal tracker platform to record food intake over the last month was used by 34.2% of the sample. A total of 85.3% of the participants who had tracked their food intake were women ($p < 0.001$) and 33.3% ($p = 0.018$) had a doctorate. It has been previously shown that women and more educated participants are likely to be better respondents to online dietary intake measurements [55], which is according to our results. Women college students have manifested as those who track calories more so than men [56,57], and highly educated citizens were revealed to use more mobile health applications [58]. Women were shown to be better respondents to the online surveys requesting data about their health-based app use [59]. More women than men have been identified as users of apps from healthy lifestyle websites for nutrition information, weight loss, and physical activity [59].

The prevalence of smoking habits in adults in the USA was determined to be 18% in 2012, and it continues to decrease [60]. In this study, the vast majority of the sample did not smoke, and there were no differences between the group that recorded their food consumption and the one that did not; thus, we can eliminate tobacco as a factor that could influence BMIs [61].

Participants who used any meal tracker platform had higher BMIs (median: 24.9 (Q1: 22.7–Q3: 27.9), $p < 0.001$), despite being engaged in more vigorous physical activity (median: 240.0 (Q1: 135.0–Q3: 450.0), $p = 0.007$) and complying with the recommendations on the amount of vigorous physical activity for health benefits from the World Health Organization (more than 75 min per week) [62]. Although it has been postulated that exercise is one of the keys to maintaining a healthy weight, the amount and type of physical activity that should be performed to achieve improvements is still subject to discussion [63]. A recent review showed that exercise protocols based on high-intensity interval training with a slow volume that require less time, however, favored better cardiorespiratory adaptations than continuous moderate physical activity, yet they did not provoke changes in the body's composition in normal, overweight, or obese adults [63]. However, it has also been shown that vigorous physical activity may be more beneficial than moderate physical activity in reducing waist circumference and visceral adiposity; however, this was observed in adults who are overweight or obese [64].

Thus, the tracking of food intake in our study is not related to a more healthy weight because, according to the BMI categories [65], participants who tracked their food intake were almost overweight (BMI between 25 and 29.9), while those participants who did not (median: 23.6 (Q1: 21.5–Q3: 26.7)), stayed not-so borderline of the normal BMI category (between 18.5 and 24.9). This is in agreement with the results of a recent review, which found that the effectiveness of multicomponent technologically mediated interventions for weight management in obesity showed promising results; however, the isolated use of an app received presumably less positive outcomes [66]. A recent review of intervention studies using smartphone apps has analyzed the effects on anthropometric, metabolic, and dietary outcomes. It has highlighted weight loss in adults being overweight and obese for 3 and 12 months, although with minimal long-term effectiveness [67]. A recent study on overweight or obese adults, who were advised to self-monitor their dietary intake for 8 weeks with an app, has found that if the frequency of self-monitoring was consistent, weight loss could be achieved in the short term [68]. Another recent study has shown that using tailored weight and calorie goals provided by professionals to track a person's food intake with a mobile app can produce clinically significant weight loss [69]. Thus, by only using the isolated online tracking of food intake, the maintenance of a healthy weight does not seem to be effective, though, previously, it has been shown that electronic dietary records were better than traditional methods for BMI reduction [49]. However, if there is professional support, the results improve. Anteriorly, it has been stated that in order to progress to healthy dietary behaviors, having simple knowledge of the facts is not enough. It would be necessary to develop favorable convictions towards alimentation [70] and have the professional support of a dietitian's skills to obtain behavioral change and sustainable weight reduction [71]. In fact, app users have declared that having professional support for using the apps may be interesting [39]. It has been demonstrated that a combination of care with digital apps-based tools and support by health professionals is effective for healthy weight achievement [72]. The factors included in these interventions, which conditioned the best results in weight management, were as follows: self-management, particularly in the first phases of the interventions; early education in nutrition and diet; and totally online support messages from health professionals [72].

Participants who used meal tracker platforms of any type not only had higher BMIs but also invested more hours a week on Instagram when looking over nutrition or physical activity (median: 2.0 (Q1: 1.0–Q3: 4.0), $p = 0.028$). The time of social media consumption has been shown to be correlated to the augmented sitting time on non-business days [73], and a higher BMI has been associated with more time spent sitting [74].

It might be supposed, however, that these almost-overweight participants sought help via technology or apps to track their food intake, and information on the web to try to achieve a healthier weight. It seems that they were aware of the benefits of a healthy weight and turned to new technologies in search of support to achieve it. This is a fact that might be confronted by health professionals, given that it might show that health services are not offering all the necessary support to educate populations in healthy nutritional behavior or that people even prefer not to consult health professionals because they might feel stigmatized [75]. It has been shown that the most habitual origins of stigma in overweight and obese adults come from doctors, classmates, store clerks, companions and fellow workers, and also from younger teachers and nurses; however, the increased frequency of stigma is not associated with BMI [75]. Therefore, it is relevant that health professionals consider improving their communication skills, avoid inappropriate comments and show comprehension and empathy [75] to favor those people concerned about their weight who turn to professionals for help.

Limitations

This study is subject to some limitations. It is based on a cross-sectional study method; thus, any causality can be referred to as relations with significant results. However, due to the scant bibliography that exists so far on the subject, the results found may be a good starting point for the future development of prospective longitudinal studies to clarify the repercussions of populations' generalized use of meal-tracking platforms. Previous studies have shown that during weight loss interventions, to guaranty ad-herence, to track the food intake diary, at least in two occasions must be achieved [76]. In our study, the number of times or the frequency at which the participants tracked their food intake was not registered. The fact that the use of a meal tracker platform is not related to a better BMI might be related to an inconstant adherence to the tracking habit in our study. Participants were questioned only about their usage of the meal-tracking platform over the last month to facilitate a concrete response and not provoke an inferred response because the event would not be concretely recalled [77]; this might also be considered a short period where the monitoring of changes in BMI can occur. Millennials are the predominant generation represented in the study. Previously, it has been stated that older adults are less prone to adopt the use of digital health technologies [78], but this fact might compromise the representativeness of our sample to other populations with a more balanced representation of the different generations. The sampled participants have a high and homogeneous internet literacy. Expanding the survey link through universities might have conditioned the access to the survey link to highly educated individuals. Thus, the results might be generalizable only to populations with similar characteristics.

5. Conclusions

United States of America residents with an Instagram account who had used any meal tracker platform to record their food intake over the last month were predominantly highly educated women, contemplating that the primary route of expansion of the survey link was through universities and that the predominant generation represented in the sample were Millennials. They had higher BMIs, despite the fact they were engaged in more vigorous exercise and invested more hours a week on Instagram looking over nutrition or physical activity, which might show that these participants rely on new technologies in search of their optimal weight.

Author Contributions: Conceptualization, H.J.T.-V. and J.M.T.-M.; methodology, H.J.T.-V., M.C.V.-P. and C.H.-G.; formal analysis, M.O.L.-L., S.M.-G. and S.M.-B.; investigation, H.J.T.-V.; data curation, M.O.L.-L., S.M.-G. and S.M.-B.; writing—original draft preparation, H.J.T.-V., M.O.L.-L., M.C.V.-P. and C.H.-G.; writing—review and editing, H.J.T.-V., M.C.V.-P., M.O.L.-L., S.M.-G. and C.H.-G.; visualization, S.M.-B. and J.M.T.-M.; supervision, J.M.T.-M. and C.H.-G. All authors have read and agreed to the published version of the manuscript.

Funding: This research received no external funding.

Institutional Review Board Statement: The study was performed considering the ethical stipulations of the Declaration of Helsinki. It was approved by the University of Zaragoza via the Academic Commission of the Doctoral Program in Health and Sports Sciences (protocol code: "Impact of Instagram on the lifestyle and physical activity in the United States of America" 2 July 2019).

Informed Consent Statement: Volunteer informed consent was given by all the participants in the study.

Data Availability Statement: The datasets presented in this study are available on request from the corresponding author. All data covered by this study are included in this manuscript.

Acknowledgments: The authors acknowledge participants for their disinterested collaboration.

Conflicts of Interest: The authors declare no competing interest.

References

1. World Health Organization. Obesity and Overweight. Available online: https://www.who.int/health-topics/obesity#tab=tab_1 (accessed on 4 November 2022).
2. NCD Risk Factor Collaboration (NCD-RisC). Worldwide trends in body-mass index, underweight, overweight, and obesity from 1975 to 2016: A pooled analysis of 2416 population-based measurement studies in 128·9 million children, adolescents, and adults. *Lancet* **2017**, *390*, 2627–2642. [CrossRef] [PubMed]
3. Bhaskaran, K.; Dos-Santos-Silva, I.; Leon, D.A.; Douglas, I.J.; Smeeth, L. Association of BMI with overall and cause-specific mortality: A population-based cohort study of 3·6 million adults in the UK. *Lancet Diabetes Endocrinol.* **2018**, *6*, 944–953. [CrossRef] [PubMed]
4. Guh, D.P.; Zhang, W.; Bansback, N.; Amarsi, Z.; Birmingham, C.L.; Anis, A.H. The incidence of co-morbidities related to obesity and overweight: A systematic review and meta-analysis. *BMC Public Health* **2009**, *9*, 88. [CrossRef] [PubMed]
5. Vallgårda, S.; Nielsen, M.E.J.; Hansen, A.K.K.; Cathaoir, K.Ó.; Hartlev, M.; Holm, L.; Christensen, B.J.; Jensen, J.D.; Sørensen, T.I.A.; Sandøe, P. Should Europe follow the US and declare obesity a disease? A discussion of the so-called utilitarian argument. *Eur. J. Clin. Nutr.* **2017**, *71*, 1263–1267. [CrossRef]
6. Santoro, E. Social media and medical apps: How they can change health communication, education and care. *Recenti Prog. Med.* **2013**, *104*, 179–180. [CrossRef]
7. Tricas-Vidal, H.J.; Vidal-Peracho, M.C.; Lucha-López, M.O.; Hidalgo-García, C.; Lucha-López, A.C.; Monti-Ballano, S.; Corral-de Toro, J.; Márquez-Gonzalvo, S.; Tricás-Moreno, J.M. Nutrition-Related Content on Instagram in the United States of America: Analytical Cross-Sectional Study. *Foods* **2022**, *11*, 239. [CrossRef] [PubMed]
8. Tricás-Vidal, H.J.; Vidal-Peracho, M.C.; Lucha-López, M.O.; Hidalgo-García, C.; Monti-Ballano, S.; Márquez-Gonzalvo, S.; Tricás-Moreno, J.M. Impact of Fitness Influencers on the Level of Physical Activity Performed by Instagram Users in the United States of America: Analytical Cross-Sectional Study. *Int. J. Environ. Res. Public Health* **2022**, *19*, 14258. [CrossRef]
9. Tricás-Vidal, H.J.; Lucha-López, M.O.; Hidalgo-García, C.; Vidal-Peracho, M.C.; Monti-Ballano, S.; Tricás-Moreno, J.M. Health Habits and Wearable Activity Tracker Devices: Analytical Cross-Sectional Study. *Sensors* **2022**, *22*, 2960. [CrossRef]
10. Bert, F.; Giacometti, M.; Gualano, M.R.; Siliquini, R. Smartphones and health promotion: A review of the evidence. *J. Med. Syst.* **2014**, *38*, 9995. [CrossRef]
11. Timon, C.M.; Astell, A.J.; Hwang, F.; Adlam, T.D.; Smith, T.; Maclean, L.; Spurr, D.; Forster, S.E.; Williams, E.A. The validation of a computer-based food record for older adults: The Novel Assessment of Nutrition and Ageing (NANA) method. *Br. J. Nutr.* **2015**, *113*, 654–664. [CrossRef]
12. Vereecken, C.A.; Covents, M.; Haynie, D.; Maes, L. Feasibility of the Young Children's Nutrition Assessment on the Web. *J. Am. Diet. Assoc.* **2009**, *109*, 1896–1902. [CrossRef] [PubMed]
13. Kaiser, B.; Stelzl, T.; Finglas, P.; Gedrich, K. The Assessment of a Personalized Nutrition Tool (eNutri) in Germany: Pilot Study on Usability Metrics and Users' Experiences. *JMIR Form. Res.* **2022**, *6*, e34497. [CrossRef]
14. Eldridge, A.L.; Piernas, C.; Illner, A.-K.; Gibney, M.J.; Gurinović, M.A.; de Vries, J.H.M.; Cade, J.E. Evaluation of New Technology-Based Tools for Dietary Intake Assessment-An ILSI Europe Dietary Intake and Exposure Task Force Evaluation. *Nutrients* **2018**, *11*, 55. [CrossRef] [PubMed]
15. Timon, C.M.; Blain, R.J.; McNulty, B.; Kehoe, L.; Evans, K.; Walton, J.; Flynn, A.; Gibney, E.R. The Development, Validation, and User Evaluation of Foodbook24: A Web-Based Dietary Assessment Tool Developed for the Irish Adult Population. *J. Med. Internet Res.* **2017**, *19*, e158. [CrossRef] [PubMed]
16. Carter, M.C.; Albar, S.A.; Morris, M.A.; Mulla, U.Z.; Hancock, N.; Evans, C.E.; Alwan, N.A.; Greenwood, D.C.; Hardie, L.J.; Frost, G.S.; et al. Development of a UK Online 24-h Dietary Assessment Tool: myfood24. *Nutrients* **2015**, *7*, 4016–4032. [CrossRef] [PubMed]
17. Albar, S.A.; Alwan, N.A.; Evans, C.E.L.; Greenwood, D.C.; Cade, J.E. Agreement between an online dietary assessment tool (myfood24) and an interviewer-administered 24-h dietary recall in British adolescents aged 11–18 years. *Br. J. Nutr.* **2016**, *115*, 1678–1686. [CrossRef]
18. Zenun Franco, R.; Fallaize, R.; Lovegrove, J.A.; Hwang, F. Online dietary intake assessment using a graphical food frequency app (eNutri): Usability metrics from the EatWellUK study. *PLoS ONE* **2018**, *13*, e0202006. [CrossRef]
19. Koch, S.A.J.; Conrad, J.; Hierath, L.; Hancock, N.; Beer, S.; Cade, J.E.; Nöthlings, U. Adaptation and Evaluation of Myfood24-Germany: A Web-Based Self-Administered 24-h Dietary Recall for the German Adult Population. *Nutrients* **2020**, *12*, 160. [CrossRef]
20. Koch, S.A.J.; Conrad, J.; Cade, J.E.; Weinhold, L.; Alexy, U.; Nöthlings, U. Validation of the web-based self-administered 24-h dietary recall myfood24-Germany: Comparison with a weighed dietary record and biomarkers. *Eur. J. Nutr.* **2021**, *60*, 4069–4082. [CrossRef]
21. Hasenböhler, A.; Denes, L.; Blanstier, N.; Dehove, H.; Hamouche, N.; Beer, S.; Williams, G.; Breil, B.; Depeint, F.; Cade, J.E.; et al. Development of an Innovative Online Dietary Assessment Tool for France: Adaptation of myfood24. *Nutrients* **2022**, *14*, 2681. [CrossRef]
22. Lindroos, A.K.; Petrelius Sipinen, J.; Axelsson, C.; Nyberg, G.; Landberg, R.; Leanderson, P.; Arnemo, M.; Warensjö Lemming, E. Use of a Web-Based Dietary Assessment Tool (RiksmatenFlex) in Swedish Adolescents: Comparison and Validation Study. *J. Med. Internet Res.* **2019**, *21*, e12572. [CrossRef] [PubMed]

23. Barchitta, M.; Maugeri, A.; Agrifoglio, O.; Favara, G.; La Mastra, C.; La Rosa, M.C.; Magnano San Lio, R.; Agodi, A. Comparison of Self-Administered Web-Based and Interviewer Printed Food Frequency Questionnaires for Dietary Assessment in Italian Adolescents. *Int. J. Environ. Res. Public Health* **2019**, *16*, 1949. [CrossRef] [PubMed]
24. Alturki, R.; Gay, V. The Development of an Arabic Weight-Loss App Akser Waznk: Qualitative Results. *JMIR Form. Res.* **2019**, *3*, e11785. [CrossRef] [PubMed]
25. Ji, Y.; Plourde, H.; Bouzo, V.; Kilgour, R.D.; Cohen, T.R. Validity and Usability of a Smartphone Image-Based Dietary Assessment App Compared to 3-Day Food Diaries in Assessing Dietary Intake Among Canadian Adults: Randomized Controlled Trial. *JMIR mHealth uHealth* **2020**, *8*, e16953. [CrossRef] [PubMed]
26. Hendrie, G.A.; James-Martin, G.; Williams, G.; Brindal, E.; Whyte, B.; Crook, A. The Development of VegEze: Smartphone App to Increase Vegetable Consumption in Australian Adults. *JMIR Form. Res.* **2019**, *3*, e10731. [CrossRef]
27. Arab, L.; Tseng, C.-H.; Ang, A.; Jardack, P. Validity of a multipass, web-based, 24-hour self-administered recall for assessment of total energy intake in blacks and whites. *Am. J. Epidemiol.* **2011**, *174*, 1256–1265. [CrossRef]
28. Arigo, D.; Jake-Schoffman, D.E.; Wolin, K.; Beckjord, E.; Hekler, E.B.; Pagoto, S.L. The history and future of digital health in the field of behavioral medicine. *J. Behav. Med.* **2019**, *42*, 67–83. [CrossRef]
29. Rivera, J.; McPherson, A.; Hamilton, J.; Birken, C.; Coons, M.; Iyer, S.; Agarwal, A.; Lalloo, C.; Stinson, J. Mobile Apps for Weight Management: A Scoping Review. *JMIR mHealth uHealth* **2016**, *4*, e87. [CrossRef]
30. Nikolaou, C.K.; Lean, M.E.J. Mobile applications for obesity and weight management: Current market characteristics. *Int. J. Obes.* **2017**, *41*, 200–202. [CrossRef]
31. Khazen, W.; Jeanne, J.-F.; Demaretz, L.; Schäfer, F.; Fagherazzi, G. Rethinking the Use of Mobile Apps for Dietary Assessment in Medical Research. *J. Med. Internet Res.* **2020**, *22*, e15619. [CrossRef]
32. Chen, J.; Bauman, A.; Allman-Farinelli, M. A Study to Determine the Most Popular Lifestyle Smartphone Applications and Willingness of the Public to Share Their Personal Data for Health Research. *Telemed. J. E Health Off. J. Am. Telemed. Assoc.* **2016**, *22*, 655–665. [CrossRef] [PubMed]
33. Fallaize, R.; Zenun Franco, R.; Pasang, J.; Hwang, F.; Lovegrove, J.A. Popular Nutrition-Related Mobile Apps: An Agreement Assessment Against a UK Reference Method. *JMIR mHealth uHealth* **2019**, *7*, e9838. [CrossRef] [PubMed]
34. Teixeira, V.; Voci, S.M.; Mendes-Netto, R.S.; da Silva, D.G. The relative validity of a food record using the smartphone application MyFitnessPal. *Nutr. Diet.* **2018**, *75*, 219–225. [CrossRef] [PubMed]
35. Evenepoel, C.; Clevers, E.; Deroover, L.; van Loo, W.; Matthys, C.; Verbeke, K. Accuracy of Nutrient Calculations Using the Consumer-Focused Online App MyFitnessPal: Validation Study. *J. Med. Internet Res.* **2020**, *22*, e18237. [CrossRef] [PubMed]
36. Siniarski, A.; Sobieraj, P.; Samel-Kowalik, P.; Sińska, B.; Milewska, M.; Bzikowska-Jura, A. Nutrition-related mobile applications—Should they be used for dietary prevention and treatment of cardiovascular diseases? *Nutr. Metab. Cardiovasc. Dis.* **2022**, *32*, 2505–2514. [CrossRef] [PubMed]
37. Beasley, J.; Riley, W.T.; Jean-Mary, J. Accuracy of a PDA-based dietary assessment program. *Nutrition* **2005**, *21*, 672–677. [CrossRef]
38. Tosi, M.; Radice, D.; Carioni, G.; Vecchiati, T.; Fiori, F.; Parpinel, M.; Gnagnarella, P. Accuracy of applications to monitor food intake: Evaluation by comparison with 3-d food diary. *Nutrition* **2021**, *84*, 111018. [CrossRef]
39. Lieffers, J.R.L.; Arocha, J.F.; Grindrod, K.; Hanning, R.M. Experiences and Perceptions of Adults Accessing Publicly Available Nutrition Behavior-Change Mobile Apps for Weight Management. *J. Acad. Nutr. Diet.* **2018**, *118*, 229–239.e3. [CrossRef]
40. Martinon, P.; Saliasi, I.; Bourgeois, D.; Smentek, C.; Dussart, C.; Fraticelli, L.; Carrouel, F. Nutrition-Related Mobile Apps in the French App Stores: Assessment of Functionality and Quality. *JMIR mHealth uHealth* **2022**, *10*, e35879. [CrossRef]
41. McCaig, D.; Elliott, M.T.; Prnjak, K.; Walasek, L.; Meyer, C. Engagement with MyFitnessPal in eating disorders: Qualitative insights from online forums. *Int. J. Eat. Disord.* **2020**, *53*, 404–411. [CrossRef]
42. Hahn, S.L.; Linxwiler, A.N.; Huynh, T.; Rose, K.L.; Bauer, K.W.; Sonneville, K.R. Impacts of dietary self-monitoring via MyFitnessPal to undergraduate women: A qualitative study. *Body Image* **2021**, *39*, 221–226. [CrossRef] [PubMed]
43. Hahn, S.L.; Hazzard, V.M.; Loth, K.A.; Larson, N.; Klein, L.; Neumark-Sztainer, D. Using apps to self-monitor diet and physical activity is linked to greater use of disordered eating behaviors among emerging adults. *Prev. Med.* **2022**, *155*, 106967. [CrossRef] [PubMed]
44. Liu, S.; Perdew, M.; Lithopoulos, A.; Rhodes, R.E. The Feasibility of Using Instagram Data to Predict Exercise Identity and Physical Activity Levels: Cross-sectional Observational Study. *J. Med. Internet Res.* **2021**, *23*, e20954. [CrossRef] [PubMed]
45. Soto Alvarez, J. Importancia del tamaño de la muestra en la investigación clínica. *Rev. Clin. Esp.* **1995**, *195*, 444. [PubMed]
46. Cade, J.E. Measuring diet in the 21st century: Use of new technologies. *Proc. Nutr. Soc.* **2017**, *76*, 276–282. [CrossRef] [PubMed]
47. Moguel, E.; Berrocal, J.; García-Alonso, J. Systematic Literature Review of Food-Intake Monitoring in an Aging Population. *Sensors* **2019**, *19*, 3265. [CrossRef]
48. Kori-Lindner, C. Ethical principles for medical research involving human subjects: World medical association declaration of Helsinki. *Klin. Pharmakologie Aktuell* **2000**, *11*, 26–28.
49. Dimock, M. Defining Generations: Where Millennials End and Generation Z Begins. Available online: https://www.pewresearch.org/fact-tank/2019/01/17/where-millennials-end-and-generation-z-begins/ (accessed on 9 January 2022).
50. Oliveros, E.; Somers, V.K.; Sochor, O.; Goel, K.; Lopez-Jimenez, F. The concept of normal weight obesity. *Prog. Cardiovasc. Dis.* **2014**, *56*, 426–433. [CrossRef]

51. Huang, D.; Huang, Y.; Khanna, S.; Dwivedi, P.; Slopen, N.; Green, K.M.; He, X.; Puett, R.; Nguyen, Q. Twitter-Derived Social Neighborhood Characteristics and Individual-Level Cardiometabolic Outcomes: Cross-Sectional Study in a Nationally Representative Sample. *JMIR public Heal. Surveill.* **2020**, *6*, e17969. [CrossRef]
52. Van Gelder, M.M.H.J.; Bretveld, R.W.; Roeleveld, N. Web-based questionnaires: The future in epidemiology? *Am. J. Epidemiol.* **2010**, *172*, 1292–1298. [CrossRef]
53. Kim, Y.; Park, I.; Kang, M. Convergent validity of the International Physical Activity Questionnaire (IPAQ): Meta-analysis. *Public Health Nutr.* **2013**, *16*, 440–452. [CrossRef] [PubMed]
54. Craig, C.L.; Marshall, A.L.; Sjöström, M.; Bauman, A.E.; Booth, M.L.; Ainsworth, B.E.; Pratt, M.; Ekelund, U.; Yngve, A.; Sallis, J.F.; et al. International physical activity questionnaire: 12-Country reliability and validity. *Med. Sci. Sports Exerc.* **2003**, *35*, 1381–1395. [CrossRef]
55. Galante, J.; Adamska, L.; Young, A.; Young, H.; Littlejohns, T.J.; Gallacher, J.; Allen, N. The acceptability of repeat Internet-based hybrid diet assessment of previous 24-h dietary intake: Administration of the Oxford WebQ in UK Biobank. *Br. J. Nutr.* **2016**, *115*, 681–686. [CrossRef] [PubMed]
56. Embacher Martin, K.; McGloin, R.; Atkin, D. Body dissatisfaction, neuroticism, and female sex as predictors of calorie-tracking app use amongst college students. *J Am. Coll. Health* **2018**, *66*, 608–616. [CrossRef] [PubMed]
57. Jabour, A.M.; Rehman, W.; Idrees, S.; Thanganadar, H.; Hira, K.; Alarifi, M.A. The Adoption of Mobile Health Applications among University Students in Health Colleges. *J. Multidiscip. Healthc.* **2021**, *14*, 1267–1273. [CrossRef]
58. Amer, S.A.; Bahumayim, A.; Shah, J.; Aleisa, N.; Hani, B.M.; Omar, D.I. Prevalence and Determinants of Mobile Health Applications Usage: A National Descriptive Study. *Front. Public Heal.* **2022**, *10*, 838509. [CrossRef]
59. Elavsky, S.; Smahel, D.; Machackova, H. Who are mobile app users from healthy lifestyle websites? Analysis of patterns of app use and user characteristics. *Transl. Behav. Med.* **2017**, *7*, 891–901. [CrossRef]
60. Arnett, D.K.; Blumenthal, R.S.; Albert, M.A.; Buroker, A.B.; Goldberger, Z.D.; Hahn, E.J.; Himmelfarb, C.D.; Khera, A.; Lloyd-Jones, D.; McEvoy, J.W.; et al. 2019 ACC/AHA Guideline on the Primary Prevention of Cardiovascular Disease: A Report of the American College of Cardiology/American Heart Association Task Force on Clinical Practice Guidelines. *Circulation* **2019**, *140*, e596–e646. [CrossRef]
61. Wills, A.G.; Hopfer, C. Phenotypic and genetic relationship between BMI and cigarette smoking in a sample of UK adults. *Addict. Behav.* **2019**, *89*, 98–103. [CrossRef]
62. Bull, F.C.; Al-Ansari, S.S.; Biddle, S.; Borodulin, K.; Buman, M.P.; Cardon, G.; Carty, C.; Chaput, J.-P.; Chastin, S.; Chou, R.; et al. World Health Organization 2020 guidelines on physical activity and sedentary behaviour. *Br. J. Sports Med.* **2020**, *54*, 1451–1462. [CrossRef]
63. Sultana, R.N.; Sabag, A.; Keating, S.E.; Johnson, N.A. The Effect of Low-Volume High-Intensity Interval Training on Body Composition and Cardiorespiratory Fitness: A Systematic Review and Meta-Analysis. *Sports Med.* **2019**, *49*, 1687–1721. [CrossRef] [PubMed]
64. Armstrong, A.; Jungbluth Rodriguez, K.; Sabag, A.; Mavros, Y.; Parker, H.M.; Keating, S.E.; Johnson, N.A. Effect of aerobic exercise on waist circumference in adults with overweight or obesity: A systematic review and meta-analysis. *Obes. Rev. Off. J. Int. Assoc. Study Obes.* **2022**, *23*, e13446. [CrossRef] [PubMed]
65. Division of Nutrition Physical Activity and Obesity from National Center for Chronic Disease Prevention and Health Promotion. Defining Adult Overweight & Obesity. Available online: https://www.cdc.gov/obesity/basics/adult-defining.html?CDC_AA_refVal=https%3A%2F%2Fwww.cdc.gov%2Fobesity%2Fadult%2Fdefining.html (accessed on 1 August 2022).
66. Allman-Farinelli, M.; Gemming, L. Technology Interventions to Manage Food Intake: Where Are We Now? *Curr. Diab. Rep.* **2017**, *17*, 103. [CrossRef] [PubMed]
67. Chew, H.S.J.; Koh, W.L.; Ng, J.S.H.Y.; Tan, K.K. Sustainability of Weight Loss Through Smartphone Apps: Systematic Review and Meta-analysis on Anthropometric, Metabolic, and Dietary Outcomes. *J. Med. Internet Res.* **2022**, *24*, e40141. [CrossRef]
68. Payne, J.E.; Turk, M.T.; Kalarchian, M.A.; Pellegrini, C.A. Adherence to mobile-app-based dietary self-monitoring-Impact on weight loss in adults. *Obes. Sci. Pract.* **2022**, *8*, 279–288. [CrossRef]
69. Patel, M.L.; Hopkins, C.M.; Brooks, T.L.; Bennett, G.G. Comparing Self-Monitoring Strategies for Weight Loss in a Smartphone App: Randomized Controlled Trial. *JMIR mHealth uHealth* **2019**, *7*, e12209. [CrossRef]
70. Jezewska-Zychowicz, M.; Plichta, M. Diet Quality, Dieting, Attitudes and Nutrition Knowledge: Their Relationship in Polish Young Adults-A Cross-Sectional Study. *Int. J. Environ. Res. Public Health* **2022**, *19*, 6533. [CrossRef]
71. Haas, K.; Hayoz, S.; Maurer-Wiesner, S. Effectiveness and Feasibility of a Remote Lifestyle Intervention by Dietitians for Overweight and Obese Adults: Pilot Study. *JMIR mHealth uHealth* **2019**, *7*, e12289. [CrossRef]
72. Schirmann, F.; Kanehl, P.; Jones, L. What Intervention Elements Drive Weight Loss in Blended-Care Behavior Change Interventions? A Real-World Data Analysis with 25,706 Patients. *Nutrients* **2022**, *14*, 2999. [CrossRef]
73. Alley, S.; Wellens, P.; Schoeppe, S.; de Vries, H.; Rebar, A.L.; Short, C.E.; Duncan, M.J.; Vandelanotte, C. Impact of increasing social media use on sitting time and body mass index. *Health Promot. J. Austr.* **2017**, *28*, 91–95. [CrossRef]
74. Thorp, A.A.; Healy, G.N.; Owen, N.; Salmon, J.; Ball, K.; Shaw, J.E.; Zimmet, P.Z.; Dunstan, D.W. Deleterious associations of sitting time and television viewing time with cardiometabolic risk biomarkers: Australian Diabetes, Obesity and Lifestyle (AusDiab) study 2004-2005. *Diabetes Care* **2010**, *33*, 327–334. [CrossRef] [PubMed]

75. Puhl, R.M.; Brownell, K.D. Confronting and coping with weight stigma: An investigation of overweight and obese adults. *Obesity* **2006**, *14*, 1802–1815. [CrossRef] [PubMed]
76. Turner-McGrievy, G.M.; Dunn, C.G.; Wilcox, S.; Boutté, A.K.; Hutto, B.; Hoover, A.; Muth, E. Defining Adherence to Mobile Dietary Self-Monitoring and Assessing Tracking Over Time: Tracking at Least Two Eating Occasions per Day Is Best Marker of Adherence within Two Different Mobile Health Randomized Weight Loss Interventions. *J. Acad. Nutr. Diet.* **2019**, *119*, 1516–1524. [CrossRef] [PubMed]
77. Bradburn, N.M.; Rips, L.J.; Shevell, S.K. Answering autobiographical questions: The impact of memory and inference on surveys. *Science* **1987**, *236*, 157–161. [CrossRef] [PubMed]
78. Röcker, C.; Ziefle, M.; Holzinger, A. From computer innovation to human integration: Current trends and challenges for pervasive HealthTechnologies. In *Pervasive Health*; Springer: Berlin/Heidelberg, Germany, 2014; pp. 1–17.

MDPI
St. Alban-Anlage 66
4052 Basel
Switzerland
www.mdpi.com

Applied Sciences Editorial Office
E-mail: applsci@mdpi.com
www.mdpi.com/journal/applsci

www.ingramcontent.com/pod-product-compliance
Lightning Source LLC
Chambersburg PA
CBHW040749250926
51850CB00007BB/1454
9783036597782